FRANCE'S NEW DEAL

FRANCE'S NEW DEAL

From the Thirties to the Postwar Era

PHILIP NORD

PRINCETON UNIVERSITY PRESS

PRINCETON AND OXFORD

Published by Princeton University Press,
41 William Street, Princeton, New Jersey 08540
In the United Kingdom:
Princeton University Press, 6 Oxford Street,
Woodstock, Oxfordshire OX20 1TW

Library of Congress Cataloging-in-Publication Data

Nord, Philip G., 1950–
France's New Deal : from the thirties to the postwar era / Philip Nord.
p.   cm.
Includes bibliographical references and index.
ISBN 978-0-691-14297-5 (hardcover : alk. paper)   1. France—Politics and
government—1914–1940.   2. France—Politics and government—1940–
1945.   3. France—Cultural policy—History—20th century.   4. France—
History—German occupation, 1940–1945.   5. Social change—France—
History—20th century.   6. Economic development—France—History—
20th century.   7. Political culture—France—History—20th century.
8. Arts, French—20th century.   I. Title
DC389.N67 2010
944.081'6—dc22   2009038281

British Library Cataloging-in-Publication Data is available

This book has been composed in ITC New Baskerville

Printed on acid-free paper. ∞

press.princeton.edu

Printed in the United States of America

1 3 5 7 9 10 8 6 4 2

For my colleagues,

past and present, here and abroad

Contents

Acknowledgments

I want to acknowledge first and foremost three friends and colleagues who have read all or large portions of this book: Claire Andrieu, Martin Conway, and Emmanuelle Loyer. I know they do not agree with every argument laid out in the pages that follow, but this did not deter them from trying to make my book a better one. It was a time-consuming effort, but they did not stint, and I am deeply grateful to them.

The Princeton History Department has been my professional home for many years. I have benefited in the past from the counsel and criticism of my departmental colleagues, and with this book it has been no different. Peter Brown, Sheldon Garon, Jan Gross, Harold James, Arno Mayer, and Daniel Rodgers have in various ways pushed me to think about France, not in isolation, but in broader, comparative terms, and I hope I have been able to make the most of their advice.

In the years that this manuscript has been in preparation, I have accumulated numerous debts to colleagues who helped out when I had a question or got stuck, proposing something useful to read, steering me to an archive, sharing a thought or work of their own. My thanks go to Dudley Andrew, Seth Armus, David Bellos, Ruth Ben-Ghiat, Alain Chatriot, Olivier Dard, Hélène Eck, Patrick Fridenson, Jane Fulcher, Pascale Goetschel, Eric Jabbari, Richard Kuisel, Alan Perry, Nathalie Richard, Marie Scot, Debora Silverman, and Bruno Valat.

I have had a number of opportunities to publish pieces of my research or to present it at conferences and seminars. This does not happen without colleagues going out of their way to issue invitations, organize panels, or offer much-needed editorial criticism. Jean-Pierre

Azéma, Marc Olivier Baruch, Herrick Chapman, Sudhir Hazareesingh, Tony Judt, Theodore Margadant, Jo Burr Margadant, and Paul-André Rosental have all gone to generous lengths to give me a chance to present my work, and to them all I express a heartfelt thanks.

I would also like to thank a group of colleagues who have been supportive of me, not just on this specific occasion (though that too), but over the course of my entire career. They have written letters, they have helped me make contacts, they have looked out for my interests in all kinds of ways. I may have guardian angels unknown to me, but these are the ones I do know of: Annette Becker, Patrice Higonnet, Robert Paxton, and Jerrold Seigel.

It is not just from individuals that support has come but also from institutions. The American Council of Learned Societies and the Guggenheim Foundation provided essential fellowship support. My wife and I spent a glorious semester at the National Humanities Center, where I worked, as a Florence Gould Foundation fellow, at getting this manuscript into final shape for publication. Those were very happy months.

Happy, not least of all, because I spent them in the company of my wife, Deborah, who has been my constant and loving partner for so many years. She has been a joy to me.

Abbreviations

ACJF	Association catholique de la jeunesse française
ADTP	Association des directeurs du théâtre de Paris
BSEF	Bureau de statistiques et d'études financières
CATJC	Centre artistique et technique des jeunes du cinéma
CDN	Centre dramatique national
CEA	Commissariat à l'Energie atomique
CEPH	Centre d'études des problèmes humains
CFTC	Confédération française des travailleurs chrétiens
CGA	Confédération générale de l'agriculture
CGC	Confédération générale des cadres
CGE	Comité général d'études
CGI	Commissariat-général à l'Information
CGP	Commissariat-général au Plan
CGPF	Confédération générale de la production française
CGPF	Confédération générale du patronat français
CGPME	Confédération générale des petites et moyennes entreprises
CGQJ	Commissariat-général aux Questions juives
CGT	Confédération générale du travail
CLCF	Comité de libération du cinéma français
CLR	Comité de libération de la radio
CNC	Centre national de la cinématographie
CNE	Conseil national économique
CNPF	Conseil national du patronat français
CNR	Conseil national de la Résistance
CNRS	Centre national de la recherche scientifique
CO	Comité d'organisation

COES	Comité d'organisation des entreprises du spectacle
COIC	Comité d'organisation des industries cinématographiques
CPEE	Centre polytechnicien des études économiques
DGEN	Direction générale de l'équipement national
EDF	Electricité de France
ELSP	Ecole libre des sciences politiques
ENA	Ecole nationale d'administration
FNC	Fédération nationale catholique
FNSP	Fondation nationale des sciences politiques
FO	Force ouvrière
HCCPF	Haut Comité consultatif de la Population et de la Famille
HCP	Haut Comité de la Population
IDHEC	Institut des hautes études cinématographiques
IEP	Institut d'études politiques
IFOP	Institut français d'opinion publique
INED	Institut national d'études démographiques
INSEE	Institut national de la statistique et des études économiques
ISEA	Institut de science économique appliquée
JAC	Jeunesse agricole chrétienne
JEC	Jeunesse étudiante chrétienne
JF	Jeune France
JOC	Jeunesse ouvrière chrétienne
MEN	Ministère de l'Economie nationale
MRP	Mouvement républicain populaire
NC	*Nouveaux Cahiers*
OCM	Organisation civile et militaire
OCRPI	Office central de répartition des produits industriels
OPC	Office professionnel du cinéma
PCF	Parti communiste français
PDP	Parti démocrate populaire
PEC	Peuple et Culture
PME	Plan de modernisation et d'équipement
POB	Parti ouvrier belge

PTT	Ministère des Postes, télégraphes et téléphones
RDF	Radiodiffusion française
RN	Radiodiffusion nationale
RTF	Radiotélévision française
SdeF	Scouts de France
SFIO	Section française de l'internationale ouvrière
SGF	Statistique générale de France
SGI	Secrétariat-général à l'Information
SGJ	Secrétariat-général à la Jeunesse
SNCF	Société nationale des chemins de fer
SNS	Service national de la statistique
SOFIRA	Société financière de radiodiffusion
SOFIRAD	Société financière de radiodiffusion
STO	Service du travail obligatoire
TEC	Travail et Culture
TNP	Théâtre national populaire
UNSA	Union nationale des syndicats agricoles

FRANCE'S NEW DEAL

INTRODUCTION

Postwar Stories

France's Fourth Republic (1946–1958) has an unhappy reputation, and it is not hard to see why.[1] High hopes for a new constitutional order at the Liberation were disappointed. General Charles de Gaulle, who presided over France's postwar Provisional Government, wanted a break with the parliamentary ways of the old Third Republic, favoring instead the creation of a strong, presidentialist regime. The parties of the Left, however, the Socialists and Communists, suspected the general of authoritarian designs and maneuvered to stymie his plans with a double consequence. First, the constitutional overhaul dreamed of by so many résistants never took place. The Fourth Republic, like the Third, would be dominated by parliament. And second, all the political infighting prompted de Gaulle himself to withdraw from public life in January 1946, Gaullist loyalists becoming in subsequent years among the most vocal opponents of the institutions of the new regime.

The Left in turn was fractured by the onset of the Cold War. The Communists had played a role in government coalitions in the early postwar years but were driven out of office in 1947. They too as a result became staunch enemies of the parliamentary status quo. The regime thus found itself beset on all sides, and it became ever more difficult to construct stable parliamentary majorities. Prime ministers now came and went with the same velocity as in the bad old days of the unmourned Third Republic.

The return of prosperity in the fifties buoyed the Fourth Republic for a period but not enough to carry it through the crises of decolonization. No sooner had the Second World War ended than France confronted armed opposition to its imperial rule, first in Indochina, then in Algeria. The Republic managed to extricate itself from Vietnam, but it was never able to muster the political will to deal with the war in Algeria. In 1958, right-wing plotters in North Africa, fearful that civilian authorities back home lacked the determination to protect France's colonial interests, took matters into their own hands, seizing control in Algiers. Elements of the army took the insurrectionists' side, and the metropole in turn came under threat. De Gaulle, ever the providential man, stepped out of retirement. Both the military and a majority in parliament were willing enough to let him take charge, and take charge he did.

De Gaulle liquidated the old Fourth Republic and set about building the presidential regime he had so long imagined, and willy-nilly he got France out of Algeria, setting the nation on a new, post-imperial course. De Gaulle settled the great issues, constitutional and imperial, that the Fourth Republic had not, giving rise to a new political order that has remained more or less intact to the present day. De Gaulle's Fifth Republic has not yet matched the seventy-year life span of the Third, but there is no reason to believe that it will not do so in time.

This story line, appealing though it may be, has at least one major flaw. It may well be that an opportunity was missed at the Liberation to reconstruct France's parliamentary and imperial institutions, but this was not at all the case when it came to the French state's executive apparatus. In the first postwar years, a veritable alphabet soup of agencies and commissions was created, the ensemble designed to relaunch the national economy and provide France's citizenry a degree of social security they had never known before. Successive waves of nationalizations, beginning with coal mines in 1944 and culminating four years later with a rash of takeovers in the sea, air, and rail sectors, brought entire industries—energy, deposit banking, insurance, transport—under state control. In January 1946, just as de Gaulle was leaving office, he created a planning body, the Commissariat-général au Plan, assigning command of the new agency to onetime businessman Jean Monnet. The Commissariat set France on an expansionist course, bringing to the task of economic planning and forecasting a novel numerical precision thanks to the collaboration of ancillary statistical bodies like the state-run Institut national de la statistique et des études économiques (INSEE) and the private Institut de science économique appliquée. Alongside the new planning machinery grew up a network of welfare institutions. The basic groundwork for what came to be known as the Sécurité sociale was laid in the fall of 1945 in a package of decrees conceived by former résistant turned welfare administrator Pierre Laroque. The postwar French welfare state insured French men and women against the perils of sickness and old age, but more than that, it included a family-allowance scheme among the most generous in Europe. Pronatalists had lobbied hard for a family-oriented welfare state, and they lobbied just as hard (and with equal success) for the creation of a populationist think tank, the Institut national d'études démographiques or INED, which was founded in 1946 under the direction of France's most renowned statistician, Alfred Sauvy. Now, it took manpower—a cadre of trained civil servants competent in technical matters but also equipped to take a view of the whole—to run France's burgeoning executive branch. In the interwar decades, the Ecole libre des sciences politiques, a private public-policy school, had enjoyed a near monopoly on civil-service education. Sciences Po, as it was nicknamed, was semi-nationalized at the Liberation, and to round out the training of would-be public administrators, an altogether new, state-run postgraduate institution was launched in October 1945, the Ecole nationale d'administration. ENA was the brainchild of Michel Debré, a de Gaulle loyalist, and the institution he shepherded into being has come to occupy a near-dominant place in public life. ENA degree holders, schooled in a Keynesian-inflected orthodoxy that touts growth-generating investment over balanced budgets, enjoy a virtual monopoly on access to the highest ranks of the French civil service, the so-called *grands corps*.

The history of the Fourth Republic then was not just a record of failure. The state was reconstructed in the immediate postwar years; it undertook a new set of tasks (management of the economy and provision of comprehensive welfare benefits); and it performed its mission with remarkable effectiveness. ENA, INED, INSEE are still very much a part of the French institutional landscape. Antistatism grew in the Anglo-American world in the 1970s and 1980s. There were echoes of this in France but far fainter. The postwar remaking of the state had nurtured French confidence in the capacity of public institutions, and that confidence ran deep enough to slow the liberalizing wave of the Thatcher/Reagan era. From this angle, what de Gaulle accomplished post-1958 was not altogether a new departure but a building upon foundations, and solid foundations at that, that had been laid in the immediate postwar period.

But such a conclusion raises a further set of questions. Granted, the Liberation moment was one of dynamic transformation. But how is this revolution in statecraft to be accounted for and characterized? How is the story of France in the aftermath of the Second World War to be told? It is possible to isolate four major narratives (there are perhaps more), and each has variants that describe, not just the French experience, but experiences elsewhere in the postwar world, in Europe and beyond. The French case then is not just interesting in itself but relevant to more general interpretations of the postwar scene.

To Claude Bourdet, a Resistance veteran and man of the Left, the postwar years had the look of a "restoration," and it is clear enough what he meant by the term.[2] In May 1943, the Conseil national de la Résistance (CNR) drafted a "democratic charter" sketching out a reform agenda that promised the "eviction of the great economic and financial castes from the direction of the economy,"[3] and for a moment at the Liberation it looked as if this might just come to pass. Local Resistance committees and militant labor pushed hard for a takeover of key enterprises, from mines to utilities, beginning a ground-up process that culminated in 1945–1946 in a series of legislative measures nationalizing huge chunks of the French economy. Nor should it be thought France's postwar legislators had a hard time stomaching nationalization. The first elections after the war were conducted in October 1945. The largest parties—the Parti communiste français (PCF), the christian-democratic Mouvement républicain populaire (MRP), and the socialist Section française de l'internationale ouvrière (SFIO)—received between them roughly three-quarters of the votes cast, and all three were pledged to the CNR program.

Yet the promise of a post-capitalist France never materialized. Bourdet himself laid heavy blame on de Gaulle. De Gaulle, as Bourdet saw him, was a man of the establishment, a general who liked command and hierarchy. Resistance experience had moderated de Gaulle's conservative instincts, but once he became head of government, now surrounded by ministers and bureaucrats rather than résistants, he reverted to type. The christian democrats too had a part to play in this drama. The MRP leadership had Resistance experience, but its electorate was more conventionally right-wing, composed of Catholics and conservatives who had nowhere else to turn, the parties of the traditional Right having compromised themselves during the Vichy years. In France's second legislative elections in the summer of 1946, the MRP garnered the most votes, and it proceeded to brake France's leftward turn. Then came the Cold War, which drove the Communists to the margins of public life, splintering the French Left and making possible a politics of capitalist reestablishment. No wonder Bourdet, who had harbored such high hopes for a France made new, wrote in disappointed tones of a France restored.

This story of hopes deceived is one that German historians, in particular German historians of left-wing persuasion, will recognize, for did not events in the German West follow an almost identical pattern? It is not so much that there was a formidable German Resistance, but there were antifascist committees that sprang up in the war's aftermath, composed of sundry leftists and liberals, men of goodwill who wanted a Germany remade. In the West, however, the American and British occupying authorities bypassed the anti-fas as they were called, and the logic of such a choice was simple enough. To Anglo-American military men and administrators, grassroots leftists did not seem the right materials, in either political or practical terms, with which to get a prostrate Germany up and running again. It made more sense to turn to men of substance who had knowledge of government, even if the men in question had Nazi-era records that did not bear close scrutiny. The Anglo-Americans in Germany, like de Gaulle in France, blocked the path to a more revolutionary future.[4] The onset of the Cold War and concomitant rise of Konrad Adenauer's Christian Democratic Union (CDU) settled the matter. In the immediate postwar years, Christian Democrats had dabbled in anticapitalist rhetoric, but the party's line had begun to liberalize in the late forties under Adenauer's prodding. The change of heart was formalized at the CDU's Düsseldorf congress in 1949, which made explicit the party's conversion to free-market principles. The cartel capitalism of Wilhelmine days did not come back to be sure (indeed, an anticartel law was passed in 1957), but the new Germany proved itself hospitable to concentrated industry, settling into an "oligopolistic" mode dominated by large firms that operated in circumstances of regulated competition. The new order may not have replicated the past but very much echoed it.

The restorationist thesis, of course, has not gone unchallenged in recent and even not so recent historiography, though the nature of the challenge comes in several varieties. In the German case, it has been pointed out, the war ended in the destruction of Germany's Junker and military elites, making possible a genuine and unprecedented liberalization of public life. The American presence may have frustrated grassroots antifascism, but it brought with it as well a model of managerial capitalism that, not right away but over time, eroded older, more authoritarian habits of business administration. "Americanization" from this perspective had a salutary impact, helping West Germany to recast itself, to find its path toward a once-elusive democratic stability.[5]

It is possible, of course, to write another, more rueful finale to the Americanization narrative. What was the American model after all? In the 1930s, it was the New Deal, a mix of welfare, antimonopoly, and regulationist measures that hemmed in the free market without ever replacing it. But this model had been scaled back by the end of the war, a process, some historians claim, that was already well under way in the late thirties. The first years of the Roosevelt presidency had witnessed a hesitant economic recovery that sputtered out in 1937–1938, and the renewed downturn created an opening for anti–New Deal forces to regroup. The war itself enhanced the powers of the New Deal state but at the same time obliged New Dealers to negotiate common ground with business interests in pursuit of a military-centered productivism. Big business was back, and after the war it launched a well-funded counteroffensive against New Deal statism that got a helpful political leg up as the Cold War set in.[6] The New Deal regime was not washed away in the process, far from it, but it was reoriented along Fordist lines. Government and the corporate sector, the Fordist argument went, had a common interest in market expansion through increased productivity. Produce in quantity; pay a living wage; sell at prices within reach of the average working man: such was the Fordist formula, and in practice it worked wonders, flooding the nation with goods that a now-expanding consumer market snapped up.[7] This was the America that came to Europe after the war, managerial, productivist, but above all consumerist, and on some accounts it proved an irresistible force.[8]

The Americanization story takes on yet darker hues when applied in the French context. Here, the critical moment is the signing of the Blum-Byrnes accord of 1946. Years of occupation and war left France devastated and impoverished. In 1946, the French government sent a delegation to Washington led by the socialist intellectual Léon Blum to negotiate debt relief and a financial aid package. The US government drove a hard bargain, striking a deal that, some have argued, reduced France to a state of fiscal dependency, and not just fiscal dependency, for the Blum-Byrnes accord included a provision that opened the French market to US films. The coming of the Marshall Plan in 1947 deepened yet further France's reliance on the United States. On this account, the France that emerged from the war was different indeed from what it had been before, but the change was not a welcome one. France was reduced to an economic satellite of the United States, its culture beleaguered by Hollywood films and what was called at the time "coca-colonization."[9]

But it may be that Americanization loomed less large in postwar European history than the coca-colonization story supposes. Take Great Britain as an example. The first postwar elections there in 1945 returned a Labor Party majority for the first time ever, which set to work reconstructing the nation with a socialist zeal. The result was a spate of nationalizations that made public employees of an estimated two million workers. The explosion of the public sector was accompanied by a series of parliamentary bills—the National Health Service Act, the National Insurance Act, the New Towns Act, all passed in

1946—that laid down the basic building blocks of Britain's welfare state. There would be public health care for the sick and infirm, national pensions for the old, "council housing" for families in need of decent homes.[10] British historians have wrangled about aspects of the welfare story: did welfare-state construction impede Britain's economic modernization; were the progressive "activators" who built the welfare state out in front of a public much less socialist in orientation?[11] But such differences no more than nuance the still-basic plotline, that of Britain's postwar rebirth as a welfare state.

And in the domain of welfare-state construction, the French would do the British one better. France had its own nationalizations, and as we have seen, it boasted a national health and pension scheme as well. But France had something that the British did not, the Commissariat-général au Plan.[12] To be sure, Britain had planist aspirations that found expression in the Town and Country Planning Act of 1944, but town planning was a local and not a national affair. It shaped the landscape but not the economy. In the domain of national, economic planning, the French were pioneers, and the French pioneer par excellence was, of course, the CGP's founding father Jean Monnet.

This is a story then told not in American but in European accents; it is the story of planning and welfare-state construction; and in many versions (though not all), it comes with an upbeat, social democratic ending. From this angle, the postwar era and, indeed, the decades that followed appear less a restorationist debacle or an Americanist triumph than a "social democratic moment" that embarked postwar Europe on a new and progressive course.[13]

But was socialism in fact the big story in the postwar West? Laroque was a career bureaucrat, Monnet a businessman turned public administration mover and shaker. Neither was a party man, let alone a card-carrying member of the SFIO. If they were the heroes of the postwar era, then the postwar era was about state institution-building as carried out by the state's own servants. This line of argument suggests a fourth rebirth-of-Europe narrative, centered not on restoration, America, or the forward march of labor but on the rise of technocracy.

In the case of France, this is an old theme, albeit one that has gotten a number of interesting rewrites in recent historiography. The old narrative went more or less as follows. Interwar France, led or, better, misled by incompetent politicos and parliamentarians, had slid into decadence. What more convincing proof than the ignominious defeat of 1940 and the subsequent humiliations of the Occupation? But at the Liberation, a new cadre of administrators—men like Laroque and Monnet, Debré and Sauvy—took charge. The institutional initiatives they launched and the energy and policy-making ambitions they brought to their work bootstrapped a backward, small-minded France out of its Malthusian past and launched it on a course of unprecedented economic and demographic growth. The question of the plan, Monnet had argued in 1946, was a question of modernization or decadence. In choosing the plan, the French had opted for a progressive, expansionist future shaped by Monnet and his technocratic heirs, the future graduates of ENA.

It will be noted how absent politics are from this account, but of course that is the whole point. Once expertise trumped parliamentary bickering, once the competent took over from the politicians, that is when France got its house in order. Recent versions of the technocracy story, however, have attempted to read the politics back in. In October 1945, de Gaulle set up the Commissariat à l'Energie atomique (CEA), a state agency to oversee the development of atomic resources, whether for civilian or military purposes. Raoul Dautry, who had compiled a distinguished record of state service in the 1930s first as director of the national railways and then in 1939–1940 as minister of armaments, was named the CEA's first administrator-general. Nominated CEA high commissioner (in effect Dautry's right-hand man) was Frédéric Joliot-Curie. Now, Joliot-Curie was a Nobel Prize–winning physicist and a Resistance veteran, but he was also a Communist. The coming of the Cold War did not lead to his immediate ouster; that was to come in 1950, consequent on the scientist's opposition to construction of a nuclear device. Dautry died in 1951 and was replaced by Pierre Guillaumat, like his predecessor an engineer and graduate of the prestigious Ecole Polytechnique. Guillaumat's tenure in office witnessed a further weeding out of communist personnel in the CEA's employ. Weapons-grade plutonium was in due course produced at CEA atomic reactors (France would get the bomb

in 1958). And on the matter of labor relations, the CEA proved itself a
not so willing interlocutor. As one historian has put it, the Commissariat "did not welcome labor unions" at its reactor sites, refusing militants
"entry" to certain military plants altogether until the early 1960s.[14]

Technocracy in a word may present itself as above politics, but
technocratic experts in practice do not like power sharing with labor
unions, and they like Communists even less. Historians who want to
make explicit the politics lurking behind the neutral-sounding "technocracy" have cast about for an alternative label. The term "technocorporatism" has been proposed. It grows out of a study of Electricité
de France (EDF), France's state-run electrical power industry. Liberation authorities created the EDF after the war by nationalizing most
of France's power-generating firms. Unions were a force to contend
with at the new entity, but it was run at the top by technocratic men
who, over time, reasserted the prerogatives of expertise. Pierre Massé
is pointed to here as the main culprit, a polytechnicien and mathematical economist who became EDF president in the midsixties after
a stint running the Commissariat-général au Plan. Massé was no union
buster but a self-styled "man of action" who believed in profit maximization, and Massé's ambition, according to one historian, was to create
a corporate culture to match, with experts on top, labor below, and
both bound by an agreed-upon commitment to principles of competence and productivity. Hence the phrase "technocorporatism."[15]

Hybrid terms like technocorporatism are not unknown in other
historiographies. One critic of mainline British historiography has
argued that the real postwar story was not so much welfare-state construction as "technonationalism," the continuity of Great Britain's
long-standing resolve to maintain its status as a "warfare state." Britain's military buildup in the late thirties escalated during the war,
and once the war was over the military effort did not flag. Nor was it
just that spending levels remained high. The state was unwavering in
its commitment to enlisting science and technology in the enterprise.
The Labor Party had a majority in parliament, but an expanding mil-
itary-industrial complex stayed in place alongside: a network of arse-
nals, laboratories, research-and-design facilities, some state run, oth-

ers privately owned but state funded, which was overseen by a phalanx
of procurement officers, military men, and senior civil servants.[16]

The British warfare state may be a fine example of technonationalism at work, but there is a better one still, though it will be necessary
to leave the shores of Europe to find it: that of Japan. The Japanese
state, since the Meiji restoration, had pledged itself to freeing the nation from dependence on foreign knowledge and invention, to that
end borrowing and domesticating Western technological design on a
grand scale. In the interwar decades, such technonationalism took
an ever more militarist turn, Japanese manufacturers like Toyota,
Nissan, and Isuzu devoting themselves wholesale to vehicle production for the armed services.[17] After the 1945 surrender, the structural
relations among Japan's major players—state, science, and industry—did not alter much, technonationalism remaining the order of
the day. What changed was that Japan's political economy was now
converted to purposes of civilian production, though at critical junctures, the Korean War for example, Japanese industry could be put to
work turning out war-related matériel, in this instance to supply the
US military effort.[18]

There is no shortage of ways then to think about the postwar years
and about postwar France more particularly. But which way or mix of
ways makes the most sense? That is the task the present volume means
to take on, but with an added twist or two. In German history, the
year 1945 is often presented as a caesura, a *Stunde null* or zero hour.
What came after was all new, bearing little resemblance to a past that
had been razed by wartime violence. The story recounted here, by
contrast, will begin in the 1930s and encompass the war years. From
this angle, the Liberation moment does not stand alone facing toward the future but comes at the end of a longer history, representing a denouement as much as a fresh start.[19]

This approach allows a battery of critical issues to be addressed.
There is first of all the "Vichy before Vichy" question, although how
it gets posed is not always the same. It is possible to ask just how much
the troubled thirties prepared the way for Vichy, incubating a vision
and cadre of personnel that would come into their own under Pétain.

At stake from this perspective is just how much Vichy itself was integrated into the stream of French history, whether it was an isolated, exceptional phenomenon or one rooted in often long-standing traditions of French public life. But it is also possible to put the question another way, asking just how much the authoritarian policies of the Vichy regime were anticipated by an authoritarian turn in the policies of a declining Third Republic. This problematic worries less about Vichy and its place in French national history than about flaws in the republican tradition itself—flaws that may still be at work in France's present-day Fifth Republic.[20]

There is an obvious correlative to the *Vichy avant Vichy* question, and that is the question of 1944 itself: just how much did preceding events prepare the way for what was accomplished (or not) at the Liberation? On the one hand, this means asking how the Resistance thought about the postwar order and then in the event set about bringing its plans to realization.[21] The Liberation authorities, however, were not dealing with a tabula rasa but with the remains of an outgoing, discredited regime, Vichy. Was Vichy erased, its institutions, policies, and personnel wiped away, or were there holdovers? In a word, was there a *Vichy après Vichy*?[22] Once again, depending on how the issue is cut into, the interpretive emphasis shifts. Was the France born of the war a Resistance creation, with all the heroic resonances such a distinguished pedigree evokes, or was its ancestry more mottled with varying doses of Vichy admixtures?

But, of course, a long-term perspective may cast doubt on just how critical specific dates were in the first place, whether 1940 or 1944. Perhaps there were continuities that spanned the moments of rupture, secular trends that might have been inflected this way or that by events but whose fundamental direction was not altered for all that. This is a claim sometimes made about France's obsession with birthrates and the family, which from the late nineteenth century through the 1960s seems to have been an unbudgeable feature of French political culture.[23]

Historians of Japan have coined the phrase "transwar" to describe the period 1930 to 1950.[24] The usefulness of the idea in the French context is evident, raising as it does the question of just what difference major regime changes—in this instance, from democracy to dictatorship and then back to democracy again—made. But there are dangers in such a perspective as well, for it might well create an interpretive bias in favor of continuity, collapsing oppositions—between republican and Vichyite, résistant and collaborator—that were of capital importance to the men and women of the era. The transwar approach has its advantages, but it also poses a serious risk of erasing moral boundaries that were drawn in sacrifice and blood.

A second twist: transwar histories of France have been done before, though they tend to zero in on a particular sphere of state activity, the management of the economy, say, or financial policy. The net will be cast wider in this volume. The institutional creativity of the Liberation years was quite remarkable, encompassing not just planning and social security but many other domains as well: statistical science, demographic and family policy, the education of elites—and the list might be extended yet further. All these subjects will be taken up in the pages that follow.

But more than that: the issue of cultural policy and institution making will also come in for treatment. Mention cultural policy, and it is not so much the Liberation as 1936 and 1959 that come to mind. Léon Blum's Popular Front government is still memorialized as a moment of cultural adventure when a socialist-leaning state encouraged an upwelling of youthful and antifascist expression in a dizzying variety of media.[25] As for 1959, it marks the founding of France's first Ministère des Affaires culturelles, a cabinet-level portfolio assigned the task of making France's cultural patrimony available to as wide a swath of the citizenry as possible. That post was occupied for an eventful decade by one of the nation's intellectual luminaries, André Malraux, whose flair for publicity and self-dramatization were well suited to the job.[26] But a handful of scholars have made a plea for the equal importance of the postwar period.[27] The late forties, after all, witnessed the state-sponsored creation of five new regional theaters. Radio was nationalized. And in the film industry, the parastatal Centre national de la cinématographie (still operating today) was set up to help organize and fund movie production, a crucial development to the survival of a French cinema.

The mid-to-late forties mattered when it came to cultural institutions, but mattered in what way? For the men and women of the era,
it seemed that they were started on something unprecedented. The
Third Republic had been laissez-faire to the point of negligence in
cultural matters. Vichy had been reactionary and traditionalist. But
now, in the postwar years, an opportunity for a new beginning had
arisen. A reconstructed state might place culture, once a preserve of
the lettered few, at the disposal of the general public, democratizing
"the best that has been thought and said" in the service of popular
uplift.

Looking at cultural policy in the long run and side by side with
economic and administrative policy will do two things. First, it will
complicate the narrative of cultural renewal.[28] The men and women
of 1944 thought they were starting anew, but they were not; they owed
something to the past, and it was not just to the Popular Front that
they were indebted but to Vichy itself. Second, it will suggest the ways
in which economic and cultural reconstruction were connected. The
nation's rebirth out of the ashes of the war entailed not just a modernization of productive life but a cultural reawakening, the one like the
other intended to serve a common purpose, the reassertion of France's
presence in the world. Indeed, rebirth of a nation might have been a
suitable title for the present volume, were it not that the phrase has
such unhappy connotations in the American context. The breadth of
the reconstruction process gave the French an energizing shot of national purpose whose effects would not dissipate for decades.

It is a truism about the French that they are a statist people. Alexis
de Tocqueville said it long ago, and because he had generous things
to say about the United States, Americans are disposed to believe
him, and not just Americans. The French too think of themselves in
these terms, and they can cite an illustrious list of state builders, from
Jean-Baptiste Colbert of old regime days to Napoleon Bonaparte, to
prove the point. It remains a near reflex in France to label any centralizing gesture Jacobin. Yet how much does this old saw about the
Jacobinical French conceal? Would any of the state builders of the
Liberation era have embraced the label Jacobin (let alone Colber-
tiste or Bonapartist)? Not many. No, the post-1944 project was some-

thing original, though what descriptive label to affix to it remains to be worked out. In any event, what happened then was not just one more expression of an eternal French statism. Indeed, the state builders saw themselves as pioneers who were taking the nation in a fresh direction, correcting the political defects of preceding regimes, the Third Republic above all. There was a good deal of mystification in such a self-presentation, as will be seen, but there was enough truth in it to sustain the point that the rise of the state in France was not an inevitable, linear process. Rather, state building unfolded in punctuated bursts, each conditioned by the historical moment in which it occurred.[29] The postwar period was one such state-building moment, and attention has to be paid to the political alignments, conjunctural rather than permanent, that made it possible.

Part I

THE FRENCH MODEL

The word "liberalism" does not have strong positive connotations in French public discourse. It is associated with the individualist, free-marketeering ways of the Thatcher/Reagan years, with an Anglo-Saxon model that celebrates the growth-creating potential of unbridled entrepreneurship. No, the French have a model of their own, a third way between the savage capitalism of the English-speaking peoples and the command economies of the now defunct East bloc.

The state stands front and center in the French model. It is the owner of a vast nationalized sector. It invests. It plans. The plan, however, is not a diktat but a blueprint of goals and targets worked out in concert between civil servants and private interests, both business and trade union. And there is a similar mix of top-down and bottom-up elements in the design of France's welfare state. The system, which provides a full battery of benefits from health care to pensions, operates under the state's general tutelage, but it is made up of numerous *caisses* or funds, financed by a mix of employer and employee contributions and managed by representatives of the contributing parties themselves. A whole separate apparatus exists to disburse family-support payments, *allocations familiales* in French, but it is similar in constitution to the health-care and retirement programs and, in its postwar heyday, of equal weight in the overall structure of the welfare system. In 1946, an estimated half of all Social Security benefits took the form of family allocation payments.[1] The range of the state's activities, however tempered by interest-group representation and participation, is impressive indeed. All this, of course, requires bureaucratic manpower, a first-rate senior civil service; and France in fact

boasts just such an elite, the graduates of the state-run Ecole nationale d'administration.

The French model—part "concerted economy," part "parental
welfare state," part "technocracy"—has come under intense pressure
in recent decades. Portions of the nationalized sector have been sold
off; the plan is but a shadow of what it once was; an aging population
threatens the fiscal viability of the welfare state; and public complaints
about the castelike character and aloofness of the nation's bureaucratic elite have multiplied. Yet, despite all such strains, the French
model has remained intact in its general outlines.

Attached as the French are to this model, it has not existed from
time immemorial but was put together, as we have seen, in a burst of
institutional creativity just after the Second World War. Now, it is tempting to look on the Liberation moment as one of dramatic rupture.
The war and Occupation had created a breach that allowed a new
generation of decision makers—men like Debré, Laroque, Sauvy,
and Monnet—to rise to positions of power. They brought with them
a youthful energy and a forward-looking élan that to date had been
lacking in French public life. France had grown old and cautious in
the thirties; the national economy had flagged; and the Third Republic, reliant on peasant and small-owning constituencies resistant to
change, lacked the dynamism to jump-start a stalemated public life.
But come the postwar moment, the stalemate was broken open, clear-
ing the way for fresh faces and fresh ways of thinking.[2]

Yet how new were the new men? Laroque in 1934 wrote a regular
column for *L'Homme nouveau,* a short-lived journal of corporatist
opinion, which debated schemes for a reorganization of French social and political life. It turns out that Debré, a recent graduate of
France's premier policy-training institute, Sciences Po, also wrote for
the paper, though just an article or two. He is better remembered for
his role in the Daladier administration of 1938. In the face of a looming Nazi menace, Prime Minister Edouard Daladier had committed
himself to a crash program of rearmament whatever the cost. To this
end, he set about diluting existing legislation that limited the wage-
earning week to forty hours. Debré, in tandem with Sauvy, helped to
draft the relevant decree-laws. Daladier also had occasion to call on

Monnet's expertise. Monnet was an international financier with invaluable contacts in the Anglo-American world. France needed weaponry, and in 1938 Daladier dispatched Monnet to Washington to purchase aircraft from the Americans. The movers and shakers at the Liberation were often young men (not Monnet, however, who was born in 1888), but that did not mean they were without pasts.

The same may be said of the institutions they created. From a certain angle, the new order at the Liberation appears a direct working out of Resistance plans. The Conseil national de la Résistance had envisioned a state takeover of critical industries in the name of the public good; it had made an explicit pledge to insure all French citizens against the vicissitudes of modern life; and then these commitments were made good once France was restored to itself. Yet not all the institutional innovations of the Liberation era were de novo inventions. Monnet's plan was not the first of its kind. The wartime Vichy regime had generated two such projects of its own, a ten-year plan conceived in 1941 and the so-called *tranche de démarrage* of 1944, which began to imagine how a postwar France might set about relaunching its economy. Sauvy's INED had antecedents in a Vichy institution as well, the Fondation Carrel, a state-funded population-research institute. Sauvy, in fact, had a passing connection himself to the Fondation Carrel, and he recruited a substantial chunk of INED's senior staff from Fondation Carrel ranks.

The mixed ancestry of the postwar order raises the vexed question of how its political significance is to be understood. It is tempting, once again, to interpret the Liberation makeover as a Left triumph. In 1936, France had experienced a Popular Front government, an administration of Socialists and Radicals who, with Communist backing, pledged themselves to a democratization of public life in the name of antifascism and a new deal for working people. The CNR's program resurrected this vision, and, from this perspective, the Resistance's triumph at the Liberation represented a kind of second coming of the Popular Front. On this account, the Liberation looks like a social democratic moment, and that is how many historians have understood the postwar order, not just in France, but in much of Western Europe as well.[3]

But there are problems with this way of looking at things. At the level of party politics, the Resistance coalition was not quite the same in composition as its Popular Front predecessor. In 1944, Socialists and Communists stood at the forefront, but not the Radicals, now replaced by an altogether new partner, the christian democrats (as represented by the Mouvement républicain populaire), who had been a marginal presence on the political scene in 1936. And just below the partisan surface, at the administrative level where institutional architects like Monnet, Laroque, Sauvy, and Debré went about their business, the classic Left was much less in evidence. Indeed, not one of the four—neither Monnet the businessman, nor any of the technocrats in waiting (Laroque, Sauvy, and Debré)—was a leftist stalwart. The same observation, of course, applies to General de Gaulle himself, until the war a career officer, who harbored a lifelong suspicion of party men of all colorations. The French model was in part the product of social democratic aspiration, but other forces were at work as well whose identifying characteristics remain to be sorted out.

A trio of arguments will be spun out in the text that follows, which will address the issues raised above. The new elite at the Liberation was not so new. In the 1930s, these individuals can already be found at work, networking, editing little reviews, forming associations, all aimed at devising alternatives to the existing institutional order, judged too parliamentarist in political constitution and too laissez-faire in economic policy. Socialists played a part in these imaginings, but even more so competing currents that are not so easy to situate on the Left/Right spectrum. They are sometimes described as non-conformist, articulating an above-party critique of the "established disorder," which pinned hopes for a national renaissance on various third-way schemes that would enable France to blaze a path to a brighter future, neither capitalist nor communist in design.[4] The "nonconformist" label, however, does not do justice to the full range of critical activity in the thirties, which encompassed an important technocratic wing composed of engineers and enlightened business-men and a less well-known Catholic subculture anchored in an awakening laity intent on a re-Christianization of public life. The debate that these various currents engaged in, moreover, was not just idle chatter but had an impact on policy, not just in the Popular Front era, but above all in the run-up to the war.[5] The Republic, decadent as it was supposed to be, had a capacity for reform, although in certain aspects the reform in question anticipated Vichy as much as what came after.

Vichy, indeed, will play a major part in this story. Nonconformists, technocrats, and lay Catholics poured into Vichy service and there set to work—in an authoritarian context shadowed by an exigent occupying power—building the new France they dreamed of. They had some success at the enterprise, and a portion of what they built was preserved at the Liberation. But it also began to dawn on many (in fact, most of these third-way hopefuls) that Vichy was not in the end the vehicle of national redemption they had anticipated. They began to peel away, switching allegiance from Pétain's regime to the Resistance. The phenomenon casts an interesting light on the Resistance itself. In the popular American imagination, Free France appears the natural reflex of a freedom-loving people in the face of a vicious Occupation. But it is worth remembering just how variegated the Resistance phenomenon was. The movement contained elements that, however anti-German, were more ambivalent about Pétain himself, objecting not to Pétain's National Revolution per se but to the attempt to make it happen in an Occupation context. The Resistance contained elements, however anti-Vichy, that espoused an elite-led, technocratic vision of national regeneration, which echoed certain themes of Vichyite rhetoric. And the Resistance contained as well a Christian component that reviled Vichyite racism but aspired to a moralization, a purification of public life that resonated with many Catholics at first drawn to Vichy. The sometime proximity between Vichy and the Resistance vanished during 1942–1944, as Pétain's regime degenerated into fascist squalor and as the Resistance itself clarified its democratic commitments. But it was a proximity that, while it lasted, permitted crossovers and that stands as a reminder, if one is needed, that the Resistance was a house of many mansions, anchored on the Left but home as well to dissidents of various stripes, some of them ex-Vichyites.[6]

The variegated composition of the Resistance is critical to keep in mind when looking at the political struggles of the Liberation era. The Left was very much a presence in postwar councils, pressing a vision of its own centered around nationalizations, economic dirigisme, a unitary welfare system (with family allocation funds not separate but rolled in), and the replacement of established institutions like Sciences Po with a new school of public administration. The Left push was powerful, and pieces of its agenda were enacted, but just pieces, and the reason why is plain enough. The Left met with opposition—from entrenched interests, from Vichy holdovers who dodged the postwar purges, and, of paramount importance, from fellow résistants. Gaullist loyalists, christian democrats, and ex-Vichyites turned résistants did not share in the Left's understanding of what the postwar order ought to look like, and they maneuvered with increasing success to thwart the Left's project, substituting one of their own— less dirigiste, more familist, and more elitist in construction.

Little wonder that left-leaning veterans of the era remember it as a moment of "restoration."[7] Yet the word is not an apt one, for the postwar order did represent a new departure. The "newness" of it all was in part a rhetorical gesture, the self-mythologizing gambit of a postwar elite bent on legitimating itself and its "modernizing" project. But there was truth to the claim as well, for that elite did lay the institutional groundwork for an astonishing economic burst, the so-called *trente glorieuses*, which propelled France out of its peasant and small-owning past into a twentieth century of planning, welfare, and technocratic management.[8] Perhaps it is best then to speak, not of a restoration, but of a conservative, state-centered modernization, so successful in execution, it might be added, that there are few in France today who want to see the "French model" undone.

CHAPTER 1

The Crisis of the Thirties

Technocrats in Waiting

Depression-era France seems to have little to recommend it. There was to be sure the bright spot of the Popular Front, but the Blum experiment did not last long, and its successes were partial at best. It is rather France's failures that stand out. The Third Republic, to all appearances, proved incapable of generating an effective response to the critical challenges of the day: at home, a deepening economic slump that sharpened class tensions; abroad, the rise of an aggressive Germany intent upon a radical revision of the international order. But the idea of French paralysis, or "immobilism" as it has sometimes been called, does not tell the whole story.

Critiques of prevailing economic policy proliferated in the thirties. They came, of course, from socialists and trade unionists who had little use for a laissez-faire liberalism, which, so far as they could see, had landed France in a depression. And liberal orthodoxy, it seemed evident enough, had no answer to the crisis, save a budget-cutting mania, which, killing demand, just made matters worse. No, what France needed was a plan: to iron out the irrationalities inherent in a market system driven by egotistical profit-seeking and to guarantee the working man a fair share in an economy geared to the interests of capital. But the Left was not alone in voicing complaint. Maréchal Lyautey, a career military officer and onetime resident-general of Morocco, gathered around himself a circle of protégés in the early thirties. Here, the accent was on the redemptive potential of energetic leadership. The standard-issue French businessman—prudent and risk-averse—lacked the firmness of purpose to right a foundering economy. A new generation of executives, men of action with the moral wherewithal to bring subordinates along, was the "one thing needful" in a France grown slack in purpose. Nonconformist opinion, sometimes Catholic in coloration, did not disagree but placed greater emphasis on organization. The anarchy of the laissez-faire economy set employer against employee. A corporatist system, on the other hand, held out the promise of restoring a modicum of order to the marketplace. Workers and managers, brought together by a tutelary state, would hash out wages and prices, creating as they did so a harmonizing bond among the producing classes, a "community of labor," which would inject a note of humanity into an otherwise cold and indifferent system. More technocratic-minded critics of liberal orthodoxy worried no less about labor relations; they too spoke of humanizing the economy. But there was less hostility to the market and the individual entrepreneur. The problem was to manage irrational behavior: to foresee economic calamities before they occurred and then correct for them. This required planning, a capacity for economic forecasting, which in turn presumed an adequate statistical grasp of the economy's ups and downs. It is not surprising then that so many proponents of the technocratic critique were graduates of France's preeminent engineering school, the Ecole Polytechnique, which boasted a curriculum that placed a premium on mathematical facility. Indeed, the principal locus of technocratic thinking in the thirties was an association nicknamed X-Crise, so called because students matriculated at the Polytechnique—polytechniciens—were known familiarly as "les X."

Liberal orthodoxy came in for withering criticism from multiple directions. Among the critics numbered socialists of various stripes, but there were others as well: self-styled leaders of men, nonconformists, Catholic corporatists, technocrats, all of whom came eager and credentialed. They were not figures of power, but they would become so, and their rise dates, not from the war or the postwar years, but from the thirties. It may just be that the Third Republic, for better or for worse, was not so blocked as sometimes supposed.

The French socialist party, the SFIO, had long confronted an ideological dilemma. It imagined itself a revolutionary body, the vanguard
organization of a radiant socialist future, yet it at the same time went
about the more mundane business of running candidates for parliament and sponsoring reform legislation. A minority within the party
latched on to planning as an avenue out of the reform versus revolution conundrum. A planned economy was a concrete project that
might be realized in the here and now through practical political activity, but it also represented an advance on the existing order, a step
toward the socialist utopia of tomorrow. Would-be socialist planners
crystallized into a formal tendency in 1931, taking the name Révolution constructive. Georges and Emilie Lefranc were the animating
spirits of the group, which attracted just a handful of adherents, not
more than a dozen at first, but they made up in quality for what they
lacked in number. Claude Lévi-Strauss, just getting started as an ethnologist, belonged, and so did Robert Marjolin, an up-and-coming
economist with good connections outside socialist circles. As a student, Marjolin had done a year's training in economics at Yale University. On return to France, the patronage of a teacher, sociologist
Célestin Bouglé, got him a posting at the Centre de documentation
sociale. The Centre was lodged at the Ecole normale supérieure, and
there Marjolin worked alongside star *normaliens*, among them Raymond Aron and Jean Stoetzel, who, like Marjolin himself, were thinking their way toward a more social-scientific understanding of how
the modern socioeconomic order functioned. Marjolin's distinctive
mix of talents drew him to the attention of Charles Rist. In the
midthirties Rist had founded a think tank, the Institut de recherches
économiques et sociales, and though a convinced free marketer himself, he was keen to recruit the best minds to the enterprise. Rist invited Marjolin to sign on, and Marjolin did not hesitate to do so.[1]

The Révolution constructive group had intellectual heft, and it
had a cause. Planning was very much in vogue in the early thirties,
thanks in good part to the efforts of Belgian socialist Henri de Man.
De Man may not have been the first to concoct a plan. His, like so
many others, envisioned a mixed economy, part state-owned, part
private. But de Man's signal achievement was to persuade the Belgian

socialist party, the Parti ouvrier belge (POB), to adopt the idea. This happened in December 1933, and the event galvanized Lefranc's team, which arranged to have de Man's Plan republished in France. The SFIO majority, however, remained unmoved, "reserved, not to say hostile" to the whole concept of planning, as trade unionist René Belin put it. The party in fact made a point of slapping down the planners at its 1934 Toulouse congress. Lefranc's faction found allies in more venturesome comrades like André Philip and Jules Moch, but that was not enough to counterbalance the opposing weight of party chief Léon Blum.[2]

The trade-union movement, by contrast, proved itself far more receptive. The POB's conversion to planning roused sympathetic stirrings in French syndicalist ranks. The Fédération des fonctionnaires published a version of de Man's plan with favorable commentary from union officers, among them Robert Lacoste. The Fédération belonged to the Confédération générale du travail, France's largest national labor organization, and the CGT in turn began to take an interest. In January 1934, Belin, a member of the CGT executive, sketched a plan that he circulated among member organizations.[3] CGT secretary Léon Jouhaux constituted a study committee to come up with a more detailed version, appointing Lacoste, of course, but also fellow-traveling intellectuals like Lefranc and the polytechnicien Louis Vallon.[4] The committee wrote up what came to be known as the "Plan de la CGT," which was in due course adopted at the CGT's 1935 congress. The CGT's plan called for, in Lacoste's words, an "économie dirigée." Like the Révolution constructive plan, the CGT's imagined a two-sector arrangement: a public sector composed of nationalized industries from banking and insurance on down and a private sector governed, not by market forces, but by state directive. But who was to formulate such directives? On the CGT's scheme, that task fell to the Conseil national économique, an already existing institution that the CGT intended to redesign. In its present form, the CNE was a consultative body that brought together labor and management spokesmen under the auspices of the Ministère du Travail. The CGT wanted to bolster the CNE's executive capacity, to invest it with all necessary authority to intervene in the economy in the interests of harmonizing industrial activity; and the CGT wanted to formalize and extend the CNE's representative character, to make it a true "emanation of all the organized economic forces of the Nation."[5]

It was not just on the trade-union Left that the notion of planning caught on. Dissident socialists, *néo-socialistes* as they were called, seized on the idea too, though taking it in a less dirigiste, more corporatist direction. The "néos" were onetime SFIO members expelled from the party in 1933. They had urged the SFIO to join coalition cabinets, a strategy that ran against existing party policy. Until the Popular Front turn, Socialists, anxious to hold on to their working-class constituency, refused to enter into compromising political bargains with bourgeois partners. The néos had taken note of Hitler's rise to power, of the German demagogue's manipulation of nationalist rhetoric to rally a frightened middle class, and they urged the SFIO, in the interests of combating fascism, to respond in kind, a political departure that the party, proletarian and antinationalist, was unwilling to swallow. The néos, led by Marcel Déat, a war hero turned ardent pacifist, did not attract a substantial following. The events of 6 February 1934, however, kindled in them hopes that the situation might be turned around. A financial imbroglio implicating prominent politicians, the Stavisky scandal, had come to light, sparking a march on parliament, followed by a night of rioting that left almost a score dead. The néos plotted how they might tap into such massive but inchoate discontent.

The problem was to hone a message. The néos had launched a review, *L'Homme nouveau,* just prior to the Stavisky riots. This was the chosen vehicle, the "ideological laboratory" as one historian has called it, for cooking up the neosocialist appeal.[6] The paper understood itself as the standard-bearer of a new political class, "Team France" in Paul Marion's ringing phrase. *L'Homme nouveau* cited with approval the dictum of litterateur Abel Bonnard: "A nation can save itself without the help of a great man, it cannot do so without the existence of an elite." That saving elite once formed, its task was to "kick down the door" of a decrepit parliamentarism, "sweep out the thieves" within ("Down with the thieves" was a slogan bandied by the rioters of 6 February), and replace the lot with an "Etat fort."[7] Nor did the review settle just for sloganeering. It defined the strong state as "corporatist" in constitution and set about thinking through just what a practical corporatism entailed.[8]

This is where Pierre Laroque came in. Laroque was a Sciences Po graduate who had entered the junior ranks of the Conseil d'état. In 1931, he landed a post as chef de cabinet to then minister of labor Adolphe Landry. The connection was not just the result of happenstance. Laroque had an established expertise in managing the medical costs of social insurance, very much part of the Ministère du Travail's brief. No less relevant, there was a family tie. Laroque's father knew Landry's son-in-law, the Radical politician César Campinchi.[9] Laroque's record of public service and his work with insurance funds and doctors' unions had awakened him to what the state, working in collaboration with organized interests, could accomplish, and this experience was reflected in a series of articles he drafted for *L'Homme nouveau.*

France, Laroque diagnosed, suffered from an excess of individualism, the unavoidable consequence of a mind-set, "the ideology of 1789," that was all too prejudiced against intermediary bodies. In the present day, however, such bodies—trade unions, insurance funds, mutual-aid societies—were essential to the reordering of a social organism that had grown lax and incoherent. The problem was that existing unions and syndicates lacked both numbers and unity. They did not command large followings; they fought among themselves, sometimes with violence. The corporate world required a firm guiding hand that the state alone was in a position to provide. Yet the present-day state itself, weakened by parliamentary tussling, by "the evolution of liberalism," lacked the authority requisite to its tutelary task. It is not hard to detect an authoritarian impulse at work here, but Laroque, ever the measured civil servant, kept it in check. France needed an "Etat fort," but he did not specify how this was to come about. He noted that, in fascist regimes, the state dictated to corporations, which in turn dictated to constituents. Laroque, however, employed the vocabulary of arbitration and coordination when talking about state/corporation relations. On the matter of trade-union organization, on the other hand, he took a tougher stand. In this domain, the state might want to insist on strengthening union authority, not just over members, but over all workers in a particular sector, whether they wanted it or not. The particularism of individual interests had to be combated, even if this entailed "the limitation if not... the suppression of syndical liberty."[10]

It is not so surprising that the Left, at the outset of the depression decade, might explore dirigiste or even corporatist antidotes to the current crisis.[11] But the Left was far from alone in its critique of the prevailing disorder.

Maréchal Lyautey may be counted among the more renowned members of France's political establishment: a career military officer, a celebrated colonizer, a onetime minister of war. On his death in 1934, he was buried where he had served, in Morocco. In the wake of Moroccan independence, Lyautey's body was returned to France, where it now lies interred at the Invalides.

Lyautey early on carved out a public persona for himself as a leader of men. In 1891, he authored an article in the prestigious *La Revue des deux mondes* titled "Le rôle social de l'officier," a study of military authority, understood not just as an exercise in top-down command but as a spiritual dominion earned through self-discipline and moral example. A lifetime's experience came to persuade Lyautey that the qualities demanded of an effective military officer were no less essential to good leadership in the civilian world.

The year 1920 witnessed the founding of two new associations, the Equipes sociales and the Scouts de France (SdeF). Both organizations were Catholic, and both engaged Lyautey's attentions. Robert Garric, a war veteran, wanted to re-create in peacetime the social solidarity he had known at the front and to that end founded the Equipes sociales. The Equipes brought together laborers and young bourgeois Catholics in a spirit of common moral and educational endeavor. The kind of "go-to-the-masses" Catholicism that Garric preached, with an accent on youth and social exchange, was attractive to bright, eager souls like Simone de Beauvoir who came from good families but hankered for something more than a conventional life. And it appealed to Lyautey as well, who involved himself in the Equipes' study circle in working-class Belleville, laboring there alongside much younger men like Hyacinthe Dubreuil and Raoul Dautry, the former a trade unionist, the latter an engineer in the railroad industry.[12] Lyautey's encounter with the Equipes sociales may have been tangential; it was less so with the Scouts de France. The Fédération nationale des Scouts de France devoted itself, like Garric's Equipes, to the team spirit but with a more military and crusading twist. The Catholic scout movement conceived of itself as a twentieth-century reincarnation of "ce vieil idéal de la chevalerie chrétienne." Troops named themselves after champions of old, the spotless Bayard, the crusading Saint-Louis. Indeed, a militant purity was taken to be the very essence of scouting. The English scout pledged himself to cleanliness, but his SdeF counterpart went a step further, vowing to be "pure in body, thought, word, and deed." And the movement took as its emblem the *croix potencée* atop a shield. This had been Godefroy de Bouillon's blazon in crusading days, later taken up by the Knights of the Holy Sepulcher.[13] Throughout the interwar years, the position of *chef Scout* was occupied by a series of generals, and topping the SdeF hierarchy was its honorary president, none other than Lyautey himself.

The Equipe sociale and the scout troop both dedicated themselves to the collective, but Lyautey believed that every collective needed a *chef*, a leader who by word and deed helped to fuse the group into a team. In the early thirties, an aging Lyautey assembled a leadership team of his own, inviting round to his rue Bonaparte apartment half a dozen promising young men to ponder France's future.[14] Their number included Dautry and Garric, of course, but also the engineer and Catholic youth leader Georges Lamirand, former prime minister André Tardieu, and Lyautey's comrade in arms from colonial days, Colonel François de La Rocque, now the leading light of a rabble-rousing veterans' organization, the Croix de feu. These men did not have great faith in parliamentary institutions. Garric expressed sympathy for the 6 February demonstrations, and Croix de feu leaguers were numerous in the ranks of the rioters that day, though de La Rocque himself hesitated to endorse the disturbances. Parliament was the very embodiment of ineffectuality, a useless talking shop. What France needed was not deal-making politicians but men of action, *chefs*. And that's how Lyautey's acolytes imagined themselves, none more so than Dautry.

Dautry published a volume in 1937, *Métier d'homme.* The text was at once a salute to Lyautey and an update of the maréchal's message. It took the World War One infantry captain as its model of command, the officer who elicited obedience not by pulling rank but by force of character. Yet who, Dautry asked, were the leaders of the present day, the elite of the twentieth century that lay ahead? His answer came loud and clear: the leader of tomorrow was the engineer. In modern business, it was the engineer turned executive, versed in the "science of man," who had the skills and authority necessary to bring harmony to labor relations. What was true of business was true a fortiori of the modern state, which now more than ever needed the engineer's mix of technical competence and decision-making authority. Only a state so commanded, exempted from debilitating partisanship, could take charge of public affairs and, arbitrating among "coherent interests," effect a "revolution of order."[15] In Dautry's hands, Lyautey's paean to leadership took a technocratic turn. The spiritual qualities of the *chef* remained as ever preeminent but now melded with a vocabulary of science and expertise, the whole wrapped in a statism of corporatist coloration.

Dautry worked close to power. He was a member of Prime Minister Pierre Laval's brain trust in 1935, a squad of tough-minded budget cutters that included the brilliant career civil servant Yves Bouthillier and Claude-Joseph Gignoux, an economic journalist with close ties to the business world.[16] And throughout the thirties, as a railroad executive, Dautry lobbied hard to rationalize the hodgepodge of state-owned railway lines, an effort that culminated in 1937 in the formation of a single, unified state train service, the Société nationale des chemins de fer (SNCF).

It would seem that Dautry's world was far removed from that of the little reviews that were home to the so-called nonconformists. Yet the distance was not so great. Dautry's *Métier d'homme* was published in a series edited by a young philosopher, Henri Daniel-Rops, who, like Dautry, had been a regular at Lyautey's conclave of young leaders. But Daniel-Rops was also a founding member of a key nonconformist organ, *L'Ordre nouveau.*

There was an overlap in ideas as well. The nonconformist move-

ment mixed themes of spiritual renewal with grand schemes of economic reform accenting planism and/or corporate organization.
There was less talk of leadership than among Lyautey's crowd, but
the same insistence on risk taking and valor. As might be expected of
a movement of the young, nonconformists touted not so much their
technical mastery as their revolutionary élan, but even so they counted
an expert or two in their ranks like the economist François Perroux,
who could talk in more than generalities about practical solutions to
the present crisis. Yet, whatever the nuances distinguishing the various currents of nonconformism, all shared in a common and deep-
seated antipathy to liberalism and parliamentary democracy.

Plans, edited by the obstreperous young lawyer Philippe Lamour,
may be taken as a case in point. The review got started in 1931 and
made plain from the very first where it stood. The world was divided
into two parties, on the one side "the democrat individualist party,"
on the other side "the party of Youth." The former had built its fortunes on principles and institutions now grown outmoded: parliament, private property, Freemasonry, the "myth of liberty," and "a
so-called Greco-Latin culture." The latter meant to sweep away such
passéiste clutter. It was committed to fashioning a communal ethic
consonant with the demands of a machinist civilization and, on the
basis of that ethic, erecting a more rational social order. The new
ethic would be Sorelian, placing a premium on energy, youth, and
violence (Hubert Lagardelle, a surviving disciple of Georges Sorel's,
served on the review's editorial board). And the new order? Lamour
cited as an instance of what he had in mind the work of the architect
Le Corbusier. In July 1931, Le Corbusier published in *Plans* a vision
of the "Ville Radieuse," a modern city like New York but disciplined à
la Cartésienne in a way that the clamorous, turbulent, "dantesque"
New World metropolis was not. This was just the sort of thing France
needed, expostulated Lamour in the very next issue, an experimental project that embodied "discipline," "order," a "Plan." Lamour
sensed a great stirring abroad that resonated with his vision of an
energized tomorrow: in the Soviet Union, in Nazi Germany, and in
the United States, the land of youth par excellence.[17]

Lamour's soft spot for US dynamism earned him a pointed rejoin-

der from Robert Aron and Arnaud Dandieu, the authors of one of
the more caustic anti-American diatribes of the thirties, *Le Cancer
américain* (1931). America to them embodied "optimistic liberalism"
in its purest form, and they had occasion to detail what they meant by
the term in *L'Ordre nouveau*, a little review they started up in 1933.
Liberalism was corruption itself. It spoke the language of freedom
and disinterestedness, yet speculators and parasites were its greatest
beneficiaries. It congratulated itself on the high-mindedness of its
culture, all the while duping honest folk—the worker, the peasant,
the technician, the intellectual—with the smoke and mirrors of advertising and parliamentary hot air. Its supposed humanism concealed a
grasping inhumanity that worked its will through Fordist regimentation and a factory regime crushing to the "human person."[18]

There was a touch of small-is-beautiful nostalgia in all this, but
L'Ordre nouveau fancied itself the paladin, not of a bygone France, but
of an alternative future. The historian René Dupuis, writing in the
pages of the review, claimed for *L'Ordre nouveau* a lineage that encompassed the French Revolution and Paris Commune as well as more
traditionalist icons like Charlemagne, Saint-Louis, and Jeanne d'Arc.
The *Ordre nouveau* cadre were ardent youth after all; Dandieu, who
would die young, had a reputation as a "redoubtable tennis player."
And they were deep believers in the upswelling of energies, in transformation from below. Of course, France needed a "planned sector"
to organize the provision of basic needs, but otherwise dirigisme had
no place in the *Ordre nouveau* scheme of things. The review execrated
the Soviet Union for its statism, championing instead a bottom-up
organization based on rooted communities, the family, the region,
but above all the free corporation.[19] It was never specified, however,
how the free corporation of *L'Ordre nouveau* imagining was to be constituted, nor what relationship it might bear to existing trade union-
ism. And while the periodical was explicit, even ferocious, in its anti-
Americanism and anticommunism, its stance vis-à-vis the Italian and
German dictatorships was much more ambiguous, alternating between expressions of sympathy and a more prudent distance-taking.

The same cannot be said of Emmanuel Mounier's *Esprit*, which
showed greater resolution in its antifascism. The review published its

first issue in 1932. Like its nonconformist confreres, it reviled the bourgeois Republic, the political expression of a misguided individualism that traced its origins to the Renaissance. To be sure, Renaissance individualism had at first shown signs of vigor, generating a series of virile types: the conquistador, the Reformation zealot, the Don Juan. But such initial energies had played themselves out, finding one last incarnation in the appalling figure of the captain of industry before settling into the mediocrity of the present day. Bourgeois life now revolved around comfort and distraction, the once-vigorous individual making do with a placid existence spent tuned in to the radio or gaping at sports events. The Republic, with its parliamentary blather, its pandering to low desires, its moneygrubbing mores, suited such "individuals" all too well, and so France got the regime it deserved, spineless and decadent, unable to make the hard choices necessary to bring vitality and order back to the public domain.[20]

So this was the task *Esprit* set itself: to effect a spiritual revolution that would "redo the Renaissance," turning France away from a dried-up individualism toward a new age of risk taking and adventure, animated not by an ethic of greed but by a selfless and exigent idealism. A reborn France, composed not of individuals but of vital human beings, "human persons" in Mounier's vocabulary, would discover a new community that bound all in a spirit of mutual regard and team solidarity.

There is a vagueness to Mounier's personalism, but the vagueness dissipates if the doctrine's Christian subtext is kept in mind. The Thomist philosopher Jacques Maritain published *L'Humanisme intégral* in 1936. It too took off from a critique of the Renaissance. Humanism and Protestant Reform, both philosophies of the individual, had fragmented the unities of the medieval world, and Maritain aspired to restore that lost coherence through imagining a Catholic humanism that did not reject the unfolding of the self but which understood that the telos of the process lay, not in individuation, but in communion with humanity and God's divine purpose. Mounier himself was a serious Catholic. He had studied with a Catholic philosophy professor at Grenoble, Jacques Chevalier, and for a period considered writing a doctorate on the Golden Age Spanish mystic John of the Angels.[21] Among the score or so who attended the founding congress of *Esprit*, moreover, were a pair of ecclesiastics, Father Maxime Gorce and the abbé René de Naurois.[22] This is not to say that the review was sectarian, but it evidenced a spiritual discipline that was appealing to ethical-minded seekers, most of them Catholic but some, like François Goguel and Roger Leenhardt, of Protestant background.

Esprit's Christian humanism armed it against the fascist temptation. Mussolini's cult of the state, Hitler's racism and neo-paganism—both ran against the grain of a review that placed the highest premium on independence of spirit and the dignity of the human person. *Esprit* did not side with Franco in the Spanish Civil War, and in the wake of the Munich crisis the journal applauded the Third Republic's stiffening resistance in the face of the fascist menace (a stance that alienated Goguel and Leenhardt, however, who remained adamant pacifists).[23]

Was *Esprit*, then, a bulwark of republican democracy against fascism? No, that would not be the appropriate conclusion, for the Christian humanism of the *Esprit* team was tempered by powerful animosities against "the established disorder," animosities against parliamentary government and free-market capitalism that in time would lead a number of the journal's contributors down authoritarian paths, nonfascist to be sure but authoritarian just the same.

Esprit styled itself a revolutionary organ, the vanguard of a mass rebellion that augured the triumph of spirit over matter. This was a non-Marxist vision, and it aligned *Esprit* with a whole range of "revolutionary heresies" (as Leenhardt called them) of the sort espoused by nonconformist journals like Déat's *L'Homme nouveau* and Aron and Dandieu's *L'Ordre nouveau*.[24] Of all such heresies, Gaston Bergery's Frontisme held a particular fascination for Mounier's circle. Little wonder perhaps, as Frontisme's original cadre included a number of *Esprit*'s own founding fathers, Louis-Emile Galey and Georges Izard. Galey and Izard, however, had begun to move out of the review's orbit in 1933, looking to take a less reflective, more hands-on approach to politics. Hence their alliance, the year following, in a *front commun* with the renegade Radical politician Bergery. Bergery's crowd backed the Blum experiment, but the Popular Front once past, Frontisme's pacifism and deep anticommunism steered it toward a more indulgent stance vis-à-vis fascism abroad and toward a more "national" understanding of what revolution meant at home. *Esprit* reproached Frontisme for its anticommunist excesses, but the review's affection for Bergery himself remained undiminished. Indeed, Bergery's take on the revolution to come was not so different from *Esprit*'s own. As *Esprit*'s house philosopher, Jean Lacroix, put it, writing in 1938: "Every revolution is national. It is not made from above but from below."[25]

Mounier's team, however, was not altogether clear as to what a national revolution ought to look like. Galey, seconded by Mounier, laid out the case for a mixed economy. It was the state's duty to meet essential needs, an obligation that justified the state's stepping in to collectivize "certain of the vital forces of production" and to run them, according to plan, not as money-making operations, but as so many *services publics*. On the matter of private-sector organization, however, Mounier was less precise. Some form of corporatist or cooperative design was called for; Mounier himself endorsed awarding multiple votes to electors, one for each of the "communities" to which a voter belonged.[26] But he was aware that there were more thoroughgoing corporatist enthusiasts in the *Esprit* ranks, François Perroux for example, who eschewed notions of a mixed economy altogether in favor of a top-to-bottom corporatist order.

Perroux had an exceptional grasp of the European scene. He read several foreign languages and had spent time in Austria on a Rockefeller grant, absorbing the wisdom of the Vienna school of economics. Joseph Schumpeter has been described as Perroux's master, and the lesson Perroux drew from Schumpeter's teaching was this: that the laissez-faire era was over. Modern economies were no longer constituted of atomized individuals but of contending social actors whose clash sparked wage-and-price disequilibriums.[27] As a solution to such instabilities, Perroux touted what he called the "communauté de travail," a collectivity composed of organized labor and its management counterparts, bargaining together to fix wage-and-price levels. The state, of course, had the right in case of deadlock to move in and enjoin agreement.[28]

Perroux expounded on this scheme in the pages of *Esprit,* for which he began writing in 1936,[29] and then at greater length in a volume published under the title *Capitalisme et communauté de travail* (1938). Perroux was no partisan of the mixed economy but a corporatist through and through, and an aggressive corporatist at that. He relished the "virile" overtones of the phrase "community of labor." He appreciated that, in certain national settings, corporatist policy had to be imposed by force majeure. Such was the case in Salazar's Portugal, and Perroux, who shared in the cult of the leader so widespread in the thirties, made no effort to conceal his admiration for the Portuguese dictator, an admiration all the greater for the high idealism of the goal Salazar pursued: "the rebirth of a nation." For Perroux was very much a national revolution man. As he put it, echoing the words of Jean Lacroix: "For those of our generation, there is no revolution that is not national."[30]

It might seem improbable at first glance, but the engineers and businessmen who gathered to X-Crise ranks in the thirties had much in common with the nonconformists. X-Crise shared in nonconformity's cult of leadership and elite regeneration. That perhaps should not come as a total surprise. X-Crise recruited its membership among graduates of the Ecole Polytechnique, and the school took a special pride in its mission: the training, not just of engineers or scientists, but of the nation's elite, a cadre of leaders who, whatever their particular field of expertise, had a generalist's grasp of wider issues, moral as well as material.[31] Members of the X-Crise group also shared in nonconformity's critique of the free market. On this score, though, they did not so much reflect the training they got as break with it, for prevailing orthodoxy at the Polytechnique, as taught by professors of economics Clément Colson and François Divisia, was laissez-faire liberalism.

X-Crise may have overlapped with nonconformism on certain points but not on all. Not on the matter of revolution for one: the engineers of X-Crise were practical men with little appetite for revolutionary posturing. As inveterate problem-solvers, moreover, they took a less jaundiced view of the state than nonconformist intellectuals, who tended to favor corporatist schemes or a mixed economy with corporatist elements. X-Crise had a corporatist wing to be sure, represented by Robert Gibrat and Robert Loustau (also members of the *Ordre nouveau* cadre), but its cast of mind was more dirigiste in character. X-Crise dirigisme, however, was of a particular sort, intended to work, not by command in the socialist manner, but by regulation and directive, patterning entrepreneurial initiative without ever supplanting it. The challenge, from the X-Crise point of view, was to set the right rules, generative of rational and efficient entrepreneurial behavior, and this required a close watch on the direction the economy was taking, a task that in turn required a wide-angle, statistical grasp of trends. It was a task, though, that the X-Crise men were more than a match for. Divisia was a partisan of the free market but also a first-rate mathematician and a founding father of econometrics in France. His students may have eschewed his liberal commitments, but they took his econometric lessons to heart, applying them to a new understanding of how to make the nation's economy run.

The Centre polytechnicien des études économiques (CPEE): such was X-Crise's formal and rather cumbersome name. It was formed in December 1931 by a trio of Polytechnique graduates, Gérard Bardet, André Loizillon, and John Nicoletis, and in its first years the organization functioned more as a debating society than as a partisan body. Liberal voices were listened to. Colson and the up-and-coming star of liberal orthodoxy Jacques Rueff were invited round to join in the general exchange of views. Socialism too got a hearing. Nicoletis was himself "very much on the Left," and he got support in X-Crise debate from SFIO party regular Jules Moch and from the planist Louis Vallon. But an X-Crise mainstream soon emerged, led by Jean Coutrot, a remarkable man by all accounts. Coutrot, a veteran of the Great War, had lost a leg in combat yet remained an avid tennis player. He was an engineer by training but also a visionary who maintained a wide correspondence with unconventional souls like himself, from the maverick Catholic theologian Teilhard de Chardin to the New Age philosopher avant la lettre Aldous Huxley.[32]

Coutrot was a firm believer in the plan. The Great War and the depression had closed an era. "An irreversible change of civilization," as Nicoletis put it, was under way.[33] It was clear enough that the old laissez-faire order, centered on the profit-seeking individual, had lost its purchase. The unmediated pursuit of self-interest, as the economic slump made all too plain, led to irrationalities and disarray. And the individual? He was a figure of receding importance, as business enterprises, once family affairs, now took on more corporate, managerial forms. Auguste Detoeuf, an electrical industry executive, addressed a well-disposed X-Crise audience in May 1936 on "the end of liberalism."[34] The plan, however, promised a way out of the present, liberal-made crisis. For the ruthless and self-destructive egotism of yesteryear, it would substitute a new guiding ethic, "la notion du service social." And in place of the once-sovereign individual it would substitute a decision-making elite, harmonized and made coherent by "a community of culture."[35]

This is just the sort of scheme to be expected of take-charge polytechniciens, but X-Crise's idea of the plan entailed more than just a power grab. First, it was understood that the "administration," however disciplined and capable, needed social partners to provide advice and consent on the formulation of economic policy. There was talk of creating a two-chamber parliament, one house based on geographical representation, a second elected by professional groupings.[36] But what form ought these professional groupings to take? Should they be corporations? Should they be voluntary bodies? All sorts of ideas were floated, but there was a willingness among X-Crise folk to keep an open mind on the subject, open enough to ask the opinion of the interested parties themselves. This meant consulting, not just with management, but with labor, and to this end X-Crise invited well-disposed trade unionists round to lecture. René Belin addressed an X-Crise assembly early on in 1937, followed later in the year by Robert Lacoste.[37]

Lacoste talked about the CGT plan and dirigisme, but his ideas on these matters were just too rigid for X-Crise tastes. Coutrot, for one, wanted a more flexible system that respected "individual initiatives." The problem was to coordinate such initiatives, to encourage business strategies that advanced the "common good" and to stymie those that did not. What the "common good" meant in this connection was a problem in itself, but Jean Ullmo (an economist-mathematician who joined the CPEE board in 1936) had a definite opinion on the subject. He wanted to maximize *"productivity* and *not profitability."* X-Crise spoke a language not of statist command but of initiative, coordination, and productivity.[38]

With this vision came a statistical passion, a faith in the power of numbers to help monitor and foresee. As Gibrat wrote to Coutrot in 1935, "Do you see, the problem of planism is also the problem of economic forecasting. Yet, about forecasting we know next to nothing at all."[39] But X-Crise intended to make up for its intellectual shortcomings. It welcomed speakers like Divisia himself, who came to lecture on econometric methods. X-Crise constituted an Equipe de conjoncture in 1936, run by a recent recruit, the demographer and statistician Alfred Sauvy. The mathematical minded in due course began to rally to X-Crise ranks. Pierre Massé, a future pioneer of linear programming, joined the CPEE board in late 1936, at about the same time as did Ullmo, who was himself an early and enthusiastic proponent of economic modeling.[40]

The antiliberal ferment of the thirties drew its energy from a variety of sources, socialist to be sure, but also Catholic, nonconformist, and technocratic. These diverse currents, so distinct in inspiration, did not exist in isolation but intersected, exchanging ideas and personnel. At no time did they all come together to constitute a single antiliberal front, but there were moments when partnerships formed, amplifying the critical voice of those involved. It was the political crises punctuating the decade—the Stavisky riots, the Popular Front, the coming of the Second World War—that determined the particular shape of each coalition, weighting it in favor of one camp or the other. With each crisis, not just did the teamings alter, but a once-marginal antiliberalism drew closer to power, moving out of debating halls and amphitheaters into the corridors of government ministries where policy was made.

The February 1934 disturbances raised the unsettling specter of civil war; at least that is how the novelist and playwright Jules Romains interpreted the event. He said as much in a public address that March, calling on all men of goodwill to make common cause to find a constructive solution to the crisis. Romains's appeal was a prelude to the drafting of a plan (yet one more), which was ready for publication in

July, hence its nickname, the "Plan du 9 juillet." The document's economic prescriptions did not go beyond the commonplaces of the moment about planning and the mixed economy. But two points about
the text do bear underlining: its technocratic parti pris and its antiparliamentarism. The first was evident in its fixation on notions of "organization, hierarchy and competence." As for the second, the Plan du
9 juillet envisioned a cut-down-to-size legislative branch, hemmed in by
an array of reinvigorated executive organs: the prime minister's office,
the Conseil national économique, the Conseil d'état.[41] But then again,
given the mix of influences that went into the 9 juillet scheme, this
outcome is not so astonishing. Neosocialists were involved in the project at all stages. Laroque helped to shape the plan, even if he did not
endorse it in the end. Paul Marion, however, did and so too the editor of *L'Homme nouveau*, Georges Roditi. Déat, though not among the
original signers, attended later meetings of the "Group du 9 juillet."
X-Crise was also well represented among the signers, contributing
four in all: Bardet, Coutrot, Vallon, and Jacques Branger. A final contingent of signatories was supplied by the antiparliamentary leagues—
the Croix de feu and Jeunesses patriotes. What is remarkable is that
the plan, vague and dubious though it was, attracted some attention
from more mainstream political organizations. Armand Hoog of the
left Catholic Jeune République put his name to the document, and
the young turk Radical Jean-Jacques Kayser turned out for a "Groupe
du 9 juillet" assembly in October.[42] Not everyone, however, answered
Romains's call, not socialist party regulars like Marjolin, for example,
who in later years dismissed the plan as "pitiful": "a pre-Pétainism of a
sort," a characterization not far wide of the mark.[43]

All the talk about plans, so noisome in the early thirties, petered
out in the Popular Front era. Two of the Front's principal partners,
the Radicals and Communists, had no interest in planning at all, nor
for that matter did Blum and much of the SFIO leadership. But the
Popular Front government that took office in June 1936 did mean to
breathe new life into a sputtering economy, and that meant striking
out in new directions. Laval's budget cutting was eschewed in favor of
reflationary policies: stimulate demand, and production would re-
awaken in response, or so the argument went. A number of erstwhile

socialist planners had a hand in shaping this change of course, Marjolin foremost, who served as an economic adviser to Blum. Moch
too, who had a hand in negotiating the so-called Matignon accords.
The Popular Front electoral victory was greeted with a strike wave of
unprecedented proportions. The Blum government, once in office,
brought together representatives from the CGT and its management
counterpart, the Confédération générale de la production française,
to hammer out a settlement, the Matignon accords, which in its final
form included a 12 percent across-the-board wage hike.

The Blum government acted to build purchasing power, and it took
steps, more symbolic in the end than consequential, to demonstrate
its general command of the economy. An altogether new ministry
was created, the Ministère de l'Economie nationale (MEN), responsible for overall coordination of economic policy. Charles Spinasse, a
Socialist, took charge. He recruited a number of X-Crise men to help
run the new ministry: Branger, Coutrot, and Sauvy.[44] Spinasse also
worked hard to build up the various agencies now attached to it,
among them the Statistique générale de France (SGF, France's main
statistical bureau) and the CNE. The Statistique générale, where
Sauvy had worked since 1923, got a new director, André Fourgeaud.[45]
As for the CNE, Spinasse had hopes of elevating it from a low-key "site
of reflection" into something grander, a kind of "professional parliament." In the initial flush of labor/management concord following
on the Matignon agreement, it might have seemed to the CNE's leadership team—Georges Cahen-Salvador, Alexandre Parodi, and Jean-
Pierre Ingrand—that this was a live possibility.[46]

None of this came to pass. Spinasse and the MEN, though energetic and innovative (an attempt was even made to reopen the debate
on planning), were not listened to.[47] The SGF was a small operation,
employing just a hundred or so personnel, and it had little authority.[48] It could gather together numbers already in the public domain,
but it had no power to compel private industry to disgorge essential
statistical information. Nor did hopes for the CNE's transformation
come to realization. Employer attitudes stiffened in the months after
Matignon. The incumbent CGPF leadership was overthrown by hard-
liners, Claude-Joseph Gignoux in the lead. With Gignoux's arrival

came a change in name. The Confédération générale de la production française was rechristened the Confédération générale du patronat français, and with that came a change in policy as well. The new CGPF cast aside the pursuit of comity in favor of a strategy of confrontation, adjourning sine die all prospect of making the CNE into anything more than an advisory body.

The Popular Front was not the moment of breakthrough that the economic nonconformists of the thirties had hoped for. But that moment would come, and it was the looming threat of war that brought it on.

It was in April 1938, the month after Hitler's Anschluss of Austria, that Edouard Daladier became prime minister. He was determined to reignite the economy, the better to sustain a rearmament drive. As he saw it, this meant rolling back certain Popular Front legislation, in particular the forty-hour week legislated by the Blum administration in the summer of 1936. Experts (even some sympathetic to the Popular Front like Marjolin) judged the law an obstacle to increased productivity, and Daladier meant to weaken its application. That task fell to Minister of Finance Paul Reynaud, who turned to his cabinet to draft the necessary decree-laws. Reynaud's cabinet was a remarkable band. Headed by Gaston Palewski, a onetime protégé of the Maréchal Lyautey, it included a number of hard-driving functionaries on their way up in the world: Bouthillier, Debré, Sauvy, and, from the fall of 1939, Claude Gruson.

Gruson, a graduate of the Polytechnique, reminisced in later years about his 1930s self: "Like almost all polytechniciens of the era, I was apolitical, that is to say, on the Right."[49] On the Right: such indeed was the tenor of the Reynaud cabinet's work. The forty-hour week was well and truly gutted, Debré authoring the relevant legislation.

Three further sets of measures deserve mention in this connection. Debré and Sauvy were staunch pronatalists, admirers of perhaps the greatest pronatalist of the day, Adolphe Landry. Landry was not just a politician but a demographer and senior figure in the Alliance nationale contre la dépopulation. Sauvy described him as "that great man," a national eminence worthy of pantheonization.[50] As a deputy and populationist advocate, Landry had lobbied energetically through

the thirties in favor of measures to extend and streamline the operation of France's burgeoning system of family allocations. The Daladier administration acted to legislate Landry's proposals by decree,
adding into the package *une allocation pour la mère au foyer*, a special
cash allowance for stay-at-home mothers. It was Sauvy, Landry's acolyte, who claimed credit for drafting the measure.[51] And Sauvy, a bureaucratic scrapper of the first order (a quality perhaps to be expected
in an avid rugby man who knew his way around a scrum[52]), made
headway on a second front as well: the battle for statistics. In November 1938, he composed a decree that compelled businesses to fill out
SGF-circulated questionnaires, with financial penalties, albeit minor,
provided for in case of noncompliance. Sauvy deployed these new
powers to compile an industrial census, not the first of its kind but
the most complete to date, which would be ready for publication in
1941. Nor was this all. The Daladier administration created a new
organism attached to the SGF, an Institut de Conjoncture, charged
with assembling indexes of production and employment, the building blocks of any national accounting system. This was just the sort of
statistical forecasting agency X-Crise had dreamed of, and so it was
fitting that Sauvy, an X-Crise man, was placed in charge, all the more
so as it was he who had authored the decree-law establishing the Institut in the first place.[53]

The Daladier agenda was to restore order—in the workplace, the
family, the economy—and the prime minister turned with increasing
frequency to experts like Gruson, nonpartisan but on the Right, to
help out. The number of such experts in government did not de-
crease as the threat of war metamorphosed into outright hostilities.
Just the opposite. In September 1939, Daladier created a Ministère
de l'Armement responsible for all war production, appointing a non-
politician, Raoul Dautry, to the post. Dautry's tenure in office is noteworthy on several accounts.

First, he made gestures, more cosmetic than substantive it should
be said, toward reestablishing labor/management concord. The evis-
ceration of the forty-hour week had provoked the CGT into strike
action, which the Daladier administration had repressed with energy.
But now that war was declared, labor, even if still nursing its wounds,

had to be brought back on board. In the fall of 1939, Daladier made a conciliatory gesture toward the working poor, reestablishing the Secours national, a relief agency private in character but funded out of tax monies, to help the neediest. The job went to Dautry's old comrade in arms Robert Garric.[54] Dautry himself, as minister of armaments, played a vigorous part in attempting to reestablish the social peace. The first week of October, he invited round to his office businessmen and "responsible" trade unionists for common deliberations. The result was a signed agreement, the so-called Majestic Accords, which promised "confident collaboration" between labor and management in war production. The agreement did not bind anyone beyond the handful of signatories (among them Jouhaux), but it proved useful to Dautry. It gave the appearance that he had lined up worker support behind the war effort, and this at no cost to his own ministerial authority, which he wielded by all accounts with exceptional energy and effectiveness.[55]

There is an ongoing historiographical debate about how prepared France was to go to war with Germany, but no one disputes Dautry's feats of management and executive capacity. Dautry's period of command at the Ministère de l'Armement was a practical demonstration of what effective leadership, untrammeled by parliamentary bickering, could accomplish, and that is what it was meant to be.

While Dautry deserves the bulk of the credit for this achievement, he did not act alone but with a team of like-minded experts. He invited Jean Bichelonne, a former star student at the Polytechnique and an X-Crise fellow traveler, to become his technical director. As circumstances dictated, Dautry tapped a range of young talents for special missions and advice, from the planist Robert Lacoste on the Left to the auto executive (and Louis Renault's nephew-in-law) François Lehideux on the Right. Resolution, command, and problem solving were the qualities Dautry valued. It was a creed he had learned at Lyautey's side in the early thirties. And not just he, but the likes of Garric and Lamirand as well. What then more natural than that Dautry should turn to such old friends for assistance in running his ministry, naming the former as director of social services and the latter as manager of a munitions facility.[56]

Daladier departed office in March 1940 and was replaced by Paul Reynaud, but the change did not stanch the flow of technocrats into public service. Reynaud too had a predilection for experts, though experts, it should be said, of a none too reliable political orientation. The new prime minister appointed Paul Baudouin to run his war cabinet. Baudouin was an inspecteur des finances who had made a career in banking. He was also a fervent Catholic who looked to Salazar's Portugal as a model of the smooth-functioning state.[57] And Baudouin surrounded himself with men of similar views, Charles Célier and Henri Dhavernas among them. Both were career civil servants, and both were former Catholic scouts who retained an ongoing connection to the scouting movement. Battlefield reverses in the spring of 1940 forced the French government to relocate to Bordeaux. There Célier and Dhavernas paid a visit to the military commander of the region, the *chef Scout* General Lafont, who saluted them as the living incarnation "of a triumphant Catholicism."[58]

The self-styled innovators and nonconformist dissidents of the thirties did not pass the decade on the sidelines. They joined government ranks, first during the Popular Front but then in increasing number as the war approached. It was the national defense crisis that prompted the Republic's political elite to reexamine the liberal policies of bygone days, a process that permitted an influx of new policies and personnel. The result was a war-preparedness effort of major proportions, a *redressement* that got the economy moving again, feeding into, if but for a moment, a much-needed renewal of public confidence. But the technocratic inflection of late Republic policy, however successful on some fronts, had its worrisome side. For this was a conservative *redressement* that dictated to labor more than embracing it, that pushed hard for the most traditional family values, that effected its will through command and decree-law. More worrisome still was the orientation of the men involved. Many had future careers as ministers. Dautry, Lacoste, and Debré would all serve in that capacity, Dautry and Lacoste in the Fourth Republic and Debré in the Fifth. But the others? Baudouin, Bichelonne, Bouthillier, Dhavernas, Garric, Lamirand, Lehideux, even Sauvy: it was the Vichy regime that they would end up working for. The technocratic turn of the late thirties, then, left an ambiguous legacy. It breathed new life into 1930s France, foreshadowing the democratic statism that would become a hallmark of the postwar Republics, but it anticipated as well and in perhaps greater measure the authoritarian antiliberalism of the Vichy years that lay just ahead.

Family and Welfare

The same ambiguity is manifest in the domain of family and welfare policy. Planners fretted about France's economic backwardness, but to many critics it was the nation's failure to manage its human resources that posed the most urgent challenge. The French, it was lamented, just did not have enough children. The physical sciences had taught the mastery of matter, but the human sciences, which took the perfecting of the species as their object, lagged far behind. The result was a population grown feeble and decadent, unable to meet the demands of modern civilization and shrinking in number.

But all was not lost. There were voices ready to sound the alarm, pronatalist lobbying organizations like the Alliance nationale contre la dépopulation and social-science think tanks like Jean Coutrot's Centre d'études des problèmes humains (CEPH). The Alliance and the Centre took a scientific approach to France's human-resource crisis, but science did not preclude a concern with the moral regeneration of the nation. The Alliance, as the thirties wound down, struck up a partnership with Catholic interests, and as it did so, its demographic anxieties focused more and more on a reconstruction of family life. Coutrot's transcendentalist impulses have already been mentioned. He came to conceive the realization of human potential as a cosmic process, matter straining to raise itself toward spirit. The task of social science was to understand this movement and to construct the environments that would favor it. Coutrot over time tended to a holism with a metaphysical if not Catholic inflection, an evolution that brought him into deepening sympathy with Teilhard de Chardin and with a like-minded Frenchman then resident in the United States, the Nobel prize–winning surgeon turned eugenicist

Alexis Carrel, author of the international best seller *L'Homme, cet inconnu* (1935).

As in the domain of planning, so in that of family and welfare; the critics of the thirties did not remain on the margins but moved at decade's end into positions of influence. Daladier created an Haut Comité de la Population in 1939 to advise the government on demographic policy, and he populated the new committee with Alliance nationale officials. Carrel returned to France in 1940 to join Dautry's Ministère de l'Armement. The national defense crisis brought onetime Cassandras into power, and it created an opening as well for the policies they espoused. The Daladier administration enacted the so-called Code de la famille in 1939, a remarkable document, as will be seen, not just for its familist bias but for its punitiveness. Historians have written of the various foreshadowings of Vichy policy in the late Third Republic, of the *Vichy avant Vichy* phenomenon. The Family Code is cited as a case in point and with good cause. And yet, at the Liberation, Vichy family policy was not so much overturned as assimilated, appropriated as a building block in the creation of a new welfare apparatus. Here, as with planning, the late Third Republic left a double legacy, Vichyite avant la lettre to be sure but also anticipatory of the republican order that took shape in the postwar years.

The Alliance nationale pour l'accroissement de la population française was founded in the 1896 by the statistician and criminologist Jacques Bertillon. Alliance members, as many others in the fin de siècle, bemoaned France's declining birthrate and wanted to do something about it, but the organization was unique in the social-science perspective it brought to the enterprise. It mobilized numbers, charts, graphs, the whole apparatus of a nascent science of demography to demonstrate the perilous consequences of population decline, and that social-science commitment did not flag in the interwar decades. Sauvy first linked up with the Alliance in the twenties when it commissioned him to tabulate a number of demographic projections. Laroque joined the organization the decade following, working up an expertise on population issues that he made use of in a series of radio broadcasts on the subject in the midthirties.[59] Both, of course, considered themselves disciples of a much more senior figure, Adolphe Landry.

Landry was a man of many parts: a politician, an Alliance official (he became a vice president in 1923), and an accomplished demographer in his own right. He authored a text in 1934, *La Révolution démographique*, which tracked the arc of Europe's population from ancient times to the present. Landry sketched the process in three phases: an old demographic regime giving way to a modern one, passing through an intermediary stage along the way, a period of demographic transition defined by dropping mortality. The notion of a demographic transition still figures in the modern demographer's conceptual tool kit. Landry may or may not deserve credit for inventing the idea, but he was among the first to explore its causes.[60] Landry forwarded a copy of the book to his friend Dr. Robert Debré. Robert in turn passed it on to his son Michel, just then starting out at the Conseil d'état, who devoured the text, scribbling detailed annotations in the margins.[61]

The Alliance nationale, however, for all its scientistic pretensions, was at bottom a lobbying organization. It had a pronatalist agenda to push, which from the midthirties took at once a more militant and more conservative turn. The generation of the Great War, the Alliance pointed out, had lost its best men and was not reproducing in sufficient number. That sad fact had become all too apparent mid-decade when, for the first time, deaths began to outnumber new births. It was at this moment, in 1936, that the organization changed its name to the Alliance nationale contre la dépopulation. The mounting Nazi threat heightened the Alliance's sense of national crisis. A France that meant to stand up to the Germans required soldiers, but in a country short of fresh young men, where were the bodies to be found? The United States had replenished its population through immigration, but Alliance vice president Paul Haury rejected this option. For look, he wrote, what had happened to America: "the exploits of gangsters and child-murderers demonstrate that there is something disordered in that country, whose traditions have been swamped by a flood of too many heterogenous immigrants."

No, what France needed was "a family policy," a concerted public effort to strengthen families, large ones above all, which constituted "a veritable moral elite."[62] This was no easy task to be sure. In a "materialist and calculating society," who wanted to bear the expense of children? But well-crafted policy might counter the regnant self-centeredness of the day. What if women were enfranchised and families got extra votes for every minor child? What if the system of family allocations was better funded and extended to encompass wider swaths of the population? What if the state provided financial incentives for women to leave the workforce and return to home life? Then there would be little excuse not "to be fruitful and multiply," and France would rise again, its virtue restored, its population reinvigorated.[63]

The Alliance's embrace of an aggressive familism[64] brought it friends in Catholic circles. Indeed, on matters of family policy, the Church and the Alliance held almost identical views. It was Catholic employers who took the lead in organizing the first family allocation schemes. Labor turmoil during 1919 and 1920 had exerted a strong upward pressure on wages. Employers, Catholic employers in the lead, fought back, setting up management-run family allocation *caisses* that paid out benefits to workers with large families. The more children, the more substantial were the payments, but workers had to demonstrate a record of good character to qualify. From the employer's perspective, the arrangement offered nothing but advantages: it was controlled by management; it incentivized workers to prudent behavior; and not least of all, it might be cited in justification of capping wage increases. Why, after all, pump up pay rates when that would mean taking money away from the *caisses*, that is, out of the pockets of the neediest workers, men with substantial families? The family allocation system took off in the twenties. By decade's end, more than two hundred *caisses* existed, covering an estimated four million wage earners.[65]

The Church's commitment to the large family was matched by a commitment no less intense to the stay-at-home mother. Pope Pius XI himself said as much in the encyclical Quadragesimo Anno (1931),[66] and the pope's words were taken to heart by Catholic Action organizations like the Jeunesse ouvrière chrétienne (JOC). The pope had

wanted to steer the Catholic laity away from sterile political agitations. In 1926, he condemned the ultra-right Action française, which
campaigned under the banner "politics first." What Catholics needed
was not partisanship but spiritual renewal, the healing power of Catholic Action. The response among the Catholic laity in France was
swift and impressive, resulting in a burst of associational activism.
The JOC was created in 1927, followed by the Jeunesse agricole chrétienne (JAC) and the Jeunesse étudiante chrétienne (JEC), both
founded in 1929. Indeed, the rededication of youth to the Christian
life constituted a core ambition of Catholic Action, and the JOC for
one went at the task with an inventive zeal. JOCistes devised a coat of
arms for themselves, a young blade of wheat twined around a Maltese
Cross. This banner in hand, they marched into spiritual battle, inton-
ing the refrain of the "Chant de la JOC mondiale" as they went: "forts
de nos droits, soyons vaillants / fiers, purs, joyeux et conquérants."[67]
And the JOCistes could stage a mass event as memorable to participants as any Popular Front manifestation. JOC officials mounted a
three-day Paris gala to commemorate the organization's tenth anniversary in 1937. Present at the occasion were a trio of aspirant civil
servants, all ex-Catholic scouts: François Bloch-Lainé, Charles Célier,
and Henri Dhavernas. Bloch-Lainé recollected in later years how
staggered his companions were by the "spectacular élan" of the event,
and well they might have been.[68] The festivities on the second day
were capped by a nighttime festival of labor, which featured a parade
of trades-workers followed by a sudden blackout. A spotlight flashed,
illuminating a forty-foot cross borne by a cohort of JOCiste youth. A
choir demanded, "But where then is the architect of *la Cité?*" to which
the assembled crowd shouted in response "It is He." And, of course,
it was not just labor that the JOC feted but also the family. Indeed, the
whole first day of the tenth-anniversary gala was given over to the
theme of *le retour de la mère au foyer.*[69]

But care should be taken not to paint Catholic Action's cult of
motherhood in colors too traditionalist in hue. No doubt Catholic
activists wanted women to keep out of the workplace, but the Christian family they dreamed of was not altogether a throwback to an
outworn, patriarchal past. Father was meant to be chef de famille but

in a family reconceived, no longer as an inflexible hierarchy, but as a team. Wives submitted, but it was a "submission of love which did not entail an abdication of personality."[70] The wife, moreover, was meant to be active outside the home, not on the job of course, but doing parish work or engaging in Catholic Action. A pair of Catholic Action groups, JOC spin-offs, were in fact set up for young marrieds, the Ligue ouvrière chrétienne for husbands and the LOCF for wives, the two fusing in 1942 to form the Mouvement populaire des familles. There was concern too that female spirituality change with the times. Diocesan bulletins encouraged young women to practice retreat and embrace a Christocentric faith focused less on the infant Jesus than on the Savior's adult example. A woman who made a Christian home, took part in civic action, and practiced her religion with a mature seriousness: was she not, some asked, entitled to vote? Christian democrats, the most "progressive" of the era's Catholic factions, came out for women's suffrage as well as for the family vote, which meant the apportionment of multiple votes to large families.[71]

On the war's eve, the Alliance nationale and Catholic familists had come to hold almost identical views. The path to demographic rebirth, it was agreed, lay through a buttressing of family values, a convergence that found practical expression in growing ties between the Alliance nationale and the Church. Fernand Boverat, the president of the Alliance, paid a visit in early 1938 to the archbishop of Paris, His Eminence Cardinal Verdier. Verdier gave his blessing to the Alliance program and pledged that the clergy would crusade for it "more actively than ever." Verdier himself was invited to join the Alliance's Comité de patronage. This was just the opening salvo, for in subsequent months the Alliance published a pastoral letter from Verdier condemning "the materialist atmosphere" of the day and then later printed a pronatalist appeal signed by five cardinals of the Church.[72]

The crisis of the thirties rerouted the pronatalist movement, taking it in a familist direction that yoked demographic science to a much larger project of moral, not to say Christian, regeneration. The same coupling of the scientific and the transcendental is evident in the work of Coutrot's CEPH, though here it was not so much the fate of the family as the future of the human sciences, indeed of humanity itself, that was at stake.

The CEPH was never a large organization. It met for the first time in July 1936 at the abbaye de Pontigny, a picturesque Cistercian monastery located in the Yonne countryside that had been converted, thanks to the efforts of Paul Desjardins, into a meeting center for cultural and intellectual events. An unspecified number of participants, in all probably not more than a score, took part in four days of informal conversation, resulting in formation of a four-man executive committee that included Carrel, Huxley, the art historian Henri Focillon, and Georges Guillaume, an X-Crise engineer. A flier was later circulated that identified the objectives of the association as well as the names of eighteen *membres conseillers*. An important minority on the list—Bardet, Branger, Loizillon, Sauvy, and Ullmo—were X-Crise members. There were a handful of reform-minded, "practical" trade unionists, including Belin, Lacoste, and Dubreuil. The balance was made up of prominent personalities with a record of interest in the human sciences, from the educator Maria Montessori to André Siegfried (star lecturer at Sciences Po) to the Jesuit priest turned paleontologist and philosopher Teilhard de Chardin.[73] Not all would prove to be reliable participants in the long run, but the roster gives a rough indication of CEPH's connectedness to the various nonconformist milieus of the era.

The first Pontigny get-together was followed by five more, until the war intervened. The regular work of the organization, however, was carried on back in Paris by the CEPH's home office, which Coutrot directed, and by a trio of smaller collaborative bodies, the Groupe Humanisme économique, the Group d'Etudes psycho-biologiques, and the Institut de psychologie appliquée. All this was but too typical of *l'esprit des années trente*: the out-in-the-country casualness of the Pontigny meetings, the preoccupation with team endeavor, the search for a new humanism. What made CEPH stand apart was Coutrot's vision. He understood human history in general evolutionary terms. The potential of mankind manifested itself in a series of material and moral advances, each advance or phase characterized by an equilibrium

point, an ordering of things that permitted the maximum, most efficient expression of human energies. In the contemporary world,
however, the material and spiritual realms were out of whack. Science
and industry had unleashed productive forces of immense power, but
the human person was not at home in this brave new world. People
were overwhelmed, rather, their somatic and mental energies failing
to work in unison, their sense of self staggered by a civilization that
thwarted rather than nurtured their abilities. The disharmony that
resulted left individuals prone to a paralyzed passivity and societies
vulnerable to the yet more massive disruptions of "war and bloody
revolution."[74]

What the world needed, now more than ever, was a fuller understanding of "that great unknown: Man" in order to restore the individual's internal equilibrium, in order to harmonize selves with the
environments they lived in. This was the task Coutrot set for himself
and the "elite" of researchers he gathered around him. It was a commitment that fueled Coutrot's sympathy for all manner of schemes,
from the Montessori school to Le Corbusier's "human urbanism,"
designed to model human behavior through environmental manipulation.[75] Coutrot, it will come as little surprise, was a longtime proponent of the scientific organization of work. And, for much the same
reason, he was interested in the persuasive power of advertising.
CEPH struck up a partnership with the founder of L'Oréal, "our
friend [Eugène] Schueller." Coutrot enthused about L'Oréal's soap
ads. Here was "applied psychology" at work, the shaping of human
desire via imagery and suggestion.[76]

There was a cold, manipulative rationalism to much of this, but it
was a rationalism not inconsistent with more metaphysical impulses.
Coutrot expressed sympathy for Aldous Huxley's experiments with
"spiritual exercises" and Zen meditation. Peace of mind, Coutrot believed, was the first step toward peace on earth.[77] For similar reasons
he was drawn to the philosophy of Teilhard de Chardin, who understood human evolution, not just as an organic phenomenon, but as a
spiritual one, the sentient self rising first to consciousness and then
to union with the spiritual principle itself, Jesus Christ. The Christian
denouement of the process may not have gripped Coutrot, but he

did appreciate Teilhard's insistence on the evolutionary and ascendant arc of spirit. Scientific rationalism and the Christian worldview,
Coutrot concluded with some amazement, were not antithetical but
complementary. Or as he expressed it in a letter to Antoine de Saint-
Exupéry (himself a Teilhard aficionado): "Recent contacts have shown
me that French Catholic thought, after two thousand years of evolution, has arrived at the exact same conclusions we engineers have
arrived at, reasoning on a purely objective basis."[78]

Coutrot's CEPH then was a complicated mix of things. It was a
think tank, governed by a strong-minded individual but which at the
same time placed a premium on collaborative research. It was inspired by a holistic vision that aimed, through scientific means, to
achieve a total renovation of the human species, and yet, for all Coutrot's science talk, he never forgot the importance of spiritual and
metaphysical concerns.

In all these respects, Coutrot's project dovetailed with the ambitions of Dr. Alexis Carrel, in the interwar decades among the most
celebrated medical researchers in the world. Carrel's high reputation
rested on two pillars. He was a pioneer in organ transplant work, garnering a Nobel Prize in 1912 for his research in the field. It was as a
Frenchman based in America that Carrel won the award. He was an
employee at the time of the Rockefeller Institute, a position he had
taken up some half-dozen years before. Indeed, Carrel spent much of
his adult life in the United States, where he developed a friendship,
both affective and professional, with Charles Lindbergh. Carrel, indeed, was expecting Lindbergh and his wife to dinner the very night
the Lindbergh baby was kidnapped.[79] The two men worked as well as
socialized together, collaborating on the development of a device to
keep organs alive outside the body. Over time, however, Carrel's passion for the laboratory dissipated, and he turned more to scientific
popularization, an enterprise, as it happened, at which he excelled.
The publication of *L'Homme, cet inconnu* (1935), a best seller on two
continents, transformed him at a stroke into a celebrity scientist.

The book's hard-edged, often repellant eugenicism was very much
of its era. Industrial civilization was eating away at the fiber of humanity. The machine enslaved; radio vulgarized; comfort-giving amenities

enfeebled. The process of natural selection would in normal circumstances have pared away the accumulating rot, but the medical sciences, motivated by a sentimental humanitarianism, had found ways to keep the weak alive, to prolong the lives of the unadapted. The overall quality of the population deteriorated in proportion, and, worse still, the process was abetted by the democratic spirit of the age, which imputed equal worth to all citizens and empowered the mass of mankind, however unfit, to rule. Yet egalitarianism ran counter to the natural order of things. In a right-ordered society, it was not majorities who took the lead but the exceptional few who imposed their will by force of personality. Carrel in fact had a special appreciation for the forceful personality, for it was "the passion to conquer" that made possible great things: "It led Pasteur to the renovation of medicine, Mussolini to the reconstruction of a great nation, Einstein to the creation of a universe."[80]

And, Carrel believed, great things still remained possible. The problem was to reconstruct an elite, to train the best in a physical and spiritual discipline that would enable them to take charge. Leadership mattered to Carrel. He liked his American secretary to address him as "chief." When Carrel himself cast about for models of what leadership meant, he turned not just to contemporary examples, like Mussolini and Einstein, but to historic ones: to the knights, monks, and guildsmen of the middle ages. It was the modern-day equivalent of men such as these that Carrel was looking for, "an ascetic and mystic minority" with the spiritual ascendancy to take command and restore to a weakened mass its fast-diminishing "virility."[81]

Carrel did not want for ideas on how to toughen up a degenerating species. On the epidemiological front, he recommended improved diet and a regimen of exercise. On the eugenic, he talked about requiring marriage-bound couples to undergo a prenuptial exam. On the whole, Carrel eschewed negative, disciplinary measures, but he did countenance the whip for criminals and the gas chamber for the most hardened convicts. For the moment, these were just ideas. Human engineering was no simple matter but necessitated a fuller understanding of the species and what made it tick.

Two further points bear making in this connection. First, Carrel's understanding of the human sciences encompassed more than just epidemiology and eugenics. The human person was a physical or reproductive organism, but more than that: he had a spiritual dimension as well, a capacity for aesthetic, moral, and religious experience, for beauty, love, and grace. Nor were the material world and mind unconnected realms. They interacted, and Carrel took a special interest in all forms of such interaction, from hypnotic suggestion to clairvoyance to telepathy. In 1902, Carrel had witnessed a faith healing at Lourdes, sparking in him a lifelong interest in the power of prayer to comfort and to mend.[82]

Second of all, Carrel had some notion, albeit imprecise, as to how to bring into being the new "science of man" he deemed so essential. He delivered a speech to the Phi Beta Kappa society at Dartmouth in 1937 outlining what he had in mind. The Rockefeller and Pasteur Institutes, Carrel reflected, studied disease, which was all fine and good, but what about preventive medicine? What about an institute, as Carrel put it, for "the prevention of mental and organic deterioration and for the improvement of the individual and of civilization"? In France, there was a growing interest in precisely such an enterprise. Raoul Dautry for one had called for a new "science of man," and there was a group, Carrel went on, that had met just last year at Pontigny "to try to coordinate the elements of a complete knowledge of man."[83] CEPH, for a moment, might well have appeared to Carrel as just the kind of human sciences think tank he was looking for, but his connection to Coutrot's organization was never more than passing.[84] Carrel's name, which figured on the CEPH's executive board into the fall of 1937, was dropped soon thereafter. Carrel himself sent in a formal resignation to Coutrot later that year, expressing his "deep sympathy" for Coutrot's efforts but explaining that he just did not have the time to get involved in the way he should. Carrel, in the meantime, never attended a Pontigny meeting. On the other hand, he and Coutrot stayed in contact up to the outbreak of the war, and Carrel kept track of the goings-on at CEPH via correspondence with a younger confederate and CEPH associate, Dr. André Missenard.[85]

Carrel felt CEPH's gravitational pull, but it never drew him away from the project he cherished most, the founding of a "Center for

the Study of Civilization," with himself in charge. What he needed to
this end were patrons and allies, and Carrel busied himself as the
decade wound down trying to drum up both. To American backers,
he sketched in plans for an "Institute of Man," which he envisaged as
an all-male operation (Carrel was a deep misogynist), run by a nu-
cleus of "native-born Americans."[86] To French friends, he proposed
an "Institut national pour la Rénovation française." Missenard volun-
teered to help line up collaborators, and he felt that he had found
one of top quality in André Siegfried. Missenard was a researcher in
his own right who studied the impact of climate effects on human
evolution. Siegfried was author of a celebrated text on how geography and milieu patterned electoral behavior. The two men, holist
each in his own way, hit it off over a lunch, and Carrel, informed of
the encounter, waxed enthusiastic about Siegfried's possible contribution to the "centre de synthèse" of which he dreamed.[87]

Coutrot and Carrel had much in common. They both understood
the contemporary crisis as a consequence of modern man's inadapta-
tion to industrial civilization. The species, both believed, needed re-
fitting, and it was up to experts—engineers and scientists—to figure
how this was to be done. Coutrot managed to assemble a team of experts for the job; Carrel got no further than the planning stage. But
each understood the experts' task in much the same way: to arrive at
a new understanding of "Man," a creature of metaphysical as well as
organic appetites, and to concoct schemes to reconfigure the human
environment in order to realize humanity's physical and moral potential. The kinds of schemes Coutrot canvassed had a New Age feel;
not so Carrel's, which had a hard eugenicist edge.

The differences between the two extended into politics as well.
CEPH was very much embedded in the nonconformist milieu. Its
membership overlapped with that of X-Crise. It sought out collaborators among trade-union planists. And it dabbled in a spirituality appealing to independent-minded Catholics like Teilhard. On the war's
eve, *Ordre nouveau*–group veterans Robert Aron and Alexandre Marc
made an effort to rally what remained of the nonconformist movement. The results were modest but not uninteresting. In August 1938,
a meeting was convened at a mountain retreat near Gap in the French

Alps. It was, in its way, a typical nonconformist event, mixing intellectual exchange with the out-of-doors life. And who was represented
there? The *Ordre nouveau* group, of course, *Esprit* in the person of its
music critic Henri-Irénée Marrou, and CEPH in that of Coutrot.[88]
There was subsequent discussion of drawing up a charter for the *fé-
dérés*, which was the name the group went by. Marc invited Coutrot to
help and instructed him to contact the representative of the "feder-
als" in Paris, Paul Flamand, codirector of the Le Seuil publishing
house.[89] X-Crise engineers, planists, nonconformist intellectuals, independent Catholics: such were the human ingredients of the CEPH-
ian milieu.

Carrel's political associations were of an altogether different sort,
more hard-line and right-wing. That is not surprising given the powerful hatreds that motivated him, animosities that were just between-
the-lines glimmerings in his published work but which blazed with a
ferocious intensity in private correspondence. He despised what he
called "the imbecility of democracy." Demagogy, the democratic
"virus" par excellence, had sapped France's energies, reducing "this
great country" to second-rank status. In the Third Republic, it was
the "spirit of small shopkeepers" that reigned. All great enterprises
were reduced to moneygrubbing "deals." Popular government, Carrel wrote in September 1938, "kills the great races, slowly but surely,"
and such was bound to be France's fate without a saving authoritarian
kick in the pants.[90]

Carrel was no more indulgent toward Jews. He referred to them in
a 1940 letter as "that garbage [crapule] which has infiltrated France
these last 20 years."[91] When his friend Lindbergh sidled up to the
Hitler regime in the late thirties, causing a public outcry, Carrel at-
tributed the aviator's plunging popularity to "Russian and Jewish propaganda." The Munich crisis of 1938 raised the specter of a new
round of hostilities with Germany. Carrel, who had no quarrel with
Hitler, blamed the confrontation on the usual suspects: "we are being
pushed into this war by the Soviets and the Jews."[92] The war did indeed come. Carrel returned to France to help his country through
the crisis, and he was invited to deliver a radio address by the Daladier administration, but he hesitated: "To speak on the radio, yes. But

the Jews control the radio. I can't say there what truly needs to be said."[93]

As the preceding makes all too plain, Carrel's anti-Semitism was often paired with an anticommunism just as passionate. Daladier's crushing of the CGT's 1938 strike elicited a telegram of congratulation from Carrel to the prime minister. Not long thereafter, he wrote to a friend of the urgency of suppressing the Communist Party altogether. And just on the eve of the war, Carrel went a step further, advocating the roundup of all Communists and their internment in "concentration camps."[94]

Carrel's prejudices situate him on the Right, but what kind of Right was he attracted to? Carrel liked demonstrations of force, a predilection that prompted him to a definite appreciation of the era's strongmen. In 1937, he looked to Italy and to Germany as Europe's best hope against the disintegrative effects of "machine civilization and Russian communism."[95] In early 1938, Carrel received a fan letter from a German doctor, vaunting Hitler's efforts "to keep the race pure and the bloodstream healthy." Carrel replied in appreciative terms: "I am following with profound attention the innovations of your Führer. . . . The organization of special schools for the training of leaders appears to me to be a great idea."[96] As a resident of New York City, Carrel noted with disappointment the mounting American indignation at the conduct of Europe's dictators. Reared on an intellectual diet of Washington and Lincoln, he despaired, the Americans just did not understand "that Hitler, Salazar, Mussolini express the defensive reaction of nations that want to go on living."[97] France too had its hard-faced men who exalted the nation above all, and Carrel was drawn to them just as he was to the likes of Mussolini. On a visit to France in 1935, he attended a meeting of de La Rocque's Croix de feu and came away impressed by the moral conviction of the militants he encountered there. Later in the decade, Carrel's attentions drifted away from the Croix de feu to Jacques Doriot's more radical, indeed fascist, Parti populaire français, which the good doctor praised as a welcome "small light on the horizon." The PPF in fact claimed him as a member in 1938. Carrel, however, was never a man of fixed loyalties. He was just as prepared in 1938 and 1939 to commend Daladier's energies and determination as Doriot's.[98] What counted most to him was a resolve that expressed itself in hard-fisted policy.

Yet force was not all that mattered. Carrel was in his peculiar way a believer. As a youth, he had attended Jesuit school in Lyon (in the company of Claude-Joseph Gignoux, who was, in many respects, Carrel's temperamental match), and that training left a lifelong imprint. In the thirties, Carrel spent stretches each year vacationing in Brittany. There, he took an interest in the local branch of the JOC, whose manifestations of faith and goodwill gave him reassurance as to the moral vitality of the local population. In the case of a second Catholic youth organization, Coeurs vaillants, interest turned into outright patronage, Carrel agreeing to preside over the neighborhood section. Back in France in 1940 to help in the war effort, Carrel fell in with a crowd of like-minded men whom he found "very interesting, such as Garric, Dubreuil, [Georges] Duhamel."[99]

Scientists of all kinds—demographers, human engineers, eugenicists—took a deepening interest in family and population issues over the course of the thirties. The relevance of this phenomenon to the present discussion is threefold. In the minds of many, from Boverat to Coutrot to Carrel, the physical regeneration of the nation entailed a concomitant spiritual revival framed in often explicit religious terms. The political center of gravity of this new familist Weltanschauung tilted to the Right. To be sure, the profamily coalition featured old republican warhorses like Landry, but it encompassed as well nonconformists à la Coutrot, an important Catholic Action contingent, and outright authoritarians in the Carrelian mold. Such was the climate of the thirties that this odd assortment of familist bedfellows enjoyed ever closer ties to governing circles as the decade drew to its close. Republican officialdom turned to them, inviting them into government, consulting them on legislation, with the unsurprising result that the regime's welfare policies took a sharp familist turn.

It was the Daladier administration of 1938–1940 that opened the breach. The gestures were small at first. In August 1938, the prime minister placed the microphones of state radio at the disposal of Alliance nationale spokesmen. Boverat organized a series of talks on population matters, which ran through the fall of that year. In March

1939, it was Landry's turn to get airtime with a radio lecture on "the demographic revolution." That same spring, the postal service issued a pair of stamps: one, for letters, depicting a baby at its mother's breast, and the other, for postcards, representing a baby in its cradle. The government earmarked a portion of the proceeds from stamp sales to fund the Alliance's pronatalist crusade.[100]

Such intersections took a yet more official turn in February 1939 with Daladier's decision to constitute an Haut Comité de la Population (HCP), a policy advisory board attached to the prime minister's office. The committee consisted of five persons, expanded to seven in April 1940, and it was presided over by a career civil servant, the conseiller d'état Jacques Doublet. Three points bear making about the HCP's composition. First, its scientific bona fides were beyond question. Landry belonged, as did Sauvy, who was one of the April 1940 add-ons. Second of all, Daladier, though leader of the anticlerical Radical Party, did not scruple to appoint a representative of the "Catholic and conservative Right" in the person of Senator Georges Pernot.[101] Pernot was president of the Fédération nationale des Associations de familles nombreuses, a Christian counterpart to the Alliance nationale.[102] And it was in the name of a religion-inspired familism that Pernot had spearheaded passage of the 1932 family allocation bill, one of the decade's most significant items of welfare legislation. The law did not alter how family allowance funds were run. They remained, as before, under employer tutelage, but it did enjoin all employers, like it or not, to affiliate to a local *caisse*, thereby adding an element of universal obligation to a system once particularist and voluntary. The third point, however, is that in the final analysis it was neither science nor religion that enjoyed the upper hand at the HCP but the Alliance nationale. Four appointees were also Alliance members: Boverat, Doublet (who joined the Alliance in November 1939), Landry, and Pernot (a man of many affiliations).[103]

The HCP turned out to be just a stepping-stone for Pernot. Daladier was succeeded by Reynaud in the early spring of 1940. Reynaud undertook a cabinet reshuffle that June, creating in the process a brand-new administrative portfolio, the Ministère de la Famille, and it was Pernot who was nominated to the post. The defeat of France intervened, however, before the new minister had any chance to leave a mark.[104]

Nor was it just Alliance men, like Boverat and Pernot, whom the government tapped for expert advice and leadership. Carrel respected Dautry, and the admiration proved to be mutual. In the early months of 1940, Dautry, as minister of armaments, appointed Carrel an *haut conseiller technique*, allocating the requisite funds to enable the doctor to set up a research lab. And Carrel's brief? To study questions of surgical technology and "social biology." Carrel was delighted. He had nothing but contempt for most of the ignorant do-nothings in charge of France's war effort, but not for Dautry, who brought to the Ministère de l'Armement a much needed can-do spirit: "There is activity there, enthusiasm, just like in America."[105]

Not just personnel but policy too began to change in the run-up to the war. A series of decree-laws in the summer of 1938 shored up family allocation benefits in the agricultural sector and extended the program to altogether new strata of the population, from shop employees to artisans. In the fall came the Sauvy/Debré decree awarding cash bonuses to stay-at-home moms.[106] All this, however, was but an overture to the main show, which was the enactment of the Code de la famille in July 1939. There are several critical points to make apropos the code. The first touches on how the legislation was crafted. The HCP itself undertook the task, and the decree it drafted was made law in almost every particular with an important exception. The HCP wanted a family vote clause, but on this point the Daladier administration, so amenable in all other respects, balked. Second and most obvious, as the code's very name attests, it was a piece of profamily legislation. To be sure, the decree mandated the teaching of demography at all levels of the education system, but its major thrust was not populationist but familist. Hence its numerous provisions for beefing up the family allocation system; hence its recapitulation of the bonus for stay-at-home moms principle. The Republic intended to push up the birthrate, but more than that: it wanted to bolster a particular family form—the married couple, dad at work and mom in the house, surrounded by a numerous (and legitimate) progeny.[107] Not least of all, the regime was prepared to apply punitive measures to get its way. This is the third important feature of the code: its disciplinary character, which stiffened repressive measures against abortion, which made the sale of certain kinds of alcoholic beverages more difficult, and which created a whole catalogue of punishments for "outrages to good morals."[108]

The Republic had indeed begun to take on a new look in the late thirties. It had for decades pursued pronatalist policies, but now natalism came cloaked in a familist and disciplinary rhetoric. What had made the change possible was the national defense crisis, which facilitated a rapprochement between the Alliance nationale and like-minded Catholics and which brought both into an ever more official partnership with the Daladier administration. It is easy enough to draw a straight line from here to the Vichy era. Pétain did not alter the Republic's profamilist course but just pursued it with a more punitive vigor. Coutrot played only a minor part at Vichy (he died in 1941) but not so Carrel, who at long last got the institute he coveted with a name Coutrot might well have appreciated: the Fondation pour l'Etude des problèmes humains, known more familiarly as the Fondation Carrel.

Yet that is not how Michel Debré saw matters. In his memoirs, he extolled the Code de la famille (which he claimed to have had a hand in formulating) and then in the next breath leapt to a celebration of General de Gaulle's "family policy" at the Liberation. Debré too drew a straight line, but one that bypassed Vichy, connecting the Third Republic right to the Fourth.[109]

Both interpretations contain a kernel of truth. In the domain of family policy, the Daladier years were indeed a prelude to Vichy, and in some respects though not all Vichy practice set the stage for the Liberation. But no lines, either in nature or in history, are ever ramrod straight. Vichy's family policies were a good deal more disciplinary than the Third Republic's, and the difference involved, it will be argued below, was more one of kind than of degree. The Fourth Republic, moreover, did not just pick up where Vichy left off, as will be seen, but steered family policy in new directions. It is possible to trace an arc of continuity from the late thirties through the forties to the Cold War era, but it is important at the same time to note the points

of discontinuity, the deviations and course corrections that were undertaken as France moved from republic to dictatorship and then
back to republic again.

Sciences Po

The old laissez-faire order had begun to wear away in the 1930s, as
the state assumed new powers to intervene in economic and welfare
matters. The erosion was no less evident in the area of elite education. Here, the dominant institution was the Ecole libre des sciences
politiques, Sciences Po for short.

Sciences Po was founded in 1872 by Emile Boutmy. France had just
experienced a cataclysmic military defeat, and Boutmy blamed the
nation's battlefield setbacks on failed political leadership. Sciences Po
was intended to make good that failing, to incubate a new generation
of public servants who would oversee France's recovery to greatness.

From the outset, the school enjoyed the patronage of the nation's
liberal establishment, "liberal" signifying in this context not so much
a commitment to laissez-faire doctrine (though that too) as to a moderate liberty, "constrained," in Alexis de Tocqueville's words, "by be-
liefs, mores, and laws."[110] Hippolyte Taine delivered the Ecole libre's
inaugural public address, and Albert Sorel, of the Académie française,
organized the first lesson. At Boutmy's death in 1906, stewardship of
Sciences Po passed to Anatole Leroy-Beaulieu, who was descended
from a distinguished family with old ties to that stalwart of nineteenth-
century French liberalism François Guizot.[111] Leroy-Beaulieu himself
died in 1912 and was in turn succeeded by Eugène d'Eichthal, son of
the Saint-Simonian Gustave d'Eichthal. The d'Eichthal family, Jewish
by origin, had long since converted to Christianity. Eugène understood the school's mandate much as Boutmy himself had: the nurture of a governing class steeped in "une culture libèrale," of an elite
"worthy of the name," as he phrased it in a commemorative essay that
appeared in *La Revue des deux mondes* in 1927.[112]

Sciences Po's success at its self-appointed mission was nothing short
of remarkable. In the interwar years, the school, a private institution,

charged annual fees in the range of 850 to 1,500 francs. The substantial costs of enrollment restricted the student body to a well-to-do few, never more than 2,000–2,500 all told, recruited in the main from the Parisian upper middle classes. The school itself was located in a bourgeois neighborhood, on the rue Saint-Guillaume in the VIIe arrondissment, which furnished it a sizable portion of its pupils. Sciences Po awarded students a diploma after two years of general education. A significant minority continued their schooling, taking a third year of more focused tuition aimed at preparing them to sit the admissions exams set up by each of the state's *grands corps*. In these tests, Sciences Po students swept aside all competition. Between 1901 and 1935, the four major *grands corps*—the Inspection des finances, the Conseil d'état, the Cour des comptes, and the Corps diplomatique—admitted a total of 740 new recruits. Of these, 685 or 92.5 percent had studied at Sciences Po. To be sure, not all were Sciences Po diploma holders. A number had taken part in the school's third-year exam preparation program but no more than that. The fact remains, nonetheless, that the ranks of *la haute fonction publique*, of France's senior civil service, were dominated in the interwar decades by men who had been trained at Sciences Po.

In the troubled thirties, when so many of France's established institutions and practices came under intense critical scrutiny, is it any wonder that Sciences Po—liberal, private, bourgeois—got its fair share? It was the Popular Front Left that led the charge. In 1937, Jean Zay, Radical deputy and minister of national education in Blum's Popular Front government—a post he would occupy until 1939—formulated a bill providing for creation of a state-run Ecole d'administration. Zay made no secret that the new school was expected to supplant Sciences Po as the principal, even exclusive, training ground of future *hauts fonctionnaires*. The Zay bill made its way through the Chamber of Deputies but got little further. The Senate considered the measure and then never voted on it. In this instance, then, the liberal establishment, the *désordre établi*, appears to have fended off its critics and come out at the far end of the debate unscathed and unregenerate.

Yet such a conclusion would be overhasty, for from the midthirties the Sciences Po administration, led first by René Seydoux and then by his youngest brother Roger (there was a middle sibling François), embarked on a program of self-reform. The project was in part formulated to fend off the Popular Front challenge, but it had internal determinants as well. The Seydoux brothers wanted to create a Sciences Po more in tune with the times. To that end, they sought out a rapprochement between their institution and the University; they attempted to craft a more rigorous and up-to-date curriculum; and they worked to modulate Sciences Po's long-standing commitment to laissez-faire pieties. This is not to say that the Ecole libre abandoned its laissez-faire traditions outright, but it did open itself to the reforming currents of the day, to the technocratic wing of the nonconformist movement in particular. The great moment of transformation would await the Liberation, when Sciences Po was partly nationalized and a postgraduate ENA created, but the point still remains: in this domain, as elsewhere, the process of transformation began before the war, and the impresarios of change were not men of the Left but an amalgam of professionalizing establishmentarians like Roger Seydoux and technocracy-minded newcomers who, as will be seen, were themselves often recent Sciences Po graduates.

Sciences Po had, indeed, become a hidebound and conventional place in the decades after the Great War. An aging d'Eichthal still presided over the school's fortunes. He was assisted by a Conseil d'administration populated by a dozen or so establishment figures. Maréchal Lyautey joined the Conseil in 1928, died six years later, and was succeeded by Maréchal Philippe Pétain. Jules Cambon, a dean of France's ambassadorial corps and longtime board member, passed away in 1935. The marquis de Vogüé, president of the Suez Canal Company and of the Société des agriculteurs, was enlisted to replace him. Typical in many respects of the depression-era Sciences Po board member was Henri de Peyerimhoff: a conseiller d'état, a respected business magnate who headed the Comité des houillères, and, in politics, a backer of the Fédération républicaine, mainstay of the "classic Right."[113]

In matters of economic doctrine, the school had a reputation as a "bastion of liberal capitalism," nor was the label undeserved. Sciences

Po's professor of political economy, Clément Colson, was described by an unsympathetic former student as the "Doctor Pangloss of economics" who radiated a laissez-faire optimism even in the midst of the depression.[114] When Colson stepped down, his chair was taken over by a disciple, Jacques Rueff, a rising inspecteur des finances who was just as "ferociously liberal" as his mentor.[115] It was not that teachers like Rueff were out of touch with the latest thinking in economic theory. Rueff had read Keynes all right, but he did not take the Englishman's work seriously and conveyed as much to his students.[116]

Sciences Po's "liberalism," of course, consisted in more than laissez-faire partisanship. André Siegfried, far and away the Ecole libre's star teacher, is a case in point. Siegfried's course on economic geography was a staple of the Sciences Po curriculum, drawing more students than the school's lecture halls could accommodate, until a new building was constructed in the mid-1930s. What was it about Siegfried that appealed? As an intellect, he was a complicated figure. Siegfried was an acute observer, open to foreign cultures, who knew and wrote about the Anglo-American world with an unmatched familiarity. At the same time, he fretted about the new civilization rising across the Atlantic, the United States, whose mania for machines and production he found threatening to Europe's greatest achievement, the autonomous and critical-minded individual. Siegfried's reputation as a scholar rested on a massive study, the *Tableau politique de la France de l'Ouest* (1913), which pioneered the field of electoral geography. Through an analysis over time of voting behavior and its material determinants—topography, property regime, patterns of settlement—the *Tableau* demonstrated the deep-rooted and enduring connections between region and political opinion. But in later work, Siegfried succumbed to the temptation to present regions, and not just regions but entire peoples and civilizations, as bearers of a distinctive soul, fixed in character. Such a point of view lent itself to reductionist, at times negative, stereotyping that targeted Jews and nonwhites. Such tensions were characteristic of a particular strain of French liberalism, enlightened and critical minded but anxious about the fate of an old-world Europe beleaguered by American enterprise and peoples of swarthy complexion.[117]

Siegfried's students may or may not have shared such ambiva-
lences, but they very much esteemed the man. He was remembered
as "un esprit latin," an elegant figure who lectured from notes, lor-
gnette in hand.[118] It was a manner he hoped in some measure to pass
on to his pupils. He explained to students preparing for Sciences Po's
exam in economic geography what he wanted them to learn: "a general economic culture," how to situate that culture in the ensemble of
knowledge, and how to express themselves in "a civilized vocabulary."
"It is essential," he concluded, "that such habits of mind become as
though second nature."[119]

In matters of *tenue*, however, Siegfried's students did not have
much to learn. Uneven entrance standards—the baccalaureate was
not required for admission—combined with substantial fees resulted
in a student body that was select in background and tastes. Sciences
Po had an acknowledged snob appeal. It was a good place to see and
be seen, to share a cigarette with the right sort and to talk over the
latest production at the nearby Théâtre du Vieux-Colombier. The atmosphere was cliquish, social relations patterned by preexisting ties
inherited from childhood days or the lycée. Paul Delouvrier, a future
inspecteur des finances who attended Sciences Po in the thirties, recalled how hard it was to fit in. He was from a family of ecclesiastics,
and religion mattered to him. It was not unusual for students to study
for a law degree at the same time that they prepared for the Sciences
Po diploma. Delouvrier was no different, except that he chose to sit
in on lectures, not at the Ecole de droit, as was the customary practice, but at the Institut Catholique (Delouvrier also did tutoring for
Garric's Equipes sociales). But what set Delouvrier most apart was his
middling provincial origin. As he characterized the Sciences Po student body: "it was the right-wing Parisian bourgeoisie, where I had no
entry."[120]

It did not help either that he was unfamiliar with the rules of smart
dressing. The Sciences Po crowd were indeed a well-heeled bunch.
Chroniclers of the era argue about the students' precise fashion preferences, but all insist that a certain formality, "une parfaite correction," reigned. The young ladies were decked out in hats—the school
had begun to admit women in 1919—and as for the gentlemen, they

sported ties and suits of "the most perfect cut," complemented, as Bloch-Lainé remembered it, with derby hats and umbrellas.[121]

Students understood that a Sciences Po education was in part about style. They valued the diploma as a "brevet of culture." Graduates who sought entry into the senior civil service took preparatory courses in their third year to gear up for the *grands corps* exams. These courses, nicknamed *grandes écuries*, were run by career functionaries on loan from their respective corps. Delouvrier's *grande écurie* was taught by one of Sciences Po's star alumni, Maurice Couve de Murville (of the Inspection des finances). It proved an unhappy experience for Delouvrier. Couve set a practice exam, inviting students to discuss the virtues and limits of planning, and Delouvrier, under the influence of Henri de Man's Belgian example, had the poor judgment to argue the proplanning side, a heterodox point of view that earned him a reproof from his teacher.[122] But the most intensive cramming was conducted in smaller, informal groups, known as *petites écuries*. A "little stable" consisted of a dozen or so self-selected students who met under the supervision of a junior civil servant not many years past the exam himself. In such intimate gatherings were nurtured professional connections that might last a lifetime. The tutorial Laroque organized in the early thirties included a clutch of good friends, Michel Debré, Jacques Rebeyrol, and André Ségalat among them, all destined to work together in the governments of the postwar era.[123] Here too, aspiring bureaucrats learned the tricks of the ordeal that awaited them, "the *spirit* and the *style* of the test," as one put it.[124]

The test itself was an intimidating affair. The Inspection des finances exam, for example, consisted of a written portion followed by an oral; the writtens were conducted in the dining hall of the Ministère des Finances itself, and, until, 1937, the dress code required all aspirants to wear formal attire throughout. No wonder the inspectorate was renowned for its esprit de corps, its sense of itself as "an academy, a tradition, a force."[125] No wonder too that types who lacked the proper grooming and background had such difficulty getting in. Pierre Uri, an Ecole normale graduate with the agrégation to his credit, thought about preparing for the Inspection des finances exam at Sciences Po. He talked to a school official who was impressed by Uri's credentials but then asked after a moment's hesitation: "are you not an Israelite?" An affirmative reply brought a cold shower of discouragement: "Well then, it's not worth the effort of trying." Rueff, indeed, was said to be the sole Jew who belonged to the Inspection, and his was a wholly exceptional case, related as he was by marriage to Maréchal Pétain.[126]

Is it any surprise then that the school and its graduates had such a reputation for right-wing leanings? Science Po's board of directors was a veritable who's who of France's business establishment, brightened up by the seven-starred sparkle of the occasional maréchal. The students were conservative, "bourgeoisie parisienne de droite," to cite Delouvrier once again. And the faculty were not much different. This is not to say that there was uniformity of opinion in the professorial ranks. Elie Halévy for years taught a course on the history of socialism, which was a revelation to maverick students like Daniel Guérin, who went on to a career of Marxist and later gay activism. Laroque, himself something of a misfit, remembered happy visits to the Halévy country home where he met Marjolin, Parodi, and the young Raymond Aron. But Halévy's easygoing tolerance was counterbalanced by the harder line of Raphaël Alibert, a professor of public administration who talked of the Republic as "the whore" and did not scruple to communicate such views from the podium.[127] Halévy and Alibert, however, were more outliers than mainstream figures, the pole ends of a spectrum whose middle ground was occupied by liberals like Rueff and Siegfried. It should be remembered, though, that Rueff and Siegfried were liberals in the French mold, elite men of enlightened views who saw themselves as guardians of social-science truths endangered by the distorting impact of mass politics, whether socialist or democratic.

No, Sciences Po in the thirties was no training ground for public service–minded democrats. So at least thought Jean Zay, who did not hesitate to accuse the school's graduates of a lack of "democratic zeal." So too thought Marc Bloch. France's "strange defeat" in 1940, as he saw it, had multiple causes, not least among them the doubtful loyalty of a Sciences Po–trained civil service that had held the Republic it served in contempt. Of course, Zay and Bloch were both leftists, a parti pris that may have clouded their judgment. Yet Bloch-Lainé, a Sciences Po–trained *haut fonctionnaire* himself, saw matters in much the same light. France's prewar civil-service elite, he wrote, "was not so democratic in its attachments as to reject absolutely a little experimenting with authoritarianism if undertaken for the public good."[128]

This was the institution the Popular Front set its sights on, intending to replace it with a state-run establishment. Zay set to work on the project within weeks of taking office. On 1 August 1936, he drafted a general proposal, calling for creation of an Ecole d'administration. Zay's *exposé des motifs* bristled with thinly veiled broadsides aimed at Sciences Po. Modern administration, the minister explained, required a technical expertise not taught at any existing educational institution. More serious still, he went on, the current, private system of civil-service training was altogether unrepublican. It gave advantage to "a narrow, privileged class whose interests might not coincide with those of the nation as a whole."[129]

Zay established an interministerial committee to work out the details of his proposal. The bill that resulted envisioned a multilayered training process. Students fresh out of lycée would enter first a state-run Ecole d'administration. Ecole graduates were expected to work for a period of years in low-ranking civil-service posts. They might then compete, alongside graduates from other state schools, for admission to a Centre des hautes études administratives, also state run. The top finishers at the Centre would then be guaranteed positions in the senior civil service without even having to pass a qualifying exam to earn the honor.[130]

There was no place in this scheme for a private institution like Sciences Po. Zay's interministerial committee included a young conseiller d'état, Michel Debré, not long out of Sciences Po himself. Debré was an ardent booster of a state-sponsored Ecole d'administration, but Zay's anti–Sciences Po bias exasperated him. The school had rendered signal services to the state, yet Zay and his associates seemed motivated by a reckless "will to destruction."[131] Debré's reading of the situation was not off the mark. The Zay bill was submitted to the Chamber of Deputies' Commission de l'enseignement in February 1937, and Zay appeared before the body on the twenty-fourth to argue the legislation's merits. Gustave Doussain, the Commission's *rapporteur*, later recounted the tenor of the minister's remarks to Sciences Po officials. Zay, it seems, had not minced words, putting it to the Commission that "the Ecole des sciences politiques is called on to disappear."[132]

Sciences Po was not idle in the face of such threats. The school equipped itself, first of all, with a new management team. The change had begun before the coming of the Popular Front but reached its denouement just as the Zay bill was taking shape. In 1929, the Ecole libre's Conseil d'administration appointed René Seydoux to the post of secretary-general, in effect elevating him to d'Eichthal's second in command. D'Eichthal died in early 1936 and was replaced by a veteran civil servant, Paul Tirard, who shared authority with an altogether new body, the Comité de direction. René Seydoux left the Ecole not long thereafter to take a job with his father-in-law, Maurice Schlumberger. His youngest brother, Roger, succeeded him, becoming secretary-general in November 1936. Tirard was a man old enough to contemplate retirement, but René and Roger Seydoux represented a generation just starting out, with promising careers ahead that would in fact play out well into the post–Second World War era.[133]

Sciences Po's new administration worked out a two-pronged strategy in answer to the Popular Front's legislative assault. On the one hand, the school set about armoring itself against Left criticism, doing what lay in its power to deflect or delay the progress of the Zay bill. On the other, it maneuvered to short-circuit the parliamentary process altogether, approaching Zay directly in an attempt to work out a negotiated settlement. Neither strategy met with much initial success.

Sciences Po's efforts to armor itself included a public-relations component. In a show of social conscience, the school established the so-called Fonds Boutmy in May 1937, a scholarship fund earmarked for the support of a few score meritorious students.[134] Sciences Po also made overtures to the University in an effort to demonstrate its openness to public institutions. The dean of the Paris Law Faculty, Sébastien Charléty, was invited to chair the school's curriculum committee, the Comité de perfectionnement. Charléty signed on in October, and he was a strategic choice on two counts. First, Sciences Po and the Faculté de Droit recruited from the same pool of students. As we have seen, the typical Sciences Po man doubled as a law student, taking courses at the Faculté de Droit in preparation for a *licence* even as he pursued a diploma at Sciences Po. Second, Charléty had useful connections outside the academic world. France's newspaper of record, *Le Temps*, would prove itself a valued champion of Sciences Po's interests. Charléty joined the paper's administrative board in 1938, reinforcing the school's ties to the establishment press.[135]

Even as the school spruced up its image, it lobbied parliament hard to hobble the Zay bill. School authorities sought an interview with Doussain, who insisted that he had no intention of causing harm to Sciences Po. Indeed, Doussain went on, a solid minority in the Chamber, perhaps even a majority, felt much the same, and Zay had been made aware of the fact.[136] In November 1937, however, Doussain made no reference to any of these discussions when he reported the Zay bill out of commission. The school's partisans did not abandon hope. Roger Seydoux composed a circular letter to sympathetic deputies, trying to line up support. A trio of loyalists were identified: Anatole de Monzie, Jean Mistler, and François Piétri, who exhorted Zay not to move ahead with undue speed. Additional backing came from the administrative departments of the Ministère des Finances and of the Ministère des Affaires étrangères.[137] Such pressures resulted in a minor amendment to the Zay bill and slowed its parliamentary progress but little more.

Sciences Po's efforts to strike up a dialogue with Zay were even less fruitful. From the outset, Sciences Po authorities gave thought to conciliatory strategies. A note, drafted in mid-August 1936 (René Seydoux himself may have been the author), contemplated conceding civil-service exam preparation to Zay's proposed Centre des hautes études administratives. What Sciences Po wanted in return was a fair chance to compete against the new Ecole d'administration for access to the Centre. The note, in fact, sketched out a quid pro quo. Sciences Po would abandon its third, exam-preparation year, provided the state reciprocated, recognizing the Sciences Po diploma as equivalent to a University degree and permitting Sciences Po graduates to vie on an equal footing for admission to the projected Centre des hautes études administratives.[138] For the moment, though, such thoughts were confined to internal memorandums.

Tirard mentioned none of this when he went to see Zay for the first time on 14 January 1937. The meeting was perfunctory and not at all encouraging. As the pressure on Sciences Po stepped up in subsequent months, the school administration steeled itself to offer a deal. On 15 November, just as the Doussain commission readied its final report, Tirard wrote to Zay proposing a "solution de collaboration." Ten days later, a delegation was dispatched, consisting of Tirard, Pétain, and Alexandre Celier, a senior figure in the banking world, to put the school's case to the minister. The meeting took place on 25 November.

Tirard underlined that Sciences Po was trying to mend its ways, to enable all worthy students to attend thanks to a generous scholarship program. The school, he continued, had no objection to the proposed Centre des hautes études administratives. All it asked was that Sciences Po students be afforded the same opportunity as graduates of state-run institutions to win admission to the Centre. Zay listened to Tirard's arguments and gave indications of flexibility. A few days later, he informed an unidentified member of parliament that he was willing to work with Tirard. And then contact was interrupted.[139]

So matters stood when the Zay bill came to a vote in January 1938. Sciences Po had presented the minister a choice: pursue the legislative path in the face of determined although not insurmountable opposition, or come to the bargaining table and negotiate. For the moment, Zay stuck with the parliamentary option. The Chamber took up the Zay law on 27 January. The debate was bruising for Sciences Po partisans. Communist and Socialist deputies lambasted the school as an antidemocratic bastion, a tool of "powerful interests" that bred in its students a "caste mentality" and perpetuated "the owning classes' stranglehold on the administrative machine." France's system of civil-service training stood in urgent need of purification, and the Zay bill, it was claimed, would cause the first cleansing winds, a "souffle républicain" in the words of the Communist Georges

Cogniot, to blow. The Popular Front majority in parliament was still intact, and the Chamber ended up voting the legislation through by a lopsided margin of 422 to 137.[140]

Zay, it appeared, was well in control of the situation. Yet, in the year that followed, he would perform an about-face, abandoning the legislative path in favor of Sciences Po's offer of collaboration. There were three factors that might account for the change in course. The obstacles the Zay bill encountered in the Chamber, even if minor, helped to soften the minister's resolve. In March 1938, Zay was ready to engage in a third round of talks with Sciences Po officials. He had a "cordial" meeting with Seydoux and Tirard on 2 March. There was discussion of a signed "convention" between the state and Sciences Po, and Zay asked Seydoux and Tirard to spell out what terms might be acceptable. A memorandum was forwarded to the minister on 21 March. The document invited the state to nominate representatives to the school's scholarship committee. In exchange, the state was summoned to fund one hundred additional scholarships and to accept Sciences Po representation on the governing board of the new Centre des hautes études administratives. In June, Zay met again with Seydoux and Tirard. He acknowledged receipt of the memorandum, signaled that the state wanted a say not just in scholarship selection but in staff appointments as well, and promised to formulate a counterproposal. Months passed, however, and the promised document never materialized.[141]

All the while, the amended Zay bill ground forward on its parliamentary way. The skeptical reception it encountered in the Senate Commission de l'enseignement must have added to Zay's worries about the project's ultimate fate. Sciences Po representatives appeared at least twice before the Senate's Commission, once on 16 February 1938 and again on 16 June, and they pitched a strong case in the school's defense. Sciences Po, it was claimed, was not hostile to reform but just the reverse, a fact borne out by its evident willingness to bargain with Zay. The school indeed made a point of sharing with the senators the details of its dealings with the Ministère de l'Education nationale. From Sciences Po's perspective, the outcome of the February meeting was heartening. "There is no doubt as to the opposition

of Senate moderates," summed up a school document. The June results were even better. Senators Pierre Jossot and Aimé Berthod, the
president and the *rapporteur* of the Commission, communicated to
Tirard their shared preference for an "agreement" and claimed that
"an important part of the Commission" was of the same view.[142] Just
in case the Zay bill ever worked its way out of commission, Sciences
Po officials busied themselves in late 1938 identifying and courting
"sympathizers" in the Senate at large.[143]

An impending Senate fight must have given Zay pause, even more
so in the closing months of 1938, when the national political climate
took such a decisive turn to the Right. Daladier's accession to office,
the Munich crisis, and then the gutting of the forty-hour work week
signaled a sea change in national priorities. War preparedness, not
social reform, had now become the central business of government.

The new mood suited Sciences Po. In the face of Left critiques, it
had always billed itself a national asset, "part of the intellectual patrimony of France,"[144] and now it had a chance to demonstrate just how
serious its patriotic credentials were. Not long after Munich, school
officials began discussing the creation of a chair in national defense.
By January 1939, the chair had been scaled back to a course, but the
project had lost none of its patriotic resonance, for the "faculty member" placed in charge was none other than Philippe Pétain, the hero
of Verdun (and an officer who still enjoyed a reputation as a republican loyalist). Pétain delivered the inaugural lecture on 3 February
1939 before an audience of eight hundred.[145]

Troubles in the Chamber, looming opposition in the Senate, and
the rightward turn in the political conjuncture persuaded Zay to explore the path of negotiation. In January 1939, he invited Sciences
Po representatives to attend talks. The Ecole's Conseil d'administration considered how to respond. An accord, it was concluded, was
well worth the effort, even at the cost of yielding a measure of school
sovereignty. Creation of an Ecole d'administration might even be
conceded, but only on terms that respected Sciences Po's fundamental interests.[146]

In the event, the school got what it wanted. It helped no doubt that
Sciences Po had important and well-placed friends. From February

to July 1939, Seydoux and Tirard—on occasion joined by Siegfried—entered into a series of conversation with Zay, Zay's chef de cabinet Marcel Abraham, and the *directeur de l'enseignement supérieur* Théodore Rosset. The school got a welcome leg up from an outside source. At the very start of the talks, Debré stepped in, penning a note to Abraham—shared in confidence with Seydoux—that laid out the terms of a possible convention, in rough outline quite close to the terms that Sciences Po itself wanted. The school, moreover, was able to count on a phalanx of sympathetic and influential bystanders whom Seydoux took pains to keep abreast of the negotiations: Berthod, Jacques Bardoux, senator from the Puy-de-Dôme, and Emile Mireaux, editor of *Le Temps*. Its troops lined up and facing a now-weakened interlocutor, Sciences Po was in a position to bargain from strength.[147]

The deal worked out was all that Sciences Po could have hoped for. To be sure, the school gave ground on certain issues. From early on, it had been willing to allow the state a role in the selection of scholarship students. In an April 1939 communication to Zay, it went further, envisaging the creation of a new organ, a Commission des études, slated to include three state representatives, of whom two would be from the University. The Commission would have the authority to review certain senior faculty appointments, which in turn would be vetted by the minister of education. Even in curricular matters, the school was prepared to show flexibility, however limited in scope, inviting the state to help set up exam juries for certain categories of students.[148]

On the major point, however, Sciences Po got its way. The Zay bill had imagined a two-story structure of civil-service education: at the top a Centre des hautes études administratives, at the bottom an Ecole d'administration. At the outset, Sciences Po had hoped to insert itself on the ground floor as a rival of the Ecole d'administration. Over the course of the 1939 negotiations, however, it got a good deal more, shunting aside the Ecole d'administration altogether and substituting itself as the feeder institution for the new Centre.[149] Zay, it seemed, would get his two-tier system but now reconfigured: the Centre at the top and at the bottom Sciences Po, linked to the state but still independent.

The convention, however, was never signed, although for its part

Sciences Po felt the deal had been all but struck.[150] This was, moreover, a deal the school did not want to let slip away. Zay left office in September 1939 as war mobilization got under way, to be replaced by Yvon Delbos. Tirard had a meeting with the new minister in December in the hope of keeping the convention talks alive, but to no avail.[151]

The story of the Zay bill is instructive on several counts. It illustrates first and foremost Sciences Po's formidable powers of self-defense. The institution was embedded in a network of relations, social and political, that it knew how to mobilize to significant effect. No less remarkable was Sciences Po's strategic flexibility. It gave ground or pushed back in accordance with the changing *rapports de force*, but more than that: it manifested a clear willingness to rethink its institutional personality. A private institution par excellence, Sciences Po had by the outbreak of the war begun to develop official ties to the University. In its dealings with Zay, moreover, the school made plain that it was amenable to accepting yet closer ties to the state, provided the terms were right, and to this extent Sciences Po's liberal antistatism was starting to become a thing of the past. Last of all, the prewar moment anticipated in critical respects what was to come later. The all but signed convention of 1939 envisaged a two-tier edifice, almost identical in overall design to that in fact created at the Liberation. But then again, is there any reason to be astonished by such an outcome? So many of the players involved in the Daladier-era negotiations, from Siegfried to Seydoux to Debré, would still be very much on the scene in 1945.

Yet it was not just Sciences Po's institutional status that had begun to evolve in the run-up to the war but also its understanding of its mission and how to go about accomplishing it. The administration grasped that the school had grown stuffy and unimaginative. The Seydoux brothers embraced professionalization as an antidote, seeking at the same time to adjust Sciences Po's curriculum and staffing to address the most urgent problems of the day. As these changes began to take hold, the school edged away from the laissez-faire orthodoxy of old, taking its first, exploratory steps toward a more technocratic future.

The process got started under René Seydoux. Sciences Po's enrollments went up in the expansive years following the Great War. To accommodate a growing student body, a new building was erected, equipped with a spacious entry hall and an amphitheater named after the school's founding father, Boutmy. The facility was completed in October 1934. Additional funds were allocated in 1935 to fit out the basement as a *salle des sports*.[152] At the same time, the school moved to tighten its admissions requirements. The principal concern was how to evaluate applicants lacking the baccalaureate. It was decided that they be asked to sit a special entrance examination, and the elder Seydoux contemplated excluding nonbacs from the applicant pool altogether.[153]

The profile of the faculty began to change at the same time. Dautry, manager of the state railway service, was hired in 1937 to teach a course on public transport. That same year, the name of an up-and-coming scholar of foreign relations, Pierre Renouvin, appeared on the Sciences Po masthead for the first time. Elie Halévy died in 1938. He was replaced by Maxime Leroy, who had as thorough an understanding of the French trade-union movement as any senior academic. There was movement in the junior ranks as well. In 1932, Sciences Po offered courses on public finance taught by Wilfrid Baumgartner and on private finance by Henry Davezac, both assistant professors. A third junior colleague, Auguste Detoeuf, headed a team-taught *conférence d'application* on problems of industrial and commercial organization. Three years later, Detoeuf had occasion to lecture Sciences Po audiences on a subject dear to him, "the death of liberalism." Last of all, there was Laroque. From 1933, he ran a prep seminar at the school for the Conseil d'état exam. Such dutifulness was repaid in 1937 when the school, awakening as Laroque put it to social issues, awarded him a course of his own devising on industrial relations.[154]

Three observations may be made apropos this roster of appointments. It is clear, first of all, that the school was determined to add depth and weight to its academic credentials. Renouvin and Leroy were serious scholars who went on to publish work still in use today. Second, the appointments indicate a willingness on Sciences Po's part to freshen its curriculum: to temper its traditional liberalism and take on the now-pressing problems of economic organization, state

interventionism, and labor/management relations. In the process—
point three—the school implicated itself in wider currents of social
science and technocratic reflection.

Jean Stoetzel, an Ecole normale graduate with an enduring interest in social psychology, pioneered opinion polling in France. He had
spent time at Columbia University in 1938, making the acquaintance
of America's first pollsters and tracking with avid attention the Gal-
lup surveys published by the *New York Times*.[155] On return to France,
Stoetzel set up a polling operation of his own, the Institut français
d'opinion publique (IFOP), and began to organize a series of what
he called *sondages* or "soundings." These earliest exercises are interesting for several reasons. First, for the subject matter chosen: Stoetzel wanted to know how the French assessed Daladier's handling of
the German threat; what they thought about the nation's declining
birthrate; whether they would vote today as they had in 1936. Stoetzel's
findings were more suggestive than definitive, given the crudeness of
the sampling techniques used, but they do paint a recognizable picture of the Daladier moment. German aggression, the foreign-policy
poll concluded, had awakened "the national conscience." On the
birthrate crisis, opinion endorsed active state intervention to shore
up the family, favoring positive measures, a generous family-allowance policy for example, more than negative ones. As for voting,
Stoetzel observed a modest but undoubted rightward shift in the
public mood.[156]

The question is, though: who did Stoetzel think might be interested in such results? IFOP of the prewar years had no clients, but
that suited Stoetzel well enough. He did not think of himself as a
businessman but as a student of society, the trailblazer of a new kind
of knowledge. That knowledge had a double value, intrinsic and util-
itarian, of potential interest to fellow social scientists and to policy
makers looking to find a way forward. These were, indeed, the two
constituencies Stoetzel appealed to. IFOP set up a society of friends
to seek out backing for its activities. A six-man board was placed in
charge. Two of its members were University professors; two, including Laroque, were career civil servants. IFOP circulated a missive to
contemporary personalities of note, soliciting interest and contribu-

tions. Just two men outside IFOP's immediate circle of supporters replied: Jean Coutrot and Roger Seydoux who sent in a check with a letter attached proposing more regular contacts.[157]

Stoetzel's association with Sciences Po was no more than glancing at this juncture, but it was to strengthen over time. He would in fact join the school's faculty right after the war, bringing to consummation a relationship that had taken its first, hesitant steps in the late thirties. Sciences Po's prewar IFOP connection was a straw in the wind but no more.

With the *Nouveaux Cahiers* group, however, the school developed much closer ties. The group got its start in the midthirties as a luncheon gathering, presided over by Davezac, an electrical industry manager. The regulars included Baumgartner and Detoeuf, plus the polytechnicien turned banker (and X-Crise member) Jacques Barnaud, Baumgartner's father-in-law Ernest Mercier, and the railroad executive Guillaume de Tarde. The Popular Front's coming to office added a note of urgency to the exchanges, persuading the most committed among the group of the need to publish a review. Detoeuf hosted the preparatory meeting in October 1936, and the journal itself, titled *Nouveaux Cahiers*, began to appear in March of the next year. Detoeuf, it should be added, was an ardent proponent of disarmament, with the result that the new review's editorial board included, alongside the expected technocratic types, a handful of pacifist intellectuals like the physicist Francis Perrin.

It was, then, a small cadre of forward-thinking businessmen, a number of them pacifists, many with Sciences Po affiliations, that got the *Nouveaux Cahiers* project off the ground, and the journal's preoccupations reflected this fact.[158] First, on the matter of pacifism: *Nouveaux Cahiers* published a pair of articles in 1937 by Simone Weil under the title "Ne recommencons pas la Guerre de Troie." Weil was a friend of Detoeuf's. She had wanted to experience firsthand the hardships of factory work, and to land a job, it was to Detoeuf she turned, who employed her at a Paris plant of the electrical company he directed. The two had many differences but few, at this juncture, when it came to foreign policy. Weil's articles invoked Jean Giraudoux's recent *La Guerre de Troie n'aura pas lieu* (1935), a dramatiza-

tion of the saber-rattling blunders that had landed Greeks and Tro-
jans, despite the best efforts of wise heads like Hector and Odysseus,
in a pointless war. The topicality of Giraudoux's play in a France once
more faced with a resurgent Germany does not need spelling out,
and Weil's allusion to it makes plain enough that she took Giraudoux's pacifist message to heart. Nor was Weil speaking only for herself. Hitler's annexation of Austria in March 1938 angered many in
France, but not Detoeuf. Let Germany expand eastward, he wrote,
and let France, now a second-rank power, remain true to its nonmar-
tial vocation as "a country of well-being."[159]

The review, however, was not so hands-off when it came to France's
internal affairs. Detoeuf was a firm believer in managerial authority.
A well-run business required a boss who knew how to command, who
understood, as Detoeuf phrased it, the "métier de chef." And what
was good for the factory was good for the state. In early 1939, *Nouveaux Cahiers* organized a debate on a much-favored theme of the
thirties, the reform of the state. The standard issues were hashed
over: how to rein in quarrelsome and free-spending parliamentarians; how to fortify the disciplinary hand of the executive branch. But
this time, the discussants pushed the debate a little further than usual,
contemplating, in emergency circumstances, the setting up of a provisional dictatorship as the Romans had done in ancient times. It is
interesting to note in this context who participated in the debate:
Davezac, Detoeuf, de Tarde, but also a young newcomer to the Sciences Po faculty, Jacques Chapsal. Not only that, the event was reported on in the February issue of *Nouveaux Cahiers* by Bernard Serampuy, the pseudonym of François Goguel, himself a future luminary
of the Sciences Po faculty.[160]

Sciences Po was very much in evidence at a second *Nouveaux Cahiers* debate as well. This time the subject was public-service education.
The periodical commissioned a panel to come up with a set of proposals for discussion. The committee was composed of *Nouveaux Cahiers*
regulars like Detoeuf and de Tarde but also included Robert Lacoste
and Michel Debré (as well as Guy de Carmoy, a career civil servant who
will be discussed later). The scheme the panel put forward, perhaps
no surprise given Debré's presence, looked a good deal like that

pushed by Sciences Po in its negotiations with Zay: a two-tier system, with a new state-run Ecole nationale d'administration at the top and a clutch of undergraduate-level feeder schools (of unspecified identity) at the bottom. Who, it might be asked, took part in the discussion that ensued? A whole raft of Sciences Po faculty, Davezac, Laroque, and even Roger Seydoux himself.[161]

The Ecole libre, under the direction of the Seydoux brothers, had begun to break out of the old liberal mold. Rueff was still the senior man when it came to economic doctrine, but now other, more interventionist voices were heard in the classroom. At the same time, Sciences Po made a concerted effort to burnish the seriousness of its academic purpose. It was not just a finishing school for general-culture dilettantes but an institution with standards, high-quality facilities, and teaching personnel to match. As the school's faculty became less orthodox in profile, so its involvement in the technocratic and nonconformist reform currents of the day deepened. Not least of all, the Sciences Po administration undertook a difficult rethinking of its relationship to the state. The school remained jealous as always of its autonomy but was more willing now than ever in the past to enter into partnership with public authorities, all the better to pursue what still remained its core mission: the formation of a civil-service elite equipped to guide the nation into an uncertain future.

The Third Republic began to drift away from its liberal parliamentary moorings in the thirties. The catalyst of change was in part the Popular Front, born of the depression and its attendant social dislocations, but just as critical, if not more so, was the role played by the Daladier administration. In the name of national defense, it introduced into public life new levels of interventionism that placed the state front and center of a national policy of *redressement*. With the new policies came new personnel, not the leftist experts of Popular Front vintage, but a mix of technocrats and nonconformists, spiced with the occasional Catholic Action militant. Leadership and teamwork, organization and family-mindedness, physical and spiritual regeneration, the formation of a sporting and manly elite: these were the watchwords of the day. The Republic's rightward turn reenergized the nation, preparing it, as well as any Western nation was prepared, for the war that lay ahead. The executive-driven revival of the prewar years, however, was an ambivalent phenomenon, engineered at the top by committed republicans like Daladier but run lower down by a civil-service cadre of oftentimes less democratic conviction.

With the defeat of 1940, France's parliamentary order, which had been taking on water for a decade, foundered altogether. Its shipwreck created opportunities for interventionists of every stripe who set about remaking a fallen nation in an image more to their liking. As Vichyites, résistants, or sometimes Vichyites turned résistants, they got down to the business of bringing into being the postliberal France they had so long hankered for.

CHAPTER 2

The War Years

L aissez-faire liberalism came under fire in the thirties from both
Left and Right: from a Popular Front that built up the state in the
name of social justice and democratic brotherhood, from a Daladier
administration that cobbled together an interventionism of its own
in the name of national discipline and war preparedness. The war years
were in critical respects a continuation of this struggle. The Republic's old political elite, burdened by the responsibility of defeat, was
sidelined. Social democracy gravitated to the Resistance. And the
Daladier-era technocrats aligned themselves with Pétain's National
Revolution.

This is, of course, too schematic a scenario. There were technocrats in the Resistance and socialists at Vichy, but more than that.
Vichy-style technocracy was a complex phenomenon. It was authoritarian and racist, dirigiste in its iron-handed management of the
economy, punitive and moralizing in family policy, and elitist throughout. Yet the Occupation years were also a boom time for number
crunchers, pollsters, and demographers, in a word, for social scientists of all kinds. Under Vichy auspices, they gained unprecedented
access to power, profiting from the opportunity to push projects long
in gestation. The planners got a plan, two in fact. France's state statistical services were overhauled, expanded, and put to altogether novel
uses. Carrel assembled the social-science think tank he had so long
lobbied for. As for Sciences Po, now as ever an antechamber to power,
it continued on its professionalizing path, distancing itself further
from its laissez-faire past even as it drew closer to the state. Not all

these policy and institutional innovations would be so easy to scrap at the Liberation.

All the more so as a number of Vichy administrators, disillusioned with the Pétainist regime, switched sides over the course of the war. Couve de Murville is but the most celebrated instance. A senior figure in Yves Bouthillier's Vichy-era Ministère des Finances, he made his way in 1943 to Algiers, joining forces first with the dissident general Henri Giraud and then with de Gaulle himself. Or take the case of Aimé Lepercq, a businessman who occupied a post in Vichy's economic administration but later enlisted in a Resistance group, the Organisation civile et militaire (OCM). He wound up at the Liberation as de Gaulle's choice for minister of finance. Or take that of Laroque himself, who worked through Vichy's first months at René Belin's Ministère de la Production industrielle et du Travail then to be fired in December 1940 because of his Jewish ancestry. Laroque in subsequent months made contact with a whole series of Resistance organizations, among them the Comité général d'études (CGE, of which Debré was a principal), before taking off for London in 1943.

These trajectories are interesting for several reasons. First, for the sometimes circuitous pathways they identify between Vichy and the Resistance. Giraud was a career officer of conservative, not to say far Right, views. The OCM's chief spokesman, Jacques Arthuys, had belonged in the thirties to de La Rocque's Croix de feu. As for the CGE, it had gotten its start in 1942 under the name Comité des experts, and the experts involved included some familiar faces—Debré, Parodi, and Lacoste—as well as a pair of up-and-coming christian democrats, the law professors François de Menthon and Pierre-Henri Teitgen. These were not organisms of the Left (though left-wingers, like Lacoste, were to be found in their ranks). They were, rather, more establishmentarian or technocratic in orientation. The Resistance, like Vichy itself, was not a bloc but a composite of multiple currents, communist and social democratic but also nationalist, nonconformist, and Catholic. These not-so-Left elements came to play a more influential role over the course of the war in the higher councils of the Resistance. Yet how could it be otherwise in a movement presided over by a maverick nationalist if ever there was one, General Charles de Gaulle himself? Now, for many on the not-so-Left, engagement in the Resistance was a transformative experience, converting them away from old prejudices and, in some cases, making full-throated leftists of men who had once been anything but. Yet the transformation was not always total, and in many cases old preoccupations and predilections persisted.

The Resistance as a result secreted more than one project for national renewal. To be sure, the Left was very much present, but it was not alone, finding itself in competition with technocrats, whether of a nonconformist or more confessional variety, who had a vision of their own. It was a vision born of the troubled thirties, which had made its policy debut in the Daladier years and then, in a more authoritarian variant, gotten a thorough tryout under Vichy. Purged by the war and Resistance experience of its most noxious elements, it would get a third and more successful chance at the Liberation.

Dirigisme

Vichy and the Resistance both eschewed the laissez-faire liberalism of Third Republic days, but there, it would seem, the similarities ended. The Pétain regime imposed a dirigiste straitjacket on the national economy, but why? To restore discipline where a rampant individualism had once reigned, to preserve an agricultural sector that was valued as the seedbed of French national virtue, and to manage the shortages created by defeat and Occupation. A mix of ruralist authoritarianism and technocratic pragmatism determined Vichy policy, which may have had its innovative aspects but which was at base more reactive, not to say reactionary, than forward-looking. Resistance dirigisme was of an altogether different cut. Yes, it was the state's job to run the economy but in consultation with the interested parties rather than by fiat. The object of state intervention, moreover, was not the management of penury but the promotion of expansion. France had lost in 1940 because it was a backward, rural nation, ill equipped for modern mechanical warfare. The sooner France turned its back on its peasant past and came to terms with the industrial age the better.

This opposition, of course, is too stark. Vichy was authoritarian all right, but its policies were not always reactionary. The Resistance made the cause of industrial expansion its own but not always in the name of social democracy. Not least of all, there was a flow of personnel and ideas from one side to the other. It was a one-directional flow to be sure, repentant Vichy administrators heading abroad to join Free France or underground to join the domestic Resistance. The result was the fashioning of a third-way statism, neither socialist nor Vichyite. It was in part an amalgam of the two: consultative and expansionist, but still guided from the top by managers and civil servants bandying the technocratic catchphrases of the nonconformist thirties—the importance of leadership, the social role of elites, the value of team play. Yet it also had an original component, for statist as it was, it made room for market forces in a way that socialists and Vichyites either would not or could not do.

René Belin was appointed minister of industrial production in July 1940. "Somebody after all must captain the ship," as he justified himself in later years. The phrase, of course, was not Belin's but taken from Jean Anouilh's *Antigone* (1944), and the speaker is Creon, the Theban king, agonizing late in the play over the cruel duties imposed by the responsibility of power.[1] Belin's cruel duty was not to command Antigone's execution but to reorganize the French economy, and he set about assembling a crack team for the job. On Bouthillier's recommendation, Belin appointed the X-Crise veteran Jacques Barnaud as his cabinet director. The two senior posts in the ministry went to Jean Bichelonne and Henri Lafond, both polytechniciens. Belin had wanted Lepercq for Lafond's position, the secrétaire-général à l'énergie, but Lepercq was locked up at the time in a German POW camp and unable to serve (he would soon be released but not until October). As for Laroque, it took some convincing to bring him on board. Belin explained to him the ministry's brief, "a strict control of the economy," necessitating "a sort of syndical institutionalization." This smacked of fascism to Laroque, who had "little sympathy" for the regime in any case, but he still agreed to take on the job, bowing to Belin's argument that, under the circumstances, no other course of action was available.[2]

But what did "a sort of syndical institutionalization" mean in practice? Belin's team, Laroque included, set to work drafting the defining legislation. The law that resulted, enacted on 16 August 1940, closed down confederated trade-union and employer associations (Laroque was upset by this provision[3]) and in their place erected a system of so-called Comités d'organisation (COs). Under the scheme, a Comité was set up in each major branch of industry or commerce. It had extensive powers: to undertake a census of industrywide resources, to propose production schedules, and to set rules regulating competition, quality, and pricing. COs funded themselves through a tax on member firms, but the state retained ultimate authority over the CO network. Comité officers were appointed by the minister of industrial production and answered first to him.[4] In the event, appointments went to experienced business executives, many of them veterans of employer interest-group politics. But Belin, for all that, did not see himself as a tool of monied interests. The men he turned to, as he saw it, were not so much "capitalists" as "Grands Commis." "Managers" was the term he used, borrowing from the English. By managers, Belin meant men who knew how to lead, commanding personalities like the Renault executive François Lehideux (head of CO for automobiles) or the mining engineer Aimé Lepercq (in charge of coal). Indeed, Lepercq was but one of a significant contingent of engineers recruited to staff the CO administrative apparatus. Auguste Detoeuf (electrical equipment), Robert Gibrat (electrical power), Pierre Ricard (foundries), Raoul de Vitry (aluminum): all were polytechniciens, and all signed on in one capacity or another to Vichy's CO experiment.[5] As the names attest, the CO executive corps included a fair sampling of X-Crise and *Nouveaux Cahiers* graduates.

It was soon realized that the COs, however well led, did not always work in concert but competed among themselves for scarce resources, all the scarcer given Germany's expropriative appetite for French industrial assets. The Germans themselves were conscious of the problem, and at their prodding, an Office central de répartition des produits industriels (OCRPI) was set up in September 1940 to coordinate the parceling out of raw materials to the various COs. Placed in charge was Jean Bichelonne, an administrator *hors pair*, it seems, who was able to work long hours and command the respect of even the most exigent fellow civil servants. Claude Gruson worked for Bichelonne through the spring of 1941, then taking a leave of absence for health reasons. Gruson did not think of himself as a Vichyite, but even in later years he professed an abiding loyalty to Bichelonne's memory.[6] Nor was François Bloch-Lainé a National Revolution partisan, yet he too, for a period, was willing to work under Bichelonne's direction. Bichelonne was a numbers man, which made him a perfect choice for OCRPI chief. The office's principal job after all was stocktaking and resource management, quantitative enterprises both. Bichelonne was aided in these tasks by a statistical bureau set up at the Ministère de la Production industrielle under the direction of Dufau-Peres with Jean Prévot in charge of the bureau's survey services. Bichelonne's team set about inventorying the nation's industrial holdings, a project for which Bloch-Lainé was tapped, but Bloch-Lainé discovered that the Germans would also have access to the inventory, prompting him to quit and return to a less exposed post at the Ministère des Finances.[7]

Bichelonne, good technocrat that he was, did not content himself with narrow problem-solving but wanted a grasp of the whole. To this end, he set up a Conseil supérieur de l'économie industrielle et commerciale in June 1942. The Conseil brought together a sampling of France's best and brightest to ponder what course to chart for the nation's economy. Bichelonne assigned direction of the council to Gérard Bardet, yet another X-Crise alumnus, who in turn drafted what one historian has described as "the elite of the technical world" to help out. The elite in question included a lineup of well-known faces: Detoeuf, Lepercq, Henri Davezac, Claude-Joseph Gignoux, but also some less familiar ones like Professor of Law Gaëtan Pirou and Roger Boutteville, head of the CO for electrical energy.[8] Council debates, it seems, turned in circles, but Bardet's team did manage to patch together a report in 1943. The document endorsed the principle of planning, a bold enough conclusion, but insisted at the same

time that France's economy, however restructured, retain a substantial agricultural sector. Ruralist impulses were hard to shed, even for
the most assertive of self-styled modernizers.[9]

It has been maintained that Bardet's Conseil entered, not at first
but over time, into discreet communication with the Resistance.[10]
The claim is a plausible one, and Lepercq was in all likelihood the
contact man. The Germans, in dire need of manpower as the war
dragged on, arm-twisted the Pétain regime into imposing a labor
draft, the Service du travail obligatoire or STO, in February 1943.
Lepercq let it be known that he opposed the measure, a gesture of
defiance that got him fired in August. He had joined the Organisation civile et militaire some months earlier, through the intermedia-
tion of a business colleague, Pierre Lefaucheux, and so for a brief
transition period straddled the Vichy/Resistance divide.[11]

The Ministère de la Production industrielle, however, was not the
sole or even the most important site of planning activity at Vichy.
Bouthillier's Ministère des Finances tried its own hand at the task.
Bouthillier assembled a team of economic experts, a Conseil d'études
économiques, that met twice a month. In composition, Bouthillier's
Conseil was not so different from Bardet's, though perhaps it had a
stronger social-science component. Vitry and the ubiquitous Detoeuf
belonged, but so too the economist François Perroux and statistician
Alfred Sauvy.[12] Alongside the Conseil functioned a second body answerable to Bouthillier, though it was not his particular creation.
This was the Direction générale de l'équipement national (DGEN),
headed by François Lehideux. Over the course of 1941, working in
great haste, DGEN elaborated a ten-year investment plan, the first
official planning document of its kind. The scheme was not meant
for immediate application but for postwar use once peacetime conditions had been restored. Lehideux's planners understood the urgency of updating the nation's economic infrastructure. How else
was France's great-power status to be restored? All the same, there
was hesitation to take an expansionist view. The DGEN plan imagined a France still in large part agricultural, still reliant on its own
resources, still operating in circumstances of shortage and need. But
perhaps this was to be expected, given that Lehideux's advisers—

Boutteville, Detoeuf, Lepercq, and Guillaume de Tarde among them—
were drawn from the same pool of dearth-conscious technocrats so
numerous in all ranks of the Vichy economic administration.[13]

From this angle, the characterization of Vichy economic policy
as a shortage-managing dirigisme appears all too apt. The state sat
astride a huge command apparatus that doled out resources that
were in short supply. Corporate bodies, endowed with regulatory and
price-setting authority, relayed state policy downward. In the DGEN
plan, market forces had a role to play. The state invested, but private
initiative took over after that. Yet this was a plan for the future, and
the future, as DGEN imagined it, was still haunted by conditions of
penury. Much of the Vichy system, of course, was ad hoc, an improvised response to the hard conditions imposed by military defeat and
a bloodsucking Occupation. But it was not all improvised. The men
who put the system together were not standard-issue civil servants,
adjusting to unforeseen circumstances. They had been active for a
decade or more beforehand, concocting technocratic schemes, more
or less statist, more or less corporatist in design. Vichy gave these men
a long-hoped-for chance, and they seized it. The regime's authoritarianism troubled some, Laroque for example, but for most this was
an unanticipated opportunity to try out the organizational and planning schemes they had debated at X-Crise symposia or in the pages of
nonconformist organs like *L'Homme nouveau* and *Nouveaux Cahiers*.
What is striking, though, is how weighed down these logic-proud
technocrats were by the vision of a France still rooted in the soil, pow-
ered by seasonal rhythms rather than the boom-and-bust cycles of an
industrial economy.

Yet that is not the whole story, for the Vichy economic project was
not only about command and shortage. It was also about statistics
and forecasting, and in this domain there were signs that a more
growth-oriented understanding of the economy was beginning to
break through.

Vichy undertook at first a gradual and then over time more accelerated buildup of the nation's statistical services. In November 1940,
a new demographic service was created under the direction of René
Carmille. Carmille was an interesting amalgam. An old soldier and

ardent Pétainist, he was someone the regime could count on. But Carmille was also a polytechnicien who had taught at Sciences Po, a man with technocratic ambitions, and he set about realizing them with a characteristic zeal. In December of 1941, Carmille's service absorbed the old Statistique générale de France and Sauvy's Institut de Conjoncture, creating a new entity, under Carmille's overall direction, the Service national de la statistique (SNS). In 1940, an estimated 150 persons worked in the state's statistical services. By war's end, that number had shot up to 7,000.[14]

And it was not just that the SNS grew in numerical terms; it grew in its range of activities as well. In March 1942, Carmille created a polling service, which he persuaded France's premier pollster, Jean Stoetzel, to run. That fall, arrangements were completed for setting up an Ecole d'application to train SNS personnel in the most up-to-date statistical techniques. The project had influential backers, among them the Polytechnique's pioneering econometrician François Divisia. The new school, once up and running, proved a "major innovation," a disseminator of much-needed skills, both practical and theoretical. It indeed continues to function to the present day, though under a new name, the Ecole nationale de la statistique et de l'administration économique.[15] Carmille's own work at the SNS will be discussed in the next section, on welfare and demography. In the present context, it is Sauvy's contribution that merits closer inspection.

Sauvy worked throughout the war at the SGF and Institut de Conjoncture. He never resisted. Anything that smacked of plots and illegality, he explained, just ran counter to "my whole bourgeois education." Yet neither did Sauvy collaborate, though recent research demonstrates that the SGF performed certain limited statistical services on the Occupier's behalf.[16] Sauvy meant to keep a low political profile, the better to concentrate on what he felt was the principal task at hand, the assembling of the statistical data necessary to steering a managed economy. In 1941, he completed the industrial census begun before the war. He brought on board two proficient numbers men, Jacques Dumontier and Jean Vergeot, to help out with a second project tabulating the costs of the Occupation.

Sauvy's greatest catch, however, may have been André Vincent.

Vincent, like Sauvy, believed that the era of laissez-faire economics had long passed. Dirigisme in one form or another was here to stay. Vincent's great conceptual breakthrough was to imagine the French economy as a kind of business writ large in need of a bookkeeping system not so different in design from that employed by individual firms. Vincent published *L'Organisation dans l'entreprise et dans la nation* in 1941, laying out what he meant by "national accounting," the first usage of the term in a French context. The problem was, as the social scientists put it, to operationalize the concept, and that is what Sauvy invited him to do, working within SGF ranks.[17] Such statistical explorations may not have borne immediate fruit, but after the war it was to Sauvy's SGF statisticians that Jean Monnet would turn when he began to put together his own planning team.[18]

Sauvy's SGF represented one critical site of statistical experimentation in the Vichy years, but it was not the only one. In January 1944, François Perroux founded an independent economic think tank, the Institut de science économique appliquée (ISEA). There is much debate about how Keynesianism came to France, but ISEA in most accounts is identified as one of the critical conduits.[19] The claim, however, poses an immediate puzzle. How did Perroux, a Catholic corporatist at last sighting, come in the end to a sympathetic appreciation of the English economist's far from corporatist theories?

The route was not a simple one. The onset of the Occupation found Perroux an economics professor, lecturing at the Sorbonne and running a seminar at the Ecole pratique des hautes études. Among his students was Pierre Uri, an educator at loose ends, who had been barred from teaching because of his Jewish background. Uri was an avid pupil and credited Perroux with making an economist of him. And Perroux took the young man under wing, taking him round to meet "the unforgettable father Maydieu" at the Dominican house on the rue Latour-Maubourg. The house was a place of sociability for Uri (it may have helped that his wife came from a very Catholic family), but it also proved a place of refuge, for it took him in when rumors of Gestapo roundups drove him into hiding.[20] The fruit of Perroux and Uri's friendship was a slim volume, *Communauté et société*, which the two men published together in 1941, Uri employing the

nom de plume Rémy Prieur. Uri claims that he had already begun to
work his way through Keynes's *General Theory of Employment, Interest
and Money* by this time, but there is little evidence of this in the text,
part critique of laissez-faire individualism, part celebration of the
healing power of community. A true collectivity, Perroux and Uri remonstrated, was bonded by love, not contract, citing the Catholic
Church as a shining example of what they had in mind. The authors
promised to commit themselves to community building, persuaded,
as the text's anonymous introduction trumpeted, that "by doing the
good work of community, we will be contributing to the National
Revolution."[21]

The two men parted company at this juncture, Uri heading south
to the comparative security of the unoccupied zone, Perroux remaining in Paris, where he soon got involved in Alexis Carrel's Fondation
française pour l'étude des problèmes humains. The Fondation Carrel was chartered in November 1941. Perroux became its secretary-
general the following September, remaining in that post until December of 1943. In addition to his administrative responsibilities,
Perroux ran the Fondation's Department of Biosociology and had
occasion, in the spring of 1943, to present a talk to the department's
"financial team" on Keynes and the problem of full employment.[22]

The connection between monetary policy and labor markets does
appear to have been a major point of interest to Perroux, or at least
that is what ISEA's early history would seem to suggest. Carrel and
Perroux, both domineering personalities, did not get on, prompting
Perroux to leave the Fondation and strike out on his own. It was at
this juncture that he formed ISEA with financial help from the
Banque de France. Perroux wanted to bring a mathematical precision hitherto lacking to the study of political economy, but he had
theoretical interests as well. A Groupe d'études sur la théorie économique was attached to ISEA, managed by Jean Bénard, a young economist Perroux had brought over with him from the Fondation Carrel. A number of the group's members, like Henri Bartoli and Bénard
himself, were also résistants. Résistants or not, though, all seem to
have shared a fascination with Keynes. A senior civil servant, Jean de
Largentaye, had translated *The General Theory* in 1942, but the text

was not easy to obtain. Bénard's crew made do without, translating Keynes's masterwork themselves as they went along. It made a difference that their number included Jean Domarchi, who had defended a thesis on Keynes's thought in December 1943 under the supervision of Perroux and Pirou. In the present context, it is worth adding that Domarchi would have a hand in a second translation effort, helping to bring out the first French-language version of William Beveridge's *Full Employment in a Free Society* (Eng. 1944, Fr. trans. 1945).[23]

One final fragment of evidence bears citing, touching on the work of Jan (Jean) Marcewski. Marcewski, a Polish national, completed a dissertation on Nazi monetary policy in the summer of 1941. It was a quantitative study of how Hitler's minister of finance Hjalmar Schacht had managed, using financial means, first to get a depressed German economy moving again and then to prepare it for what turned out to be a victorious (at that time) war effort. Marcewski, as he himself put it in later years, interpreted Schacht's manipulations as an "inspired anticipation of Keynesian theory." Perroux, who was supposed to sit on Marcewski's jury but did not for unexplained reasons, still read the work and was much impressed. Marcewski himself, an ardent patriot, took up Resistance work and was arrested and deported. Repatriated after the war, he turned to Perroux for help, and Perroux accommodated, hiring Marcewski at ISEA.[24]

ISEA then was well positioned at the war's end. Its chief, Perroux, had been a Catholic corporatist and National Revolution partisan, but he had begun to evolve. It is not that Perroux abjured Pétainism, but he did take a step or two back. Take a look at the ISEA staff, which included a fair number of experienced résistants in its ranks. As for Perroux's corporatism, it receded to make way for a Keynesian-inflected monetarism that took full employment as its objective. In one critical respect, though, Perroux had not changed at all. He always styled himself a humanist. *Economie et humanisme*—that was the name of the study group he had taken part in founding in 1941 with the former naval officer turned Dominican father Louis Lebret. In corporatist days, as in the more Keynesian present, Perroux's principal antagonist always remained the same: free-market liberalism and its disintegrative and demoralizing effects. The Institut he created may not have shared all the master's philosophical presuppositions, but it did share his antipathy to classical economics. It was indeed a Keynesian hotbed (Uri too joined the ISEA team at the end of 1944, as soon as he felt safe to move back to Paris). More than that, ISEA researchers had been at work for years, thinking about the ways state financial policy might be applied to stimulate economic activity and promote employment, and they brought to the enterprise an exceptional mathematical acumen. Here then was an institution with unusual intellectual assets, and so it is little wonder that ISEA (and Perroux as well for that matter) managed to navigate the shoals of the Liberation without difficulty to emerge in the aftermath a critical player in the shaping of postwar economic policy.

It was not just Perroux who began to evolve in the Occupation's closing months but DGEN too. Lehideux left the agency in the spring of 1942. The institution, though now marginalized, stuck by its planning ambitions and, in fact, began work on a shortened version of its ten-year plan sometime in 1943. The nomination the following January of Frédéric Surleau as DGEN director gave the project a boost. Surleau was a Dautry protégé, an engineer turned *haut fonctionnaire* who knew how to get things done. A plan, the so-called *tranche de démarrage*, was ready to go in the spring of 1944, and it was an interesting document for several reasons. The *tranche de démarrage*, like DGEN's first plan, was designed for postwar use, but it is the dissimilarities between the two documents that are most telling. The *tranche* adopted a two-year time frame, not a decade. It was practical in its concerns about reintegrating returning POWs and rebuilding destroyed infrastructure, but it had a more forward-looking dimension as well. It was clear now, as it had not been in the spring of 1942, that the Allies were going to win the war, a prospect that gave promise of a new start for France. The *tranche* was, like its predecessor, an investment plan, but now it was not agriculture but industry and transport that were designated the prime recipients of the state's largesse. This project was not about managing shortage but had "a modernizing fervor" to it, which helps explain why postwar planners paid attention to its prescriptions. Pierre Mendès France, minister of national economy in de Gaulle's postwar Provisional Government, printed the *tranche* in November 1944, making sure it was then circulated to potentially interested colleagues.[25]

Vichy gave rise, then, to more than one form of dirigisme. The state corporatist variant, associated with the Ministère de la Production industrielle and Bichelonne's OCRPI, occupied the institutional center stage. But in the wings a second project was starting to take shape as the war's end approached. It lacked coherence as yet, but its constituent pieces had begun to articulate themselves at the SGF, at Perroux's ISEA, and at the DGEN. Industrial expansion, not an outmoded ruralism, was the objective. And the means? Keynesian monetary policy and a state investment plan informed by a full national accounting of the French economy's assets and requirements. These various pieces, however, would not come together until after the war, and it was not a National Revolution holdover who pulled off the feat but Jean Monnet. Monnet may not have been a first-hour résistant, but he was, from 1943 on, a senior figure in the Algiers-based Comité français de libération nationale presided over by General de Gaulle.[26]

All of which raises the question: how did the Resistance itself imagine France's postwar economic order? The interior Resistance had a clear view on the subject. In March 1944, the Conseil national de la Résistance (CNR), a federation of the most important Resistance organizations, issued an action program. The document, more a set of guidelines and objectives than a detailed road map, envisioned a French economy run according to plan. How the plan would work in practice was not spelled out, but this much was certain. The trusts and financial combines of yesteryear would not profit. The CNR indeed proposed that a wide swath of industry, from energy to banking, be "return[ed] to the nation." No, it was not capitalists but the working people of France who would be the prime beneficiaries, consulted in the elaboration of the plan and included as never before in industrial management. "A real economic and social democracy": this was the future that the CNR mapped out for the nation.[27]

A social democratic dirigisme had powerful partisans among the Free French abroad as well. The key figures here were André Philip and Pierre Mendès France. Philip joined de Gaulle in London in mid-1942. He was already a seasoned résistant by then, a man of ability and character with deep roots in a socialist milieu that de Gaulle, in need of backing, was anxious to rally to his side. De Gaulle made good use of Philip, naming him the Free French commissaire à l'intérieur and dispatching him later that year to Washington to plead the Gaullist case to President Roosevelt. Philip was no less active on the postwar planning front. In December 1941, de Gaulle created a study commission to hash over solutions to France's most pressing economic and social problems. The Socialists George Boris and Robert Marjolin both took part, in due course joined by Philip himself once he had settled in London.

The early months of 1944 found Philip hard at work on a comprehensive report charting a new, dirigiste future for France's postwar economy. He was now minister in charge of relations with Free France's proto-parliament, the Algiers-based Assemblée consultative provisoire. Assemblée members fed Philip ideas, but it was from more expert-oriented bodies that he got the most help. Philip put together a series of study commissions, among them a commission on economic problems that included among others Jean de Largentaye (a career civil servant and translator of Keynes's *General Theory*), Louis Vallon (associated with the CGT plan in the 1930s), and Pierre Mendès France. The Philip report, completed in July 1944, called for a planned economy from top to bottom. It envisioned a two-sector scheme: a nationalized sector under more or less direct state administration and a nonpublic sector, which, though still in private hands, remained subject to tight government supervision. The state, in Philip's scheme, arrogated to itself all major investment and resource allocation decisions, relaying them downward to the private sector through "industrial groups" that bore a more than passing resemblance to Vichy's COs. Planning and the overall direction of the economy were invested in a rejuvenated Ministère de l'Economie nationale (MEN), and the overriding object of the enterprise was expansionist. The war had made plain to Philip, as to many, that the future lay, not with the reassuring but old-fashioned cadences of an agriculture-based economy, but with the dynamism of an industrial one. Now, all this calls to mind the socialist plans of the thirties but with certain striking differences. Defeat had taught the urgency of industrial growth; from Vichy were learned practical lessons in state oversight and management of the private sector; and an incipient Keynesianism suggested how investment policy might be applied to promote expansionist ends.[28]

It fell to Mendès France to make a first effort at translating such hard-earned wisdom into practice. He took over at the MEN in September 1944. Mendésiste policy in the immediate postwar years is best remembered for its fiscal rigor. The MEN proposed wage and price controls, rationing, and an extended workweek. The idea was to dampen inflation, not as an end in itself, but as a prelude to relaunching the economy, and this was not to be a haphazard but a planned exercise. Mendès France appointed Boris to run the MEN's planning agency, and it was in this context that Boris, acting on his minister's behalf, reprinted Vichy's *tranche de démarrage*. Mendès France, moreover, meant for the MEN plan-in-the-making to have teeth. He envisioned a huge nationalized sector, encompassing the financial and energy industries, and a private sector operating under the tutelage of CO-like organs dubbed Offices professionnels.[29]

The socialist dirigisme of the 1930s had lacked detail and contour. Not so the Liberation-era variant, which, tempered and reconfigured by wartime experience, knew what it was about. Yet, important as the socialist dirigiste current was, it does not tell the whole story of Resistance thinking about France's postwar economic future.

Consider, for example, the case of the Organisation civile et militaire. At first glance, the organization seems very much in accord with the CNR's social democratic line. Its September 1943 cahier declared that the Resistance was at base "republican" and "socialist" in orientation. What such commitments meant in economic terms had been spelled out the preceding spring in a collective statement drafted by a team of OCM members, including its founder, the business executive Maxime Blocq-Mascart (the organization had come into existence in December 1940). The statement was unequivocal in its advocacy of "the methods of a planist economy," and the OCM's planning ambitions came with a distinct dirigiste flavoring. The scheme it proposed placed the state in the forefront, formulating directives that were then handed down to the organized professions, each headed in turn by a state-appointed "prefect."[30] But there were limits to the OCM's statism, for below the level of the organized profession, individual firms and the managers who ran them were conceded a certain margin of maneuver. The plan laid out a set of objectives; the organized profession and relevant business executives hammered out an agreement fixing production targets and pricing; but after that, it was up to the managers how to proceed. The market did not have much place in such an arrangement, but civil servants and executives did, little surprise perhaps as OCM contained a fair mix of technocratic cum managerial types: Lefaucheux, Lepercq (from 1943), Jacques Rebeyrol (Michel Debré's friend from Sciences Po days), and, of course, Blocq-Mascart himself.[31]

OCM's project then was more technocratic than socialist. It came wrapped, moreover, in a rhetoric that called to mind nothing so much as the third-way discourse of 1930s nonconformity. The OCM made clear from the very start that it repudiated the old Third Republic. Parties and party wrangling had rotted away democracy. What was needed was "a new order," a democracy rejuvenated not by politicians but by "chefs puritains": "the good, the pure, the ardent, the sincere," who would bring to public life a new spirit born of the Resistance, "a constructive mystique."[32] The OCM's talk about purity spilled over at times into an all too familiar xenophobia. Blocq-Mascart, for one, had little liking for immigrants, singling out Jews in particular, who, in the depressed thirties, had "encumbered" certain professions, taking jobs away from native Frenchmen. Not just that—Jews had a tendency to stick together, a castelike impulse that had found expression in the Popular Front, led by a Jew who surrounded himself with Jewish cronies. The wider Resistance chastised Blocq-Mascart for such remarks, and in later years he acknowledged that it had been impolitic at the time (June 1942) to raise "the Jewish question," a formulation that suggests, however, that he still did not get where the real problem lay.[33]

In any event, this was not the stuff of social democracy, and, indeed, the social democratic way was not at all what the OCM had in mind. It sought, rather, a French national path, a via media, as a 1941 OCM document put it, between German state worship and "Anglo-Saxon mercantilism."[34] OCM recruited its share of technocrats, but it also counted a few third-way enthusiasts in its ranks. Arthuys perhaps does not qualify for the label. He was more inclined to the Croix de feu hard Right. But the epithet does fit Georges Izard, Mounier's onetime condisciple and a veteran of 1930s third-way politics, who just after the Liberation became the OCM's secretary-general.[35]

In certain respects, the OCM's agenda tacked closer to Vichy-style technocorporatism than to the socialist statism espoused by a Philip or Mendès France. It was still a dirigiste vision, however, and as such occupied a space closer to the Resistance mainstream than did, say, the Comité général d'études, which understood France's future in much more market-oriented terms.

The CGE was founded in the summer of 1942, the result of a negotiation between law professor François de Menthon and Jean Moulin, de Gaulle's emissary to the Resistance on French soil. It began work under the name Comité des experts, which was changed the year following to Comité général d'études. The membership over time expanded to nine: Paul Bastid, Jacques Charpentier, René Courtin, Michel Debré, Robert Lacoste, Pierre Lefaucheux, François de Menthon, Alexandre Parodi, and Pierre-Henri Teitgen. From the outset, the CGE enjoyed direct and regular contacts with London. There was every reason for de Gaulle's entourage to take a close interest in the Comité's work, for the CGE had assigned itself a most ambitious task: mapping out France's economic and constitutional future for the postwar era.[36]

The CGE's privileged status, none too modest agenda, and self-styled expertise earned it the suspicion of other Resistance organizations. Pascal Copeau, a senior figure in the domestic Resistance, dubbed the CGE "the synarchy of professional Catholics," a dig at Menthon and Teitgen, who were both professors of law and christian democrats.[37] Copeau was himself the son of a reborn Catholic, the celebrated interwar dramaturge Jacques Copeau, and so might have thought himself in a position to know. Indeed, the CGE's Catholic component ought not be dismissed outright. In the spring of 1943, Free France dispatched a delegate, Francis Louis Closon, to make the rounds of the domestic Resistance. Closon was a man of faith himself, a Catholic of forward-looking views, who hit it off with Menthon when the two met in Lyon, then the site of CGE headquarters. The conversation, as Closon recounted it, reflected the doubleness of the progressive Catholic perspective, at once critical of the old Republic and of Church orthodoxy: "We didn't have a hard time liquidating the spirit of the IIIe [République], the weakness and disorder of those sad, final years, the deep-seated anticlericalism of the French Left and the bourgeois clericalism of the conservatives."[38]

Copeau's assessment, however, while not wrong, is exaggerated. For every Catholic in CGE ranks, there was a republican of mainstream convictions. Paul Bastid is an example, a Radical in good standing who had served in Blum's Popular Front administration. In the spring of 1943, the CGE began to publish a record of its activities, and to whom did it turn for editorial assistance? To Marc Bloch, in many ways the very embodiment of *l'esprit républicain*.[39] In political terms, what is most striking about the CGE is its centrism. No Communist belonged and just a lone Socialist, Lacoste, who, as a veteran of the technocratic circuit of the thirties, was not a standard-issue leftist. And there was no one at all who hailed from the far Right.[40]

In the end, it was less the politics of the CGE members that mattered than their know-how and competence. A number were lawyers or law professors: Bastid, Charpentier, Menthon, and Teitgen. The rest, Lacoste apart, were technocratic types like the engineer turned business executive Lefaucheux, or Courtin, the professor of political economy, or Debré and Parodi, who, already in the thirties, had begun to make their mark as policy-minded civil servants. It is perhaps worth mentioning in this connection that Pierre Laroque, yet one more policy-minded *haut fonctionnaire*, had a more than passing encounter with the CGE. Once fired by Vichy, Laroque had taken refuge in the southern zone. He sent his family into hiding when the Germans occupied all of France in November 1942, finding a safe haven for them with the help of Guy de Carmoy, an acquaintance from Science Po days (and a senior Vichy film official). It was about this time that Laroque made contact with the CGE, attending a number of meetings, until in the spring of 1943 Moulin and Parodi thought it better to remove him to London, where for a period he served as liaison between Free France and the CGE.[41] The CGE, in a word, well deserved its initial moniker, Comité des experts, and the expertise in question came seasoned with a distinct mix of technocratic and christian-democratic flavorings.

As for the policies it espoused, these too represented a mix. The CGE has been called a "school of neo-liberal thought," and it is not hard to see why.[42] Courtin, assisted by Menthon and Teitgen, drafted a report in November 1943 outlining plans for a restructuring of France's postwar economy. The report envisaged a limited round of nationalizations, acknowledged an ongoing need for state regulation and rationing (at least so long as shortages persisted), and endorsed the setting up of an investment council that would steer public monies, according to plan, toward industries essential to recovery. The aim was to get the economy moving again and at the same time to reshape it, guiding France away from an agricultural vocation now outdated toward a more expansionist future. Yet here is where Courtin's underlying liberalism came into play. For, once economic activity did begin to pick up, he believed it then behooved the state to step back, allowing the market to take over. Planned investment, rationing, and the like were on this account helpful but no more than temporary expedients, stepping stones to a remarketization that would open up and air out the French economy, integrating it over the long term into the wider (i.e., Anglo-American) world. Little wonder that one socialist critic dismissed the Courtin report as a rehash of the "classic liberalism of Sciences Po."[43] But the criticism was not quite on the mark, for Courtin showed himself willing to countenance a degree of state interventionism, both temporary and long-term (in the shape of nationalizations), that a Colson, for example, would never have been able to stomach.

But economic policy making, whether liberal, neoliberal, or otherwise, was not all that the CGE was about. The Comité also wanted to remake France's political institutions. *Refaire la France* was indeed the title of a slim volume Debré coauthored with fellow civil servant Emmanuel Monick during the war years. The text, written under the Occupation, resonated with the themes that informed Debré's work for the CGE, which in fact patterned his entire political career.[44] France's destiny was democratic, the book made clear, but what France required above all was "a virile and disciplined form of democracy." In all domains, private and public, new elites were called for, willing to cooperate and think beyond individual interest. In no area was this need more pressing than in that of public administration. *Refaire la France* urged creation of a state-run school of public administration, and in this it is not hard to detect Debré's influence at work. The same may be said of the text's ringing endorsement of a strong executive. France craved a genuine "Chef d'Etat," a chief of state who did not answer to representative bodies but was, rather, in a position to rein parliament in with the threat of dissolution.[45] Debré used the expression "republican monarch" to describe what he had in mind. The phrase first appeared in a CGE report, but it was a report he wrote with the text of *Refaire la France* lying at his elbow.[46] It is hard to see what is liberal about any of this. On the contrary, Debré's constitutional proposals were cast in the antiliberal phraseology of 1930s technocracy, a perspective that set little store by liberal shibboleths like parliament, party, or the individual, pinning its hopes instead on a team-spirited public-service elite working under the command of an above-politics *chef.*

In economic matters, the OCM was dirigiste, the CGE more market-oriented. But both embraced state interventionism of a novel sort, and both spoke in a language shot through with the polarities and catch phrases of the "neither right nor left" 1930s. Of course, this is a language that Vichy itself spoke, and so it is not altogether astonishing that the occasional Vichy official—Lepercq, Laroque, even Lefaucheux (said to have seen service on a Vichy CO himself)—made his way into the Resistance via the OCM's or CGE's good offices. Socialist dirigisme enjoyed pride of place in much Resistance thinking, but alongside it sprang up competing currents, curious intellectual amalgams like the OCM's nonconformist dirigisme or the CGE's market-friendly technocratic statism. These were minority phenomena but of importance because of the men associated with them—policy intellectuals and civil servants who, though small in number, were well placed to make a disproportionate difference.

The same phenomenon is observable apropos the overseas Resistance. Social democratic dirigistes like Philip and Mendès France were prominent figures, but they were not without competitors. De Gaulle, of course, had his own aspirations, centered on a restoration of French grandeur. As he saw it, the state and effective leadership were essential to this goal, together providing a strong guiding hand that would push a slow-moving France into the machine age. De Gaulle understood that a modern economy was a prerequisite to greatness, but how to go about the business of modernization was not what he knew best. He had advisers to help him out, of course, among them Hervé Alphand, a career diplomat who joined the general in London. There, in 1942, Alphand drafted a memorandum that, in its effort to sanction interventionism without doing undue violence to free-market principles, bore some resemblance to Courtin's CGE project. In the event, however, de Gaulle's most consequential interlocutor on economic matters turned out to be Jean Monnet, and with the general's backing, Monnet in due course managed to outmaneuver all his policy-making rivals, Philip and Mendès France not least of all.[47]

It is tempting to think of Monnet as the liberal Atlanticist par excellence, a friend of the United States, a believer in market forces, a modernizer. None of this is false, but it glosses over the complexity of Monnet's achievement.

It is worth remembering first of all that Monnet did not begin as a Gaullist. After the defeat in 1940, he stayed on in Britain, doing supply work for the British government, which in this connection sent him to Washington. Washington in turn dispatched Monnet to Algiers in March 1943 to advise General Giraud, Roosevelt's choice to run a now-liberated French North Africa. Several points bear making about Giraud in the present context. He was first of all a onetime Pétainist, a man of traditional conservative, not to say reactionary, views who surrounded himself with like-minded establishment figures—imperial administrators and military officers. But Giraud was also an anti-German patriot who wanted to fight the Occupier. It was this determination that brought him to North Africa, where he meant to take command of a French army of liberation. The Americans liked him and placed him in charge.

So too did many French *hauts fonctionnaires*, both Vichyite and not, who rallied to Giraud as a partisan of a strong, effective state, an establishment figure more reassuring than the renegade (and lower-ranking) de Gaulle.[48] Couve de Murville is an example of the one-time Vichyite turned Giraudist. He quit the Vichy administration in 1943, departing in late March for North Africa, where he entered into the general's service. René Mayer, by contrast, if not an out-and-out résistant, was never a Vichyite, yet he too at first rallied to the Giraudist camp. Mayer was a conseiller d'état and company executive, a deal maker who worked at the intersection of business and politics. He had made a mark in the late Third Republic but as a Jew had no future at Vichy. Mayer fled France and then in 1943 made his way to Algiers to join forces with Giraud.

Like Couve and Mayer and for similar reasons, Monnet was drawn to Giraud. Bloch-Lainé writes of Monnet's "weak-spot" for the general.[49] The insinuation is not a fair one. Monnet respected the military man, but that is all. He backed Giraud because he believed him to be the best instrument to unify a too-fragmented Resistance movement, and he did what he could to moderate Giraud's reactionary impulses, cajoling the general into delivering what Giraud himself described as the first democratic speech of his life. On the other hand, Giraud, in the brief period he ran the show in liberated North Africa, balked at rescinding Vichy-era legislation that stripped Algeria's Jewish population of its French citizenship. This was a hard blow for Monnet to take, but he took it. The general, after all, represented institutional stability, the continuity of the state, and as such stood in the path of the egomaniacal de Gaulle, whose maverick ambitions Monnet feared might open the door to dictatorship or, worse, a communist takeover.

Giraud's proconsular career, however, did not last long. He was pushed aside by a far more astute de Gaulle, and as de Gaulle moved center stage, Monnet reconsidered where he himself stood. It was now de Gaulle who appeared to be the surest guarantor of national unity and the state's interests, and so Monnet switched from one general to the other, as did Couve and Mayer for that matter. Perhaps too much should not be made of Monnet's Giraudist episode, but it does suggest a *prise de position* that was not just liberal in orientation but statist as well.[50]

As does the entourage Monnet began to put together. In Algiers, he assembled an informal discussion group that began to think about postwar plans. Mayer belonged, joined by Alphand (who had relocated to North Africa) and Robert Marjolin, whom Monnet had known from work done together in 1940 London. Etienne Hirsch rounded out the team. An engineer by training, Hirsch had made a career as a chemical industry executive. He was, it seems, among the few who heard de Gaulle's 18 June call to Resistance, which he answered without hesitation, taking off for London and from there, in 1943, following the Free French government to Algiers.[51]

Monnet's first "committee of experts" did not last long. It broke up when he was sent on a mission to Washington late in the year, but it would be in part reconstituted in November 1945. Monnet had just returned from the United States. He had a clear understanding of the difficulty of France's present predicament and a rough idea of the way forward. Monnet had in fact laid out the situation to de Gaulle in a conversation earlier that year:

> You speak of greatness... but today the French are small.
> There will only be greatness when the French are of a stature
> to warrant it. That is how they are. For this purpose, they must
> modernize themselves—because at the moment they are not
> modern. They need more production and greater produc-
> tivity.[52]

The path to greatness lay through "modernization" and "greater productivity," objectives that were not realizable, as Monnet saw it, without a plan. He called on the counsel of Hirsch and Marjolin. The three met from November on at the Hotel Bristol and after a month's feverish labor produced a sketch for a "Plan de modernisation et d'équipement." It was a bare-bones document, but certain points were clear. The French economy, to grow, could no longer afford to hunker down behind protectionist barriers but had to open itself to the world. Growth in turn required coordination and consent of the sort that experts alone could not provide. A successful plan required the input of all interested parties—industrialists and trade unionists as well as state representatives. The document was submitted to de Gaulle, head of France's Provisional Government. De Gaulle was taken with the project, which was in general outline consonant with his own views, and, in January of 1946, decreed into existence a new government agency attached to the prime minister's office, the Commissariat-général au Plan, with Monnet in charge.

From such a cursory chronology, it would seem Monnet's Planning Commission was an accomplishment of parthenogenic proportions, the brainchild of a modernizing avant-garde that bootstrapped itself, thanks to de Gaulle's patronage, into a position of rare influence in the freewheeling months after the Liberation. Yet who were the first planners? Monnet's team, thanks to the intercession of de Gaulle's cabinet chief Gaston Palewski, set up shop in a fine old mansion on the rue de Martignac. The core trio—Monnet, Hirsch, Marjolin—were all men of enlightened views, businessmen, engineers, and experts who had fought on the right side during the war.

But as the team added new members, its political pedigree took on a more varied hue. Let's start with Monnet's chef de cabinet, Félix Gaillard. Gaillard in the fifties made a career as a Radical Party politician, but it was not as a Radical that he began. In 1940, fresh from school, he joined first the Chantiers de la Jeunesse and then the Compagnons de France, both Vichy youth groups, both headed by former Catholic scouts, General de La Porte du Theil in the case of the Chantiers, Henri Dhavernas in that of the Compagnons. Gaillard was at this juncture a confirmed Pétainist and had occasion to declare as much in an article published in the Compagnons de France periodical *Métier de chef.* The Third Republic had been a rotten regime, he wrote. Not so Pétain's, which, "authoritarian and hierarchical," represented a salutary "revolution against egoism." Gaillard's brush with the Vichy youth movement ended when he returned to his studies to prepare for the Inspection des finances exams. He sat them in the spring of 1943 and not long thereafter, for reasons unexplained, entered into the Resistance.[53]

Paul Delouvrier, placed in charge of the Plan's Financial Department, followed a trajectory similar in many respects. He had prepared for the Inspection des finances exam alongside Dhavernas. The Vichy regime under way, Delouvrier was recruited into Dhavernas' Compagnons. Delouvrier was a Pétainist but no collaborator; he believed the maréchal was playing a double game, pretending to work with the Occupier, all the while preparing a counterstroke. But it was not just Pétain's stature as national hero that attracted Delouvrier to Vichy. He was "haunted by the deliquescence of the French body politic," and, as he saw it, there was but one antidote to the rot of the Third Republic, "a strong State, an effective government." Delouvrier believed he saw in Vichy the iron hand he was looking for. He later wondered about his youthful self: "Was there lacking in me perhaps a certain democratic spirit?"[54] Like Gaillard, Delouvrier in the end lost faith in the Vichy project and passed into the Resistance.

So it went as Monnet's team expanded. It is not that every new enlistee had a dubious or uncertain past, but several did. This is true of a number of the statisticians and economists associated with the Commissariat in its early phases. Sauvy, as might be expected, was tapped for advice, but he was a busy man and soon dropped out of the picture. Not so Sauvy's disciples at the SGF, who established more enduring links to the Plan: Jean Vergeot, whom Hirsch identified as "my deputy," and Jacques Dumontier.[55] Monnet lined up recruits, not just from Sauvy's stable, but from Perroux's as well. Uri, for a period after the Liberation, worked at Perroux's ISEA but then jumped to the Plan, which occasioned a falling out with his possessive erstwhile mentor. Or take the case of Jean Ripert, a young economist who worked at the Plan as a member of Vergeot's team. Like Uri, Ripert had been electrified by Perroux's wartime lectures. He was not a Pétainist, but the Third Republic "made him vomit" (that is his own characterization), and he belonged to a group "much influenced by Uriage," Vichy's leadership-training school. Ripert acknowledged that Perroux, though fascinating, was an ambiguous type, and just as ambiguous, he conceded, was his own Uriage-inspired circle of friends, which had "its kind of 'National Revolution' side."[56]

Monnet's Planning Commission then was not just a club of market-oriented, Atlanticist modernizers but a much more complex mélange. Vichyites turned résistants belonged, as did several who had served the maréchal's regime without interruption, albeit in technical, that is, "nonpolitical," posts. There is no reason to think the Plan's senior leadership was antidemocratic. Quite the contrary. Yet, among Monnet's junior colleagues, there numbered more than one with a professed weakness for an authoritarian statism intended to waken France from the political decadence and economic torpor of Third Republic days.

This perspective casts a somewhat different light on the Planning Commission's celebrated "working style." The Plan's rue de Martignac digs came equipped with a dining room that became the site of informal, working meals. The fare was simple and the atmosphere relaxed, facilitating conversation and free exchange. Such unpretentious simplicity suited the planners, who, as Commission member Jean-François Gravier recollected, did not at all think of themselves as bureaucrats. Monnet wanted to re-create the easygoing but productive sociability he had become acquainted with from Anglo-American experience. Jean Fourastié, an early recruit to the Planning Commission, remembered that lunches were short, "on the American model" as he phrased it. Bloch-Lainé, a sometime visitor to the rue de Martignac, spoke of the meals in much the same terms. Cheese and salad courses were served together, he recalled, "as in Anglo-Saxonia."[57] But perhaps the sociability was not all "Anglo-Saxon" in character. Bloch-Lainé, after all, was an old Catholic scout. Fourastié was likewise a product of the interwar Catholic youth movement, a member of the Association catholique de la jeunesse française. A sometime student at Sciences Po, he had then entered public service, occupying a second-rank, technical position at the insurance industry CO during the war. Gravier's itinerary was not so different. He took youthful inspiration in part from Maurras, in part from a "Christian personalism." The brand of Christian personalism that attracted him, though, was not so much Mounier's as Perroux's, and indeed, during the Occupation, Gravier found employment, under Perroux's direction, in the Biosociology Department of the Fondation Carrel.[58] The Planning Commission's peculiar working style may have had Anglo-American antecedents, but it was not altogether a novelty to many in Monnet's entourage. Whether from adolescent days in Catholic youth groups or from more recent experience in the

Vichy administration, they had already had an encounter with the rough-and-ready ways of a team-spirited camaraderie.[59]

The Liberation did not resolve the question of France's future direction. To be sure, Vichy-style dirigisme was finished, but what was to take its place? A socialist dirigisme, ensconced in the MEN, was poised to stake its claim, but it had a competitor, a small team of planners gathered about Monnet. This would appear to be an unequal contest. The MEN project was much more in the Resistance mainstream. Monnet's was an eclectic potpourri, a third-way statism as it has been labeled here. The Monnet scheme was liberal and modernizing in its willingness to open the French economy to international markets, and it was full of consultative promise, though just how consultation was to be organized remained unspecified. Yet Monnet's project also had a strong statist flavoring. It was after all a plan, concocted in the first instance by experts, economists, and statisticians, many of whom harbored second thoughts, if not more, about the effectiveness and viability of parliamentary institutions. Monnet's team, to be sure, had a mystique and esprit de corps, itself a peculiar mix of ingredients, part Anglo-American and part nonconformist, but what else did it have going for it? De Gaulle's support, but then again, de Gaulle withdrew from the political scene in January 1946, not many weeks after legislating the Planning Commission into existence. Despite the odds, of course, Monnet's Plan would survive, but how and in what form remain to be seen.

Welfare, Family, and Population

It is puzzling how little thought the Resistance devoted to welfare and population-planning policy. To be sure, London-based Free French officials took cognizance of the Beveridge Report on Social Insurance and Allied Services when it was published in 1942. Beveridge's scheme envisioned a single state-administered insurance fund that would mete out a range of benefits to all, and the Resistance committee in charge of such matters saluted the report as "meriting our special attention." Yet the Free French came up with no equivalent project of their own. Nor were they much more inventive when it came to population issues. The syndicalist Adrien Tixier addressed the Assemblée consultative provisoire in January 1944. To general applause, he called for a determined and well-funded "protection of the family," touting the Daladier-era Code de la famille as "a monument" that required, not demolition, but building upon. The interior Resistance was of a similar mind.[60] The Comité général d'études, of course, counted Michel Debré among its number, a hard-core pronatalist, and so it is not surprising that the CGE took the population question to heart. It called for creation after the war of an interministerial commission to coordinate population policy. This commission would in turn get help from two organs: a Conseil supérieur de la Population composed of experts and an Haut-Commissariat à la Population presided over by a high commissioner recruited from the ranks of the permanent civil service. As for welfare, the CNR made known its views on the subject in no uncertain terms. Its March 1944 action program promised a "complete Social Security plan," guaranteeing the "means of existence" to all citizens in need, administered by the interested parties themselves in conjunction with the state.[61]

There was consensus then but little precision as to what had to be done at the Liberation. France needed a comprehensive and participatory social security system and a family-defense policy to match. This left a wide latitude for independent action to the men who would take charge of policy making after the war. They did not, however, confront a tabula rasa.

Vichy had been active in the welfare and population domains, and the legacy it left was an ambiguous one to say the least. In certain respects, Pétain's regime just added to what had come before. The pro-family coalition that had gained such influence in the Third Republic's final years gained yet more under Vichy, a regime that fetishized motherhood and the hearth with a sentimentalizing fervor all its own. But all was not sentiment under Vichy. Family policy had already begun to take a punitive turn in the Daladier era, and Pétain's regime gave the disciplinary screw several additional and violent turns. Vichy's decision to make abortion a capital offense is but the most egregious example of this development. At times, however, there was scientific method to the regime's madness. René Carmille's SNS took on the problem of population management with an imaginative statistical zeal. And then there was the Fondation Carrel, which styled itself a research institute of a novel kind, dedicated, in Carrel's own words, to the "systematic construction of civilized man in the totality of his corporal, social, and racial activities."[62]

Liberation officials made policy but not in circumstances of their own choosing. They confronted a mottled landscape of practices and institutions inherited from the Third Republic and from Vichy too, and it is the contours of this preexisting landscape that the present chapter will set about sketching in.

Welfare reform was not the Vichy regime's strongest suit. In the late summer of 1940, Belin's Ministère du Travail did come up with a plan for a major overhaul of existing institutions. Laroque worked on the project, alongside Francis Netter, a less senior official who, it seems, handled the bulk of the work. Both men were of Jewish descent; Laroque was soon fired for racial reasons; the more junior Netter managed to evade dismissal but had to maintain a low profile. All the same, the project they drafted did get circulated. It called for a fusion of France's myriad social insurance and family allowance regimes into a single, state-managed system of social security.[63]

This represented a dramatic break with the status quo in two critical respects. Reform legislation in 1928 and 1930 had expanded the state's role in the overall management of health and old-age insurance but did not abolish existing grassroots insurance funds managed by mutual-aid societies and *syndicats agricoles*. The 1928 and 1930 laws integrated local-level *caisses* into a national system that operated under the state's general supervision, but the *caisses* still retained a measure of decision-making autonomy, which they guarded jealously and effectively thanks to the lobbying efforts of pressure groups like the Fédération nationale de la mutualité française, well-connected to the Radical Party, and Jacques Le Roy Ladurie's conservative and corporatist Union nationale des syndicats agricoles (UNSA). The Netter/Laroque scheme aimed to root out such entrenched interests, elevating the state to a dominant role in welfare administration.

The state was scripted to play a dominant role in the administration of family allowances as well. The family allowance system had ramified in the 1930s. The Popular Front extended benefits to rural workers, a reform that met with massive noncompliance from cash-strapped farmers who had little inclination to pay welfare costs in the midst of a depression. In an effort to ensure more enthusiastic peasant participation, the Daladier administration took steps to cover as much as two-thirds of the required premiums out of public funds, a huge financial investment, of which Le Roy Ladurie's UNSA was a prime beneficiary.[64] The family allowance system was a world apart, a large one at that, and Netter and Laroque intended to fold it into a single, unified regime.

Belin pushed the Netter/Laroque proposal, but to no avail. It was just too radical, and Vichy contented itself with building on Third Republic precedents. It extended pension benefits to a substantial number of the once uncovered; it imposed a special tax on agricultural products, setting aside the proceeds to shore up the finances of the rural family allowance system; and it gave institutional expression to the growing separateness of rural welfare, taking away responsibility for agricultural social insurance from the Ministère du Travail and assigning it to the Ministère de l'Agriculture. From 1939 to 1944, the number of French men and women receiving welfare payments jumped from 11.4 million to 15.7 million, but the overall contours of the system did not change.[65] Private interests remained important in managing it; family allowances were handled under a distinct regime; and rural France continued to evolve down its own separate path.

Up to a point, the same observation holds true for family policy. The Vichy familist apparatus bears a marked resemblance to that of the late Republic, although not in every detail. Under Vichy, as before, there was a distinct government agency specializing in family matters, the Secrétariat d'Etat à la Famille et à la Santé, which got a beefing up in 1941 and a new name, the Commissariat-général à la Famille. The post was occupied by a series of personalities, many with no more than a fleeting interest in family policy. Mounier's former teacher Jacques Chevalier, who served in the position from February to August 1941, was an exception. He had solid familist credentials and indeed named an Alliance nationale man, Paul Haury, as his cabinet director. Haury himself was an unabashed Vichyite and had declared as much in an Alliance nationale publication, execrating the old Third Republic—its individualism and parliamentarism— even as he talked up the virtues of Maréchal Pétain's National Revolution.[66]

The Chevalier/Haury team, moreover, reached out to the familist movement. In June, it decreed creation of a Comité consultatif de la Famille, inviting representatives from various profamily organizations to join. Now, in certain respects, the Comité consultatif had the look of a successor body to the Daladier-era Haut Comité de la Population. The new Comité came into existence the very day the HCP was dissolved, and there was an overlap in personnel between the two. Jacques Doublet, Georges Pernot, and Alfred Sauvy belonged to the new as to the old organization. Yet what is perhaps most striking about the Comité consultatif was not so much its HCP antecedents as its rootedness in the profamily milieu. The Alliance nationale boasted that it had five delegates on the Comité consultatif, including Alliance president Paul Lefebvre-Dibon (Lefebvre-Dibon took over the presidency from Boverat, who had dropped out of sight in 1940).[67] And, of course, Catholic family interests were represented as well: in the person of Pernot, for example, who straddled the secular and religious worlds, and in that of Robert Prigent, the general secretary of the Catholic Action Ligue ouvrière chrétienne. The Ligue changed its name in 1942 to the Mouvement populaire des familles. Prigent too was to experience a change of heart, shifting allegiance from Vichy to the Resistance. The timing of the switch is not certain, but it was no later than 1943, when he can be found militating in the ranks of the OCM.[68]

The partnership of lay and Catholic familism that had begun to crystallize in the prewar years was formalized under Vichy (though, as Prigent's defection attests, the partnership had its points of vulnerability). This coming together took place not just within government institutions but also without. The regime encouraged France's numerous profamily associations to join forces, an effort that gave birth to a new umbrella organization, the Centre de coordination et d'action des mouvements familiaux, founded in October 1940. The Alliance nationale, the Fédération nationale des association de familles nombreuses, and like-minded groups all sent representatives to the Centre, which, in July 1941, was extended official governmental recognition.[69]

The family movement had never been more united or better positioned to get what it wanted than under Vichy. But what did it want? The regime made a cult of motherhood, and the familist movement did its best to help out. It had been the custom since the midtwenties for the state to award medals to mothers of large families. The ceremony was conducted on Mother's Day, and 25 May 1941, the first Mother's Day feted under the new regime, was no exception. The Centre de coordination organized a gala of its own to honor medal recipients, a matinee at the Comédie française that featured a two-act play, *Le Chant du berceau*, plus inspirational readings from the poetry of Victor Hugo and Charles Péguy. The maréchal did not attend the event, but he did deliver a stirring radio address celebrating the mothers of France who, like Mary, the Mater dolorosa, endured in the face of adversity and loss. The Alliance nationale was thrilled. Its house review recapped recent triumphs in the field of family policy, talked about how needful effective leadership was, and then concluded with a Pétainist flourish: "That *Chef*, we have him: it is the Maréchal Pétain."[70]

Of equal importance to the Alliance nationale was a thoroughgoing application of the 1939 Family Code, and in this domain too Vichy did not disappoint. In 1940, it forbade the advertising of aperitifs, whether by billboard or poster, in the press or on the radio. In 1941, it built up the benefit system for stay-at-home mothers, extending the payment, now renamed the *allocation de salaire unique*, to nonworking moms in the agricultural sector.[71] And in 1942, the regime mandated demographic instruction in all primary schools, and then the year following it added a demographic component to the national high school curriculum as well. The Alliance nationale itself was invited to help draw up the new programs of study. These various measures were noted and applauded in the Alliance nationale press.[72]

In all these respects, Vichy practice looks more like an extension of late Third Republic policy than a fresh departure. The new regime's familist apparatus resembled in basic design the institutional edifice first erected under Daladier. Daladier had reached out to the profamily movement to recruit policy-making personnel, and Vichy did the same. As for policy itself, the Code de la famille remained for Vichy, as for Daladier, a founding document, the constitutional touchstone of a new familist era.

It is important, though, not to forget the points of difference, some minor, others less so. The profamily coalition of the Vichy years was much more weighted to the confessional side. Chevalier, Pernot, Prigent were all products of the Catholic milieu. It mattered as well that certain personalities on the secularist end of the coalition experienced a partial eclipse during the war years. Boverat did in the end resurface. He involved himself once more in Alliance affairs but did not regain the prominence of bygone days. As for Landry, he was persona non grata under Vichy. A Radical deputy, he had abstained in July 1940 rather than vote Pétain *pleins pouvoirs*. Nor did Landry buckle to the regime afterward. On the contrary, he aided and abetted the Resistance and busied himself getting the Radical Party, dissolved by Vichy, up and running again.[73]

A more forceful religious presence in profamily ranks did alter the tonality of the movement's rhetoric. The old strain of scientizing pronatalism did not disappear, but the accent was now more on maternal devotion and sacrifice, a frame of mind very much in tune with Vichy's own way of thinking.[74] The regime indeed took an array of steps to insure that women, nolens volens, lived up to domestic expectations. It made home economics a curricular requirement in the public schools; it created obstacles to public-sector employment for married women; it forbade divorce in the first two years of marriage. Such measures were of course not just rhetorical gestures but legal imperatives. There had been a ferocity to profamily oratory in the late Republic. The Alliance nationale likened abortionists to traitors who, as such, deserved no better than the firing squad.[75] But now, under Vichy, with normal democratic restraints removed, it was easier to translate such words into deeds. Two abortionists were in fact executed under Vichy law and sixteen sent away for life. Late Republic familism was a complex amalgam. Vichy did not so much add to the mix as accentuate certain of its ingredients: its religiosity, its lachrymose maternalism, its violence.

The familist movement still cared about population science, but it was no longer in the vanguard of demographic research, as it had been in Landry's day. In this domain, the baton was passed to new institutions, to René Carmille's SNS first of all. The SNS maintained two principal offices, one in Paris headed by Henri Bunle, where Sauvy's Institut de Conjoncture was also based. The second was headquartered in Lyon. The latter housed the demographic service, which was Carmille's special area of interest. There was a rivalry between the two offices, the Paris branch styling itself a more artisanal, research-oriented operation in contrast to Carmille's factory-like Lyon bureau. The factory metaphor was in certain respects an apt one. Carmille, as already noted, expanded the staffing of the SNS, assigning a large chunk of the new personnel to the demographic service. He was a firm believer, moreover, in the counting power of machines. Carmille wanted to create a demographic profile for every Frenchman that could be summed up in a numerical code. That code, punched onto perforated cards, might then be tabulated and collated by machine, allowing classifications and comparisons just too complex to compile by manual methods.[76]

And what was the principal object of Carmille's number-crunching enterprise? Census taking: the SNS compiled a census of demobilized military personnel and a yet more extensive professional census of all persons born between 1876 and 1927 resident in the unoccupied zone. Neither, it turns out, was just a neutral, academic exercise.

The professional census, completed in the summer of 1941, posed several categories of question, the answers enumerated in a thirteen-digit code. The section on nationality included the query "are you of the Jewish race?" The SNS implicated itself in the regime's racial policies, though not always with enthusiasm. It did help devise statistical means to identify Algerian Jews, whom the regime targeted for denaturalization. On the other hand, when Vichy's Commissariat-général aux Questions juives (CGQJ) turned to the SNS regional office in

Clermont-Ferrand for assistance in processing police data on the local
Jewish population, the office dragged its feet. The same mix of solici-
tousness and foot-dragging characterized the SNS response to the
Ministère de la Production industrielle's demands for help compiling lists of potential STO conscripts. The STO labor draft got started
in February 1943. The ministry wanted information on draft-age
youths, and the SNS made available the relevant documentation from
the 1941 census. By springtime, however, Carmille's organization had
grown less forthcoming, leaving STO recruiters more and more to
fend for themselves.[77]

The SNS's course correction may have had a connection to Carmille's own evolving sympathies. He was a Pétainist who never broke
faith with the maréchal himself. Carmille, like so many in the Pétainist camp, execrated the liberal individualism of the nineteenth century. He also seems to have been an anti-Semite of the conventional,
establishment type, accepting of Vichy's racial policies but without
the persecutory zeal of the CGQJ. Yet Carmille was at the same time
an unbending patriot. The census on demobilized military personnel
was itself a patriotic act. Carmille wanted a record of all ex-soldiers,
the better to mobilize them against the Germans when the time came
for France to stand up for itself once again. The census was ready for
use in April 1942. The Germans occupied all of France in November,
and not long after that, Carmille had the document destroyed, lest it
fall into enemy hands. The STO could not have sat well with a patriot
of Carmille's sort, and indeed, sometime in 1943, he established contact with the Marco Polo Resistance network. Carmille then was a
man of dual loyalties, a "Vichysto-résistant," who believed himself
true to Pétain even as he plunged into Resistance work. And the Resistance commitment was a serious one, leading to Carmille's arrest
in February 1944 and eventual death in deportation.[78]

Bunle took over direction of the SNS after Carmille's departure,
and Bunle made great claims for the organization's Resistance bona
fides. The SNS, he maintained, had funneled information to the
Resistance—the names of the recent dead, for example—to assist in
the fabrication of false identity papers. On the other hand, the SNS
was slow to shake off its racist past. It did not suppress the racial

component of the thirteen-digit identity number until mid-May 1945, and regional offices were still using Vichy-era census questionnaires, complete with racial references, into the middle of that same year.[79]

This then was the organization the Liberation-era governments inherited. It had obvious liabilities. The SNS had been headed by a Pétain loyalist, and the institution had implicated itself in the implementation of some of the least savory aspects of Vichy policy. At the same time, the SNS was in a position to vaunt its patriotic, if not Resistance, credentials. It had lost a chief in the fight against the Occupier. Not least of all, there were the bureau's institutional assets: its large, trained staff, all those machines, Sauvy's Institut de Conjoncture, the accumulated census data, that ever so useful thirteen-digit identity number. It would not be so easy for the Resistance, once in power, to turn its back on such an array of resources.

Nor would it be so easy to decide what to do with a second Vichy-era institution, the Fondation Carrel. Carrel was no Vichysto-résistant but an unyielding man of the National Revolution to the very end. He was at the same time a first-rate institution builder, a match and then some in this respect for Carmille. He would create under Vichy auspices a social-science think tank of an altogether novel type, "dedicated," as a Fondation document put it, "to the construction of civilized men."[80] Postwar France, as much as Vichy, had an interest in the demographic reconstruction of the nation. Would it want to disassemble Carrel's oeuvre, which had already made such a signal contribution to the cause?

It took some time to get the Fondation functioning with a staff that met the chief's, that is, Carrel's, high standards. Carrel was last encountered in 1940, employed at Dautry's Ministère de l'Armement. The impending defeat of France prompted Carrel's return to the United States in May. He returned to his native country in early 1941, dispatched on a medical mission by the Roosevelt administration. The visit took him to Vichy, where he met with the new US ambassador, Admiral Leahy. Carrel made a stop at his Breton family retreat as well, and there reconnected with André Missenard. Missenard, seconded by Mme. Carrel and Dom Alexis Presse (a clergyman described as exercising "a great influence on Carrel"), bent every effort to per-

suading the doctor to remain in France. Carrel agreed on condition
that the government furnish him, in Missenard's characterization,
"the necessary tools of labor." Carrel himself had a definite idea of
what he had in mind. "I want to instigate," he wrote to an old friend
in June, "the organization of a sort of Institute for the regeneration
of the individual and the race."[81] Missenard got to work mobilizing
on Carrel's behalf. Back in Paris, he contacted André Gros and
Jacques Ménétrier, both MDs. The trio in turn lobbied various Vichy
officials of their acquaintance—Baudouin, Bichelonne, Lehideux—
and such efforts produced results.[82] In November 1941, the Vichy
government promised a substantial sum to set up a Fondation française pour l'étude des problèmes humains. Carrel was named regent.

Carrel then set about finding space and personnel for his new operation. On the matter of space, he installed himself in a building on
the rue de la Baume that had been the property of the Rockefeller
Foundation. Carrel was aware that the move might not sit well with
Rockefeller officials Simon Flexner and Alan Gregg. Flexner was retired director of the Rockefeller Institute and Gregg chief medical
officer at the Rockefeller Foundation. Carrel wrote to his American
secretary, asking her, in tones at once boastful and ingratiating, to
explain to them what he was up to:

> Please tell to Dr. Flexner that I have a wonderful opportunity
> to apply on a large scale what I learned during those many
> years at the Institute. Also to Dr. Alan Gregg that his plan for a
> National Institute of Health will be realized.[83]

Gregg, it appears, was unmollified. He did not reply when informed
of Carrel's real-estate grab, and Carrel's secretary sensed "disapproval"
in Gregg's silence.[84]

Carrel encountered difficulties as well assembling what he felt to
be a loyal staff. The day-to-day running of the Fondation Carrel was
assigned to the secretary-general, a post occupied in the Fondation's
first months by Ménétrier. In September 1942, however, Perroux
took over the position, and then the troubles began. Carrel came to
detest Perroux, whom he described as "a defective" and "a paranoid."
It took Carrel months of battling, aggravated by incipient health

problems, to get rid of the economist, but Perroux was at last pushed out in December 1943.[85] He was succeeded by Roger Peltier, who proved a capable and, as will be seen, durable administrator.

Carrel now had the team he wanted, and he was exultant. The Fondation, he wrote on New Year's eve 1943, "is taking off."[86] There should be no mistaking, moreover, that this was a Pétainist institution, at the top at least. Carrel met with the maréchal three times, and he was in good odor with Laval as well. In the spring of 1943, Laval approached Carrel about becoming Vichy minister of public health.[87] Carrel's refusal ought not be taken as a sign that he had doubts of any kind about the regime's legitimacy. In April 1944, Pétain paid a visit to Paris, and the newsreel footage of the event made it appear he had been welcomed by enthusiastic crowds. The maréchal's "triumphal reception" pleased Carrel. "What an unexpected blow," he exulted, "to de Gaulle, and the traitor Giraud." And there was Carrel the month following, at lunch with the director-general of the SNCF, railing against France's decline and degeneration. Georges Duhamel, who was present on the occasion, did not disagree but wondered whether it might not be better to hold one's tongue until the Germans left. Carrel felt otherwise.[88]

Carrel, moreover, understood the institutional project he was embarked on very much in National Revolution terms. The interwar decades had left France diminished. The Fondation set itself the task, in Missenard's words, of studying "the causes of French weakness and the necessary remedies."[89] Carrel himself had a reasonably clear idea of how this was to be done. He felt an intense pride in the high quality of the research staff he had assembled, young men in the main, most of them under forty. "I have surrounded myself," he boasted, "with an elite," a leaven that would over time enable the nation to rise again. But that leaven's power depended on teamwork, "something new for the French," as Carrel put it.[90] The Fondation Carrel was organized in six departments, which in turn broke down into a score or so *équipes*. All the talk about France's failings, about elite redemption and team spirit, was very much of the Vichy era, but what about the Fondation's actual work? Did its research agenda fit the National Revolution project?

The answer here must be yes. Take the Population Biology Department as a first example. André Missenard, Carrel's right-hand man, headed the unit. Missenard in turn was at pains to solicit the collaboration of the Alliance nationale, and indeed the Fondation had genuine success working out the modus vivendi it sought, recruiting three senior Alliance nationale members to its ranks: Fernand Boverat, Jacques Doublet, and Paul Vincent. In a pair of notes drafted in October 1942, Missenard outlined what he hoped his department would accomplish. The problem, he wrote, was to improve the quality of France's population, and in this connection he perorated on the virtues of scouting and the vices of women's work. It was obvious to any disinterested observer that healthy parents made for healthy babies, but the problem was how to ensure the healthfulness of parents. To this end, Missenard recommended sterilizing, voluntarily or otherwise, the carriers of "hereditary taints." At a minimum, the state had the right to require engaged couples, prior to marriage, to secure medical certification attesting to their general health and genetic status. Vichy, in fact, enacted just such a requirement. From December 1942, all about-to-be marrieds were placed under obligation to obtain from a doctor of their choosing a "prenuptial certificate." The measure, need it be said, won the wholehearted approval of the Fondation Carrel.[91]

The quality of the nation's human breeding stock came up once again in debates about immigration. The *équipe population*, quartered in the Population Biology Department, handled this area of research. Robert Gessain, a doctor and physical anthropologist, presided over the *équipe*, which included at least one personality well known to historians, Louis Chevalier. Chevalier's real passion at this juncture was not immigration but regions, understood as organisms like the *Ouest* of André Siegfried's magisterial *Tableau politique*. The region, as Chevalier conceived it, was a living entity more real than the artificial departmental units into which France had been divided since the French Revolution. Chevalier had wanted to create a biogeography team to study the problem but was turned down and had to settle for a research post under Gessain's direction. What Gessain's team proposed to do was to examine immigration in terms of the potential assimilability of diverse immigrant populations. At stake was nothing less than the protection of the "hereditary patrimony of the fatherland" (Gessain's words). The wrong sort of immigrant threatened to pollute the national gene pool, and the wrong sort were the unassimilables. In a speech to Chantiers de la Jeunesse officials, Gessain gave a clear indication of just who the offending parties were: "racial elements that have been mongrelized or negritized or Judified," the very sorts who had in recent decades battened on an unsuspecting and weakened France by the hundreds of thousands.[92]

But the Fondation's population talk was not just eugenicist and racist in character. The Population Biology Department maintained a natality team that included Boverat, who served as secretary. Boverat in fact published a brochure under Fondation Carrel auspices titled *Une Doctrine de la natalité*. And the Fondation's natalism was not only of the hand-wringing, hortatory variety. It had a serious, scientific dimension. Gessain's research squad included a young polytechnicien, Jean Bourgeois (later Jean Bourgeois-Pichat), who came recommended by Vincent. Bourgeois was a mathematizer with a penchant for charts and graphs that at times made his work hard to understand for the less numerate demographers of an earlier generation. Under Gessain's supervision, Bourgeois set about studying the evolution of the French birthrate and came up with a startling conclusion. Since 1941, there had been an "impressive augmentation of legitimate fecundity." The French were starting to reproduce once again, the first, uncertain glimmerings of a phenomenon that would over time come to be known as the "baby boom."[93]

The Fondation Carrel understood itself as a handmaiden to the regime, a policy-oriented body that would supply Vichy officialdom with serviceable scientific knowledge to aid in the monitoring and remodeling of the national population. That was very much how Jean Stoetzel saw his role at the rue de la Baume. Stoetzel joined the Fondation Carrel in the spring of 1942 and would remain on board until the end. He took charge of the institute's polling and statistical services and in that capacity conducted a pair of surveys before the year was out, the most significant (completed in late fall) canvassing popular attitudes toward reproductive policy. The results revealed an interesting mix of attitudes, both punitive and indulgent. Yes, answered 71 percent of the respondents, abortion was a serious crime and ought to be treated as such. At the same time, 89 percent favored the protection of unwed mothers and illegitimate children.[94] Stoetzel was at pains to underscore the scientific character of his work. He did not promise one hundred percent accuracy but a statistical certainty within a calculable margin of error. Polling was a science, but more than that it was a useful science with policy implications, provided the authorities took notice. And a wise "sovereign," Stoetzel insisted, would do just that, for was not the art of governing the art of managing "the popular consciousness"? "There is no government," Stoetzel wrote in 1943, "however authoritarian it may be, and perhaps even more so the more authoritarian it is, which is not preoccupied, at least on certain questions, with securing the accord of public opinion."[95]

Stoetzel never did get the ear of the Vichy government. The Fondation's *équipe travail*, however, had more success. The team was part of the Labor Department headed by Gros, who, in collaboration with Ménétrier, had published a volume on industrial medicine in 1941. "Medical technocrats" that they were, Gros and Ménétrier believed that managing the "human factor" (i.e. the health and well-being of the shop-floor worker) was critical to the functioning of a harmonious, productive business enterprise. In July 1942, Vichy enacted a law requiring all large-scale industrial organizations to set up medical and social counseling services. The Fondation Carrel is said to have played a part in inspiring the policy. What is certain is that the labor team had a hand in its execution.[96]

This then was the organization the Resistance inherited at the Liberation. Carrel, the Fondation's director, was an arch Pétainist and the Fondation itself a willing collaborator in the Vichy regime's racial and eugenicist policies. On the other hand, Carrel's staff, composed in large measure of doctors and polytechniciens, was first-rate.[97] Most were serious social scientists, embarked on research projects that dealt with a range of matters—from demographic trends to opinion polling to industrial hygiene—of potential interest to postwar policy makers, whatever their political views. What to do with Carrel and the Fondation would not be an easy choice.

Vichy did, indeed, leave an equivocal legacy in the domain of welfare and population policy. Much of what Vichy did had a familiar, familist look. Yet the regime also pushed the profamily line with a disciplinary and sometimes lethal vengeance, driving women out of the public domain as best it could. Birthrates and reproduction remained, as before the war, a subject of preoccupation but now with noxious racial and eugenicist admixtures. Where the regime did innovate was in population management, creating or sponsoring new institutions, like the SNS and Fondation Carrel, that brought a maturing statistical insight to bear on demographic and related issues of great moment to the state. Postwar authorities might well want to think twice whether it made good sense to jettison the Vichy past altogether. And if they opted to pick and choose among policies and institutions, they would still have to sort out what was worth saving and what not. Such were the questions, not at all simple ones, that Liberation-era policy makers confronted.

Sciences Po

The postwar policy makers also had to decide what to do with Sciences Po. The Left had a clear enough idea how it wanted to proceed. In late February 1945, Sciences Po's old nemesis, the Communist Georges Cogniot, submitted a resolution to the Assemblée consultative provisoire. The text ticked off the usual list of anti–Sciences Po accusations: the school catered to the few; its curriculum did not correspond to modern realities; it was a tool of "the global trusts." But a new and explosive charge had been added to the standard brief. Sciences Po, the resolution read, had "supplied the *cadres supérieurs* of treason and of collaboration with the enemy." Under the circumstances, the people's representatives had a right to confiscate the school's assets and turn them over to a new institution that would be "national and democratic."[98]

Cogniot's, moreover, was not a solitary voice. All proposals relating to civil-service reform had to be examined by the Assembly's Commission sur la Réforme de l'Etat, which counted among its member-

ship Pierre Cot, a former young turk of the Radical Party and Léon
Blum's erstwhile minister of aviation. Cot, a man of leftist views, was
known to have it in for Sciences Po. So too did Assembly member
André Philip, a Socialist and résistant, who harbored a particular dis-
trust of *la haute fonction publique*. In 1945, he penned a preface to a
book on the reform of the state in which he echoed almost charge for
charge Cogniot's indictment of the civil-service regime *en place*. And
then the following year he floated a proposal—which came to nothing—to abolish the Inspection des finances outright.[99] From a certain
angle, it might well have appeared that the old Popular Front coalition, drawing fresh vitality from its Resistance exploits, was re-forming,
this time to finish off the job begun in 1936: the demolition of Sciences Po and the erection in its place of a new Ecole nationale d'administration.

At first glance, Sciences Po seemed to be vulnerable indeed to such
attacks. The catastrophe of 1940 presented Sciences Po with a series
of dilemmas: how to manage the Germans; how to deal with Vichy;
how to regulate its internal affairs in a setting of war and occupation.
In the first instance, Sciences Po made every effort to establish "correct relations."[100] In the second, a more intimate and symbiotic relationship developed: Vichy recruited into its service a raft of Sciences
Po faculty, and Sciences Po in return invited Vichy officials to teach
and to speak. And in the third? Reforms of a professionalizing cast
remained as before the war at the top of the school's agenda, although now pursued with a Pétainist inflection. This was not the kind
of record designed to protect the school against a concerted assault
from the Left.

And yet, on closer inspection, Sciences Po's record proves to have
been more mixed. In 1942–1943, the school began to distance itself
from the Vichy regime. Ties with the Resistance were cultivated, and
by war's end Sciences Po was in a position to insist on its genuine
contribution to the fight against the Occupier. It was a contribution,
moreover, that won the school backing in influential Resistance circles, from the CGE for example, which shared in Sciences Po's ever
more technocratic orientation. At the Liberation, Sciences Po was
neither as retrograde nor as reactionary as the Left portrayed it, and

it had well-placed friends into the bargain. In the fight then shaping up, the old Ecole libre was perhaps not so vulnerable after all.

The Germans closed down Sciences Po on 26 July 1940. Roger Seydoux telephoned and then met with Karl Epting of the German embassy to work out conditions for the school's reopening. Before the war, Epting had worked at the German Institute in Paris, and Seydoux and he had first become acquainted at that time. Vichy authorities were also approached. A letter inviting Pétain's intercession was drafted although not sent. Sciences Po officials did meet with General de La Laurencie, Vichy's representative in the occupied zone, and with the new minister of national education Emile Mireaux, an old friend, to discover what they knew of German intentions.[101]

These communications made two points clear. The Occupation authorities were unhappy about the anti-German bias of elements of the school's curriculum. Nor did they care for certain—unidentified—instructors on its teaching staff. The school promised to be responsive on the first issue. It had on its own initiative dropped Pétain's course on national defense. Jacques Benoist-Méchin, a well-known Germanophile and right-winger, was asked to lecture on aspects of contemporary German history. It does not appear, however, that he ever took up the invitation. A course *was* offered, though, on "German unity," taught by René Dupuis, a onetime member of the *Ordre nouveau* group.[102]

On the question of personnel, the Sciences Po administration is supposed to have given assurances of its intention to discharge "undesirable" faculty. Jacques Rueff, who was Jewish, did leave the school's service. The Gestapo made plain that it would not allow him to teach in Paris, obliging the veteran economist to quit the rue Saint-Guillaume. He headed south in search of a safe haven. Sciences Po's exact role in this parting of the ways, however, is not clear. Rueff's case apart, the school overall seems to have found ways to spare itself hard choices. Michel Debré, of Jewish descent, was just the sort of colleague the Germans would have targeted. With André Ségalat, he ran an *écurie* under Sciences Po auspices to gear up candidates for the Conseil d'état exam. In 1940, however, the *écurie* was convened not on school premises in Paris but at Clermont-Ferrand in the unoccupied zone, out of German reach. The school also opened a branch campus in Lyon. Jacques Chapsal—now Seydoux's secretary-general and right-hand man—Raoul Dautry, Henri Davezac, and André Siegfried all relocated there in the early years of the Occupation. Baumgartner, who was reputed to be persona non grata with the Germans, divided his time between the capital, which was dangerous for him, and the safer terrain of the Lyon campus.[103]

To placate Occupation authorities, the school pledged itself to good behavior, adjusting its curriculum and reshuffling its teaching staff. Such exertions proved sufficient, and Sciences Po was allowed to reopen in the late fall of 1940. Unlike the Germans, the Vichy regime was disposed in Sciences Po's favor, as well it might have been. Pétain still sat on the Conseil d'administration. Vichy's first two ministers of justice, Raphaël Alibert and Joseph Barthélemy, were high-ranking Sciences Po faculty. Alibert had taught at the school in the 1930s. Barthélemy, when called to Vichy's service in 1941, was still an active member of the teaching staff and had to take a leave of absence to assume his government duties. The school sent faculty to work at Vichy: Davezac and Detoeuf, who had both taught courses at Sciences Po before the war, were appointed to top posts at the electrical industry CO.[104] And the school welcomed to its halls Vichy officials, both current and former, as speakers and colleagues. In January 1942, Bichelonne, soon to become minister of industrial production, delivered an address to the school, a defense of dirigiste economics titled "L'Etat actuel de l'organisation économique française." Two months later, it was the turn of Jean Borotra, a senior official at the Education Ministry, who discoursed on the pedagogical virtues of sport (Borotra was himself a former tennis great, one of the Four Musketeers who brought the Davis Cup home to France in the late twenties). That same March, the school hired Henri Dhavernas for a junior post, and in July awarded a chair to Jean-Jacques Chevallier. Chevallier, like Borotra, was an athletic man, a passionate cyclist, but it was his intellectual and oratorical skills that set him apart. He was a much-feted speaker at the Vichy-sponsored Ecole des cadres at Uriage, and at Sciences Po he packed the students in, filling the Boutmy amphitheater and drawing applause at the end of every lecture.[105]

Once the school's status vis-à-vis the Germans had been sorted out and Vichy's benevolent patronage assured, Sciences Po turned to its own affairs. Before 1940 was finished, the school had subjected its governing structures to an overhaul. Tirard was named president, in effect kicked upstairs to a more honorific post. The old Comité de direction was at the same time dismantled, leaving Seydoux alone in charge of the day-to-day running of the school.[106] The sitting Conseil d'administration also underwent a shake-up. A trio of long-standing members, among them the marquis de Vogüé, were dropped. It was proposed to fill the seats made vacant with five replacements: Baumgartner; Georges Pichat, vice president of the Conseil d'état; Pierre-Eugène Fournier, president of the national railway company, the SNCF; Georges Ripert, dean of the Paris Law School; and the rector of the University of Paris, who attended a council meeting or two but then stopped coming. Baumgartner was interned by the Nazis in 1943. Three of the other new members, however, were destined to play important roles at Vichy—Fournier as director of the agency that oversaw the management of "aryanized" Jewish property in the southern zone, Pichat as president of the Secours national, and Ripert as Vichy minister of education. The purpose of such reshuffling was twofold: to clean out older, nonparticipating members and to substitute for them a more dynamic, less business-oriented team with ties to the University and to state administration.[107]

Sciences Po, indeed, was keen to formalize its links to the Sorbonne. In the early months of 1941, a convention was concluded between representatives from the two institutions and ratified by ministerial decree in June. Under the terms of the agreement, the dean of the Faculty of Law and the dean of the Faculty of Letters were accorded ex officio status on Sciences Po's governing board. The rector of the University himself was not expected to serve, but the convention did confer on him authority to nominate delegates to Sciences Po organs dealing with curriculum oversight and examinations. The Sorbonne in return granted Sciences Po the right to affix the University's name to its diplomas.[108]

Tougher standards had been an ongoing preoccupation ever since Seydoux joined the school administration in 1936. Two changes were effected in this domain during the Occupation years, both with Vichy overtones. No sooner had Sciences Po reopened in 1940 than the administration imposed a physical education requirement. The object? To boost student morale and habits of discipline. Borotra, who paid a visit to the school in March 1942, inspected the athletic program and came away much impressed.[109] In 1941, a second new requirement was imposed. All incoming male students, with certain exceptions, were now expected to possess the bac. As for women applicants, bac holders or not, they were obliged to take a special entrance exam, which proved no mere formality, as more than half who sat it actually failed. The school did not want "young ladies" who came there "for reasons of snobbery." The Vichy regime, moreover, had placed restrictions on female employment in the state administration. Sciences Po officials saw no point in training women for jobs that did not exist.[110]

Last of all, the school continued to rework its curriculum the better to reflect what it understood to be the present economic realities. Sauvy was hired to teach a course on conjunctural economics in 1940. Louis Chevalier came on board as a junior professor the following year and François Bloch-Lainé (himself a Sciences Po alumnus) at the same rank in 1942.[111] In the 1941–1942 academic year, Siegfried offered a course on American civilization, analyzing Taylorism and Fordism as the avatars of a new, post-bourgeois "technical age."[112] Of perhaps greater moment was Sciences Po's decision to appoint Gaëtan Pirou to replace the now-absent Rueff. Pirou, recruited from the Faculty of Law, was no orthodox liberal but a convinced dirigiste. This did not mean he repudiated the laws of supply and demand, not at all. But the market stood in need of a firm hand, of a "political power extremely strong," which, informed by a vision of the whole, by a plan in a word, would be in a position to impose "order and general discipline." These were the lessons Pirou taught in his course, "Economie libérale et économie dirigée," and they represented a dramatic departure from the laissez-faire orthodoxy of the old Sciences Po.[113]

In the thirties, the school had begun to temper its former economic liberalism in favor of more directive approaches, a reorienta-

tion that made possible a first rapprochement with circles of technocratic reflection. This process was accelerated during the war. Seydoux
first met François Perroux in 1944, "under the Occupation" as Seydoux put it. Perroux was just then getting ISEA up and running, and
he wanted Sciences Po's backing. Seydoux proved an obliging interlocutor, and in due course a gratin of school faculty—Detoeuf, Pirou,
Sauvy, Siegfried himself—were drawn into ISEA's orbit.[114]

Sciences Po in the meantime kept up its *Nouveaux Cahiers* connection. The defeat of 1940 had dispersed the group, but it reformed in
August under a new name, the Comité d'études pour la France. The
Comité d'études was presided over by NC veterans Guillaume de Tarde
and Auguste Detoeuf, and like the old NC it hosted regular meetings
to debate the issues of the day. The gist of its debates was communicated to the government, which was no more than natural given the
participation of various Vichy officials—Surleau for example—in the
Comité's proceedings. The body understood itself as a think tank,
generating real solutions to real problems. And it turned out to be a
most successful enterprise, with affiliates outside Paris and a membership numbering in the hundreds. André Isambert, a *Nouveaux Cahiers* founder, ran the Lyon chapter (known as the Comité d'études et
d'informations), which he had gotten started at the instigation of Seydoux. Sciences Po was indeed very much a presence in the ranks of the
Comité d'études, which counted both Seydoux and Siegfried as members as well as a number of school faculty like Detoeuf and Sauvy.[115]

The Comité was a private organization with excellent contacts
in ruling circles. The Conseil supérieur de l'Economie industrielle et
commerciale, on the other hand, was a regular administrative agency,
set up in 1942 under the auspices of the Ministère de la Production
industrielle. The Conseil was conceived as "an organism of study and
propaganda," and an old X-Crise man, Bardet, placed in charge. He
staffed the agency, as already noted, with the best technical minds,
including a trio of Sciences Po faculty: Davezac, Detoeuf, and Pirou.[116]
Wherever the nation's economic future was being planned, there Sciences Po faculty and administrators were on hand to lend advice.

Yet, however close the ties between Sciences Po and Vichy, the connection did not prove unbreakable. Consider the trajectories of Sieg-

fried and Seydoux. Siegfried in the first years of the Occupation continued to print articles in the pro-Vichy *Le Temps*. But he was also
known to dabble in activities of a more oppositional nature. Paul Bastid, no friend of Vichy, as we have seen, ran a discussion group that
met in Lyon in the early years of the Occupation. The old republican
Left set the tone, but Bastid's circle included a smattering of more
centrist types, the christian democrat Champetier de Ribes for example, and, from time to time, Siegfried himself. Siegfried was active
as well in a second gathering, animated by Jean de Traz, which began
as a discussion group but which by 1942 had begun to relay intelligence to the Free French in London.[117]

Seydoux's trajectory was similar. In the first years after the armistice, he appears to have kept up contact with Epting. But to Sciences
Po undergraduates like Jean Lacouture, Seydoux made no secret of
his dislike for Vichy. The Allied invasion of North Africa in 1942
prompted the Germans to occupy the southern zone of France. Jean
Chauvel, a senior official at the Ministère des Affaires étrangères, resigned his post, taking with him a number of younger colleagues, including Seydoux's brother François. Chauvel intended to create a
veritable shadow ministry that would chart out French foreign policy
for a post-Vichy future. He approached Seydoux for assistance, who
made Sciences Po premises available for planning meetings.[118]

The year 1942, and the German occupation of the southern zone
in particular, appears to have been a turning point. Pétain's name
still figured on the roster of Sciences Po's Conseil d'administration in
July. By year's end, it had been dropped.[119] In 1943–1944, the school's
involvement in oppositional activity deepened. Barthélemy, having
stepped down as minister of justice in the spring of 1943, sought to
resume his teaching responsibilities at the rue Saint-Guillaume. The
school refused to take him back. More consequential still were the
school's efforts to preserve its students from the labor draft imposed
in February 1943. The STO conscripted military-age youth for labor
service in Germany, and Sciences Po wanted no part of the operation, attempting to dissuade students from answering the call, falsify-
ing records, and providing cover to help those who did not want to
go. Such obstructionism earned Seydoux a frigid interview with min-

ister of national education Abel Bonnard in May. Bonnard would not shake Seydoux's hand, treating him to a mixture of reproach and imprecation about Sciences Po's general political posture.[120]

Seydoux, however, was undeterred by Bonnard's threats. Over the course of 1943—the precise timing is uncertain—Seydoux struck up a collaboration with Philippe Viannay, a student turned journalist who managed a major Resistance newspaper, *La Défense de la France*. Viannay furnished Sciences Po students and personnel with forged documents; Seydoux supplied Viannay information and contacts in the civil-service and business worlds.[121]

The Resistance in fact was coming to recognize in Seydoux a useful go-between in its dealings with France's administrative and economic elites. In October 1943, Admiral Gabriel Auphan, onetime Vichy minister of the navy, got in touch with Seydoux in the hope of working out a rapprochement with the Resistance. Seydoux hosted a pair of meetings between Auphan and Resistance representatives Debré and Teitgen, but the negotiations came to nothing. Seydoux's interventions were more effective in the case of Jean Prouvost. The defeat of 1940 had found Prouvost, a textile magnate and press lord, in the post of minister of information, a position he continued to occupy for a brief period under Vichy. He was publisher as well of a much-read newspaper, *Paris-Soir*, which did not cease publication until 1943, well after the German occupation of the southern zone. As the Liberation neared, Prouvost grew anxious about the ambiguities of his wartime record and approached Seydoux, who then called in Debré. Prouvost ended up making a substantial cash contribution to the Resistance, getting in return a receipt that helped to bail him out at the Liberation.[122] The Seydoux-Debré connection was activated yet once more in the spring of 1944. Debré, now a senior Resistance official, was charged with putting in place the administrative apparatus of a post-Vichy France. Future prefects were designated, and Debré then met with them clandestinely in batches, region by region. The Gestapo almost broke up one such gathering, the delegates taking refuge on Seydoux's invitation in a room at Sciences Po.[123] It is not clear how much Vichy authorities knew of such goings-on, but they knew enough to conclude that Sciences Po harbored "Gaullist and Anglo-

Saxon sympathies" and that Seydoux himself was the man most responsible for this state of affairs.[124]

The school had been Pétainist at the armistice; in 1942–1943, it
turned to the Resistance. In certain respects, though, Sciences Po's
underlying commitments remained unchanged throughout. Pétain
was looked to as a figure of authority who, in partnership with competent elites, might yet set the nation's house in order. The maréchal,
however, had not been up to the task. Nothing made that fact more
patent than German occupation of the southern zone, crushing testimony to Pétain's inability to preserve even a semblance of national
sovereignty. But perhaps de Gaulle might succeed where Pétain had
failed. Yes, a Gaullist triumph would bring parliamentary institutions
back to France but, it was hoped, a representative order now disciplined as it had not been in the chaotic thirties: by the authority of a
Gaullist executive, by the expertise of an administrative elite purified
and hardened in the fires of the Resistance.

These were indeed the cherished themes of the Resistance currents with which Sciences Po aligned itself. The notion of a "virile
and disciplined form of democracy," of course, lay very much at the
heart of the CGE's project, and Sciences Po did indeed count a number of well-disposed colleagues in the Comité's ranks: Paul Bastid,
Siegfried's comrade in arms from war days in Lyon, Teitgen, and not
least of all Debré.

Then there was Philippe Viannay's *Défense de la France*. The first
issue of Viannay's paper appeared in August 1941. It was anti-German
but not anti-Vichy, persuaded (much like Delouvrier) that the maréchal was engaged in a double game. Viannay in the end gave up on
Pétain but not until the spring of 1942, and even then he did not
definitively opt for de Gaulle until the following year. The new Gaullist commitment, though, was sincere and deepened when a member
of the general's own family, his niece Geneviève, joined the group in
1943.[125] The paper wanted a democratic future for France, but the
democracy it imagined was "authoritarian and progressive." The nation stood in dire need of forceful executive action. What substitute
indeed was there for the "living" authority of the true leader who
imposed himself by force of will? The Resistance had cast up such a

leader, and it had cast up "a new elite" as well, "des hommes purs, des hommes efficaces," who delighted in risk taking and shunned the careful materialism of the petty-minded.[126]

Sciences Po might well believe that it had little to fear from the Liberation. To be sure, it could be held accountable for certain failings in the early years of the Occupation, but it had from 1942 on more than made amends, compiling a modest but nonetheless estimable record of Resistance. And it had made some influential Resistance friends along the way: journalists and experts who were poised to occupy strategic positions of command in the postwar order. Such men had institutional renovation on their minds, but so too did Sciences Po authorities, and the two visions of reform were not incongruent. The disciplined democracy envisioned by a Viannay or Debré left ample room for an elite institution like Sciences Po. Nor did Seydoux, so intent on reorganizing the school along professional, technical-minded lines, want anything different. This compatibility of views assured that there would be a remaking of Sciences Po at the Liberation, but a remaking undertaken in accordance with and not against the school's wishes.

In the event, that is how matters started out. In the fall of 1944, interested parties in the Provisional Government and Conseil d'état began to explore schemes for creation of a state-run Ecole nationale d'administration. The gist of these discussion was communicated to Sciences Po administrators at a meeting in September.[127] Sciences Po readied itself to respond. Seydoux was absent at the time. He had enlisted in the Leclerc Division at the Liberation and so was away at the front for much of the fall. Chapsal, however, stepped into the breach, meeting with government officials, sending round to them all the documentation pertaining to the Seydoux-Zay negotiations of 1939.[128] More important still, the school remodeled its leadership team yet again. In the first week of January 1945, Tirard submitted his letter of resignation, pleading ill health. Siegfried was persuaded to step in as Sciences Po president. The old Conseil d'administration took the occasion to resign en masse. Siegfried then proceeded to appoint his own men to the board, a mix of old faces and new. Baumgartner, now released from internment, was kept on, joined by

newcomers like Georges Duhamel, secretary of the Académie française. Gone were the discredited Pétainists Pichat and Ripert.[129]

Duhamel was a kindred spirit to Siegfried in many ways. Duhamel's
institution, the Académie française, was packed with Vichy sympathizers and would-be collaborationists, but he had maneuvered with surprising success to preserve it from compromising actions. Siegfried
might well have imagined that he had played a not dissimilar role at
Sciences Po. The two men, moreover, were both exponents of a nine-
teenth-century enlightened creed that vaunted the rationality and
refinements of Western civilization but worried about twentieth-
century threats to that achievement: fascism, communism, and Amer-
ican-style mass society.[130]

Without fanfare, Sciences Po had begun to clean house, burnish-
ing its Resistance credentials and in the process casting itself as a
standard-bearer of Western values. Indeed, the French delegation
dispatched to San Francisco in the spring of 1945 to attend the founding conference of the United Nations included the school's two most
senior administrators, Seydoux and Siegfried. The creation of a new
Ecole nationale d'administration loomed on the near horizon, but
Sciences Po had little apparent reason to fear it would lose from the
change. It was in contact with de Gaulle's Provisional Government; it
had made its position known; it was negotiating in good faith.

Then came Cogniot's late February bombshell. The Left, reenergized by its Resistance struggles and with the PCF in the lead, had its
own plans for how to educate France's future elites, plans that did
not include Sciences Po. There was then a squaring off at the Liberation between the reform-minded in France's establishment and the
Resistance Left, the fate of Sciences Po hanging on the balance. In
practice, the confrontation turned out to be one-sided. The Left was
routed, and Sciences Po got a reform it could live with. The Liberation might be thought a time when a Left ascendant had the resources, both moral and political, to recast France's destiny as it desired. As will be seen, things did not quite work out this way.

The war years at once illuminated and muddied France's path forward into the postwar era. Vichy represented a sharp break with the

nation's democratic and republican past. Liberal parliamentarism was rejected with a mixture of nausea and contempt. A strong state, guided by a *chef* working in tandem with an elite defined not by partisanship but by expertise: such was the Vichyite ideal of good government. Self-styled "experts" did indeed pour into government service in the Vichy years, and they brought with them an agenda that had been roughed out in a decade or more of preceding debate. There was agreement on certain points. The era of laissez-faire was over. A strong family was the building block of any future national revival. Leadership was all, provided, of course, leadership was of the right sort, combining technical skills with a moral and physical discipline that commanded respect and obedience. Within this common framework, there was ample room for argument. In a directed economy, what role, if any, did corporate bodies have to play? When it came to family regeneration, who had the clearest understanding of how to proceed, the Catholic Action militant or the science-minded population manager? As for leadership, what qualities mattered most in the making of the true *chef,* the virtues of the good scout or the competence of the technocrat?

The Vichy regime, at once united and riven, generated a remarkable range of institutional innovations: the DGEN with its plans, the corporation-like COs, Carmille's SNS, the Fondation Carrel. And the Vichy-era ambience left its imprint on a number of independent initiatives as well. Perroux's proto-Keynesian ISEA is a case in point, and Seydoux's Sciences Po too for that matter, in the process of recasting itself along technocratic lines.

Vichy's legacy was a complex compound of rhetorics, initiatives, and practices. It might be thought easy enough for the résistants who acceded to power in the war's aftermath to decide what to keep and what to discard from the mix, and in certain respects it was. No one wanted to replicate the pro-business, authoritarian dirigisme that characterized Vichy-style economic planning. The Resistance was not immune to xenophobic expressions, but overall it eschewed a biologizing racism of the kind institutionalized at the Fondation Carrel. There was, moreover, an emergent consensus in Resistance ranks to break Sciences Po's near monopoly on civil-service training.

In certain respects, however, it was not so easy to decide what to do with the Vichy past, and this for several reasons. There were Resistance currents first of all that, like their counterparts at Vichy, had been touched by *l'esprit des années trente*.[131] Such résistants had little use at all for laissez-faire policy; they believed in family values; they talked of leaders and teams, of elites made pure. To be sure, they were democrats, but democrats who wanted a virile, interventionist state, not the do-nothing parliamentarism of "decadent" prewar days. Some résistants and some Vichyites were molded in the same intellectual crucible and in that measure held a number of presuppositions in common. The gradual and then accelerated hemorrhaging of onetime Pétainists into the Resistance cause just reinforced the presence of such forms of thinking in Resistance ranks. It is hard to affix a label to a phenomenon that encompassed such a disparate array of types: technocrats, nonconformists, Catholic Action militants, not to mention just plain nationalists. They were the not-so-Left, and the term, imprecise as it is, is not inapt, for it was in part against the Resistance Left that the group began to define itself.

This is the final point. The Left at the Liberation had an ambitious and sweeping vision all its own. It wanted extensive nationalizations and a dirigiste economy, cradle-to-grave social security, and a regime of elite education that bypassed old-line institutions like Sciences Po outright. This was more than the not-so-Left was prepared to swallow. It wanted a remaking of the state, but not such a radical departure as that envisioned by the Left. Planning made sense, but perhaps a more flexible, less dirigiste scheme was called for. Comprehensive social security was an inevitability, but the not-so-Left inclined to a system with a strong bias in favor of family values. As for elite training: to be sure, there was need for a new Ecole nationale d'administration, but that did not mean it was imperative to shunt aside a Sciences Po that had already done so much to modernize itself. Modernization was indeed the watchword of the not-so-Left, a useful catchphrase that communicated a steadfast commitment to change, but a commitment that was beyond partisanship, neither right nor left. From this perspective, there were things (and people) from the Vichy past worth salvaging. Pétain's regime had, here and there, taken steps to make

France more modern. Was it necessary then to set aside the entire Vichy legacy?

It was a certainty that the French state would get an overhaul at the Liberation, but how the process would play out was less certain. The Resistance generated multiple and competing projects of state reform, all to varying degrees marked by Vichy antecedents. Which projects would get the upper hand and which not was far from a foregone conclusion. Such battles would be the stuff of Liberation-era politics.

CHAPTER 3

The Liberation Moment

The Liberation was a moment of dramatic transformation. The state took over large chunks of the national economy. The nationalization drive got off to an uncertain start in 1944 but then accelerated in the years following. By the time it petered out in the late forties, a full million workers now found employment in France's much-expanded public sector. What was perhaps most remarkable about the process was how consensual it was, drawing support not just from the Left but from the christian-democratic MRP and General de Gaulle himself. But then again, all had signed on to the nationalization clauses of the CNR action program and felt duty-bound to stand by the wartime promises they had made.[1] A second CNR pledge was redeemed in October 1945 when Pierre Laroque's Social Security ordinances were enacted. Then came de Gaulle's decree the following January creating the Commissariat-général au Plan. The CNR program had committed itself to the idea of planning, and now this commitment too had been realized. The program had said nothing about creation of an Ecole nationale d'administration, yet this had been a Left aspiration of long standing, dating back, not just to the Popular Front, but all the way to the revolution of 1848. At that time, under the auspices of the Second Republic, a state-run school of public administration had functioned for a few brief months. It awaited the birth of yet another Republic, France's Fourth, before the project got a second chance, on this occasion with more enduring results. ENA was founded in October 1945 and has continued in operation to the present day.

The postwar moment left a powerful and long-lasting legacy, endowing France with a configuration of state institutions unique in the world. This was a Resistance achievement, no doubt about that. Yet such a claim conceals as much as it explains, for state remaking at the Liberation was not just a consensual process. As much as not, it was the outcome of intense institutional infighting, of insider battles that pitted résistant against résistant, closing out certain options even as the way was opened to others.

In grand design, the Resistance Left got much of what it wanted, but the losses and half successes need to be totaled along with the victories. In the domain of planning, it was not Mendès France's dirigiste schemes that got the upper hand but Monnet's more flexible, consultative project. The MEN was sidelined in favor of the nimble-footed Commissariat-général au Plan (CGP). Modernization and productivity were the watchwords of Monnet's new order, and it was a vocabulary that France's modernizing partners in America, men of progress but no socialists, found congenial.

The Plan may not have been a social democratic triumph, but what about Social Security? Laroque's welfare legislation assigned the management of Social Security *caisses* to joint employer-worker boards, with worker representatives in the majority. Trade unionists over time bought into the system and have counted themselves among its staunchest defenders ever since. But Social Security was not just a worker's victory, a "conquête ouvrière" as it has been called.[2] The new system did not encompass the agricultural sector, which maintained its own independent welfare institutions. Salaried employees did sign on but negotiated a special deal. And the self-employed opted out of the Laroque scheme altogether, developing a trio of distinct and separate regimes, one each for artisans, businessmen, and liberal professionals. The French welfare state was not universalist in the Beveridgian sense but corporatist, with benefits doled out not to citizens but to occupants of work-based categories. It is this corporatist dimension that has prompted social scientists to label the French welfare regime "Christian Democratic,"[3] but even this label does not capture the full complexity of the French situation. Laroque had wanted to include family allocation *caisses* in his scheme but was defeated on this point by an all too familiar coalition of profamily christian democrats and pronatalists. Family allocation institutions, as will be seen, did indeed get a reworking at the Liberation, but they still preserved, as under preceding regimes, an identity apart.

The same may be said of population management institutions. Vichy had manifested an energetic interest in this arena, which took policy-making form in a trio of state organs: the Comité consultatif de la Famille, the SNS, and the Fondation Carrel. All three were held over at the Liberation, although under new names. Population research—the enumeration, classification, and management of bodies—remained a pressing state concern, whether the state was Vichyite or republican. How workerist then was France's postwar welfare apparatus after all? It was that in part, but it was also christian-democratic, familist, and populationist.

As for the creation of ENA, it did indeed represent a striking departure. The school's graduates have come to exercise a near stranglehold on French public life and not just in the senior civil service. Since the mid-1980s, France has been governed by eleven prime ministers, seven of whom have been ENA graduates. Two out of four of the nation's most recent presidents also studied at the Ecole. The two presidents in question, of course, are Valéry Giscard d'Estaing and Jacques Chirac, neither a man of the Left. No doubt, it was the Popular Front that first mooted a remodeling of elite education, but the reform that was in fact enacted in 1945 was not of the Left's devising. Its guiding spirit was Michel Debré, ex of the CGE and in the decades to come a Gaullist stalwart. Debré, moreover, made certain that ENA's founding did not displace the alma mater he held dear, Sciences Po. To be sure, the old Ecole libre, rechristened the Institut d'études politiques de Paris (IEP), was incorporated into the nation's public University system, but this was but a half nationalization, the new IEP retaining exceptional autonomy when it came to setting fees, fashioning curriculum, and making appointments. It retained as well a major role in the formation of France's civil-service elite. Under the new postwar dispensation, the senior civil service was obliged to draft its members from the ranks of ENA graduates. But ENA was a postgraduate institution, and there were two routes into it: the first via an exam aimed at recent undergraduates, the second through an exam reserved for low-level civil servants who had accumulated a certain minimal work experience. Never more than a minority made it in through the latter path. The royal road to ENA passed through the undergraduate exam, and here Sciences Po students outperformed all competitors. Between 1952 and 1969, about half the students who sat the test but more than three-quarters of those who passed it—77.5 percent—were IEP alumni.[4] Sciences Po, never a favorite of France's social democratic Left, did more than just survive the whirlwind of the Liberation. It emerged at the far end with its privileged status re-affirmed.[5]

The Resistance Left did not altogether get its way at the Liberation. It had greatest success in the domain of nationalizations. There was a groundswell of public opinion in favor, expressed in massive voter support for Left parties and a resurgent trade-union movement. But in other domains, where the public was less mobilized, the Left ran into obstacles. It found itself outmaneuvered by civil servants and administrative insiders whose projects tempered or supplanted the Left's own. It is the task of the present chapter to identify who the Left's competitors were, and how they managed to tally as much success as they did.

Planning and Statistics

Hopes for a socialist reformation of the national economy were pinned on the Ministère de l'Economie nationale (MEN). The MEN project was an ambitious one, a Left dirigisme inspired by Popular Front ideals reworked in light of wartime experience. Its most determined proponents were Pierre Mendès France and André Philip. Mendès France held down the MEN portfolio from September 1944 to April 1945. Philip's tenure in the position was a good deal longer. From January to June 1946 and then again from December 1946 to January 1947, he served as minister of economics and finance, MEN and the Ministère des Finances having during that period been combined into one. MEN regained its autonomy after that, with Philip staying on as minister until the following October.

Planning mattered to both men. This was unfamiliar policy-making terrain, and each had to grope to find his way forward. Mendès France, on the lookout for a planning template, opted to take a closer look at the Vichy-era *tranche de démarrage* as a potential model. Philip adopted a different tack. He urged that MEN annex outright Monnet's planning Commissariat, at the time attached to the prime minister's office (he did not, of course, succeed at the maneuver).[6]

Both Mendès France and Philip, moreover, took a dirigiste, that is, a top-down approach to economic management. At the Liberation, Vichy's command structures, the resource allocation services of the OCRPI and the COs, were held over. Not intact, to be sure. The COs, for example, now called *offices professionnels*, were recast as paritary bodies with equal employer and trade-union representation, a democratizing advance on the COs of old, which had been dominated by business executives. Still, the instruments of an organized, directed economy remained in place, and this suited Mendès France, who was an advocate of an industry-driven recovery. Such a strategy entailed keeping consumer spending and, with it, inflation in check, and tight resource control was essential to this purpose. The project, however, soon came unstuck. The Provisional Government's minister of finance René Pleven (he succeeded Aimé Lepercq in the post in November 1944 when Lepercq was killed in a car accident) opposed Mendès France's austerity plans. After years of shortage and hard times, Pleven wanted to give the consumer some relief, not just in an unspecified future but right away. A dramatic meeting that next January between de Gaulle, Mendès France, and Pleven settled the matter in Pleven's favor. Reflation in due course translated into inflation, saddling postwar policy makers with debilitating financial problems it would take years to resolve, and the whole business left Socialists embittered. Jules Moch, listening to a Pleven speech in the Assemblée provisoire consultative, was heard to say: "Aren't we hearing our old teachers, Colson or Leroy-Beaulieu?"[7]

Nor was it just from liberals like Pleven that the trouble came. In

April 1946, the communist minister of industrial production Marcel Paul decided to dismantle the vestiges of Vichy's economic command apparatus, the *offices professionnels* included. Philip for one was upset by the decision and protested in the name of dirigiste principle. Indeed, when Philip's turn came to run the MEN, he brought a dirigiste heavy-handedness to the job that earned him a chiding from his old friend Monnet, who urged more supple methods of administration.[8]

Noteworthy here is the amenability of the Resistance Left to build on Vichy precedents, whether the *tranche de démarrage* or the reconstituted COs. This willingness was no less evident in the domain of statistics. The fate of the SNS hung in the balance at the Liberation. The Service, though a Vichy-era innovation, had numerous institutional assets, and it was decided to salvage it. The SNS got a new name. In April 1946, the service was transformed into the Institut national de la statistique et des études économiques (INSEE). It also got a new institutional home. The June decree elaborating the details of INSEE's creation assigned the new organ to the Ministère de l'Economie nationale, at the time attached to the Ministère des Finances.[9] This was a real coup for the still-fledgling MEN.

INSEE had first-rate staff and a leader to match. Henri Bunle, René Carmille's successor at the SNS, was pushed aside when INSEE was founded in favor of a new director appointed from the outside. He was Francis Louis Closon, a résistant of impeccable credentials and a man of real personal skills. In 1943, de Gaulle had dispatched him from London to France to rally support. Closon planned a stopover in Toulouse to contact Monseigneur Saliège, a cleric of exceptional courage who though at first well disposed to Vichy had then turned away, promulgating an episcopal letter in the late summer of 1942 that censured the regime's anti-Semitic roundups. In preparation for the Toulouse visit, Closon consulted with a good "friend" in London, the abbé René de Naurois, a nonconformist Catholic who, like Archbishop Saliège, had followed a spiritual odyssey that took him first into Vichy and then out of it.[10] Naurois was there in 1934 when *Esprit* had been launched. At the Occupation's outset, like so many in Mounier's circle, he had done a stint at Uriage, site of the Vichy-sponsored Ecole des cadres. But Naurois was an independent-minded soul who fell afoul of a regime that tolerated few deviations. He was sacked from Uriage in 1941; then finding his way into the Resistance and to London, he reconnected with Closon.

Closon knew how to work with men in spiritual motion who were shaking off discredited mental habits in favor of new ones. It was a talent he brought to bear at INSEE with considerable success. INSEE's break with its Vichy past was in certain respects slow to develop. It took until September before it discontinued using its stock of old Vichy letterhead. To be sure, there was a paper shortage at the time, but shortage does not explain the fact that, as late as 1947, eight of the Institut's nineteen regional directors were old hands who had been on the job at least since 1943. At the same time, however, the Institut was beginning to strike out in new directions. Closon instructed his staff to cultivate good working relations with Perroux's ISEA. INSEE, in fact, helped ISEA with subventions, and Perroux in turn agreed to sit on the oversight board of INSEE's new Ecole d'application. When it came to statistical practice, Closon meant for the Institut to take a backseat to none, and he felt the same way about economics. Starting in the 1947 academic year, the Ecole d'application offered an introductory course in Keynesian theory required of all first-year students.[11]

INSEE, however, had difficulty in staking out a policy-making niche for itself. The Institut looked to make its mark in industrial statistics, a natural choice given Sauvy's census-taking work in the field. But INSEE was not the only claimant around. The Ministère de l'Industrie had a statistical service of its own, the Bureau central de la statistique industrielle, directed from 1948 by the Vichy holdover Jean Prévot. It is not that the two bodies proved unable to cooperate. They worked together, for example, settling the terms of a 1951 law that regulated state statistical practice. The new legislation mandated that all state questionnaires carry the INSEE seal. Businesses in receipt of INSEE questionnaires were under strict obligation to fill them out, the state promising in return to keep the information confidential, above all from its own fiscal agencies. The management of the actual statistics collected, however, fell not so much to INSEE as to Prévot's Bureau central. Until INSEE was reorganized in the

1960s, it would never be more than a secondary player in the domain of economic statistics.[12]

It is clear enough what the component parts of the postwar social democratic project were. Mendès France and Philip looked to the Ministère de l'Economie nationale as the project's institutional base. MEN would construct a plan, imposing its dirigiste will through a network of state institutions—*offices professionnels*, resource allocation agencies, and the like. In this it would be assisted by the statistical expertise of INSEE, with back-up from associated bodies like ISEA. There was much here that harked back to the socialist and trade-union schemes of the thirties. Now, as in the past, the economy was conceived as a two-tier structure, a nationalized sector under direct state management operating alongside a private sphere supervised by the state in collaboration with professional groupings representative of employer and labor interests. But there was much here that was also new. Vichy's dirigiste experiments had taught useful lessons, defining models of corporatist and statistical organization that reformers like Mendès France and Philip were prepared, with the proper democratizing correctives, to apply to socialist purposes. And the whole now came wrapped, less in the stages-to-socialism rhetoric of the thirties, than in a new expansionist idiom with unmistakable Keynesian accents.

This was a powerful vision, but it was never realized. Some of the reasons why should already be apparent. The PCF and enlightened liberals like Pleven might have been on board for nationalizations but were lukewarm about dirigiste policy. Institutional rivals, like the Ministère de l'Industrie, demoted INSEE to second-rank status in the competition for the statistical high ground. But these are second-order explanations. In the end, what mattered most in the defeat of the social democratic vision was the successful, step-by-step advance of Jean Monnet's own project.

Monnet's triumph is a remarkable story. It owed much to Monnet's own skills as a consensus builder and talent spotter. But, at critical junctures, he was given a leg up by powerful allies—de Gaulle, the United States, the Ministère des Finances. Events too helped out, none more than the onset of the Cold War, which fractured the

French Left and sidelined what might have been a formidable impediment in the PCF. The economic management apparatus that resulted was a novel construction. Its originality, however, ought not obscure its debt in personnel, structure, and animating ethos to 1930s nonconformism and technocracy, not to mention (though in a more muted key) to Vichy.

It was de Gaulle's patronage, of course, that first brought the Commissariat-général au Plan into existence in January 1946. At the outset, the Commissariat was not expected to last out the year.[13] A cash-strapped France was about to embark on negotiations with the United States for critical reconstruction assistance. Léon Blum was named to lead the French delegation, and Monnet, who had long experience with the Americans, was designated to help. In preparation, Monnet's Commissariat prepared a text, a preliminary version of the Plan, on the current, parlous state of the French economy. The document laid out a simple argument: it was incumbent on a backward France to modernize, and modernization in turn required financial support that the United States alone was in a position to supply. It made its case with statistical backup and sketched in how investment monies might be targeted to boost industrial production and France's competitiveness in world markets. Monnet brought the document with him to the United States. The Americans liked the project and in this sense, as one historian has observed, okayed the Plan in advance of the French themselves.[14] US goodwill, however, did not translate into unstinting generosity. The Americans agreed to cancel French war debts and to tender a credit package totaling an estimated $650 million, a good deal less than the $3 billion the French had hoped for. The Blum-Byrnes accord, as it has come to be known, was signed in May, and from the French point of view it was something of a disappointment.[15]

Monnet, however, was undeterred. His Commissariat, its initial task completed, might have faded at this point, but Monnet was not about to let this happen. He set about transforming an ad hoc operation into a permanent institution, a feat he pulled off thanks in part to the Plan itself, which was ready for public scrutiny in November 1946. It was an imagination-catching document, pithy and direct, that limned a growth-oriented future for a nation at the time still reeling from war and occupation. The Plan de modernisation et d'équipement (PME), as it was called, identified six *secteurs de base*: coal, electricity, steel, cement, transport, and agricultural machinery. For each, ambitious annual production targets were set, culminating in the Plan's end date, 1950. The France of tomorrow, the document made plain, would be an industrial power, but what other choice was there? "Modernization or decadence": such were the nation's only options. The word "decadence," of course, carried a heavy ideological load, evoking the unhappy days of the Third Republic and all the ills that had attended upon them: economic backwardness, demographic stagnation, political stalemate at home, and diplomatic paralysis abroad. The Plan then conveyed an implicit pledge to make a clean break with France's prewar past, and that break was meant to be as much psychological as material. In the Plan's formulation, "modernization is not a state of things, it is a state of mind." The slogan is not hard to unpack. Sit a farmer on a tractor, Etienne Hirsch explained, and he "will no longer think like a farmer behind a horse." Embrace the machine, in a word, and new mental horizons, no longer the cautious Malthusianism of old but a forward-looking experimentalism, would open. The Plan, moreover, did intend for peasants to sit on tractors. The farm machinery section of the project envisioned a shrinkage of the rural workforce, a loss in manpower compensated and then some by farm machinery imports. The tractor park in France in fact shot up from 35,000 machines in 1938 to 165,000 in 1952, most purchased from the United States.[16] It was, then, not just a new economy that the Plan promised but a new identity. Third Republic France liked to think of itself as a nation of shopkeepers and peasants, with an accent on the virtues of smallness and the self-reliant individual. This cozy past was to be left behind in favor of a growth-oriented world populated by forward-looking men—managers, farmers, workers—who valued efficiency and cooperative enterprise. The idea of collective endeavor, of an economy run by concertation rather than a market-based individualism, was indeed central to the Plan's conception of itself. Hirsch coined the phrase "économie concertée" and made sure it was included in the text of the Plan.[17] Monnet did not like the term at first but then yielded. Péguy, he recollected, had criticized the French as an "unconcerted people." Monnet was determined to change France's image, so why not, he reasoned, build that determination into the very language of the Plan itself?

Concertedness in practice meant involving, not just the expert few, but the living forces of the nation in the Plan-making process. The more interests brought on board, the greater the project's legitimacy and chances of success. At this task, that of consensus building, the planners proved themselves past masters.

The decree that created Monnet's Commissariat also created the Conseil du Plan. The Conseil had the right to review the work of Monnet's team. Monnet appeared before the body in March 1946 to lay out France's bargaining position in the run-up to the Blum-Byrnes negotiations. The Conseil had occasion to convene again in January 1947 to approve the PME. In all, though, the Conseil did not meet often, just a handful of times.[18] Its task was as much to sell the Plan as to sit in critical examination of it. The "representative" character of the Conseil's membership was crucial in this regard, positioning the body to speak, not just for particular interests, but for the economic nation as a whole. The Conseil was composed in part of sitting ministers, in part of appointees. The appointee selection process, it appears, was managed by de Gaulle's assistant chief of staff, Louis Vallon, working in consultation with Monnet. From one angle, the choices were just as might be expected. Vallon and Monnet tapped all the major interest-group associations for recruits. The Confédération française des travailleurs chrétiens supplied the Catholic trade unionist Gaston Tessier. From the CGT came Léon Jouhaux and the Communist Benoît Frachon. Big business was represented by Paul Ricard, an official of the Conseil national du patronat français (CNPF), successor organization to the old CGPF. After the war, new organizations were launched to speak on behalf of the small-business and agricultural sectors, the Confédération générale des petites et moyennes entreprises and the Confédération générale de l'agriculture. Each contributed a member to the Conseil du Plan: the CGPME in the person of Léon Gingembre, the CGA in that of Philippe

Lamour.[19] There were a couple of figures here who had seen service at Vichy, Ricard as a CO officer and Gingembre as an aide to Bichelonne.[20] But what is more striking is the number of 1930s planists: Vallon, Jouhaux, Lamour. Ricard, it might be added, had been a member of Dautry's team at the Ministère de l'Armement in 1939.[21] And one last detail: the Conseil du Plan included experts as well as interest-group officials. In this connection, François Perroux's name was put forward and so too Georges Boris's. Monnet rejected Perroux but not, it seems, Boris, yet one more veteran of interwar planism.[22] The Conseil du Plan's "representative" composition lent its deliberations a quasi-parliamentary character, and as such its imprimatur had meaningful legitimating power. But the Conseil was not just a parliament of interests. It was also anchored in a 1930s past, a living connection to long-standing currents of economic reform, whether of a socialist or a more technocratic cast.[23]

The Plan's renowned Commissions de modernisation also had a connection to the past, though just how deep a connection remains a matter of some dispute. Monnet had promised from the outset that he did not intend to act as a bureaucrat, imposing the Plan de haut en bas. It was necessary to confer with the interested parties in the drafting process, labor as well as management. Consultation generated information and goodwill, both essential ingredients to the Plan's successful execution, and so planning commissions were formed, bodies with mixed memberships composed in varying combinations of civil servants, experts, business executives, and trade unionists. Eighteen such Commissions de modernisation were constituted prior to the Plan's ratification and an additional half dozen thereafter, twenty-four in all over the course of 1946–1947. To Claude Gruson, the new Commissions were not so new at all. Vichy's COs had, as he put it, "facilitated the change." But what truth was there in such a claim?[24]

The Commissions, like the COs, were sector based, but Vichy had divided the economy into two hundred plus sectors,[25] Monnet's scheme into just a couple dozen. Trade unionists, moreover, played a role on the Commissions de modernisation that they had been denied outright at Vichy. The difference is significant but only up to a point, for trade unionists were oftentimes outsiders on the Commis-

sions. Take the case of the Commission des carburants, among the
first created. The state had a forceful spokesman in Pierre Guillaumat, and business had one in Léon Kaplan, a Shell Oil executive and
X-Crise veteran. The CGT had its own man on the Commission, but
he did not quite occupy the same space as Guillaumat and Kaplan,
both high-powered polytechniciens. The ratcheting up of Cold War
tensions weakened labor's position yet further. In the spring of 1947,
Socialist prime minister Paul Ramadier tossed Communist ministers
out of the government. The PCF answered back, refusing any further
participation in the institutions of state. This translated into a CGT
boycott of the Commissions de modernisation. Labor had a voice on
the Commissions then, but it was not an equal's voice, and it grew
weaker over time.[26]

The Commissions bore a family resemblance to the COs, but they
were more cousins once removed than lineal descendants. The same
may be said of the business personnel who ended up serving on them,
although on this point too there is some difference of opinion. To be
sure, there is evidence of continuity. Of the nine business executives
who sat on the Commission des carburants, for example, six had sat
in Vichy days on its wartime equivalent.[27] A less case-specific approach,
however, suggests that the oil industry was exceptional. A careful
study of all Commission officers demonstrates that just five out of the
fifty-seven men concerned (as of 1947) had also worked in the CO
system. There is, of course, the example of Roger Boutteville, who
graduated from running the CO de l'énergie électrique to the presidency of the electrical industry's Commission de modernisation. But
Boutteville's was an anomalous case. He had been talked about for a
senior post in the administration of the nationalized Electricité de
France. His Vichy associations made him an awkward choice, however, so he was compensated with a lower-profile job at the Commission de modernisation.[28]

Yet there is another way to cut into the problem. Why look for a
direct, one-to-one connection between the COs and Monnet's Commissions? Just because a Commission member had no CO background did not mean he had not been employed elsewhere in Vichy's
economic command apparatus, and so it turns out to be. A survey of

the senior officers (presidents, vice presidents, *rapporteurs*) of the seven most important Commissions de modernisation reveals that a significant percentage, ten out of twenty-six, had worked at Vichy, some for a CO but others for OCRPI or the Ministère de la Production industrielle.[29] This is still a minority, albeit a substantial one. Monnet's Commissions drew on Vichy's reservoir of technocratic expertise but no more than that.

It is a conclusion that makes perfect sense in light of how the business-world commissioners were selected. They were not elected by professional associations, the kind of procedure Left planners might have favored. It was the Commissariat that designated them, and Monnet wanted men of influence, industry leaders who were "the most open to progress." The task of hunting up such a cadre fell to Hirsch, who in turn consulted Georges Villiers, president of the CNPF.[30] Villiers's reputation dated from the prewar era. He had been director of a major metallurgical firm in Lyon, a position that, post-1940, earned him Vichy's benevolent attentions. When the regime sacked Lyon's elected mayor, the Radical Edouard Herriot, it appointed Villiers to replace him. Villiers was an engineer of forward-looking views, enough so that he was tapped to join Seydoux's Lyon-based Comité d'études et d'informations. He was also a patriot whose frank anti-Germanism earned him over time the enmity of the regime he served, not to mention that of the Occupation authorities. Vichy fired him in 1943, and he was then deported to Germany. The Monnet-Hirsch-Villiers team was not about to pick planning commissioners with collaborationist pasts. On the other hand, Vichy service was not going to be a disqualification either. What mattered most was not so much a candidate's political record as his competence and attitude. Was he a man of ideas? Did he know how to bring others along? Léon Kaplan, the X-Crise old-timer with "a highly developed sense of teamwork" (the characterization is Monnet's), passed muster by such standards; so too did the Vichyite expert and administrator Roger Boutteville.[31] Indeed, it was technocratic more than political orientation that constituted the most significant common denominator of the business-world commissioners. According to the study of Commission officers cited above, ten of the twenty-six were ex-Vichyites, but a full sixteen were graduates of the Ecole Polytechnique.[32]

The Commissions de modernisation were critical to winning over France's economic movers and shakers, but Monnet's consensus-building efforts did not stop there. Persistent and destabilizing inflationary pressures threatened to undermine the Plan's realization, but Monnet had a solution. Increase output at a faster clip than wages, he argued, and inflation was bound to falter. In 1948, the Commissariat assembled a Groupe de travail, a working group, to look into the productivity question. Placed in charge was a Monnet loyalist, Jean Fourastié, today remembered as an apostle of growth second to none. It was Fourastié who later coined the term "trente glorieuses" to describe France's economic miracle, the decades-long boom that got started at the Liberation and did not stall until the oil shocks of the 1970s. In 1949, Fourastié's Groupe de travail metamorphosed into a Comité provisoire, now headed by Monnet himself, and then in 1950 into a more permanent body, the Comité national de la productivité, which was presided over by a political figure rather than a Plan insider, the christian democrat Robert Buron.[33]

This flurry of organizational activity was not without result. It was decided to organize so-called Missions de productivité to be dispatched to the United States (although not to the United States alone) to learn firsthand the most up-to-date techniques in business and shop-floor management. The first mission took off for America in the summer of 1949. In the three years following, more than two hundred such expeditions, involving several thousand participants, made the pilgrimage to the land of opportunity. It was an ambitious program, but the French and American governments did not hesitate to fund it, seeing a mutual interest in Franco-American cooperation in an era of heightening international tensions.[34]

But what is consensus building about all this? The productivity missions, like the Commissions de modernisation, were designed to involve not just the managerial few but workers as well. Missions de productivité were tripartite in composition, mixing businessmen, shop-floor laborers, and civil servants. Participation in the exercise was meant to change the participants' outlook, to teach one and all the virtues of pulling together on behalf of a common cause: enterprise, efficiency, and maximization of output. The ideological message here is not hard to decipher. France's best hope for a happy and productive future lay, not in the class struggle, but in an enlightened managerialism à l'américaine. This does not sound very social democratic, nor was it. Workers never played more than a backup role in the operation. A typical mission was made up one-quarter of trade unionists but 45 percent of management, and the CGT, of course, France's largest trade-union organization, had no hand at all in the program, which it shunned for Cold War reasons just as it shunned the Commissions de modernisation.[35] Who, for that matter, ran the program from the French end? Fourastié, a onetime Vichy official, albeit low level; Buron, a Vichy film administrator, who turned résistant in time to avoid serious troubles at the Liberation; and, of course, Monnet himself, who, though never a Vichyite, came out of the Resistance's Giraudist camp, at least at first.

Monnet's genius at bringing others along was critical to the Plan's gradual institutionalization. He embedded the enterprise in a cocoon of councils and commissions that brought together representatives from every walk of life. Labor, management, agriculture: all were invited to take part. But Monnet did not want them joining in a spirit of sectional egotism, labor looking after labor's interests, management after management's. It was essential to nurture an esprit de corps, a sense of common endeavor. A new France was under construction, and a vocabulary to match was invented, which was bandied about with a sloganeering verve that disarmed all but the most hardened ideological opponents. The Plan, expansion, modernization, productivity: who could be against such obvious and necessary goods?

But note also the limits of Monnet's consensus building. Co-option, not election, was his modus operandi, and who got selected to serve on the Conseil du Plan, the Commissions de modernisation, the Missions de productivité? In part, trade unionists, but the labor contingent grew weaker and less militant as the Cold War set in. In larger part, men known to be already on board the technocratic band-

wagon—planists from 1930s days, onetime Vichy apparatchiks, polytechniciens past and present.

The first postwar planners liked to think of themselves as an avant-
garde, but they were an avant-garde with a past. They critiqued Third
Republic ways. They talked up the virtues of forward-looking elites
and team-spiritedness. They touted statistics and the Plan itself. They
looked to the state as the indispensable instrument of the nation's
redressement. And they erected a network of ancillary councils and
commissions that were, in effect, corporatist in design. This was not
Vichy by another name: Monnet was neither an authoritarian nor a
dirigiste, and he sought out, as Vichy never did, the participation of
organized labor in all its variety (admittedly within certain limits).
But like Vichy technocracy, Monnet's postwar planning apparatus
was a recognizable descendant of interwar debates, a relationship
veiled at the time by the Plan's self-legitimating rhetoric of newness
but a family relationship for all that.

It might have looked in the first flush of the Liberation that France
would take a social democratic turn, but Monnet's savvy packaging of
the Plan steered economic policy making in a different direction.
The conversion of the Ministère des Finances to the Plan experiment
settled the matter to Monnet's advantage. This story has been well
told before, which does not make it any less extraordinary.[36] The interwar Ministère des Finances was celebrated for its budget-balancing
caution. How did it come to chart a new course, to discard the fiscal
orthodoxy of old in favor of an investment policy that gambled on
future expansion to cover the costs? There are two major pieces to
the answer.

The first touches on the uncertain state of French finances after
the war. Rampant inflation hampered reconstruction efforts, and
Monnet's team was all too aware of the problem. They had manifested an interest in a sound system of national accounting from early
on. In 1945, Robert Marjolin contacted ISEA for help coming up
with a national bookkeeping scheme. ISEA was indeed already at
work on the question. In the summer months, Perroux, accompanied by Pierre Uri and Jean Bartoli, traveled to England to consult
with the economist Richard Stone (among others) about Stone's cur-

rent research on "social bookkeeping."[37] Stone was in fact the first to come up with a national accounting model, work that in time would earn him a Nobel Prize. Monnet was able to tap into ISEA's growing expertise on the subject when in 1947 he recruited Uri over from Perroux's organization to his own. Nor did Monnet delay in putting his fresh recruit to productive use. He created a new organ, yet one more, and appointed Uri to run it. The so-called Commission du bilan was charged with drawing up a national balance sheet; Uri shouldered the task, and a hundred-page report was ready by December.[38] The document had a simple point to make: demand in the year ahead was on course to outstrip supply, creating a so-called inflation gap. Bloch-Lainé remembers Uri's balance sheet as a crude confection of modest scientific interest, but it did, he acknowledges, have "a psychological impact," sending an attention-grabbing message to policy makers: boost output, dampen demand, or else.[39]

Policy makers responded. The minister of finance René Mayer took inflation-dampening measures: large-denomination banknotes were withdrawn from circulation and a onetime compulsory levy imposed on all taxpayers. On the output-boosting end, the government earmarked a portion of the levy's proceeds for reconstruction, creating a new administrative vehicle, the Fonds de modernisation, to handle the monies. Not least of all, Uri's national accounting wizardry piqued the interest of Treasury officials, first and foremost the director of the Treasury himself, François Bloch-Lainé. Bloch-Lainé had occupied the post since June 1947. He knew Uri's work firsthand, having served alongside him on the Commission du bilan. The experience and its results made him a partisan of the national bookkeeping approach, but he wanted to go at the problem with less improvisation and more system than Uri. Bloch-Lainé turned to an old friend, Claude Gruson, to help out, placing him in charge of a research group, the Bureau de statistiques et d'études financières (BSEF), housed at the Ministère des Finances.[40]

The arrival of Marshall funds redoubled Bloch-Lainé's interest in Monnet's doings. The Marshall Plan, of course, was announced in mid-1947. The US Plan was a godsend to Monnet's own. The Blum-Byrnes credits negotiated in 1946 had proved sufficient to finance the PME through 1947 but no more. Monnet's Plan needed a cash infusion, and the Americans, it seemed, had arrived just in time to provide it. There were conditions, to be sure. The US government insisted on a rational accounting of how its cash was used, but France was now far enough down the national accounting road to be able to supply the facts and figures required. The decision was made to funnel Marshall monies through the just-created Fonds de modernisation et d'équipement, but this generated a sharp bureaucratic clash. Monnet wanted control of the Fonds; Bloch-Lainé contended this was the Treasury's prerogative, and Bloch-Lainé won out.[41]

The fiscal crisis of 1947–1948 and its Marshall Plan denouement made the Ministère des Finances into a central player in the running of the Plan. Monnet's Commissariat still plotted national investment strategy, but the rue de Rivoli now held the purse strings, and it had the requisite statistical know-how to back up its budgetary decisions. The result was twofold. The Commissariat-général au Plan was weakened, but the Plan itself, with the Ministère des Finances as an ally, was here to stay.

This final chapter in the Plan's institutionalization did not alter in any fundamental way its not-so-Left political valence. An argument, to be sure, can be made to the contrary. It would begin with the team Gruson assembled at BSEF (later the Service des études économiques et financières). The Bureau counted more than one former résistant in its ranks, Simon Nora, for example, and Charles Prou. A third Bureau member, Jean Sérisé, was a Socialist at the time (although he would later become a close adviser to Giscard), and there were also a number of Communists in the group or, at least, "people who were strongly suspected of being so." Claude Alphandéry and Jean Bénard were for sure party members, and Jean Denizet, who had worked at the postwar Ministère du Travail under a PCF minister, had a reputation as a "crypto-communist."[42] The whole BSEF team, as Gruson summed it up, was of a more or less "Left sensibility." It is not surprising then to find the group in the early 1950s linked in informal alliance with Mendès France, one of the first politicians to take up the cause of national accounting in a public way. The Bureau's progressive orientation even left its mark on its working habits. Louis-

Pierre Blanc recalled the relaxed, unbureaucratic atmosphere at
BSEF, "Harvard-like and a little over the top."[43]

But such language has an all too familiar ring. It is the same used
to describe Monnet's Commissariat au Plan team. And just as Monnet's crew turned out to be a complicated mélange, so too did Gruson's. Bénard, it will be remembered, had once worked at the Fondation Carrel, leaving to accompany Perroux over to ISEA. And there
was little enough of standard-issue leftism in Nora's Resistance commitment.

In the thirties, Nora had been an ardent Left pacifist, but of a particular sort, a youth-hostel rambler who exalted in the simple virtues
of the fresh-air life in the manner of novelist Jean Giono (during the
war a Vichy fellow traveler). Nora's family was of Jewish origin, and
during the war sought a safe haven in Grenoble in the southern zone.
There it was that Nora began to get involved in Resistance activities,
but what Resistance was it that engaged him? Emmanuel Mounier
was the presiding moral influence at Vichy's Ecole des cadres at
Uriage (located in the mountains above Grenoble). Mounier detested the Third Republic; he hankered for a purifying, elite-led *redressement national*. These were also Uriage's commitments, and for a
period they jibed well enough with the Vichy regime's own redemptive ambitions. But the Uriage band, like Mounier himself, tended to
a Christian nonconformism, idealist and independent minded, and
in due course they fell out with the authoritarians at Vichy, who had
little use for Uriage-style spiritualism, preferring lockstep obedience
to boy-scoutish elucubrations. The regime shut the school down in
1942, and many of its adherents then switched into the Resistance. It
was one of them, Joffre Dumazedier, who recruited Nora to full-time
Resistance activity, and the match proved well made. Nora, the outdoor rambler, was primed for the rigors of Resistance clandestinity.
He was, moreover, like his Uriage comrades, a firm believer in leadership education. France needed a permanent Ecole des cadres, an
Ecole nationale d'administration, and Nora conceived of the institution in quasi-monastic terms with a live-in student body decked out in
uniform garb (Uriage's *chef,* the Captain Dunoyer de Segonzac, liked
to dress up in a ski outfit).[44]

The evocation of the names of Perroux and Mounier points to an interesting characteristic of the BSEF team, the presence of a solid Christian contingent. René Froment, a statistician with MRP links, is a case in point. So too Prou, although Prou's Catholicism, inflected by pacifist conviction and the promptings of a tender social conscience, was of a less mainstream variety. Then there was Gruson himself, a Protestant much shaken in his faith by revelations of the Shoah. God existed, but He was not everywhere present in the world. The realization of the Christian ideal in the here and now was mankind's choice, and man might choose evil as well as good, genocide as well as hope. Gruson opted for hope and, indeed, understood the Plan itself as an instrument for programming hope into human existence. This is not the stuff of conventional belief. Little wonder then that the theologian most favored among BSEF Christians was a maverick spirit himself, that old cosmic visionary soon to be at the height of his reputation, Father Teilhard de Chardin.[45]

All Gruson's team were committed to *le service public*, to a public-service ethic that placed the common good ahead of self. They might have chosen more lucrative paths than the unsung labor of national accounting, but they did not, accepting, as Gruson put it, "a career sacrifice in order to move in a new, nonconformist direction."[46] The disciplined Left cadre might well see himself reflected in such a characterization, but so too might a less than conventional Christian who resonated to the idea of a sacrificial nonconformism, an idea that smacked as much of *l'esprit des années trente* as of leftist militancy.

Last of all, who was the boss of bosses at BSEF? Gruson answered to Bloch-Lainé, the ex-Catholic scout, and Bloch-Lainé was no firebrand. Not long after the war, he found himself at a dinner party with Jacques Chaban-Delmas and Maurice Bourgès-Maunoury. Chaban and Bourgès-Maunoury were looking for a way into politics and had fixed on the old Radical Party as the vehicle of their hopes, urging Bloch-Lainé to do the same. He got similar advice from Michel Debré, who had given the MRP some consideration but, finding it too "sectarian," plumped instead for the Radicals.[47] Bloch-Lainé, of course, remained loyal to *la haute fonction publique*, but it is clear enough where he would have stood had he entered the partisan arena: in the power-wielding center alongside elite-schooled types like himself. Bourgès-Maunoury was a polytechnicien, and Chaban and Debré were Sciences Po graduates.

No, it was not social democracy that triumphed in the postwar era. The nationalization wave of 1946 marked the social democratic Left's high-water mark, but after that it was Monnet and the CGP/Ministère des Finances condominium that got the upper hand. De Gaulle and the United States lent critical initial support to Monnet's project. He took it from there, building momentum in a whirl of consensus building and public-relations activity. The fiscal crisis of 1947–1948 and the infusion of Marshall Plan funds helped bring the Ministère des Finances around, a powerful and decisive ally. It was no doubt reassuring to all that the onset of the Cold War had pushed the PCF out of the decision-making process and cut back the role of the trade unions.

The postwar economic order in France may not have been social democratic, but what then was it? It is not wrong to say that the Plan was the creation of a modernizing avant-garde with strategic Atlanticist connections. The planning apparatus was staffed with eager young men, a number with Resistance experience, determined to inject a new dynamism into French economic life. They talked the talk of modernization and productivity, a language with an agreeable ring to American ears. But this line of interpretation goes just so far. For many of the planners had pasts, as depression-decade nonconformists or Vichy-era technocrats. This was just as true of the résistants in their ranks as of the nonrésistants. A heroic Resistance record compiled in the closing years of the Occupation did not preclude a preceding period of more or less faithful service to Pétain's regime. And the rough-and-ready ethos that inspirited these men came just as much out of the scout camp or Uriage as it did from the maquis. Reform-minded polytechniciens and Sciences Po grads had been bleeding into political life since the thirties, and they had begun, well before Monnet, to work out in practice their technocratic ambitions. It was a policy-making landscape littered with the debris of such past ventures that Monnet encountered. The male-bonded team, the concentration of statistical expertise, the schemes of corporatist representation, indeed, the very idea of the Plan itself: these were not de novo fabrications but surviving bits and pieces of bygone projects. It was Monnet's particular achievement to put them together into a functioning whole, and he did so with the problem-solving flair of a master *bricoleur*.

The Plan owed more than a little to past experiments, but the debt was obscured by the Plan's own parthenogenic myth making. The same, it turns out, was true for Social Security. Here too the postwar era appeared a point of new departure, and there was indeed much that was new in the welfare edifice Laroque constructed. But Laroque did not make history just as he pleased: he confronted institutions and interests too well entrenched to be ignored, which left a mark as deep as Laroque's own on welfare and population policy.

Social Security and Population Management

It is not hard to understand why the French welfare state has come to be understood as social democratic in constitution. Laroque's 1945 scheme had universalizing ambitions. It aimed to enroll all social insurance and family welfare funds into a single, nationwide regime. This regime, moreover, was designed to be self-sustaining and participatory: self-sustaining in that the various welfare *caisses* were to be funded, not out of general tax revenues, but by pay-as-you-go contributions from the so-called interested parties (i.e., workers and employers); and participatory in that it was the interested parties themselves who were charged with running the system, in particular at the local level, where *caisse* administration boards were to be composed of a mix of worker and employer representatives.

There was some skirmishing about the precise makeup and mode of selection for local Social Security *caisses*. Laroque envisioned boards made up two-thirds of workers and one-third of employers, the worker representatives designated by the most important trade unions (the CGT and christian-democratic CFTC), the employer representatives by the most important business associations (i.e., the CNPF). In October 1946, this scheme came in for a modification, but one that enhanced labor's role rather than diluting it. Thenceforth, a full three-quarters of *caisse* board seats were set aside for workers and a mere one-quarter for employers, and it would be by election, rather than designation, that board members were selected.

In the event, the Communist-controlled CGT dominated the first Social Security board elections—until, that is, the onset of the Cold War changed things (though not in all respects). The CGT itself fractured in December 1947, a significant minority splitting off to constitute the more moderate and reformist Force ouvrière. FO delegates, in coalition with christian-democratic and business partners, were now in a position to make common cause on *caisse* boards to contest Communist hegemony and did so, much reducing the CGT's influence. This mattered to be sure, but it did not alter the underlying fact that trade unions in the postwar era, whether communist or not, had become the key players in local Social Security administration.[48] What a change from earlier times, when it was mutualists and Catholic paternalists, so resistant to state tutelage, who had enjoyed the upper hand.

It is possible, however, to gloss Laroque's oeuvre in somewhat different terms, accenting less its workerism than its neocorporatist and technocratic character. As a contributor to *L'Homme nouveau* in the depression-ridden thirties, Laroque had championed state-sponsored collective bargaining as a solution to France's economic ills. At Vichy, he had pushed a scheme of welfare reform that would have confiscated *caisse* management from mutualist and Catholic paternalist control, centralizing it in the hands of the state. From this angle, the 1945 legislation looks like a reprise of what came before, a melding of long-standing neocorporatist and statist commitments in a welfare overhaul that empowered participants as members of professional bodies and that did so under state auspices. For it should be kept in mind that the state was far from absent in Laroque's new scheme: it exercised an ongoing tutelary role as inspector of the books and reserved to itself the right to annul given *caisse* decisions under the appropriate circumstances.[49] Laroque, it might be added, got help in working up the legislation from a familiar source. In 1945, as in 1940, Francis Netter was there to lend assistance, Netter the polytechnicien and sometime X-Crise fellow traveler.[50] Trade unionists embraced

Laroque's new welfare dispensation and made it their own, but the reform was in its initial design very much the brainchild of civil servants who had more than just the laboring man's interests at heart. Social stabilization was Laroque's ultimate objective, and hard-knock lessons learned in the turbulent thirties had taught him, or so he believed, how best to achieve that goal: through state-orchestrated bargaining among organized interests.[51]

In general outline, Laroque got the stabilizing, corporatist regime he aspired to, though just in general outline. Laroque was to experience disappointments on two fronts. First, on the matter of family welfare policy, he had intended to fuse the Social Security and family allocation funds into a single entity, but this never happened. Stiff opposition to the proposal arose almost at once, and it came from a predictable quarter, the pronatalist Alliance nationale.

The Alliance, its Vichy associations notwithstanding, remained a force to contend with after the war. It had taken care at the Liberation to clean up its image. The organization's wartime president, Paul Lefebvre-Dibon, stepped down in the fall of 1944, to be replaced by a new man, André Toulemon, and the following year the Alliance's house publication underwent a change of title to the upbeat-sounding *Vitalité française*.[52] Adolphe Landry's name, moreover, was included on the roster of the organization's vice presidents, a presence likely to reassure wary Resistance authorities. Yet the Alliance's housecleaning was not so thoroughgoing as all that. Paul Haury and Fernand Boverat, two Vichy-era personalities, remained on board as Alliance officers, though, as it turned out, such continuities in personnel proved in no way harmful to the Alliance's cause.

The Alliance made representations to de Gaulle's provisional government about keeping the family allocation and Social Security *caisses* distinct, and de Gaulle, who would show himself a faithful partisan of the pronatalist cause, listened. By personal decision of the general, the fusion Laroque had sought was postponed, and as of 1949 postponement turned into a permanent divorce.[53] Still, Laroque's defeat was not total. He had wanted to wrest the family allocation apparatus from Catholic employer hands, and on this score he had some success. Under the old dispensation, the family allocation *caisses* were subsidized by joint employer-employee contributions, and it was the employers who retained all the decision-making power. Under Laroque's, it was employers alone who paid in, and the *caisses* were run by committees of elected representatives, half chosen by the employers and the other half by the beneficiaries themselves. The postwar regime drained the high-handed paternalism out of the system, a salutary transformation that in time earned the regime the loyalty of its once-suspicious working-class clientele.[54]

Laroque's setback on the family front was significant but no more than partial. More serious, perhaps, was the rapid fragmentation of the Social Security apparatus, which Laroque had intended to be single and unified, into a mosaic of profession-based schemes. This was Laroque's second disappointment, and it was a major one. The power of entrenched interests explains in part what happened. Miners and railway workers, both well organized and militant, had first-rate pension schemes of their own that provided benefits superior to those on offer from Social Security, and they refused to buy in. In the agricultural sector too there was resistance. The Ministère de l'Agriculture handled all welfare issues relating to rural France, and agriculture-based interest-groups effectively bore down on the ministry to make sure things stayed that way.[55] But it was not just interests that stood in Laroque's way; it was also christian democracy.

National elections in the summer of 1946 returned a new Constituent Assembly. The PCF and SFIO, which together had accounted for the majority of delegates in the outgoing assembly, still remained central players, but now it was the MRP that enjoyed the most numerous representation. Georges Bidault, a founding member of the party, had joked to a colleague about the elections: "With the women's vote, the Bishops and the Holy Spirit, we will get a hundred deputies." In the event, the MRP returned a delegation of 161, 15 more than the Communists. No doubt, the MRP owed its electoral good fortune in part to the backing of the Church hierarchy and in part to that altogether new phenomenon, the women's vote (women took part in national elections for the first time in France in 1945), but there was more to it than that.

The example of Bidault himself provides a clue. He was a senior figure in the Resistance, a onetime president of the CNR, and the MRP leadership was indeed studded with veteran résistants like Bidault. The examples of François de Menthon, Maurice Schumann, and Pierre-Henri Teitgen come straightaway to mind. In the interwar decades, moreover, Bidault had been an active organization man, a member of the Association catholique de la jeunesse française (ACJF) and of the christian-democratic Parti démocrate populaire (PDP). In this respect, too, he was little different from his MRP confreres. There were three national elections from 1945 to 1946, two Constituent Assembly votes (October 1945 and June 1946) and one for a National Assembly (November 1946). Of the roughly 200 MRP personalities returned in these various contests, 105 were ACJF graduates and 96 former PDP militants.[56] The MRP, new though it was, had a serviceable organizational past, not to mention legitimating Resistance credentials, a one-two punch that made a huge difference at the polls.

But what did Liberation-era christian democracy stand for? True to its interwar antecedents, when Catholic Action groups had worked hard to clear space for themselves in an associational universe dominated by better-established republican and socialist rivals, christian democracy stood for pluralism. Centralization threatened to drown the particularities of Catholic associationism in a larger leftist sea, and so it is little wonder that the MRP did not much care for it. To be sure, the party was prepared to endorse the nationalizations of the Liberation era, but it was less receptive to centralizing gestures on other fronts, not least of all when it came to welfare.[57]

Laroque had wanted the entire working population covered by a single Social Security fund, the so-called *caisse unique*. Christian democrats opposed him, seconding the efforts of the Alliance nationale to hive off the family allocation system.[58] And then after that they sided with unionized white-collar workers who were reluctant to join at all. The question of enrolling salaried employees into the system arose in the summer of 1946. The CGT was not the dominant trade-union advocate in this sector but faced competition from the christian-democratic CFTC and the independent Confédération générale des cadres. The CGC, which dated back to the thirties, maintained a certain distance vis-à-vis the labor movement. It spoke of its white-collar constituency, not as proletarians, but as members of a middle class who occupied a strategic buffer zone between labor and management. Now, neither the CFTC nor the CGC much favored the government's plan to bring *cadres* under Laroque's Social Security umbrella, and in July they mounted a muscle-flexing warning strike to make their views known. Such obstructionism found a ready echo in the Constituent Assembly in the form of the now-empowered MRP. This was a formidable coalition of forces, and it was decided to strike a deal. The *cadres* agreed to join Social Security but under privileged circumstances. They were allowed to set up a supplementary regime, outside the system, that furnished additional benefits to members over and above those provided by Social Security alone.[59]

This was but a half defeat for Laroque. *Cadres* were in the end brought into the system, even if under a special arrangement. In the case of the self-employed, however, Laroque's defeat was more complete. The extension of the system to cover independents came up for debate in 1946, and once again the MRP stood up in opposition. This time, it got support from employers' organizations: from the big business union, the CNPF, and from Léon Gingembre's CGPME. Businessmen, artisans, and professionals felt they could do better outside the Social Security system than within, and they got their way. A series of 1948 ordinances created separate pension regimes for each social category.[60]

Social Security a social democratic triumph? It does not quite look that way in actuality. Laroque's neocorporatist vision did place trade unions at the heart of the system, and the unions came to embrace the role assigned to them. But they always shared power with employer representatives, and the employers' role in this dialogue amplified as the Cold War, which muted the voice of the Communist CGT, got under way. Pronatalists made sure that family allocation funds were kept separate; and christian democrats, in alliance with a varied array of professional interests, made sure that most nonworkers stayed out of the system altogether. Pronatalists and christian democrats left their stamp on the new welfare order, and lest any doubts linger about the matter, it is worth remembering just who followed Laroque as director of Social Security and how Laroque's successor got his job.

Laroque returned to the Conseil d'état in 1951. The minister of labor at the time (and it was to the Ministère du Travail that the Social Security director answered) was MRP deputy Paul Bacon. Bacon was of working-class background, a persevering man who had made a long climb to the top of the Catholic Action hierarchy. He had started out as a JOCiste and then risen to become editor at the CFTC's press organ before heading into christian-democratic politics. Bacon had played a significant role in the Resistance, but not so the *haut fonctionnaire* he appointed to take over from Laroque. That man was Bacon's sometime directeur de cabinet, Jacques Doublet, a veteran official of the Alliance nationale, a conseiller d'état with a long record of public service first under the late Third Republic and then under Vichy. Membership on Vichy's Comité consultatif de la Famille and participation in Fondation Carrel research debates had not interrupted Doublet's upward career trajectory, a rising arc that elevated him to the summit of the Social Security apparatus, a position in which he would remain until 1960.[61]

Catholic familism and pronatalism had struck up a partnership in the late thirties that proved to have sufficient staying power to outlast the compromising experiences of the Vichy era. This partnership had a formative impact on the construction of the postwar Social Security system, and its impact was no less important in a second, related domain, that of population management.

Partisans of a sound, family-oriented population policy had reason to be hopeful at the Liberation. The anticlericalism of the old Third Republic now seemed a thing of the past. After all, who was in charge of the Provisional Government at the Liberation but de Gaulle himself, a man of undisguised religious convictions? On 26 August , the very next day after entering a liberated Paris, the general marched down the Champs-Elysées en route to Notre Dame to celebrate a Te Deum. The archbishop of Paris, Cardinal Suhard, was not present at the occasion and for good reason. Earlier that summer, Suhard had taken part in the funeral services of Philippe Henriot, Vichy's mudslinging minister of information, a onetime Catholic orator turned apostle of collaboration who had been gunned down in June by a Resistance commando. Closon and André Ségalat had been dispatched

to Suhard to explain to him why de Gaulle did not want him in attendance at the Te Deum. They found a way to console the cardinal,
however, pointing out de Gaulle's friendliness to religion. Here at
last, they explained, was a statesman who made a point of attending
Catholic ceremonials, "an attitude," as Closon put it, "which we were
not at all accustomed to under preceding French Governments."[62]

De Gaulle did indeed prove himself a good friend to Catholic interests, above all when it came to formulating family policy. First, at
the administrative level, de Gaulle appointed Robert Prigent to take
over the Vichy-era Commissariat-général à la Famille. The Commissariat answered to the Ministère de la Santé publique, which from
September 1944 was headed by François Billoux, a Communist. There
was a reshuffling in April 1945. The Commissariat was rechristened
the Secrétariat-général à la Famille et à la Population, and Alfred
Sauvy succeeded Prigent in the post. Sauvy, however, showed little
aptitude for the role of bureaucratic second in command. In October, it was decided to shut down the Sécretariat altogether, and Sauvy
found himself out of a job. One more round of institutional reconfig-
uring took place at the end of the year. The Secrétariat was resurrected and turned over to Emmanuel Rain, a member of the Conseil
d'état. As for the Ministère de la Santé publique, it got a new name.
It was henceforth known as the Ministère de la Population, and it got
a new or perhaps not so new minister, de Gaulle's point man on family issues, the christian-democratic Robert Prigent.[63]

Prigent, of course, was not at all a newcomer to the family policy
scene. He had been a Catholic Action militant in the thirties and
then a Vichyite after that. As a member of Vichy's Comité consultatif
de la Famille, Prigent had worked alongside leading lights of the pronatalist movement. It was a connection he meant to keep up now that
he had become minister. The Alliance nationale celebrated its fifti-
eth anniversary in 1946. A gala was organized on the occasion at the
Grand Amphitheater of the Sorbonne. On hand to provide musical
accompaniment were the Compagnons de la Musique, an all-male
choral group specializing in folkloric material, which had gotten its
start under the aegis of the Vichy-era youth corps, the Compagnons
de France. Presiding over the festivities, much to the delight of Alli-

ance nationale officials, was the minister of population himself, Robert Prigent.[64]

The character of the event prompts two observations. The first and most obvious is the evident durability of the familist/pronatalist alliance, still viable despite an equivocal Vichy past. The second touches on just how buried that past now was. The Alliance nationale had taken steps to freshen its image. What mattered about Prigent was not his Vichy-era service but the Resistance record he had compiled as a member of the OCM. Even the Compagnons de la Musique had come in for a makeover. From 1944 to 1945, as the war drew to a close, the Compagnons were reinvented as a Free French choir, joining the theater group attached to General de Lattre de Tassigny's First Army, then fighting in the north of France.[65]

De Gaulle's elevation of population policy to a matter of ministerial importance was an innovation of note. His decision in April 1945 to create an advisory body on population and family matters attached to the prime minister's office was not. The Haut Comité consultatif de la Population et de la Famille (HCCPF), as the new body was called, had direct institutional precursors, first in Daladier's Haut Comité de la Population and then in the Vichy-era Comité consultatif de la Famille.

In the present connection, three points bear making about the HCCPF. There is no doubt that de Gaulle attached particular importance to the new organ, taking the time to sit in on its first session himself from start to finish.[66] The committee was made up of nine members plus a general secretary, and it is interesting to note that three of these ten were veterans of the profamily movement: Simone Collet (from the association La Plus Grande Famille), Dr. Maurice Monsaingeon (from the Fédération des associations des familles nombreuses), and Prigent, whose familist past requires no additional commentary.

Last of all, it is noteworthy how much the HCCPF owed both in personnel and in policy to its Vichy-era predecessors. There were new faces on the committee to be sure—Maxime Blocq-Mascart, Robert Debré, Mme Delabit—who had distinguished themselves in the Resistance or, as with Mme Delabit, in the trade-union movement (she was a CGT militant of long standing). There was also the inevitable Landry, who had not buckled to the Pétainist temptation. But what about the others? All the profamily activists—Collet, Monsaingeon, Prigent—had had a brush or more with the Vichy population-policy apparatus. Of the three committee members not yet discussed—Fernand Boverat, Jacques Doublet, and Georges Mauco—two are already known quantities. Boverat and Doublet had both seen service in prewar days, working on Daladier's Haut Comité de la Population. Boverat had kept a low profile in the first years of the Occupation but then associated himself with the workings of the Fondation Carrel. As for Doublet, he had worked for Pétain's regime throughout. He had also had run-ins with Vichy administration higher-ups, enough so to dispel Resistance suspicions of his political bona fides. Perhaps then the Vichy associations of so many HCCPF members ought not to be overstressed, mitigated as they were by later Resistance activism (Prigent) or by manifestations of halfhearted loyalty to the Pétainist regime (Doublet).[67]

Yet there is still the troubling case of Georges Mauco, the HCCPF's general secretary. It is not so much that he was a Vichy man. Mauco was a trained demographer who had worked up an expertise on immigration matters. In the 1930s and during the war, he had managed to insinuate himself into populationist networks, lining up for himself powerful patrons, Landry among them. But such associations had not earned Mauco anything more than minor policy-making positions, whether under the Third Republic or Vichy. What makes Mauco's case disturbing is not so much his Vichy service, which was second rank, as his record of right-wing racism. Mauco joined Jacques Doriot's fascist Parti populaire français in 1939 and remained a member until November 1942. In 1940, he penned an apology for the principle of a "fascist revolution," and from 1942 to 1943 contributed a series of articles to L'Ethnie française, a journal of scientific racism directed by Georges Montandon. Mauco had always been a firm believer in the nonassimilability of certain immigrant populations— "asiatics, africans, levantines" as he identified them in a prewar text. In the Ethnie française articles, however, he was less coy, dropping the code word "levantine" in favor of a more explicit anti-Semitism that identified Jewish mercantilism and effeminacy as mortal dangers to the moral and physical well-being of the French body politic.[68]

This was the man chosen at the Liberation to help manage the HCCPF. There was, as might be imagined, opposition to Mauco's professional advance, but he defended himself. He had joined the Free French armed forces in early 1944 and taken part in the fighting at the Liberation; he denied full authorship of one of the *Ethnie française* articles; and such pleadings proved sufficient. Mauco's underlying views on immigration, however, had not changed much. At the HCCPF, he argued for the internment of refugees, "fugitives" he called them, as though they were criminals on the run. On the immigration issue, moreover, while conceding the need for additional manpower to aid in the reconstruction of a recovering France, he insisted on the continuing salience of ethnic "desirability" in the vetting of would-be immigrants.[69]

On the matter of internment, Mauco's colleagues at the HCCPF thought otherwise, but on that of immigration there was greater unity of opinion. Robert Debré and Alfred Sauvy (an ex officio member of the committee) also recognized the importance of ethnic background to a sound immigration policy. Certain categories of immigrant, as they saw it, were more difficult to absorb than others, "levantines" for example, whom Debré and Sauvy characterized, invoking the well-worn stereotype, as "sometimes too cunning." But "hard to assimilate," for Debré and Sauvy, did not mean impossible to assimilate, and on this point they parted company with the more rigid Mauco.[70] Such differences, however, did not prevent the HCCPF from agreeing on a joint recommendation urging immigration officials to take into account "ethnic, sanitary, demographic and geographical" considerations when establishing immigration guidelines. It required a decision by the Conseil d'état, in this instance led by the veteran résistant René Cassin, to block the HCCPF's push for an ethnicity-based immigration policy.[71]

The point still remains, however, that the HCCPF had more than a little in common with its Vichy-era predecessor. It is not just that there were continuities in institutional form and personnel. In policy matters too there were overlaps. To be sure, the overt racism of the war years was no longer the order of the day, but family—and family understood in the most conventional terms—still mattered. Yet how could it have been otherwise, given de Gaulle's own profamily views and the postwar ascendancy (even if momentary) of the christiandemocratic MRP, which in fact styled itself "le parti de la famille."[72] Not least of all, the preservation of Frenchness still mattered. France needed new bodies to survive, but they had to be quality bodies, healthy, vigorous, and, most important of all, amenable to easy assimilation into the national mainstream. Here the major players were not so much familists as population engineers, pronatalists, and statisticians, men like Mauco, Debré, and Sauvy.

The populationist lobby was one current among many at the HCCPF, jostling for influence alongside the better-established familist/pronatalist nexus. There was one corner of the postwar state, however, where populationists like Debré and Sauvy came to exercise a more unrivaled preeminence: at the brand-new Institut national d'études démographiques. INED was created in October 1945, but was it so new as all that? Not really, for it laid its foundations on the ruins of a Vichy-era forerunner, the Fondation Carrel, whose successor INED turned out to be in all but name.

The Fondation Carrel was shut down at the Liberation. Carrel, who would have faced legal proceedings, died of a heart attack in November 1946. Missenard did indeed appear before a purge commission, headed by Dr. Bernard Lafay (who would serve a brief stint in the 1970s as president of the Paris municipal council). Lafay, however, was not an impartial figure. It seems that he had expressed, not two years before heading the purge commission, a passing interest in a Fondation Carrel affiliation. Under the circumstances it is little surprise that Missenard got off, but, though unpunished, he was now a marginalized and embittered figure in the world of population science.[73]

Yet what of the Fondation's numerous institutional assets: its building and equipment on the rue de la Baume, its administrative services, its research teams? The Centre national de la recherche scientifique (CNRS) made a bid for them, which, had it been successful, might well have steered population management in a new direction. The CNRS, a state-funded science and social-science think tank, dated back to 1939. Its first director had been Henri Laugier, a specialist in the science of work and industrial relations. At the Liberation, he was succeeded by the atomic physicist Frédéric Joliot-Curie. Both men had been militant antifascists in the thirties who then went on to distinguish themselves in the Resistance.[74] But it was not the Resistance Left that was to come out on top in the competition for the Fondation Carrel's resources.

Robert Debré had plans of his own. He dreamed of resurrecting the Fondation as a population studies institute, and Debré was a man with excellent connections. In the latter years of the war, he had joined the Resistance, serving in a variety of capacities, not least as a member of the Front National, a frontist organization started by the Communist Party in 1941. Debré was, then, in good odor in certain communist circles, which turned out to be a crucial advantage. The minister in charge of deciding what to do with the Fondation Carrel's remains was the minister of health, who in mid-1945 was François Billoux, a Communist. Billoux, "a fearful little man without character" as Sauvy dismissively described him, proved to be receptive to Debré's persuasive efforts. Billoux gave Debré the go-ahead; Sauvy was called in to help draft the relevant ordonnance; and so came into being in October 1945 the Institut national d'études démographiques (INED). Sauvy was named director, a post he would retain until 1962.[75]

Debré and Sauvy were canny institutional players. They had outmaneuvered the CNRS but did not want to alienate it altogether. In a gesture as politic as it was inclusive, Laugier was named to INED's technical oversight board (Comité technique). Nor was Laugier just the token leftist. Jean Langevin, Francis Perrin, and Paul Rivet were also tapped to serve. Langevin was the son of Paul Langevin, an atomic scientist, a communist fellow traveler (Langevin senior would in fact join the party in 1944), and a veteran antifascist intellectual from Popular Front days. Francis Perrin had a similar paternal pedigree. His father, Jean, was a Nobel Prize–winning physicist who had served in Léon Blum's first Popular Front cabinet in 1936. As for Rivet, he had made a reputation for himself both as an ethnologist and as a socialist of unyielding antifascist convictions, militating in the thirties alongside Paul Langevin to line up intellectual backing for the Popular Front and then in the early years of the Occupation taking part in the founding of the Musée de l'Homme Resistance network.[76] INED, judged on the basis of the composition of its Comité technique, would appear a lineal descendant, not of the Fondation Carrel, but of the Popular Front.

Such a conclusion, however, would be overhasty. Sauvy, first of all, made sure that the Fondation Carrel's material resources, its building and matériel, wound up in INED's hands. The new Institut was first housed in the offices of the old Fondation Carrel, rue de la Baume, although the arrangement did not last. In 1949, the Rockefeller Foundation managed to reclaim what had after all been its original property, at which time INED relocated to the rue Franklin, where it would remain until the end of the sixties.

Sauvy had greater success salvaging Fondation Carrel personnel. Roger Peltier, who had succeeded Perroux as secretary-general of the Fondation in December 1943, was kept on in that post at INED. He would not step down until 1969.[77] As for the Fondation's scientific staff, Sauvy held over a sizable contingent, although estimates differ on this point. On one calculation, Fondation Carrel holdovers—thirty persons in all—accounted for about half of INED's initial research staff; on another, the Fondation Carrel contributed thirteen of INED's original twenty-five scientists.[78] Either way, the proportion is about the same: a full 50 percent of INED's scientific personnel had once worked for Dr. Carrel's establishment.

That half, moreover, included a number of major figures who had stood out at the Fondation as they would again at INED. Sauvy's memoirs identify seven core members of the INED team: Jean Bourgeois-Pichat, Louis Chevalier, Robert Gessain, Alain Girard, Jean Sutter, Jean Stoetzel, and Paul Vincent.[79] All had had an association with the Fondation Carrel, Chevalier as a research team associate, the rest as formal members. All, moreover, would play key roles at INED, whether as contributors to the institute's new journal, *Population* (famous, among other things, for its brick-red cover), or as research supervisors. INED, like the Foundation Carrel, was organized on a departmental basis. On one account, the first batch of department heads consisted to a man of Fondation Carrel veterans.[80] And it was not just individual scientists who made the transition from one institution to the other; in a couple of instances, entire research units preserved more or less intact, Jean Sutter's nutrition team, for example, or Stoetzel's polling group.[81]

INED was born under the Fondation Carrel's shadow, and it was a long shadow at that. Sauvy began to think about retirement from the institute directorship in the late fifties. He brought Jean Fourastié on board, hoping to groom him as a successor, but the maneuver stalled, and the succession in fact went to Bourgeois-Pichat, a demographer of renown, a sometime adviser to the United Nations on population matters (1954–1962), and, of course, in Vichy days a onetime associate of Alexis Carrel.[82]

In critical respects, moreover, INED's connection to the past was intellectual as well as organizational. INED, it will come as no surprise, remained true to the demographic fraternity's long-established commitment to pronatalist policy. Bourgeois-Pichat continued his wartime studies on the baby boom, although now with a greater scientific rigor than before. Sauvy did shut down the Fondation Carrel's Biology and Architecture/Urbanism sections.[83] All the same, INED researchers, starting with Sauvy himself, continued to fret about the assimilability of immigrant populations. Sauvy and Debré published a volume in 1946, *Des Français pour la France*, that championed Jewish intermarriage as a means of breaking down Jewish isolation and the "conflicts" that resulted therefrom. Indeed, they went on to argue, assimilability was the lodestar of any immigration policy worthy of the name. France ought to pick and choose among applicants, selecting "for Frenchification those who are really suitable to become French."[84] As for urbanism, INED did not abandon the subject altogether. Sauvy got to know Le Corbusier in the immediate postwar era, an acquaintanceship that persuaded him, Sauvy, that reconstruction and "the demographic revival of France" were interconnected phenomena. Le Corbusier set to work building his celebrated *Unité d'habitation* in 1947, a residential tower block in Marseille that offered all the amenities essential to a healthful, family life on site: commissary, playground, medical services, day-care facilities. In a speech reprinted the following year in *Population*, Le Corbusier did not hesitate to frame the objectives of his enterprise in the language of the stock-breeder: "It is necessary... to create housing that can bring about the breeding [l'élévage]—that's what I say, breeding—of the species: children and adults."[85] Such language, whether from a Sauvy or a Le Corbusier, suggests an INED that had not outgrown by much the eugenicist obsessions of the Carrel era.

Add to this INED's ongoing relations with the pronatalist/Catholic alliance, and the case for downplaying the ruptures of 1944–1945 gets stronger still. Georges Hourdin, a Catholic journalist and veteran of the Catholic family movement, sat alongside Rivet and the others on INED's technical board, and from 1946 the institute supplied an annual financial subsidy to the old Alliance nationale.[86] Looked at in this light, INED appears not so much a progeny of the Popular Front as a Fondation Carrel clone.

Yet this conclusion too does not tell the whole story. To be sure, the overlap in personnel and policy between the Fondation Carrel and INED was extensive, but this did not mean that the two institutions had quite the same goals in every respect. Sauvy's INED carved out an agenda of its own that owed something to Carrel's binationalism but which, in its "modernizing" and globalist thrust, struck out in new directions.

In part, what distinguished INED was the seriousness of its science. The demographers went about mathematizing their work in ways that made it difficult for old-timers to understand. Stoetzel's lab stocked itself with the latest in tabulating machinery. Then there was the fieldwork, the assembly of multidisciplinary teams to examine the life practices of a particular locality, using the most up-to-date survey and interview techniques.[87]

The most celebrated of such studies zeroed in on an isolated Breton village, Plozévet. The project, initiated by Gessain in the early sixties, was not an INED enterprise per se. Gessain at the time presided over a scientific research board, the Comité d'analyse démographique, économique et sociale (he was also director of the Musée de l'Homme), and it was the Comité d'analyse that undertook to get the Plozévet study up and running. Still, a number of the senior men who took part in the project's planning and execution—Chevalier, Stoetzel, Sutter, and, of course, Gessain himself—had INED backgrounds.

The Plozévet study merits mentioning here for two reasons. Gessain himself picked the research site. Plozévet residents intermarried at exceptional rates, and Gessain had a long-standing interest in tracking the genetic, psychological, and social consequences of endogamy. It was the breeder's mentality that put Plozévet on the social-science map, and to this extent the study was ab initio cast in the Carrelian mold.[88] But as Gessain's research teams descended on Plozévet, they made a discovery, and this is the second point. Brittany was caught up in a spasm of social metamorphosis that was changing forever the face of rural France. Here was a theme, "the rising tide of modernity," that the sociologists involved could not ignore.[89] One of them was a young Edgar Morin, just then starting out, and the fruit of his collaboration was a book of his own, *Commune en France: la métamorphose de Plodemet* (1967). Morin's study was a brilliant evocation of a French countryside in transition, wrenched out of an archaic past by what he called a "continuous modernity."[90]

There was a tension then in the Plozévet story between a Carrelian biologism and a modernization-minded sociology. It was not resolved when the study was written up by the Annales historian André Burguière,[91] and in the present context that tension is just what makes the study apropos. It was a marker of the passing of an older, biology-based paradigm and its absorption into a new schematic that spoke the language of modernization.

INED scientists played a hinge role in this transformation, and the change played itself out, not just in INED-inspired village fieldwork like the Plozévet project, but in other research domains as well. Historical demography is a case in point. How did French men and women in the past regulate reproduction; when had they married; when and how often did they give birth? These were the questions addressed in a collective volume, *La Prévention des naissances dans la famille: Ses origines dans les temps modernes*, published in 1960 under INED auspices. The list of contributors included seasoned population scientists like Sauvy and Sutter but some new faces as well, like that of Louis Henry, who had joined the INED staff in the immediate postwar era, or that of Philippe Ariès, a nonconformist historian cum demographer who happened to publish just that same year his still-celebrated study of old regime child-rearing practices, *Centuries of Childhood*. It was not just the past that got a new look but the colonial world too. INED dispatched Louis Chevalier to North Africa to research Algerian birthrates, skyrocketing at the time.[92] And what was the upshot of such various efforts? First of all, a deeper understanding of the "demographic transition," a concept Landry had explored back in the thirties. But this deeper understanding also had practical consequences for contemporary policy making, in particular when it came to thinking about how to manage world population growth.

In the late forties, the American demographers Frank Notestein and Kingsley Davis had posited a connection between the demographic transition and economic development. In the West, the industrial revolution had preceded the transition, a sequencing that made perfect sense. It is not hard to see how an increase in productive capacity might translate into reduced infant mortality. This line of reasoning pointed the way toward a second and related set of conclusions, that excessive population growth could over time smother development. France's postwar economic miracle, the *trente glorieuses*, had fed on the baby boom: growth favoring a rising birthrate, the consumer demand of the baby-boom generation in turn fueling growth. Yet, in the underdeveloped but still modernizing third world, progress was more precarious, threatened by the growth-stifling effects of a population explosion. Modernization here required managed population growth, in a word, family planning.[93] It bears remembering in this context that it was Fourastié who coined the term *trente glorieuses* and Sauvy *Tiers Monde*. INED researchers placed themselves in the forefront of a global debate on the demographics of modernization, and so it is little wonder that INED old-timers like Bourgeois-Pichat were so sought after by world organizations like the fledgling United Nations.[94]

The postwar INED built, then, on Carrelian foundations, but it also struck out in new directions, honing its science and reworking its agenda to address not only the familiar concerns of a natality-obsessed

France but a new global agenda centered on managed growth and population planning.

Nor was INED the only institution that, via the embrace of population policy, succeeded in finding a new role for itself. INSEE had been sidelined as a major player in the planning process, but it found another domain in which to put its accumulated statistical wisdom to work: welfare and population management. In December 1946, INSEE signed an accord with Laroque's Sécurité Sociale. Under its terms, INSEE undertook to assign all Social Security contributors an identification number, which in the event turned out to be a variant on the thirteen-digit code René Carmille had devised during the war.[95]

France conducted its first postwar census in 1946, and the task of organizing it fell to INSEE. There was considerable debate as to how to classify subjects by professional activity. The minister of labor, Alexandre Parodi, issued a series of decrees in 1945, which settled the matter for the moment. Wage-earning and salaried employees were divided into five principal branches of employment. In the process, alongside familiar categories like blue-collar worker or *employé*, a new rubric was introduced: that of *cadre*, defined as a diploma holder who exercised some form of authority in the workplace. At the same time, the blue-collar category itself was broken down into five further subcategories. These were stratified by skill level, ranging from the simple manual laborer at the bottom to the semiskilled worker in the middle (*ouvrier spécialisé* or OS) to the highly skilled worker at the top (*ouvrier hautement qualifié* or O hautement Q).[96] The Parodi decrees, of course, did not solve the problems of nomenclature once and for all, and INSEE researchers set to work fine-tuning a more comprehensive professional classification scheme. Several versions were proposed, culminating in the *Code socio-profesionnelle* of 1954, completed in time for France's second postwar census carried out that very same year. The 1954 classification code was a landmark of its kind. Its descriptive terminology was not set in stone but in practice was to vary little in the decades ahead.[97]

Such a passion for classification, of course, was not just an end in itself. It enabled the state to visualize its population... and to sound it out. INSEE's Vichy-era predecessor, the SNS, had maintained a polling service, and it did not take long before INSEE itself got into the business of public opinion research. In 1946 and again in 1948, it conducted surveys in collaboration with INED on how families managed household budgets. INSEE, it seems, began polling on its own in 1950 with a study of employment, followed in 1952 by a survey of radio listeners' program preferences. Jean Porte designed the latter poll, and he understood as well as anyone how critical a well-conceived classificatory grid was to a fruitful analysis of sampling data. But then again, Porte had been himself a principal architect of the *Code socio-professionnelle*.[98]

Michel Foucault, ever the aficionado of neologisms, invented a term to describe the modern state's growing aptitude for the management of people through classificatory schemes: "governmentality."[99] From one angle, INSEE looks like an extension of its immediate wartime predecessor, René Carmille's SNS. But from another, it appears the handmaiden of a new kind of state, armed with numbers, codes, statistics of all kinds, the better to govern not so much citizens but populations.

It would be difficult to overestimate the massiveness of the Liberation-era's legacy in matters of welfare and population policy, but sizing up its significance is another matter. Was the welfare state a social democratic or workerist conquest? In part, yes. There is no doubting the Resistance's commitment, inscribed in the CNR program, to a comprehensive system of welfare provision. The Social Security regime Laroque in fact constructed, moreover, depended on active trade-union participation in the management and disbursement of benefits. But Laroque was also a man of the 1930s, marked by the corporatist currents of that not-so-bygone era. He believed that the path to social peace lay through negotiation between organized interests, and he built that "corporatist" principle into the design of local Social Security boards, composed of both labor and management representatives. That principle once admitted, however, the way was then open to the fragmentation of Social Security as every "interest" sought a regime of its own. The result was not a universalist scheme on the British model but a corporatist one that valorized professional identities first and foremost.

The splintering of Social Security was aided and abetted by a new and major political player on the scene, christian democracy. Political Catholicism positioned itself as the champion of the family, and wherever family concerns were involved, there christian democrats made their newfound influence felt. They wanted the family allowance system to be administered apart from other forms of welfare benefit, and they got what they wanted. De Gaulle proved himself a reliable and indispensable ally in this domain. The general made family and population policy a state priority, overseeing creation of an array of new institutions to address the issue: the HCCPF, the Ministère de la Population, INSEE, INED. And in every instance, Catholics were invited to take part, sometimes in starring roles, sometimes as members of the supporting cast. Yet whichever, the conclusion is still valid: men of religion in the Fourth Republic came to occupy a place in public life they had not known under the Third, and family and welfare policy was a major conduit for the change.

The new prominence of family policy in the postwar era helped to relaunch the fortunes of a second group, France's venerable and still-powerful pronatalist lobby. The Alliance nationale stood shoulder to shoulder with organized Catholicism in the postwar era, renewing a partnership first struck up in the late thirties and carried on through the war. But two additional points need making in this connection. First, that the terms of the partnership had altered. Christian activists had been second-rank players before the war, but under Vichy and again under the Fourth Republic they had gained in stature. And second, that the pronatalist movement itself was in the process of evolving. An older generation of amateurs and polemicists was passing, giving way to new men like Debré and Sauvy who defined themselves not just as pronatalists but as serious scientists, as demographers.

A wide-angle vision of welfare state construction—wide enough to encompass family and population policy alongside Social Security—adds additional layers of complexity to the question of the welfare state's origins. It is not just that there were carryovers from the 1930s, whether corporatist or pronatalist, though that was no doubt the case. But there is the further problem of Vichy's contribution. Vichy may be understood in part as a relay station, picking up causes and principles that had gotten started under the late Third Republic and passing them on to the Fourth. Daladier's Haut Comité de la Population gave way to Vichy's Comité consultatif, which in turn gave way to the postwar HCCPF. To be sure, the institutions were not identical, but they bore a strong family resemblance to one another in both composition and agenda. From the Code de la famille on down to postwar debates on immigration policy, certain preoccupations perdured: France's need for large and healthy families, for a new moral discipline, for a discriminating and discriminatory immigration policy. Under Vichy, of course, concerns about ethnic assimilability transmuted into an explicit racism, but otherwise there were significant continuities in public discourse on these subjects.

Yet Vichy was not just a relay; it was also an innovator in its own right both in statistics and in population science. Carmille's SNS and the Fondation Carrel may be taken as examples. These were Vichy creations, and they were successful enough that Liberation-era authorities thought it worthwhile to preserve them, though under new names. The SNS became INSEE and the Fondation Carrel INED. Preservation, however, did not mean stasis. INSEE and INED took off in new directions, coding and classifying, bringing to bear a scientizing rigor to the problems of France's postwar "modernization."

The postwar welfare state was in part a social democratic achievement, but it was a good deal more than that, with multiple currents—corporatist, christian-democratic, pronatalist, populationist—contributing to its design and functioning. As for the question of Vichy survivals (the *Vichy après Vichy* problem), they were numerous. Politics, institutions, and personnel were carried over from the war years into the postwar era. The mandatory prenuptial exam, a Vichy innovation, was not repudiated by Liberation-era authorities but kept on. Vichy had wanted an interlocutor qualified to speak for the family movement as a whole and so had encouraged creation of an umbrella organization, the Centre de coordination et d'action des mouvements familiaux. The Centre's representative status vis-à-vis the state was officialized into law in 1942 (the so-called *loi Gounot*). At the Liberation, the Centre disappeared but was reborn as the Union nationale des associations familiales, which moved into the same premises that the Centre had occupied during the war. Robert Prigent had had a hand in legislating the Union into existence, the same Prigent who had made the move from militant to policy adviser under Vichy and then after the war from adviser to minister.[100] But such continuities, important as they were, should not obscure just how much the Liberation inflected agendas, muting the unbridled prejudices of the Vichy years and steering energies toward a new project. National Revolution had once been the order of the day; now it was national reconstruction and modernization.

Sciences Po and ENA

The balance sheet was no less mixed in the domain of elite education. There are two ways to tell the postwar story here. The first places principal emphasis on continuity. Sciences Po, though slated for extinction by the Resistance Left, survived the storms of the Liberation. The Left got the Ecole nationale d'administration it so much wanted, and ENA graduates, depending on class standing, were assured the most prestigious jobs in the beginning ranks of the state's *grands corps*. But Sciences Po adjusted to the change, remaking itself into ENA's most important feeder school, bar none. Under the new dispensation, as under the old, Sciences Po remained a near-essential stepping-stone to a career in the senior civil service.

Yet Sciences Po survived and prospered not by remaining the same but by changing. It professionalized its faculty and teaching, eschewing the impressionistic, dilettantish ways of the prewar era in favor of a curriculum that had a more hard-edged, social-science content. The liberal orthodoxies of old were abandoned, their place taken by technocratic, interventionist approaches to public policy making. The new ENA defined itself as an Ecole d'application, meaning that it taught practical lessons about public administration. The school's students did internships in both the public and private sectors; they took courses from professors, often borrowed from the *grands corps*, who had firsthand experience of how state institutions were run. Sciences Po's ever more technocratic orientation and deepening embrace of

interventionist policy made it an excellent proving ground for ambitious young men who aspired to the kind of hands-on education on
offer at ENA.

The technocratic approach and interventionist policy were not,
however, postwar inventions. Sciences Po had been moving in this
direction for some time, the Liberation consummating a process that
had gotten its start already in the late Third Republic. As to the ini-
tiators of the change, they were neither social democrats nor leftists
but establishment insiders like Seydoux and Siegfried, who got help
at critical junctures from like-minded men in de Gaulle's Provisional
Government, from Debré first and foremost and, indeed, from the
general himself. The remaking of elite education at the Liberation
then was in part a story of survival but also in part a story of self-
transformation. The Left had a role to play in the drama, but in the
end the Left did not get the victories it hoped for.

Sciences Po, as we have seen, began to gear up for a change well
before the Cogniot bill came up for discussion in late February 1945.
The Communist assault, however, raised the stakes. At issue now was
not just the school's reform but its very existence.

Sciences Po, of course, was not without allies in the struggle, and
some powerful ones at that. By its own count, eight of the thirteen
members of de Gaulle's Provisional Government were Sciences Po
graduates.[101] The general himself was not about to allow the obstreperous Cogniot to steal a march on him in matters of state. De Gaulle
wanted a government counterstroke and turned to Debré, who was
brought on board in the first week of April.

Debré, of course, had been thinking over just such a project for
years, so it did not take him long to conduct the necessary consulta-
tions and come up with a proposal of his own. He sketched a two-tier
system, his own variation on Jean Zay's old scheme. At the top, a state-
run ENA would prime mature students to sit a single *grands corps*
exam; at the bottom, a small number of political science institutes—
the most important situated in Paris—would offer a more general
education but also prepare interested undergraduates for the ENA
admissions test. Debré laid out what he had in mind to de Gaulle on
23 May 1945. The ordinance was fine-tuned by an interministerial

committee on 4 June and approved by the cabinet as a whole four days later.

In the meantime, Debré had cabled to San Francisco, alerting Siegfried and Seydoux, who were there attending the founding conference of the United Nations, as to what was happening. The pair returned to France on 31 May.[102] It must have heartened them to learn that the minister in charge of presenting the Debré project to the Assemblée consultative provisoire was Jules Jeanneney. Jeanneney, a veteran of Third Republic Senate politics, was well disposed to Sciences Po, all the more so as his son—and cabinet director—Jean-Marcel was a loyal school alumnus.[103] The Debré project, of course, had first to make its way through the Assembly's Commission sur la Réforme de l'Etat. This was Pierre Cot's bailiwick—he was in fact designated *rapporteur* for the Debré bill—but it was not Cot's alone, for the president of the Commission was Siegfried's comrade in arms from war days in Lyon, Paul Bastid.

Sciences Po had numerous well-wishers in the Provisional Government. Its position in the Assemblée consultative provisoire was less secure but far from hopeless. In the spring of 1945, the most urgent task confronting Siegfried and Seydoux was conjuring away Cogniot's threat of demolition, and this they contrived to do, making the most of the connections and public-relations resources available to them.

First, a thirty-three-page memorandum was drafted, enumerating and then refuting point by point Cogniot's various accusations. The document went to particular lengths to demonstrate that Sciences Po had undertaken to purge itself of all Vichy taint. To this end, it was pointed out, the school had of its own volition set up an internal Commission d'épuration, chaired by Siegfried himself, which had fired compromising faculty and administrators like Georges Ripert.[104] Copies of the memorandum, accompanied by a cover letter from Siegfried, were circulated in mid-April to well over a hundred recipients, most of them members of the Assemblée consultative provisoire.[105]

Sciences Po, indeed, was determined to put on the best public face possible. This meant for starters getting rid of Vichyite faculty. It also meant a strategic watchfulness over new hires. Jean-Jacques Chevallier had taught at Sciences Po in 1942–1943 and proved himself a great hit with students. The possibility arose that he might teach again after the war, but Sciences Po's secretary-general, Jacques Chapsal, worried about the wisdom of the idea. Chevallier, he observed to Seydoux, had all the makings of an excellent colleague, but now in mid-1945 was not the time to extend him a new appointment, "for he had, in plain view of everyone, taken part in propaganda meetings and conferences in favor of the preceding regime."[106] Chapsal's cautious counsel prevailed, and Chevallier's candidacy was put on hold for the time being.

Not least of all, Siegfried and Seydoux had recourse to the press to plead Sciences Po's cause. Philippe Viannay in this context proved a useful contact. Viannay's Resistance newspaper, *Défense de la France*, had been among the most successful of its kind, with a circulation in the hundreds of thousands. It was one of the few Resistance organs to survive the Liberation in robust good health. In November 1944, it rechristened itself *France-Soir* and brought in new management in the person of veteran newspaperman Pierre Lazareff. Lazareff had worked at Jean Prouvost's mass-circulation *Paris-Soir* in the thirties and then spent the war in the United States, familiarizing himself with American ways. This was the experience he brought to bear as *France-Soir*'s new secretary-general, and the paper went on to claim a place for itself as the best-selling evening daily in the postwar era.[107] This was also the paper to which Siegfried turned in early spring 1945 for a much-needed boost. On 30 March, prior to departing for the UN conference in San Francisco, he delivered himself of a front-page interview to *France-Soir*. Sciences Po, Siegfried explained at length, had not collaborated in any way with the Vichy regime. Indeed, quite the reverse: it had worked honorably in close liaison with Resistance networks like Viannay's own Défense de la France.[108]

Seydoux too talked to the press, although the issue he addressed was not so much the school's war record as its alleged laissez-faire bias. In early June, just back from the United States, he spoke to *L'Université libre*. Yes, Seydoux conceded, free-market doctrine had in the past dominated the school's curriculum but no more; and he then proceeded to tick off the names of various "dirigistes" on the faculty: "Gaëtan Pirou, [Charles] Morazé, Davezac...."[109]

In the early weeks of June 1945, as the government readied Debré's ordinance for submission to the Provisional Assembly, Sciences
Po concentrated its lobbying efforts more and more on the individual personalities best situated to shape the outcome of the debate. At
a businesslike meeting with Jeanneney senior on 11 June, Seydoux
and Siegfried renewed Sciences Po's pledge to work with the state on
civil-service reform. An appearance before the Commission sur la Réforme de l'Etat on 19 June was much less satisfactory. Cot in particular exhibited "a pretty aggressive attitude," making plain his own
preference for Sciences Po's outright "expropriation." The next day,
Seydoux and Siegfried had an audience with General de Gaulle himself, with more reassuring results. The general dismissed Cot as prone
to "demagogic posturing." The government, he explained, had not
the least intention of doing in Sciences Po. On the contrary, the general concluded, "the school should find its place in the new organization of things."[110]

The Assemblée consultative provisoire took up the Debré proposal
the next day. Sciences Po came in for rough handling from a number
of representatives, André Philip and Cot foremost among them, who
urged state seizure of the school's library and buildings. Similar demands were made in the press by the Communist daily *L'Humanité*
and the Resistance press organ *Franc-Tireur*. Sciences Po's own assessment of the debate, however, was almost exultant in tone and for
good reason. In the Assembly, Bastid and Viannay had both borne
credible witness to the school's Resistance record. Seydoux and Siegfried had worked hard to shore up school flanks on just this point,
and they had succeeded. The Assembly as a body, moreover, issued
an endorsement of the Debré proposal, even if many representatives
felt that it did not go far enough. As for the newspapers, few echoed
Philip and Cot's confiscatory exhortations. *Le Monde* in fact spoke up
in defense of Sciences Po's interests. On the eve of the Assembly session, there had been predictions of Sciences Po's imminent demise,
but in its aftermath school authorities congratulated themselves that
the old "cadaver" had life in it still.[111]

Sciences Po had warded off the Left's attack: Debré's ordinance,
not Cogniot's proposal, would determine the school's future. All

depended now on how the ordinance was applied, and Sciences Po's leadership set to work devising an implementation scheme of its own. Discussion of the question, indeed, had gotten under way in early June, several weeks before the decisive Assembly debate. School officials conceived a two-part strategy. First, the old Sciences Po would dissolve itself, to be reborn as the Paris Institut d'études politiques (IEP). No doubt, the state would play a key role in administering the new IEP, but Sciences Po officials did not want the state to govern alone. What they had in mind, rather, was a condominium, the state working in collaboration with an altogether new body, a private Fondation of as yet unspecified composition and attributes. This was the second and in the event crucial plank of the Sciences Po plan.[112]

The state turned out to be a receptive and prompt interlocutor. Little wonder, as Debré remained in charge of the negotiations from the state's end. To senior Sciences Po administrators, he remained "Michel," a devoted alumnus and negotiator of unalloyed "good faith."[113] All concerned, moreover, felt under time pressure. There was a new academic year to prepare for, and elections for a new Assembly—this one Constituent rather than Consultative—were scheduled in October, which might well complicate what was now a constructive political climate.[114] It did not take long for an agreement to be arrived at. The terms, in fact, had been settled before the autumn was out, and on all points the state proved accommodating to Sciences Po concerns.

Debré from the outset was attached to the idea of a Fondation, or Fondation nationale des sciences politiques (FNSP) as the institution came to be known.[115] There was much give-and-take over the composition of the FNSP board. The government at first insisted on a majority of state nominees but then hesitated, leaving the matter unresolved for the moment. The initial ordinance of 9 October envisaged a governing board composed of up to thirty members. Fifteen would be designated by the state. As many as fifteen but no fewer than ten would be selected by the outgoing Sciences Po administration. Not left undecided however, was the identity of the FNSP's first president. On 12 September, the state announced its intention to appoint André Siegfried to the post.[116]

Definition of the FNSP's actual mandate generated a fresh round of debate. On one point there was agreement: the FNSP would take charge of managing the Sciences Po endowment, devoting a portion of the income to the advancement of political science—the publication of a review, of monographs, and so on—and the balance to the running of the IEP itself, the upkeep and expansion of its library facilities, for example. But what role would the FNSP have in IEP governance?

The answer came in three parts. On 12 September, the state made public its selection for the new director of the IEP, Roger Seydoux. Seydoux was to be assisted by a Comité de perfectionnement. The Comité's composition in turn was fixed by a decree of 9 October, which provided for a board of seventeen members: two ex officio (the president of the CNRS and the new director of ENA), two selected by the state, seven by the University, and five by the FNSP itself, plus one IEP old boy. The remaining details of FNSP-IEP relations were settled by a convention of 27 October, hammered out between Sciences Po and University representatives. The first article of the document spelled out in lapidary terms that the FNSP was responsible for the "administrative and financial management" of the new IEP.[117]

A final, though minor, piece of the puzzle was put in place at the beginning of November. Debré's major interest in the new architecture of civil-service education was the Ecole nationale d'administration. Sciences Po administrators had no say in the shaping of the new institution, although, as it turned out, they would have a bit part in its actual functioning. Sciences Po and ENA representatives signed a convention on 2 November, naming the FNSP's president and senior administrator as ex officio members of ENA's Conseil d'administration.[118]

The rough outline of these various arrangements had come into focus as early as the final week of July 1945, such that Sciences Po was ready then to submit the package to its backers for their review. Diehards like Davezac were outraged at the concessions made to the state, but cooler heads like Emmanuel Monick and Henri de Peyerimhoff —the latter now retired from the school's Conseil d'administration but still an influential figure—were delighted, "surprised that it was possible to obtain so much."[119] The Sciences Po governing board approved the deal in early September; the Provisional Government followed suit a few days later; and then came the flood of ordinances and decrees.[120]

Consider how much, indeed, Sciences Po had been able to obtain: parity or near parity on the FNSP board, a controlling hand in the IEP's finances, a say in its pedagogical affairs, and even a voice, however faint, in the governance of ENA. Not least, the state had named two Sciences Po old-timers, Siegfried and Seydoux, to pilot the new FNSP-IEP complex.

The tidings got even better as the new machinery cranked into motion. In the event, the actual size of the FNSP board was set at twenty-seven, conferring on state appointees a slim majority. But note whom the state designated as its representatives: the University professors Jules Basdevant and Jean-Jacques Chevallier, both onetime Sciences Po faculty; the conseiller d'état André Ségalat, a Sciences Po alumnus who had codirected with Debré a Sciences Po *écurie* at the beginning of the war. Add to this that the state's fifteen nominees included the director of the IEP himself, at the time Seydoux, and it becomes clear that the new FNSP board remained very much in the hands, not of the state's agents, but of Sciences Po loyalists, however reform-minded they might have been.[121]

The state's dominion over the IEP was greater, although far from undiluted. All senior faculty appointments required the sanction of the Ministère de l'Education. The selection of the junior faculty, however, remained the exclusive prerogative of the director, Seydoux, who was succeeded in the post by Chapsal in 1947. A new system of state scholarships was expected to leaven the elitism of the Sciences Po student body. The grants, while more numerous and generous than the old Boutmy scholarships, did not suffice to support students lacking other resources. Sciences Po remained a fees-based institution, its finances administered by a quasi-private Fondation, its students recruited from the ranks of the better-off. As such, it constituted an anomaly within the state-run University system.[122] True, the school no longer launched its students straight into the *grands corps*, that distinction having passed to ENA. But Sciences Po did contrive to make itself into a gateway school for would-be ENA students. Still partly private, still a critical way station in the civil-service training hierarchy, in both respects the new Sciences Po looked much like the old.

Yet, at the same time, much had changed. The IEP was now in name and, to a degree, in fact a state institution. Of greater importance, the education it had to offer was more professional in cast than it had ever been. To be sure, the school still cared about imparting a general, liberal culture to its students, but that liberalism was becoming ever more interventionist in skew.

Sciences Po had long made a practice of inviting serving civil servants to teach courses. That was how Bloch-Lainé and Sauvy had come to join the faculty in the Occupation years, and the two continued to teach at the school into the Liberation era, now no longer the young turks they had once been but the acknowledged architects of a new, modernizing state. Nor were they exceptional cases. Sciences Po welcomed Fourastié and Laroque to its teaching ranks in the postwar era and Pierre Massé too, head of the state-run Electricité de France and a future director of the Plan.[123] A member of the class of 1962 who went on to prepare for the ENA entrance exam remembers the technocratic partiality of the instruction he received:

> And so progressively, I came to embrace the values proposed to us.... That is, that in our country there are problems, and to deal with them, there is a State. This State has a certain legitimacy, a technical capacity which is called upon to resolve these problems.[124]

To be sure, the school also called back to its teaching ranks old hands like Jacques Rueff, who remained an unregenerate free marketeer, scoffing at Keynes in class as "un zozo." But Keynes's star was very much on the rise, Rueff's derision notwithstanding. In 1946–1947, François Perroux taught a course on the history of economic doctrines that featured, as Perroux himself put it, "a confrontation... between neoclassical theory and Keynesian theory." All first-year students, moreover, were required to take an introductory lecture in political economy, and Keynesianism, not laissez-faire orthodoxy, enjoyed pride of place on the syllabus, at least as political scientist Jean

Meynaud constructed it in the late 1940s. According to one historian, Keynesian theory was not just taught and studied at Sciences Po but "impregnated the courses and exposés," indeed, the entire program of study.[125]

The can-do Keyensian *fonctionnaire*, however, was not the sole model of professionalism the school held up to students. The IEP hired and promoted a cohort of academic social scientists who would leave an enduring imprint on their field. The names of Chapsal and Meynaud have been mentioned. Maurice Duverger joined the faculty after the war. Jean Stoetzel was named professor in 1946 and Jean Touchard promoted to the same rank the following year. Such high-caliber personnel made Sciences Po the best place in postwar France for systematic research into things political, from elections to polling studies to political theory.

François Goguel, who joined the IEP professorate in 1948, carried forward Siegfried's pioneering explorations in electoral geography, elevating psephological analysis into a subdiscipline in its own right, complete with the maps, charts, and statistical tables to prove its scientific rigor. The text that made Goguel's academic reputation, *La Politique des partis sous la Troisième République*, appeared in 1946. The book was more impressionistic than a good deal of his later work (it appears that much of it was composed while he sat out the war in a German POW camp). But it had a serious argument to make, one that would echo across Goguel's entire career. A close analysis of Third Republic voting patterns, he demonstrated, revealed the existence of two political parties in France, a party of order and a party of movement. Each party—what was at issue, in fact, was less an actual partisan formation than a Weltanschauung or temperament—had its own network of regional strongholds, and this geography, though not invariable, had changed little over time. Jean-Marie Domenach, who reviewed the book for *Esprit*, had no trouble deciphering what he took to be Goguel's core message. Under the Third Republic, the close balance of the two parties had immobilized public life, but now, in the postwar era, a moment of potential "unblocking" had come. Push on with "the anticapitalist revolution," Domenach exhorted, promote "the technical aspect of things" and the worker's cause, make France all in all a more civic-minded place, and then the "established order" (or, as Mounier himself used to call it, "the established disorder") would yield at last to the forces of movement.[126]

Not all of Goguel's colleagues, of course, understood electoral politics in quite the same geography-based, progressive-minded terms, not Jean Stoetzel for one. Stoetzel's experiments in polling disclosed a political reality much more indeterminate than Goguel's. There was a floating vote, not fixed in its commitments, and such fluidity left opinion-shaping politicians critical room for maneuver.[127] As for progress, Stoetzel, like Goguel, believed in *la technique* but not in the service of anticapitalism. After the war, Stoetzel made a serious effort to modernize IFOP's polling equipment, acquiring the latest punch-card processing machinery and then, in 1956, a computer. IFOP's house publication, *Sondages*, got an update as well. Alain Girard, Stoetzel's colleague from Fondation Carrel days, was brought on board as managing editor.[128] All such innovations, of course, cost money. IFOP contracted out its services to American military authorities during the Liberation. It conducted listener polls for state radio in the late forties. From here, it was but a short jump to market research pure and simple, and IFOP took the leap in the 1950s, partnering with the Institut pour l'étude des marchés en France et à l'étranger to set up IFOP-Etmar. The alliance proved a lucrative one. IFOP-Etmar supplied the private sector, now in full expansion, with the marketing expertise it more than ever needed, and the private sector returned the favor, paying IFOP-Etmar handsomely for its services.[129]

Goguel did not much care for opinion polling, which he found lacking in the human touch, but Stoetzel had an ally on the Sciences Po faculty in Raymond Aron. Aron, like Stoetzel, became a Sciences Po professor in 1946, teaching a regular course on elites and social classes.[130] It is, of course, as a political theorist that Aron, the social scientist, is best remembered. Young *normaliens* might tout Sartre, but Sciences Po had a master thinker of its own in Aron. And while Sartre cited Marx, Aron answered back, invoking the classics of continental social thought: Durkheim, Weber, and, not least of all, Tocqueville.[131] Even in the "soft" discipline of social theory, the postwar Sciences Po made its mark.

The school might well imagine itself the premier social-science institution in France. It had the teaching staff to make the case, and it
had the institutional connections as well. The first national political
science organization in France, the Association française de science
politique, was founded in 1949. Siegfried presided over the new organ,
succeeded by Chevallier (who had rejoined the Sciences Po faculty by
then) and Goguel. From 1951, the Association published the *Revue
française de science politique*, for many years the sole specialist periodical of its kind. Here too the Sciences Po imprimatur was evident.
School faculty edited the journal—Meynaud and Georges Lavau, for
example—and, over time, the publications of the FNSP's research
laboratories came to dominate its pages. Stoetzel, alongside half a
dozen Sciences Po colleagues, served on the RFSP's editorial board.
In 1959, however, Stoetzel branched out to found a journal more in
tune with his own intellectual interests, the *Revue française de sociologie*,
which in due course became a flagship publication in its own right.[132]

Not least of all, the ambience of Sciences Po had undergone a
none too subtle transformation. Students remained conventional in
dress, but gone was the buttoned-up formality of the 1930s, the bowler
hats and umbrellas. The fashion détente had its effect even on the
faculty. Chapsal pedaled to work on a bicycle, clips around his ankles,
exuding the rough-and-ready air of the Boy Scout.[133] That Sciences
Po had become less snobbish did not mean, of course, that it was any
the less an establishment institution. After all, both Aron and Siegfried were regular columnists at France's most prestigious conservative daily, *Le Figaro*. But the school's enduring establishment bias was
now tempered by a more questing, even religious impulse. Chevallier
had left Uriage days long behind, yet not altogether, transmuting the
disciplined spiritualism that had been an Uriage hallmark into a less
authority-minded but still Christian commitment. "Liberal, Christian-
Democrat": that was how the future Russianist Alain Besançon, then
a student, characterized Chevallier, concluding, "such was the tone of
the school." The scoutlike Chapsal, it was rumored, was active in the
affairs of his local parish church. And Goguel published his analyses
of the first postwar elections in the pages of Mounier's *Esprit*. The
Christian existentialism that *Esprit* dealt in may or may not have ap-

pealed to all Sciences Po undergraduates, but it did to at least one: Pierre Elliot Trudeau.[134]

Sciences Po did more than just survive the Liberation. It beat back a Left offensive and then, working in close collaboration with a cadre of sympathetic state negotiators, remade itself. Critics had inveighed against the school's general subservience to business interests, outmoded liberalism, and snobbish dilettantism. The school now changed its orientation, distancing itself from the private sector in favor of the University and state administration. The institution that resulted was a peculiar hybrid. In principle, Sciences Po had been absorbed into the state, but in practice it retained considerable autonomy. Along the way, the school sharpened its professional and technocratic profile. As in prewar days, aspirants to the nation's senior administrative ranks had to pass through its classrooms, but a Sciences Po education was no longer what it once was. The school remained a training ground for the privileged few, but the elite it formed were to be the best and brightest, educated by political scientists and civil-service experts to wield the instruments of state. A general, liberal culture counted as always: a sense of the Western tradition and of France's special place in it. But there were now new realities and values to contend with—efficiency, modernity, grandeur.

It is tempting to tell the story of the Liberation as a moment of rupture, but that is not Sciences Po's story. Still, perhaps it was ENA's. ENA did not want to be a school in the traditional sense. Its three-year curriculum placed a special and novel emphasis on lessons learned outside the classroom. All first-year students were required to perform internships in a provincial prefecture; and all third-year students had to spend time working at a business, whether in the public or private sector.[135] It is not hard to sort out the intent behind such arrangements. Book learning was fine, but France's future *hauts fonctionnaires* needed more than theoretical knowledge: they needed the kind of practical know-how that came from firsthand contact with the hard realities of administrative decision-making. It mattered too that France's future civil servants knew something of the nation, not just the well-appointed ministries of the capital city, but the more modest offices of *la France profonde*, where real-life problems got solved. A man of decision who understood the nation's problems not just in the abstract but from the ground up: such was the model of the new-style civil servant ENA meant to incubate.

There was a Resistance flavoring to the school's insistence on action-oriented service to the nation. Indeed, ENA, in its first years, made an extra effort to recruit former résistants to student ranks and not without success. Every incoming class had the right to vote itself a nickname, and the first class at ENA chose to call itself "Fighting France." Simon Nora was a member of that rather select group, eighty-six students in all, and he remembered the Resistance spirit then so strong at the school: "At the Liberation, I moved over almost directly from the maquis to ENA, and I have to say that I did not feel out of my element."[136]

Indeed, the best-informed studies of the school present it as in effect a Resistance creation, a practical working out of principles embodied in the CNR charter.[137] The evidence to back up such a claim is powerful. ENA, after all, was the brainchild of Michel Debré, a key member of the CGE. The school's director in its first twenty years was Henri Bourdeau de Fontenay, like Debré a distinguished résistant, as were a number of ENA faculty, as we will see.

So it may be true that Sciences Po (however spruced up) was something of a holdover from the past, but not so the brand-new Ecole nationale d'administration. This way of looking at the matter, though, exaggerates the differences between the two schools. There were, in fact, points of intersection between them. First, at the teaching level: like Sciences Po, ENA did not have a full-time faculty but invited wise old hands—both academics and civil servants—to teach classes in their particular area of expertise. Louis Armand, director of the SNCF (and a Resistance veteran), was appointed to lecture on technology. Aron was brought on board just after the war to offer a survey in the history of political ideas that devoted several weeks to the explication of Keynes's ideas. Aron persuaded the ENA administration to hire Pierre Uri as well. Uri, like the others, taught what he knew, a course on national revenue, which was attended by at least one future minister of finance: Valéry Giscard d'Estaing.[138] The likes of Armand and Uri were soon joined by other men of experience: Wilfrid Baumgartner, Jean Fourastié, Jean-François Gravier.[139] ENA made sure, in a word, that its students were exposed to the doctrines, practices, and personalities that were shaping the new postwar state. At the same time, it bears pointing out how many ENA faculty—Aron, Baumgart-ner, Fourastié—also had IEP connections.

The same may be said of the students. ENA's first classes included a fair share of young people who had graduated from Resistance ac-tivism rather than from a *grande école*. But that moment passed, and the *grandes écoles* in due course reclaimed their preeminence. In the 1950s and 1960s, an estimated three-quarters of students admitted to ENA had studied at Sciences Po.[140] But this ought not come as a sur-prise. Sciences Po adjusted its "stable system," now to prepare stu-dents for the ENA admissions exam, and the exam itself, a mix of written and oral exercises, was just the sort of thing Sciences Po stu-dents excelled at. The writtens included a general culture essay along-side more technical material. And what of *le grand oral*, as it was called? An agency of the Ministère des Finances prepared a handbook to help ENA applicants prepare for the ordeal. The document featured short snippets that summed up the life and work of authors the stu-dents might be asked about. The author list included Camus and Sartre, both leading lights of the postwar intellectual Left, but the longest snippets were devoted to less typical figures: the eccentric theologian Teilhard de Chardin, Robert Brasillach, a fascist, and the Catholic novelist turned résistant Georges Bernanos.[141] The ENA man, it was plain enough, was expected to be more a cultured person than an intellectual, more a seeker in spiritual matters than a *gau-chiste engagé*.

But did the ENA student body in fact live up to such expectations? Surveys of ENA graduates from the postwar period are revealing in this respect. Students, it seems, favored the movies over theatergoing when it came to recreation. As for reading, it was newspapers, more than books, that were the preferred genre. Almost everyone kept up with *Le Monde*, and just under a third read *Le Figaro*. Intellectual peri-odicals were a minority taste, but it is interesting to note, nonetheless, where ENA students turned when they were in the mood for chal-lenging reading. Pierre Bourdieu has made the claim that it was *Esprit* that they liked best, though it has been countered that *Esprit* was the preference of just a handful and that in the matter of periodical reading the real student favorite was in fact the mendésiste *L'Express* (which began publishing in 1953).[142] Now, the mendésisme of *L'Express* was not the socialist dirigisme Pierre Mendès France had pushed so hard for immediately after the war. It was, rather, a modernizing creed, youthful but realistic, that promised a reconciliation of planification and the marketplace. Such then was the "spirit" of the ENA student body in its first, postwar incarnation: a pragmatic, growth-oriented statism that was leavened by a high-minded, not to say spiritual, earnestness.

It is hard to affix a political label to such a potpourri. It was not classic Right, which was much more favorable to private enterprise. But neither was it communist: the first classes at ENA included a handful of communist students, but the state in due course clamped down on the admissions process. Post-1947, "the communist Enarque," never a common breed, became a rare bird indeed.[143] In a sense, as one historian of ENA has put it, the peculiar "ideological syncretism" that characterized the school in its first years situated it outside politics: "above parties... *ni de droite, ni de gauche*."[144]

Such a conclusion prompts two further observations. The ENA creed—a faith in technocracy tempered by an above-politics public-spiritedness that at times shaded into a more or less explicit religiosity—was not so different from the new mood at the IEP. The two institutions shared not just faculty and a cadre of students who passed from one school to the next but also a certain tone. Or as one young man who attended both institutions put it: "The ideas I encountered at ENA ... differed hardly at all from those I had learned at Sciences Po."[145] Nor did the similarities end there. ENA, in the progressive spirit of the postwar era, admitted women, but then again, Sciences Po had been doing just that since the end of the Great War. And ENA, following the Sciences Po example, accreted a "stable" system of its own. ENA's "conférences," as they were called, were study groups led by school graduates who had gone on to better things. The atmosphere was personal and lively, but the common objective was serious: prepping students for the end-of-studies exam that determined their future prospects and placement in *la haute fonction publique*.[146] There was even a physical dimension to the symbiosis between the IEP and ENA. ENA set up its headquarters, provisional at first, on the rue des Saints-Pères. Debré expected the school to relocate to Versailles, but the move in the end never took place. The rue des Saints-Pères, as it turns out, was just one street over from the rue Saint-Guillaume. The Ecole nationale d'administration and Sciences Po backed onto each other. Students graduating from one institution to the next had but to cross a common courtyard.

The second observation touches on ENA's political antecedents. The phrase *ni de droite, ni de gauche* gives a moment's pause, for it evokes, not so much the moral clarity of the Resistance, as the more ambiguous commitments of 1930s nonconformism. And, in fact, the ENA faculty contained a sprinkling of onetime political odd men out: Fourastié's past was anchored in Catholic Action; the young Gravier, as we have seen, straddled the border between a Christian personalism and the Maurrasian Right; and Uri was a Perroux acolyte. In wartime, Fourastié found employment as a Vichy civil servant and Gravier as a researcher at the Fondation Carrel. It is worth remembering in this context Nora's Uriage connection. To be sure, the Uriage men Nora joined forces with were pulling away from Vichy en route into the Resistance, but they still thought of themselves, Uriage-style, as a leadership elite with a moral mission to regenerate a nation grown decadent. Nora was himself a convinced partisan of leadership education on the Uriage model. ENA was not quite the quasi-monastic institution he had envisioned, but it was close enough to excite his enthusiasm. Uriage veterans, moreover, might well take satisfaction in the kind of student that ENA trained. To be sure, ENA products took too serious an interest in the movies, but they did know their Teilhard. They were also readers of *Esprit* and *Le Monde*, both edited by men, Emmanuel Mounier and Hubert Beuve-Méry, with an insider's knowledge of what Uriage had been all about.

None of this is to say that ENA was not a Resistance creation. It was that, but the school was not constructed out of nothing. It was built on intellectual foundations laid in the 1930s. Debré himself, of course, was in part a product of that decade's technocratic awakening. Catholic Action and nonconformism too, it has been suggested here, made a contribution to shaping the new school's personality. This intellectual mix lived on after the war, cycled through the Resistance of course, but cycled through Vichy as well.

The cycling-through process, however, and this point must be insisted upon, was transformative. Thirties critiques of national decline were laced with an antiparliamentarism that in too many cases spilled into a rejection of republican democracy itself. Come the Liberation, however, and the antidemocratic impulses of old had much dissipated. "Neither right nor left" in the 1930s had meant a rejection of the "established disorder," a search for a third way between parliamentary democracy and its pagan, state-worshipping rivals: communism and fascism. In the 1940s and 1950s, ENA's above-politics stance placed it between mendésisme on the Left and a Giscard-style progressive conservatism on the Right.[147] There was no flirting with authoritarianism here, just a commitment to a France that would be modern, strong, and republican at the same time.

Emile Boutmy had committed himself to endowing France with a cohesive and high-minded civil-service elite and enjoyed remarkable success at the enterprise. The *hauts fonctionnaires* schooled at Boutmy's Sciences Po, however, were not always at home in the Republic they served. It is not necessary to rehearse again the multiple defects they imputed to the old Republic—incompetence, petty-mindedness, demagoguery. The disaffection ran so deep that few senior civil servants mourned the passing of the regime in 1940. Few too resisted the temptations of Vichy authoritarianism. Yet, for a saving remnant, the Occupation years had a sobering effect. Democracy was embraced as France's destiny. The problem was to create a new Republic armored against the weaknesses of the old. Such an agenda took material form in the new scaffolding of elite education erected at the Liberation: the FNSP, IEP, ENA. The result was a new deal for *la haute fonction publique*: an expanded and more activist role in the management of national affairs. *La haute fonction publique* in return extended to democratic institutions an allegiance it had earlier withheld or extended but halfheartedly.

Sciences Po's remaking formed a critical piece of this historic compromise. The Left played a role in the process, but it was a walk-on part that consisted in the main of goading others to action. The principal architects of the transformation were, rather, the school's own administration, Roger Seydoux in the lead, seconded by civil servants like Michel Debré. Seydoux had from the outset wanted to professionalize Sciences Po: to raise academic standards for students, to recruit teachers who understood the technocratic currents of the day, to draw the school within the University's orbit. The upheaval of the Liberation forced on Sciences Po a more intimate relationship with the state than it would otherwise have sought, but in practice the seminationalization of the school turned out to be less a demotion than, in Debré's own words, a veritable "consecration." Little wonder, as so many of the parties to the deal, on the state's side as on the school's, were themselves distinguished Sciences Po alumni. This was a conservative reform, worked out among establishment insiders. And it was a reform freighted with consequence, which helped to stabilize democratic institutions even as it edged French democracy away from the revolutionary republicanism that lay at its origins.

The French state was redesigned at the Liberation, but how is a change so major to be evaluated? The place to start is the CNR program, which mandated much of what was in fact accomplished at the war's end: nationalizations, planning, the setting up of a national Social Security system. The creation of ENA did not figure in the program's provisions, but historians of the institution are insistent that it might just as well have, so well did the school answer to the preoccupations and concerns of the program's drafters.

But the CNR charter was silent on many things, and on many others it was not specific as to how reform was to be implemented. Into the gap between intention and realization spilled politics. The Left had a clear vision of how the new postwar order should look. Mendès France and André Philip wanted planning on the dirigiste model with the state making the major decisions and imposing its will through a network of resource allocation agencies. Social Security was meant to be national and comprehensive. In the domain of population policy, the CNRS coveted what remained of the old Fondation Carrel; and in the domain of elite education, the hope was to displace Sciences Po outright, leaving the brand-new Ecole nationale d'administration in full control.

Yet this is not how things worked out. Liberation-era France got a planning apparatus, but it operated more by persuasion—*concertation* in the language of the day—than by directive. The Social Security system fragmented along corporatist lines; the family allowance regime, a critical piece of the system, was broken off and administered apart; and population matters ended up in the hands, not of the CNRS, but of INED. As for Sciences Po, it was not eliminated at all but managed with remarkable success to assure itself a pivotal role in the new elite-education hierarchy.

How are these outcomes to be accounted for? The place to begin is with the remarkable cadre of institution builders who got their chance at the Liberation: Bloch-Lainé, Closon, Debré (father and son), Laroque, Monnet, Sauvy, and many others. Not one was a man of the classic Left. They had projects of their own and proved themselves past masters at infighting.

But why should they have succeeded where Georges Cogniot, Mendès France, and André Philip did not? In many instances, it was General de Gaulle himself who made the difference. He intervened in a conclusive manner at critical junctures: plumping for Pleven over Mendès France in the reflation versus austerity conflict, giving Monnet the nod to organize the Commissariat au Plan, sanctioning a separate family allowance regime, appointing Debré to craft an elite education project to counter Cogniot's. De Gaulle did not micromanage, but he made his presence felt across a wide spectrum of policy areas.

Yet it should not be thought that the remaking of the French state was altogether an inside job. The part played by trade unions in this connection has been well understood. Monnet was at pains to bring union men into the planning process, though in minority roles for the most part. Laroque turned to union representatives to help manage the Social Security system, and here they were not just cast as supernumeraries but were essential players. Less often commented upon, however, was the centrality of the MRP in shaping France's postwar new deal. Neither the fragmentation of the Social Security system nor the familist alignment of the new welfare state would have happened as they did without the intercessions of a resurgent christian democracy. The family movement too weighed in on these issues, though, now hobbled by its Vichyite associations, it was no longer in a position to make such a decisive difference as in days gone by.

Then there was the overall international conjuncture, far more favorable to a moderate statism than to dirigiste projects of a left-wing cast. Anticommunism, always a feature of the political landscape, deepened with the intensification of the Cold War, marginalizing the PCF and weakening the Left overall in the process. Nor did the Communists help themselves. They hunkered down in a paranoid isolation, withdrawing from participation in state institutions and backing strike waves in 1947 and 1948 that incited a repressive backlash. Even as the Left fractured, the institution builders, no one more than Monnet, got a leg up when the United States announced the Marshall Plan, helping to supply the cash necessary to make France's own Plan work.

None of this, however, should detract from the institution builders' achievement. They built and built well. The argument has been made here, however, that they did not build from scratch but worked with institutions and policies already in place. They struck up partnerships with established power centers like the Ministère des Finances and Sciences Po, once-hidebound institutions that themselves had begun to evolve, casting off the laissez-faire orthodoxies of old in favor of more technocratic and Keynesian approaches. Yet even institutions less well anchored were seen to have their uses, and this despite the fact that many of them—the SNS, the Fondation Carrel, the Comité consultatif de la Famille—came freighted with a Vichyite taint. It was essential, of course, to cleanse such bodies: to purge them of their Vichy-era racism and authoritarianism. This was done, albeit with more thoroughness in certain cases than in others. The institution builders, then, did not want a clean sweep but looked to work with the powers-that-be, provided the powers were themselves ready for a change. Such a strategy built consensus, making allies out of people and interests that the Left's more radical projects turned into foot-draggers, if not outright enemies.

Yet the institution builders, though careful to build on the past, did not hesitate to deploy a rhetoric of fresh beginnings. France, postwar, had embarked on a new path, one of planned expansion that would re-energize a nation grown decadent and then crushed by defeat. A radiant future now lay ahead, modern, productive, innovative. And that future would be managed by new men, social scientists and civil servants who brought to public life hard-won qualities tempered in the fires of the Resistance: a new moral earnestness and disinterested commitment to the welfare of the whole. It helped, of course, that men like Monnet, Fourastié, and Sauvy were not just innovators but superb phrasemakers as well. Indeed, a number of their verbal inventions still resonate to the present day: the "concerted economy," "les trente glorieuses," "the Third World." They knew, moreover, how to get their message of renewal across, more often than not finding in the mainstream press—from *Le Monde* to *France-Soir* to *Le Figaro*—welcome allies. Here then was a project above politics. Its backers were not party men but prophets who promised to make the nation great again, to marry France to the twentieth century. Such talk resonated with a nation that had experienced defeat and Occupation and that yearned for a new birth. Why stick with the Left under such circumstances, a Left committed to a heavy-handed dirigisme and policies of collective austerity that conjured unwelcome images of the Soviet Union?

The institution builders' parthenogenic rhetoric was in part so effective because of what it concealed, the institution builders' own deep debt to the past. Start with the rhetoric itself. The France it meant to repudiate was a caricatured version of the Third Republic, a France of peasants and shopkeepers, of small-minded individualists who looked after themselves first and foremost. Such folk held the state in deep suspicion, but they were fortunate in that public institutions—a weak party system, a parliament populated by careerist politicians, and a corrupt press—made concerted state action all but impossible. The result was immobilism, a public paralysis that might have served the interests of individualists, careerists, and money-grubbers but that ill served the nation as a whole when it came to confront the great challenges of the thirties—the depression and the rise of fascism. But France was blessed in the postwar era by the crystallization of a new leadership elite that eschewed the individualism of old in favor of teamwork. The members of this new elite were self-less young men, risk takers who represented the very antithesis of the talkers and paper pushers who had brought public life to such a low ebb in the thirties. And they were a high-minded lot, pure and earnest, committed to family and nation, neither Right nor Left. Such rhetoric, need it be said, was not altogether new. It echoed with the tropes of 1930s nonconformism. But then again, why should there be any surprise here? For the institution builders themselves with an uncanny frequency had been active in the thirties, militating in various dissident milieus, whether nonconformist, Catholic, or technocratic.

This is not to say that the postwar overhaul of state institutions was the realization plain and simple of 1930s dreams. Those dreams had been reshaped by subsequent experience, but the subsequent experience in question was not always what postwar mythmaking might lead one to expect. To be sure, many thirties dissidents made straight for the Resistance. De Gaulle himself is a prime example. He was an above-party nationalist who never cared for the hairsplitting partisanship of Third Republic parliamentarism; he was a soldier who reflected hard in an era of führers and duces on just what real leadership meant;[148] and he was a military modernizer who, unlike stick-in-the-mud superiors, had foreseen the importance of mechanized warfare. But for every first-hour résistant, there was also someone willing to give Vichy a try. The trial period might have been short-lived, as in the cases of Laroque, Uri, and Perroux, the former two then heading into the Resistance, the latter settling into a more wait-and-see stance. Or it might have lasted the duration of the war, as with Fourastié and Sauvy. This is not to say that Fourastié or Sauvy was ever a Vichyite enthusiast, just that they worked in the regime's administrative apparatus without interruption.

So what? one might ask. The Vichy years afforded a number of onetime dissidents a chance to begin the process of institutional overhaul they had spent the preceding decade polemicizing about. The result was institutional experiments like Uriage and the Fondation Carrel, the first two Plans, and the SNS. Vichy left a legacy of institutions, policies, and personnel that postwar institution builders could not bring themselves to discard outright, in part because it was a legacy the institution builders, at least some of them, had had a hand in constructing.

Lest there be any misunderstanding, it is worth saying again that the Vichy legacy, such as it was, was not taken up unregenerate. The war had taught that France's future lay in a democratic Republic. It was a lesson even de Gaulle himself had had to learn. He got into the fight as a general rallying any and all prepared to answer his call to Resistance. "Honor and Fatherland" was the slogan he bandied, a military motto without republican connotation. But, by the fall of 1941, de Gaulle had begun to evolve. It was now for the Republic that Free France fought, and it did so in the name of "Liberty-Equality-Fraternity."[149] De Gaulle himself in 1943 would invite representatives from the political parties of Third Republic days to work with him, all in the interests of building a new national consensus. The makers of the postwar state might well want to salvage institutions from the Vichy era, but they would have to redesign them to function within a new democratic republican order. This meant cleaning them up: democratizing them, purging the most compromised personnel, muting the racism.

The postwar French state then was a new birth but not such a new birth as all the rhetoric might suggest. It had a mixed ancestry, and the mottled character of its pedigree helps to explain its very success. Most of the institutions discussed above—the Plan, Social Security, INSEE, INED, ENA—continue to function right down to the present. Politicians tinker with them at their peril. On more than one occasion in recent history, projects to pare down Social Security benefits have brought trade unions into the street. But, of course, organized labor has a stake, institutional as well as financial, moral as well as material, in how the Social Security system works, and that stake dates back to the Liberation era. It is just such a genealogy that invites interpretations of the postwar state as social democratic in inspiration. Such interpretations are not so much wrong as one-sided. For there were many other constituencies beside labor who could see their interests in the new postwar order: Catholics, *hauts fonctionnaires*, pronatalists, technocrats, and so on. These were not left-wing constituencies. On the contrary, a number of them had felt a deep distaste for the institutions of the old Third Republic, a sense of alienation that during the war tempted many for varying periods into the Vichy orbit. But now, with the coming of the postwar order, a Republic took shape that they could live with, which in fact they themselves had played a role in shaping.

Republican institutions in France have never been more stable than they are today. It is not just that the Left has lost much of its erstwhile revolutionary zeal but that the Right too, Jean-Marie Le Pen notwithstanding, has tempered its long-standing antidemocratic animus. Democratic stabilization has been a long process with many twists and bends in the road. The postwar moment, in all its complexity, was one such turning point. In important respects, it was a turning point of less significance to the Left than to the Right. Constituencies once doubtful about the virtues of republican democracy—the Church, for example or *la haute fonction publique*—were brought on board in a historic compromise. The deal, of course, came at a price. Democratic institutions enjoyed newfound and much-needed backing, but the center of gravity of republican life made an architectonic shift in the process: away from the parliamentary forms of old toward a new elite-managed statism.

It is de Gaulle's presidential Fifth Republic that is often credited with effecting this shift. Postwar parliaments after all continued to go about their business much as they had under the old Third Republic. Yet a different line of argument has been developed here. Sometimes in quiet ways, sometimes to great fanfare, the state had already begun to assert its prerogatives before de Gaulle's return to power in 1958, and to this extent the Fifth Republic did not so much inaugurate a new era as consummate a process of *étatisation* that had gotten its start at the Liberation, if not even before that.

Part II

A CULTURE OF QUALITY

No state in Europe devotes a greater proportion of its resources to the promotion of the arts than France. The construction of *l'état culturel*, as it has sometimes been called, took place in stages, and it is easy enough to identify, looking backward, critical moments in the process: the first Mitterrand presidency, which set aside an unprecedented 1 percent of the nation's budget for cultural affairs; André Malraux's groundbreaking tenure from 1959 to 1969 as France's first minister of culture; the Popular Front government of Léon Blum, which elevated state intervention in the arts, hitherto a hit-or-miss affair, into a matter of coherent public policy.

Such a genealogy gives short shrift to the Liberation era, and yet the immediate postwar years saw a sea change in the French state's relations to culture. French theater, for so long monopolized by the Parisian stage, decentralized. No one did more to advance this cause than Underdirector of Theater and Music Jeanne Laurent, who committed substantial state subsidies to the creation of five regional theaters: the Centre dramatique national de l'Est, founded in 1947 under the direction, after some initial missteps, of André Clavé; the CDN de Saint-Etienne, launched the following year under the direction of Jean Dasté; and so on. The aim was to bring the greatest works of French theater to less privileged, provincial audiences. A similar motive inspired Laurent's determined backing of Jean Vilar, who was appointed director of France's Théâtre national populaire (TNP) in 1951. And Vilar did not disappoint. He conceived of the national theater as a "service public" akin to the state-run Electricité de France and set about devising schemes to deliver a quality product to as wide a public as possible. Quality product, of course, meant masterpieces like the memorable *Le Cid*, which Vilar produced to great acclaim in his first season as TNP chief. For the classics of the French stage, the postwar years were, indeed, a veritable "golden age."[1]

The notion of a postwar golden age has been applied to the film industry as well.[2] The moviegoing public reached a peak of 430 million in 1947, dipping after that, and then stabilizing at around 400 million through the decade of the fifties, and it was not just Hollywood films that audiences went to see. France's movie industry flourished in the late forties and fifties, turning out roughly 150 pictures per year, well-crafted films that boosters with pride (and later New Wave critics with derision) lauded as a "cinéma de qualité." France's cinematic vitality owed more than a little to concerted state policy. In October 1946, the Centre national de la cinématographie (CNC) was created, a parastatal body run by a senior civil servant working in collaboration with a board of movie-industry representatives. The CNC performed a range of corporate functions, from issuing professional identity cards to monitoring box-office receipts. The state organized the motion-picture business, and it acted to keep foreign competitors, principally the United States, at bay. In the thirties, France had set a numerical ceiling on film imports. After the war, a new strategy was developed: reserving a minimum percentage of screen time for French-made movies. A first round of talks with the United States yielded the Blum-Byrnes accord of 1946. As we have seen, the principal concern of France's negotiator, Léon Blum, was to attract American investment credits, and as a result he did not drive a hard bargain on movie issues. Still, the United States did accede to the new principle of a screen-time quota, although the actual quota set was not high: French films were guaranteed just four weeks per quarter of screen time. In the wake of industrywide protests, a second round of negotiations was undertaken in 1948, raising the quota to five weeks per quarter. That same year, the government enacted a so-called *loi d'aide*. The law imposed a pair of new cinema taxes, one on movie producers, one on ticket purchasers, pledging that the revenues generated would be reinvested in the film industry itself. At a stroke, the French state made itself a major movie investor.

The state's policy vis-à-vis the radio industry was more interventionist still. In the prewar era, France boasted a dozen or so private stations; at the Liberation, all were nationalized. The national radio service, known first as the RDF (Radiodiffusion française) and then as the RTF (Radiotélévision française), never achieved the autonomous corporate status enjoyed by its British counterpart, the BBC. Instead, the state retained tight control. Radio administrators answered to bureaucratic higher-ups at the Ministère de l'Information and in the prime minister's office. The RTF's reach even extended beyond France's borders via a state-managed holding company, known in the postwar years as the Société financière de radiodiffusion (SOFIRAD), which held a controlling interest in a number of foreign stations, Radio Monte-Carlo among them. The RTF's near monopoly was disputed by a single, major competitor, the privately owned Radio Luxembourg, based just across France's northern frontier. Television was slow to make its way in France; in the meantime, radio ownership skyrocketed, the number of radio sets almost doubling from 5.3 to 10.1 million in the period from 1945 to 1957.[3] Little wonder that one radio professional was moved to call these years "the golden age of radio." What made the age all the more golden was the high-mindedness of RTF programming, which offered up the best that has been known and thought to audiences in a spirit of "radiophonic humanism."[4]

The institutional structures erected at the Liberation would endure for years to come, and a number still stand to the present day. The problem is what to make of the Liberation moment, with its penchant for the classics and cultural uplift, its rhetoric of quality, public service, and humanism? One interpretation accents the continuities between the Liberation moment and its Popular Front antecedents, the institutional achievements of the postwar era bringing to completion the experiment in socialist humanism begun under Blum.[5] A second, far less sympathetic interpretation denigrates the new postwar order as the brainchild of would-be cultural commissars, Jeanne Laurent in the lead, hell-bent on imposing minority tastes on an unsuspecting public. Worse, the very theater men to whom Laurent turned—Clavé, Dasté, Vilar—had all in preceding years been connected to a Vichy-sponsored arts group, Jeune France. From this perspective, the Liberation achievement looks less like the Popular Front revisited than the quasi-totalitarian concoction of administrative Leninists working in cahoots with Vichyite holdovers.[6]

Neither view quite captures the complexities and ambiguities of the Liberation moment. Socialists played a major part in the cultural new deal of the Liberation years, in particular in the redesign of the radio industry. Many of the institutional innovations of the Liberation era, on the other hand, had direct Vichy precursors, the CNC for example or the SOFIRAD, as will be seen. Not least of all, onetime servants of Vichy abound in all corners of the postwar arts establishment. Two caveats, however, are in order. Most of these onetime Vichyites had soured on the regime early on, passing in 1942 or 1943 over to the Resistance. They came from a variety of political milieus—Catholic Action, nonconformism, technocratic reformism. Democracy and even more so the Third Republic had not been to their liking in prewar days (a number would evolve away from this position over the course of the war itself), but few were outright fascists. A final point: there were converts to communism in the group, but the postwar cultural order was no communist stalking horse. On the contrary, its designers worked hard to confine communist influence and then, as the Cold War set in during the late forties, to eliminate it. The postwar order was not socialist, nor was it crypto-totalitarian. It represented rather a compromise that brought together a protean band—from Popular Front stalwarts to disillusioned Vichyites—behind a common program: the defense and illustration of French quality in a Europe under threat from rampant commercialization.

CHAPTER 4

Art and Commerce
in the Interwar Decades

In Search of a New Theater

France experienced a theater renaissance in the interwar decades, and Jacques Copeau was its acknowledged trailblazer. The four Paris-based directors known as the Cartel—Charles Dullin, Louis Jouvet, Gaston Baty, and Georges Pitoëff—carried Copeau's project forward, reworking it, making it their own. And a generation of younger, Copeau-trained acolytes relayed the master's promise of a new theater from the capital to the provinces, via itinerant troupes, both amateur and professional. Copeau and his emulators, different as they were in certain respects, shared a common set of dislikes, first and foremost for the boulevard theater. The typical boulevard play titillated with tales of sex and adultery but never went so far as to subvert conventional morality. Set design, direction, the actor's skill all took a back seat to sparkling dialogue that emphasized superficial wordplay over emotional depth. Critics had no trouble putting a face on the theater they so despised: it was that of Henry Bernstein, the French stage's most successful playwright in the interwar decades, renowned for the wit and eroticism of his work.[1]

To the likes of Dullin, the degrading onstage antics of boulevard theater were but the public face of a more deep-seated, behind-the-scenes corruption. Modern producers, he declared, had become mere profit seekers: men of the theater today, *garagistes* or stock-market gamblers tomorrow. They rented playhouses on spec, handed out cut-price tickets to drum up business, and hired actors, or rather stars, not for their talent but for their box-office draw. Amidst all the wheeling and dealing, Dullin wondered, what future was there for the great theaters of the boulevards but to fall "one by one... into the hands of foreigners."[2]

For the boulevard stage, Copeau and company manifested unalloyed contempt. They were critical, but less contemptuous, of naturalist theater. Naturalism's great pioneer and practitioner was the late-nineteenth-century actor/director Antoine. Antoine's naturalist theater took its themes from the commonplace experience of ordinary people. Such slice-of-life dramas called for an acting style more human, less posturing than in conventional theater, and it called for a realistic decor to match. In Antoine's favor, he had sought a cleansing break with mainstream forms. Against him, he had misunderstood the fundamental purpose of theater, which was "not to copy life" but to interpret it, even to transcend it.[3]

Here is where Copeau came in, restoring "soul" and "purity" to a theater corrupted by boulevard mercantilism, restoring the spectacular to a theater grown subservient to the mundane.[4] Copeau first made a mark in 1913 as founder and director of the experimental Théâtre du Vieux-Colombier. The theater closed down during the war but reopened afterward, Copeau adding an acting school to the enterprise. He grew ever more disgruntled with Parisian life, however, and in 1924 abandoned the Vieux-Colombier for rural Burgundy, taking with him a handful of young recruits known as the Copiaus.

Copeau's pursuit of purity led him to a thoroughgoing reconceptualization of the theatrical enterprise. The gilded splendor of the Italianate theater and the busyness of the boulevard stage were not for him. The Vieux-Colombier eschewed the customary theater chandelier in favor of more muted lighting. Copeau, a professed partisan of the *tréteau nu* or bare stage, simplified sets to the point of austerity. And he treated his actors not as stars but as troupers of equal standing, none with a special claim to any particular role. For Copeau, acting was not a matter of ego but of rigorous self-discipline. Diction mattered, of course, but he wanted players who could work with body as well as voice, for whom the text was not all. Vieux-Colombier students and the Copiaus after them were subjected to a regimen of gymnastics, mime, and improvisation. Copeau innovated in matters of repertoire as well.[5] Shakespeare, then little known to French theatergoers,[6] was a Copeau favorite. His production of *Twelfth Night*, indeed, was the crowning success of the Vieux-Colombier's opening season. Installed in rural Burgundy from the midtwenties, Copeau varied his offerings to appeal to village audiences. Molière was a reliable standard, so too plays that drew on the stock of Commedia dell'arte characters. And the occasional original piece was mixed in, such as *La Danse de la ville et des champs*, which told the seasons of country life through a mélange of stories, song, dance, and mime.[7]

Copeau, always a taskmaster, grew ever more exacting over time. In the aftermath of the war, he took to reading the memoirs of old soldiers like the Maréchal Foch and General Mangin, empathizing with their experience of command: "Those were true leaders. I understand that, I understand completely the souls of true leaders." Copeau underwent a full-dress religious conversion in the midtwenties, a reawakened faith redoubling the intensity of his near-monastic devotion to theater.[8] His single-mindedness at times created difficulties with colleagues and students, prompting them to strike out on their own. Copeau's former disciples, nonetheless, remained true to his innovating spirit, and as they migrated away from the master, the Copeau revolution cut a widening swath through the theater world.

Two of the Cartel directors, Dullin and Jouvet, were in fact veterans of the Vieux-Colombier's inaugural season. But what was the Cartel? More an informal alliance than an institutional reality. Dullin dates its origins from 1928. He staged an Aristophanes play that year and at curtain time for the dress rehearsal shut the theater doors, not allowing dilatory critics to enter. They retaliated, refusing to review or even to announce Dullin's program for the coming season. Baty, Jouvet, and Pitoëff rallied to Dullin, pledging to boycott the critics who boycotted Dullin. It seems, however, that Dullin's recollections were not quite precise. It was not in 1928 that the four directors first joined forces but the year preceding, when they published a manifesto in a theatrical journal, outlining common principles. The four pledged to coordinate programs and tours and to advertise together. Not least of all, they insisted on the importance of punctuality, and it was the strict application of that principle that got Dullin into difficulties the following year, putting the solidarity of the new Cartel to its first test.[9]

Behind the issue of punctuality lurked a more pressing and general concern: preserving the integrity of the theatrical performance against spell-breaking distractions. On this point—the stage's near-magical capacity to summon audiences out of the here and now—the Cartel directors revealed what they all owed to Copeau. They differed in the ways they pursued their common project, but in the end the differences counted for less than the similarities.

Dullin was above all a man of the classics: of Greek theater, the Elizabethans, Commedia dell'arte, and Molière. Yet he wanted to make the classics live again, renewed by a sense of spectacle that drew on all the elements of theater. Zone lighting, expressive but uncluttered set design, an ensemble cast—all such means, woven into a unified whole by the director's art, evoked a world of enchantment that brought new vitality to the masterpieces of the past. This was a collective endeavor, the work of trained and devoted craftsmen. Dullin insisted on the artisanal character of his enterprise. He named the theater he ran L'Atelier. And, alongside the theater, he organized an actors' workshop, which counted a young Vilar among its onetime students. The workshop curriculum—physical training, classes in improvisation and mime—bespoke Dullin's debt to Copeau. Indeed, the school's teacher of mime in the thirties was none other than a former Copiau, Emile Ducroux.[10]

Jouvet's debt to Copeau was more tempered but still evident. Jouvet did not care for elaborate or naturalistic stage design, preferring sets of an elegant simplicity, well lit and brightly colored. He was himself a physical actor of exceptional talent. But it was for language that Jouvet's theater is best remembered, the language above all of Jouvet's favorite playwright, Jean Giraudoux. All Giraudoux's major dramas, from *Siegfried* in 1928 to *La Folle de Chaillot* in 1945, premiered on Jouvet's stage, and all were composed in a sparkling, lyrical prose that none knew better than Jouvet how to phrase and deliver.[11] There was, moreover, more than a touch of nonconformism to Jouvet's repertoire, which included, in addition to Giraudoux's expanding oeuvre, Jules Romains's *Knock*. Giraudoux wrote of the pleasures of this world, of its passing beauties, of love and the briefness of life. But his plays often had an edge: *Siegfried* counseling Franco-German reconciliation, *La guerre de Troie n'aura pas lieu* (1935) warning (in vain) against the coming of war. They contained negative caricatures as well—petty-minded officials, sophistical intellectuals, real-estate speculators (*les mecs* as Giraudoux called them in *La Folle de Chaillot*)—who betrayed life in the name of abstractions or in pursuit of gain. Romains's *Knock* was biting in its own way, sending up the hygienic regimentation of modern life, personified in the character of Dr. Knock, a medical martinet who rattles off fantastic diagnoses and imposes no less fantastic cures on the credulous inhabitants of a country town.

Dullin's cult of craftsmanship, Jouvet's poetical nonconformism, both were protests against a mechanical-minded worldliness. Pitoëff and Baty protested too, weaving theatrical moods, dreamlike or sacramental, that stood in critical juxtaposition to the real. Pitoëff and his wife, Ludmilla, were Russian-born Armenians who had relocated to France, passing first through Switzerland. They made acquaintance along the way with the progressive theater of the day, the plays of Ibsen, Shaw, and Chekhov. But the "moderns" they presented to Paris audiences were moderns reinterpreted, the psychological highlighted over the social. Pitoëff played with light and shadow, with a bare-bones decor (a rug, a stick of furniture, a door framed by curtains), to sketch "states of the soul." The psychological intensity of Pitoëff's theater of evocation astounded playgoers, not least of all a young Robert Brasillach, who all but inserted himself into the Pitoëff family circle. It was not just audiences who were swept up by the Pitoëff magic. In the late twenties, Ludmilla played the lead role in Shaw's *Saint Joan*, an experience that brought on a "mystico-literary crisis," culminating in a revival of her own religious faith.[12]

Baty had no need of a return to faith. He was a Catholic believer from first to last, and it affected how he conceived the director's craft. He likened the theater to a religious experience that fused audience and players in worshipful communion. The ancient Greeks, pagan though they were, had understood the collective, reverential dimension of theater, until Socrates came along, spoiling the wonderment with questions and cavils. The mystery plays and liturgical dramas of medieval Europe had made theater holy once again, and the new spirit of communion outlived the Middle Ages thanks to the great playwrights of the Elizabethan stage and of Golden Age Spain. But a fresh generation of spoilers had arisen: Descartes, Luther, Calvin, who revolted against the proper order of things "in the name of the rights of reason and the individual."[13]

Baty saw it as his task to restore the communal order of theater. In France, Cartesian individualism had fed a joyless intellectualizing, which, in drama, found expression in the idolatry of the written word. Baty, however, meant to unseat "His Highness, the word." He wanted to create works of poetry, not prose, to communicate the ineffable. Baty's sets were simple but more expressive than stark; he made dramatic use of lighting, playing with silhouette and shadow for effect, inducing mood through color (including the celebrated Baty blue); he directed actors not to declaim their parts but to play them. The art of the metteur en scène, as Baty put it, was "not to line up words, but to order color, light, gesture and voice in order to create a world, alternative to the real and yet more beautiful."[14]

The breakup of the Vieux-Colombier troupe fed recruits to the Cartel. Copeau's Burgundy team began to fray in its turn with equally creative consequences. In April 1929, a chance encounter brought together onetime Copiau Léon Chancerel with Father Paul Doncoeur, founder of the elite branch of Catholic scouting, the *Routiers* or Rovers. Doncoeur invited Chancerel to put on a Christmas play, the parts assigned to a cast of Rover scouts. Chancerel rose to the challenge and was ready to go in time for the upcoming holiday season. So began, in the humble setting of a country barn, what came to be known as the Comédiens-Routiers.[15]

The enterprise was remarkable on several counts. The players were all amateurs, young men, often no more than teenagers. For many— Hubert Gignoux, Jean-Pierre Grenier, Olivier Hussenot, Maurice Jacquemont—the experience sparked a lifelong theatrical vocation (although not for François Bloch-Lainé, who, much as he enjoyed scouting theatricals, gave them up for a more earthbound career in administration and public finance).[16] In the Copeau spirit, Chancerel set up an acting school, putting together a faculty that included at least one ex-Copiau like himself, Jean Dasté. Chancerel's curriculum stressed acting with the body; students worked with masks to undercut reliance on verbal and facial expressivity. And it downplayed the importance of individual performance. Chancerel, like Copeau, was a fervent believer in "l'esprit de troupe," whether acting ensemble or scout patrol. The commitment informed his novel insistence on choral training. Comédiens-Routiers learned to sing, to chant, to recite in unison, the emphasis falling as much on rhythm as on clear articulation.[17]

Chancerel wanted his troupers to fuse into a single, expressive whole, but more: he wanted actors and audience to fuse, for Chancerel conceived the theater, much as did Baty, as a "communion" akin to the sacred Mass, priest and congregants drawn together in holy celebration.[18] Much like Baty, moreover, Chancerel venerated classical Greek theater and the great medieval mysteries. Here were dramas of an elemental simplicity, purified of all low artifice. Perform them in the same spirit, perform them at parish halls, around campfires, in country barns, and how could audiences not be transfigured? Chancerel put on an *Antigone des Routiers*, but his repertorial preferences ran more to sacred material than to the classical: Noels, Nativity scenes, Easter cycles. At times, the sacred spilled into the epic national. Chancerel composed a life of Jeanne d'Arc, performed on the steps of the Domrémy basilica in the spring of 1938.[19] A second Chancerel text, *Terre de France, Royaume de Marie*, debuted later that year for an outdoor, pilgrim audience at Lourdes. The play dramatized, in a series of tableaux, the Virgin's special attachment to France. At times, Chancerel's theater of faith and nation descended onto less uplifting terrain. A *Terre de France* tableau excoriated the "dullness" and "gray" of Protestantism, the maleficence of the philosophes, the hateful and angry deeds of 1793. A Nativity play included a scene of Mary preparing the infant Jesus's new bed as a chorus of scout angels recited the verse:

> Joseph cut down a beech tree
> For his cradle of wood
> The Jews will trim a beech tree
> For to build him a rood.[20]

But such sentiments come as no surprise from a man who penned a paean to Antonio Salazar (founder of the Catholic corporatist Estado Nuovo in Portugal) or who drew inspiration from the classics of the French nationalist school: Péguy, Barrès, Déroulède, Maurras.[21]

Chancerel's acting troupe was amateur, and not least of all it was itinerant, committed to bringing the marvels of the stage to modest folk, young and old, who might not otherwise have access. Pioneering as scout theater was in this respect, it was not unique. Jacquemont, from the midthirties Chancerel's second in command at the Comédiens-Routiers, hankered to turn professional. Chancerel did not share in such ambitions, prompting Jacquemont to strike out on his own. Dasté soon followed, and the pair, joined by Pierre Barbier and André Barsacq, went on to found the Théâtre des Quatre Saisons in 1936. The Quatre Saisons performed the standard Molière fare but dabbled in contemporary theater as well, introducing the work of Jean Anouilh, for example. And it took to the road, mounting scenery and an easy-to-assemble stage onto two trucks and touring the countryside.[22] A second troupe merits mention in this connection: André Clavé's Comédiens de la Roulotte. The company was so christened in 1936 by its founders, a band of former Bordeaux high schoolers transplanted to Paris. It was an amateur endeavor with all the enthusiasm and earnestness of youth, amplified by the moral ardor of its chief, Clavé, a pacifist Catholic who had militated in lycée days in the ranks of the Jeunesse étudiante chrétienne (JEC). Clavé in Paris was electrified by the Cartel's theatrical innovations, and, Bordelais that he was, dreamed of exporting them to non-Parisian audiences. Such dreams came to fruition but not until 1941, when the troupe, now joined by Vilar, embarked on its first provincial tour. La Roulotte on the road styled itself a company of strolling players, parading into town squares at noontime to trumpet that evening's performance.[23]

The revolution in theater that Copeau did so much to get started was a varied phenomenon that appealed to the serious Parisian theatergoer as well as to younger and less metropolitan audiences. It was professional and amateur by turns, city based and itinerant. But always it vaunted its purity of aesthetic purpose (as contrasted to the grubbing materialism of the boulevards) and above all its aspiration to poetic spectacle. The text had its place in the new theater, but director and troupe were the principals, the former in command of all the elements of stagecraft, the latter in command of body and voice. Working together, they summoned up an alternative reality, inviting audiences, popular as well as elite, to leave behind, if just for an evening, the coarseness of the everyday.

A movement that made such a to-do about its dissident and innovatory ambitions was bound to attract the attention of arts administrators with an eye to cultural reform. The Popular Front elevated the democratization of culture to a matter of high policy. The more popularizing aspects of the new theater impressed two Blum officials, Léo Lagrange (secretary of state for sport and leisure) and Jean Zay (minister of national education and fine arts), who acted to extend a dose of patronage. Lagrange doled out a modest but meaningful subsidy to Jacquemont and Dasté's Quatre Saisons. And Zay, in an effort to shake up a national theater grown too set in its ways, appointed Edouard Bourdet to the directorship of the Comédie Française in 1936. Bourdet took the mandate with the utmost seriousness, inviting Copeau and three of the Cartel directors—Baty, Dullin, and Jouvet—to put on productions for the house of Molière in the rejuvenating spirit they had made famous. One last item in this connection: the Popular Front proposed construction of a youth center, picking out a site on the boulevard Kellermann for the project. The building complex, which included a theater studio, was opened in connection with the Paris exposition of 1937. Chancerel was placed in charge of the studio, which in due course became the new home of the Comédiens-Routiers.[24]

These intersections, however, did not signify that the Popular Front had captured the new theater for its purposes. Baty, a monarchist, and the Catholic Chancerel remained refractory. Copeau as well. André Gide paid an interwar visit to the Copeau household and

came upon Copeau's son, Pascal, assembling "grotesque photomon-
tages" of Third Republic worthies. What was the explanation for such
rough handling? The worthies in question were known for their ani-
mosity to the ultra-right Action française. Gide reproached the senior
Copeau for permitting such spiteful behavior in a young person.
What if the opposing camp, Gide asked, caricatured Copeau and his
friends with the same mean-spiritedness? To which Copeau replied:
"We would in any event cut a more noble profile."[25] It is perhaps
worth remembering in this connection that Dullin's cleansing moral
rigor, his detestation of speculators, indeed, of all elements "foreign"
to the theater, came couched on occasion in the idiom of xenophobia.

Still, it would be a mistake twice over to think of the new theater as
chiefly right-wing in inspiration. A Christian faith mattered to many
of its practitioners but not always a Christian faith traditionalist in
cast. Scurrilous hounding by the ultra-nationalist press drove a Popular Front minister, Roger Salengro, to suicide in the fall of 1936.
Dullin and Georges Pitoëff signed a petition in protest of the Far
Right's disgraceful conduct that was published in the pages of a
christian-democratic newspaper, *L'Aube*.[26] Clavé's brand of Christianity was more progressive still. He was a young man of tender social
conscience and deep antiwar convictions. It was a pair of commitments that brought him within the orbit of a Catholic splinter party,
the Jeune République, which aligned itself with the Popular Front in
the name of economic reform and pacifist principle.[27]

Then there was Jouvet, who does not seem to have been religious
at all. He was a confirmed antifascist, signing two manifestos in 1935,
which made plain his views. Jouvet's antifascism, however, was not of
the standard-issue left-wing variety. Remember that his good friend
Jules Romains was not just a playwright but the moving spirit behind
the "Plan du 9 juillet," a curious document whose technocratic and
antiparliamentarist prescriptions appealed to nonconformists across
the political spectrum. Jouvet was also known to frequent the offices
of Gaston Bergery's *La Flèche*. Bergery's circle, as we have seen, had
backed the Popular Front, but its deep-seated hostility to communism and to war led it in subsequent years to back a policy of appease-

ment vis-à-vis Europe's dictators. *La Flèche*'s pacifism was a theme with evident appeal to the director of Giraudoux's *La guerre de Troie*.[28]

The new theater was not socialist humanist in orientation. Its center of moral gravity was more Christian than secular, running from the hard-edged Catholic rigorism of Baty to the more modulated and forward-looking credo of Clavé. Jouvet was the outlier, a man of radical associations, but even Jouvet's radicalism came with a maverick, nonconformist spin. Yet it was not politics so much as the fate of the French stage that mattered most to Copeau and company, and on this question a near unanimity reigned. The center-right Daladier administration, which took office in 1938, commissioned Dullin to draft a report on theater decentralization. "The theater must be cleansed"[29]: such was Dullin's principal conclusion, but the words might have been uttered by any of the era's noncommercial directors. The money changers had muscled their way into the temple of art, and the sooner they were chased out the better.

Cinema in Crisis

Film historians, echoing contemporaries, write of the fragmentation and "anarchy" that blighted the French movie industry in the 1930s. These were, indeed, hard times for filmmakers. The onset of the slump brought financial ruin to the largest movie studios: to Gaumont, which went under in 1934, and then to Pathé-Natan, which filed for bankruptcy the next year.[30] It did not help that the French state looked on cinema, not as an art, but as a taxable luxury, siphoning off up to two-fifths of gross receipts in taxes. And then there was French cinema's great rival, Hollywood. In 1933, up to 40 percent of the movies projected in France originated in the United States. Paramount, not content to compete from afar, established a beachhead on French soil early in the decade, the Studio de Saint-Maurice. The French government made a halfhearted attempt to contain the American invasion through imposition of a numerical ceiling on foreign films, the so-called *contingentement* system. French and American film negotiators signed an agreement in 1936, the Marchandeau accords, which capped the importation of dubbed films at 188 per year. The deal, a favorable one for the United States, set aside 150 import licenses for American movies. The French market, then, was saturated with films, not just homemade, but also foreign. Theater owners, under pressure at once to move the product and to draw in crowds, took to showing double bills, even as they cut admissions prices.[31]

All the same, there was money to be made in the French film industry, but who made it and how? In movies, as in commerce, the chain demonstrated its superior market-worthiness. France had its movie-house chains, not perhaps on the scale of their US counterparts, but significant enterprises nonetheless: the Circuit Siritsky, which ran a score of theaters in the Paris area, and the Jacques Haïk chain, which included a pair of picture-palace gems fitted out for the movies of the new talkie era—the Olympia on the boulevard des Capucines, with its art-deco facade, and the nearby Rex, with its over-the-top Moorish design.[32] Film production, even in the best of times, is an uncertain business, and was all the more so in depression-era France. Financing was cooked up on a film-by-film basis. It required an agile, fast-talking producer to line up would-be backers, and what a colorful crew the producers sometimes were: directors investing their own funds, chain owners with vertical integration in mind (Haïk was a sometime producer), self-styled patrons of the arts, and speculators of all kinds. The deal makers were to be seen plying their trade at Le Fouquet's, a stylish café that doubled as a movie-business watering hole, located on the Champs-Elysées. Is it a surprise, under the circumstances, that deals fell through, pictures got half-made, bankruptcies multiplied? In 1933 alone, almost ninety production companies wound up in receivership. It has been estimated that as many as one in three companies went bust over the course of the interwar decades.[33]

Movies got made nevertheless. They were filmed in studio in most cases, rather than on location. The arrangement ensured sound quality, and, not least of all, it was a boon to set designers and lighting technicians, who came to occupy central roles in the moviemaking process. In certain respects, it was they, just as much as the directors, who created the distinctive aesthetic of 1930s French cinema, generating effects, moods, atmospheres that mimicked reality but at the same time stylized, even poeticized, its expression.[34]

And there were great successes too: the Pinkevitch-Rollmer production of Jean Renoir's *La Grande Illusion* (1937), for example, or Gregor Rabinovitch's production of Marcel Carné's *Quai des Brumes* (1938). Both films starred Jean Gabin, an everyman figure who, although not handsome, had a rough-hewn masculinity that communicated a fundamental decency, tough but tender, that has been of enduring appeal to both French and foreign audiences.[35] For France, like the United States, had its movie stars. In the thirties, it has been argued, the movie actor's task was less the representation of psychological depth than the embodiment of a social type. But there were stars just the same, and they were an essential ingredient to movie profitability. As such, they drew hefty salaries, earning a good deal more than technicians and even some movie directors, however famous.[36]

The French system, though unregulated and freewheeling, still turned out classics, as attested by the success, both commercial and artistic, of the two films mentioned above. Each in its way is emblematic of a moment in 1930s French film history, Renoir's capturing the optimism of the Popular Front era, Carné's the follow-on sense of discouragement. *La Grande Illusion* is set in a German-run POW camp during the Great War. The French prisoners plot and pull off a breakout. The principal, played by Gabin, experiences a series of reconciliations in the process: with an aristocratic fellow inmate who turns out, for all his airs, to be a decent comrade; with his fellow escapee, Rosenthal, a well-to-do Parisian Jew; and with a German war widow who harbors the fugitives before they make a final dash, out of wartorn Europe, into neutral Switzerland. The film is antiwar but not unpatriotic, hopeful that Frenchmen, in the name of a common humanity, will learn to set aside the antagonisms—social, religious, and national—which generate conflict. In *Quai des Brumes*, Gabin once again plays a soldier, Jean, but this time he is a deserter on the run. Jean meets a young woman, an orphan named Nelly, and the two fall in love. But the romance is thwarted: first by Nelly's "guardian," a louche figure, whom Jean is cornered into killing; and then by a crazed, jealous gangster who covets Nelly for himself and guns down

Jean. In a world so sordid, it seems, hard-luck types like Jean and Nelly are not fated to happiness, a pessimistic conclusion accentuated by the film's wharfside settings shrouded in murk and fog.

In film, as in theater, there was no shortage of critics to decry a creeping and corrupting commercialization. The United States, of course, was a principal target of blame. Hollywood's great dream factories brought a chilling, Taylorized efficiency to film production, cranking out movies in assembly-line quantity. The movies made were formulaic fare that dazzled, stupefied, and degraded. Such was the opinion of a range of Far Right critics like Maurice Bardèche and Robert Brasillach, who contrasted Hollywood machinism with continental production techniques that allowed directors the leeway to craft an individual moviemaking style.[37] Bardèche and Brasillach were far from alone in such thinking. Marcel L'Herbier was a veteran filmmaker who had made the transition from silents to talkies; he directed a string of movies in the thirties on military and imperial themes, among them *Les Hommes nouveaux* on the pacification of Morocco, which included footage of Maréchal Lyautey; and he was no friend of Hollywood, inveighing against "the invasion from the West," which drained French cinema of its lifeblood. France's film industry, to survive, had buckled to foreign ways, renouncing "its pure nationality." Worse, the corrosive effects of Yankee showmanship had even begun to eat away at France's moral well-being, "the healthy traditions of our way of life," as L'Herbier put it.[38] Such nationalist bluster found an echo even on the Far Left. Film director Louis Daquin (a fellow traveler who joined the Communist Party in 1941) characterized Paramount's French studio as "the factories of Saint-Maurice." Yet, he acknowledged, the "Hollywood formula," transplanted to France, had had a salutary effect, for "Hollywood's cosmopolitan perspective" prompted French filmmakers to model a national response. It came in the form of the independent studio film, which alone permitted "a national production, original and nonconformist." Indeed, concluded Communist film historian Georges Sadoul, all the great cinema of the thirties, from Renoir to Carné, had been the work of what was, in effect, a "quasi-artisanate."[39]

It was not just from Hollywood, from the West, that the invasion

came but from the East as well. L'Herbier wrote of "two coloniza-
tions" that were eating away at French cinema: American and Jewish.[40] France in the thirties experienced a wave of Jewish immigration
from troubled central and eastern Europe, and no doubt many of the
newcomers found their way into the movie industry. Anti-Semites
liked to exaggerate the role of Jews in filmmaking, claiming they
added up to a full half of all directors and roughly four in five producers. A more sober estimate has tallied the Jewish presence at 15
percent, a hefty enough share in itself.[41] A number of critics addressed
"the Jewish Question" in coded but still none too subtle terms. The
1935 edition of Bardèche and Brasillach's film history sneered at the
"adventurers of all kinds"—"rug sellers, Romanians, Arabs or Poles"—
who had taken over the French film industry. Litterateur Paul Morand authored a satire of moviemaking mores, *France la doulce*, in
1935. The producers' world he wrote of was populated by "pirates,
naturalized or not, who have found their way from the obscurity of
central Europe and the Levant to the bright lights of the Champs-
Elysées."[42]

It may not have been good form to mention Jews by name, but
Louis-Ferdinand Céline knew no such scruples. "The Jew," he wrote
in *Bagatelles pour un massacre* (1938), was the moving spirit behind
"modern civilization," behind "the standardization of everything,"
and behind "all of cinema." Lucien Rebatet, Brasillach's confederate
at the notorious right-wing newspaper *Je suis partout*, was every bit as
direct. The trip from Berlin to Paris was a short hop, Rebatet observed, and the Jews had made it, leaving the Kurfürstendamm behind to set up shop on the Champs-Elysées. As always, the Jews traded
in junk. Jacques Haïk's movie houses, piles of fake marble and gilt,
peddled a cinema to match, trash films of uncertain morals. Carné's
films were typical of the genre, all low-life tales that defiled rather
than uplifted. As for Carné himself, he was the very "embodiment of
the Jewified talent."[43]

The Jews, Rebatet concluded, had established what amounted to a
cinematic dictatorship, but was not that just their way? They had infiltrated the movie industry, and via the base demagogy of Blum, Zay,
and company they had done the same in the parliamentary domain.[44]

Nor was Rebatet alone in drawing a connection between creeping Jewish influence in politics and in cinema. The Jew, ranted Céline, had come into his own with the Popular Front. So long a lurking but disguised presence, he was now no longer afraid to show himself on the screen "such as he is," and show himself he did "en 'Rosenthal.'"[45] Yes, L'Herbier concurred, 1936 had been a turning point, for it was then that "Jewish immigrants" had taken over the movie industry, "remaking it in their image which is assuredly not our own."[46]

L'Herbier's dig is a reminder that it was not just hard-core Jew haters like Céline and Rebatet who indulged in anti-Semitic polemic but cinema professionals as well, and L'Herbier was not alone. Jacques Feyder is best remembered by American audiences as the director of *La Kermesse héroïque* (1935), a lighthearted satire that conveys its pacific message with a deft touch. The movie, set in an early-seventeenth-century Dutch town, sends up the faintheartedness of the local burgomasters who quail in the face of an approaching Spanish army, leaving their wives to handle the situation. They do so with aplomb, charming the invaders, who turn out to be more chivalrous than barbaric. There were some foreign "invaders," however, Feyder was not prepared to countenance. The director complained to a movie magazine in 1938 about his troubles finding work in France. The reason: "invading Jews who have gotten their hands on French cinema."[47]

Claude Autant-Lara, like Feyder a director, preferred the term "flood" to "invasion."[48] In the 1950s, Autant-Lara was pilloried by New Wave critics as the very embodiment of "quality cinema," and it is easy enough to understand why in light of Autant-Lara's estimable but wooden adaptation of Stendahl's *Le Rouge et le Noir* (1954). Such assaults may have contributed to Autant-Lara's growing crankiness in old age, a distemper much in evidence in his late autobiographical writings (and in his association with Jean-Marie Le Pen's Front National). Here, recounting his early days in cinema before the war, he rails with Célinesque abandon against Coca-Cola—"that Europe-killing swill" (*cette saloperie europicide*)—and "the plague" of German refugees who, post-1933, had swarmed onto the French moviemaking scene.[49] Autant-Lara describes his youthful self as beleaguered and well-nigh friendless. But not quite, for he had at least one staunch partisan in the person of Philippe Lamour. Indeed, in the early thirties just before leaving for a stint in Hollywood, Autant-Lara had collaborated on Lamour's short-lived periodical of dissident opinion, *Plans*. The *Plans* connection is an interesting one, for it suggests a prewar Autant-Lara with a critical, nonconformist edge, perhaps a more accurate portrait of the man he was then than the unhinged xenophobe who emerges from his memoirs.[50]

The xenophobic currents that crisscrossed the film industry even found expression, albeit muted and intermittent, in the movies themselves. Abel Gance is celebrated for his spectacular, triple-screen production of *Napoléon* (1928). His unsurpassed skill at orchestrating battlefield sequences was much in evidence in both the silent and talkie versions of *J'accuse!* (1919, 1937). The 1937 remake, filmed when the threat of war was once again imminent, had a particular, topical resonance. It tells the story of a World War I veteran who, in faithful remembrance of comrades lost, puts his inventor's skills to work to prevent a second armageddon. To the protagonist's dismay, the powers-that-be maneuver to turn his war-ending invention to warmaking purposes. The movie is remarkable for its intercutting of actual World War I battle footage, some of it filmed by Gance himself, and for its impassioned and unyielding pacifism at a moment of revived international tensions. On occasion, Gance's antiwar zealotry took a xenophobic turn, as it did in *La Fin du monde* (1931), which features a character named Schomburg, a moneyman and warmonger who is the very stereotype of the "refined Semite."[51]

Marcel Pagnol's *Le Schpountz* (1938) also contains a stereotype, that of the Jewish film producer Meyerboom. The picture recounts the improbable rise to movie stardom of a provincial (and Provençal) film fan, played by Fernandel with the toothy, wide-smile charm that so ingratiated him to French audiences. Meyerboom is just a minor figure in the story, and the portrait of him is harmless enough. But it is said that the original version of the film was not so benign and had to be recut to tone down the anti-Semitism. Fernandel himself, it might be added, was not immune to bouts of intolerance: delivering himself of a newspaper interview in 1937, he called for a purge to clean out the foreigners from France's film industry.[52]

There was wide agreement then that French cinema was in crisis, though the diagnoses might vary. France specialized in artisanal films with an individual style, but makers of such films were hard-pressed to find audiences in a market dominated by the Hollywood film factory. The French film industry was not in much position to compete anyhow, hobbled as it was by its own disorganization. Then, of course, there was the sneaking sense that the industry had grown corrupt, its morals debased by speculators more interested in profits than art. No doubt, there is much that is distorted in such a dire portrait. The quality of pictures made in the thirties was not so low as critics made out. Disorganization, it might be countered, even had its virtues. The fragmented character of the industry permitted small-scale team collaborations that resulted in a cinema with a coherent and distinctive aesthetic, realist in its representation of social hierarchies and types, poetic in its atmospheric effects. As for commercialization, the French made their own share of B movies and did not need Hollywood to instruct them in the matter.

Still, it would be wrong to underestimate the importance of the public debate on cinema, for that debate set the terms of policy making. Critics of the cinema scene identified a trio of problems. Industrial filmmaking practices, foreign in origin, threatened the integrity of French cinema; the French movie business was too fragmented to organize its own defense; and, anyhow, the moviemaking milieu, populated as it was by so many unsavory types, was too rotted away to stand up for French quality. To each "problem," contemporaries proposed policy solutions, although little in fact was accomplished by way of implementation, at least before the war.

In 1935, Prime Minister Pierre Laval commissioned a high-level civil servant, the inspecteur des finances Guy de Carmoy, to draft a report on the reorganization of the film industry. Carmoy recommended establishment of a film corporation run by industry professionals under state supervision. It was to be formed from an amalgamation of existing employer associations, and all film-industry employers, whether already enrolled in an association or not, would be required to belong. Carmoy envisaged an organ with near-sovereign powers—to regulate the flow of new films onto the market, to oversee the open-

ing of new movie theaters, to limit double billing—which were meant
to be used to dampen the competition so ruinous to French cinema.
Carmoy's report was completed just as the Popular Front took office
in 1936. The Conseil national économique, an advisory body of technical experts attached to the Ministère de l'Economie nationale,
okayed Carmoy's project in July, but it went no further. In a democratic republic committed to freedom of association, in an era when
worker rights were the order of the day, such a corporatist, employer-
centered scheme held minimal appeal.[53]

Parliament took up the issue at this juncture. Through the winter
of 1936 into the spring of the following year, a joint Chamber/Senate
commission met to investigate the state of France's film industry. Testimony was taken from a variety of industry professionals and interested parties, and all concurred that quality was French cinema's defining feature, essential to its survival and yet, at present, its most
endangered asset. Indeed, in this respect, the movie industry's predicament mirrored that of France itself. "Yes," a committee member
expostulated, "the problem that faces cinema is the problem that faces
all of France: we are a country of quality." How then was the problem
of quality to be solved? Tax breaks for quality films: such was L'Herbier's
recommendation. Zay suggested creating a stamp of distinction, *Film
France*, which would confer appreciable material advantages on the
movies so honored. It was an idea he had gotten from Robert Aron, a
core member of the nonconformist *Ordre nouveau* group. None of
these schemes, however, addressed the more fundamental issue of
how quality films were to be identified. On this point, consensus dissolved, and the committee's deliberations hit an impasse.[54]

Zay himself now assumed direct responsibility for cinema reform.
It was less quality protection than a moralization of the film industry
that he made his guiding aim. "The French cinema must be cleansed":
this was the language Zay used to spell out his policy objectives in an
October 1937 interview to *L'Intransigeant*. The housecleaning impulse was much in evidence in the movie reform bill Zay proposed to
the Chamber of Deputies in March 1939. The project provided for
creation of a professional identity card, a measure intended to bar
cheats and swindlers from the film business. It further provided for

institution of a state body to monitor box-office receipts, the better to keep a watch on theater owners who might not always make an honest declaration of earnings. And it envisioned a pair of schemes to rein in money-grabbing producers. Existing law sanctioned producers' claims to exclusive authorship of the films they produced. The Zay bill acknowledged the authorship rights of all the creative talents—writers and directors, as well as producers—who made a substantive contribution to the filmmaking process. Heretofore, producers conducted financial operations as they pleased, unchecked by scrutiny of any kind. The Zay bill provided for creation of a registry office charged with keeping a public record of all contracts relating to films in production.[55]

The bill made its way to parliamentary commission but progressed no further because of the war. This is not to say that nothing of moment was accomplished by way of cinema reorganization in the thirties. What the parliamentary process had failed to achieve might yet be enacted by decree. A decree of July 1939 created a professional organ to track box-office receipts. That same month, the Daladier administration promulgated a bundle of decrees, the so-called Code de la famille, which, as its name implies, was intended as a shield to family values. The code enshrined in law for the first time the state's prerogative to censor media in the name of protecting youthful morals, paving the way for subsequent establishment of a film classification system that would prohibit children's access to unsuitable movie material.[56] Such measures, however, amounted to no more than a start and a modest one at that.

None of these were Popular Front measures; they were instead the work of the Daladier administration. Even Zay's project, with its purgative preoccupations, reflected more the mood of moral retrenchment characteristic of the immediate prewar moment than the optimism of the Popular Front era. Zay, it should be remembered, took over as minister of national education in 1936, but he remained in the post well after Blum departed office, staying on through the Daladier years until the very outbreak of hostilities.

Quality, corporation, cleansing: these were the watchwords of cinema debate in the mid-to-late thirties, and they were often articulated in xenophobic or, at least, protectionist accents. Boulevard commercialism threatened theater; an unregulated market and foreign competition squeezed cinema. Was the situation any different in the radio industry?

Radio Days

French radio was still in its infancy in the 1920s. At the end of the decade, the nation counted a mere half-million receivers in all.[57] The state from the outset had laid claim to tutelary authority over the entire industry, but responsibility for regulating the airwaves was situated in a third-rank ministry: the Ministère des Postes, télégraphes et téléphones or PTT. Nor was the PTT altogether rigorous in the exercise of its duties. State broadcasting facilities were made available to fifteen stations, which varied widely in organization from locale to locale. Grassroots listeners' associations ran a number of the stations; a number sold advertising time to underwrite station finances. This hodgepodge constituted the public sector. Alongside it, a private sector had begun to emerge, the creation of tinkerers and enthusiasts like Lucien Lévy, for example, who ran a Paris-based station, Radio LL, out of business premises in the industrial XVe arrondissement. In principle, private radio entrepreneurs had to have state authorization in order to broadcast, though in practice not all private stations bothered to obtain the state's go-ahead. In principle once again, the state claimed a monopoly on ownership of broadcasting facilities but from 1928 conceded that private stations might build and own antennae of their own.[58]

Under the circumstances, the boundary between public and private was far from distinct. The state acted to clarify the lines of separation in 1928. That year's finance law imposed a cap on the number of private stations, at first set at fourteen, later lowered to thirteen.[59] A pair of measures in 1933 reconstituted the public domain. Public stations were forbidden to advertise, a prohibition phased in over a two-year period. Station financing, of course, had to be renegotiated in consequence. The state stepped forward, undertaking to cover station expenses out of the national budget. To pay for the additional expenses it had now shouldered, the state invented a new tax (the *redevance*) levied on all radio owners.[60]

The French government had gotten serious about its regulatory responsibilities at the very moment the radio business began to take off. The number of receiving sets multiplied tenfold in the thirties, hitting five million on the eve of the war.[61] A vast new market had opened. Would the PTT's public network win it over, or would the listeners tune in instead to the private stations?

Prewar public radio is remembered as at best an estimable endeavor. Few, whether memoirists or historians, speak well of its news reporting, which consisted in large part of scripted communiqués declaimed by announcers in the sententious and lofty tones of the high-minded stage actor. There was little effort to capture the immediacy of events and little of spontaneity in the presentation.[62] The talk shows, so numerous on the public airwaves (they accounted for roughly a quarter of all airtime on state-run Radio Paris in 1934[63]), were not much better. Tony exchanges on literature and matters of related cultural moment had appeal to educated audiences, but a dismaying pedantry of tone too often colored the discussions. It did not help that France's most eminent and engaging litterateurs disdained radio as little more than a "diversion for helots."[64] They shunned the talk shows, which were left to the devices of the not so distinguished. Still, state radio ran first-rate music services. It maintained a national orchestra unsurpassed in quality. For symphonic concerts, chamber music, solo recitals, indeed for all that was best in the classical repertoire, there was no better place to turn. Public radio's theater offerings were of a similar high caliber. Retransmissions from the state theaters, the Comédie française or the Opéra, were standard fare. The recording of stage performances, however, presented acoustic difficulties, and so, for productions less grand, for Odéon and Opéra comique productions, say, actors and singers were invited en masse to the studio. But it was not just the works of the state theater that public radio broadcast. Before the decade's end, Cartel productions had come to occupy a minor but not insignificant niche in state-radio theatrical programming.[65] Yet this should not come altogether as a surprise. From 1936, the director of artistic services at public radio was Wladimir Porché, a man with strong familial connections to the theater world. Porché's mother, Madame Simone, was an actress of renown, his father, François, a dramatist with Cartel connections. Dullin in fact staged a play by Porché senior, the "violently anticommunist" *Tsar Lénine*, in 1931.[66]

State radio did not eschew the variety show or light music, but its specialty was quality broadcasting designed to provide a full evening's entertainment to a public in search of uplift. As the thirties drew to a close, it dawned on programmers that this strategy might not be the winning one in the competition for listeners. To sound out audience interest, the PTT at last got around to setting up a listeners' mail service in 1937.

Private radio by contrast prided itself on its intimate grasp of what the public wanted. An ambitious young adman, Marcel Bleustein (later Bleustein-Blanchet), bought up Radio LL in 1935 and gave the station a new name, Radio-Cité. Bleustein wanted to break down the distance between radio and its listeners. Radio-Cité maintained a fleet of red radio cars that careered about Paris recording news events as they unfolded. Variety shows were taped in front of live audiences. Listeners were meant to feel as though they themselves were there on the spot, in the crowd. And, of course, Radio-Cité welcomed listener response whether in the form of phone calls or, more often, mail. Public radio was just getting its listener services up and running at a time when Radio-Cité was flooded with an estimated forty thousand letters per week.[67]

Immediacy, or at least the illusion of it, was one of private radio's trump cards. So too demotic program content and presentation. News reporting was a staple feature of private programming and for good reason. The printed press took an early interest in radio affairs. The private Poste parisien was in fact founded by a newspaper, the popular Parisian daily *Le Petit parisien*. In 1935, Bleustein struck a deal with *L'Intransigeant*, farming out Radio-Cité's news services to the paper in exchange for certain financial advantages. The bargain did not last long, but it supplied Radio-Cité with a team of innovative newsmen, headed first by Jean Antoine, son of the theater director, and then by the up-and-coming reporter Jean Guignebert. *L'Intransi-geant*'s decision to get into the radio business, however short-lived, inspired an imitator. Jean Prouvost, proprietor of the mass-circulation daily *Paris-Soir*, bought up Radio Béziers, redubbing it Paris 37 (1937 was the year the station began broadcasting under its new name).[68]

These various deals channeled a cadre of print journalists into private radio, journalists who pioneered a news style that accented reportage over chatter. Radio-Cité's on-the-spot reporting has been mentioned. The station, moreover, did not hesitate to interrupt regular programming for breaking stories. In March 1938, it got the jump on all competitors, printed or wireless, reporting on the Austrian Anschluss even before any official announcement of the event had been made. Private radio, of course, featured scheduled news broadcasts with written texts, but scripted reporting was leavened with live interviews, and, scripted or not, all the news was delivered in a speaking voice less stilted than the theatrical accents of public radio. A conscious effort was made to work out a genuine "radiophonic style," a manner of talking that, broadcast over the airwaves, would have the ring of naturalness.[69] In the domain of news reporting, private stations had to hustle for listener attention, but it was from within the private sector itself that the principal competition came, not from official radio, which Paris 37's station manager dismissed as "a negligible adversary."[70]

Private-sector dynamism was no less evident in the entertainment end of the business. Private radio did not refuse highbrow material, but it had to be ready to field listener complaints when it did so. Paris 37 turned over snippets of airtime to the printed media—*Temps Présent*, *Le Canard enchaîné*—to present cultural news of potential public interest. A *Nouvelle revue française* presentation on the playwright Paul Claudel, however, spilled over the time allotted, provoking a flood of angry mail. The *NRF* got no further airtime after that. Radio Toulouse learned a lesson of its own when it aired Debussy's *Pelléas et Mélisande*. Listeners wrote in making known their distinct preference for operetta over such weighty fare.[71] The private-sector audience wanted music, but what it liked best was shorter, more accessible pieces.

This was, indeed, the musical terrain that private radio staked out for itself. It made a specialty of the variety-show format (adapted from music hall), which featured a rapid-fire sequence of acts with the emphasis on popular song. The "singing fool" Charles Trenet, partnered for much of the thirties with Johnny Hess, performed solo for the first time on Radio-Cité's *Le Music Hall des Jeunes*. The show helped make his fortune, and it gave a boost as well to the career of an already celebrated artist, the "little sparrow" Edith Piaf, who came back to sing week in, week out.[72] Paris 37's *Bar des vedettes* had a regular of its own, Maurice Chevalier. The host of the program, the sympatico "barman" Albert Riéra, welcomed a different guest each week (among them Chevalier) for conversation and a few songs. It began as a quarter-hour show but was so popular that it got extended to forty-five minutes.[73] For Trenet, Piaf, and Chevalier, radio boosted careers begun on the music-hall stage.[74] In the case of Tino Rossi, however, the medium played a more central role, making the name of a vocalist otherwise little known.[75] Rossi's rich tenor voice and romantic evocations of his native Corsica played well to a public who had learned to savor the charms of Mediterranean life through the movies of Marcel Pagnol or the guitar playing of Vincent Scotto.

Radio nurtured and fed on the stardust dreams of its listening public. Among Radio-Cité's most successful programs was *Le Crochet radiophonique*, an amateur-hour show sponsored by Monsavon, a L'Oréal soap product. *Le Crochet*, following the American model, was staged before a live audience that was invited to vote for the hook (*le crochet*) when an act was not up to standard. A jury, presided over by an established celebrity, selected the winning artist of the day, and the show wound up on a note of general good humor with the star performing a song of his own.[76] Radio and *la chanson populaire* sustained each other, and, on the radio end, it was the private sector that profited most from the alliance.

In the domain of variety programming, state radio was an also-ran. When it came to game shows, it did not even bother to compete, leaving such vulgarities altogether to its commercial competitors. The most celebrated game show of the prewar era was the Poste parisien's *La Course au Trésor*. Listeners competed in a treasure hunt, racing to be first to deliver to the broadcasting studio the various obscure objects itemized by the show's announcer, Pierre Dac. In Radio-Cité's *Les Fiancés de Byrrh*, soon-to-be-married couples competed for listener sympathy, and to the winners went a basketful of prizes, from the all-expenses-paid honeymoon to useful household goods.[77]

The commercial stations in fact made a quite conscious effort to target romance- and family-minded audiences. French radio, like commercial radio in the United States, had its soap operas, none more enduring than Radio-Cité's *La Famille Duraton*.[78] The show portrayed the daily-life joys and cares of a typical French family, the eponymous Duratons, through dramatizations of the family's lunch table conversations. Papa was a civil servant, Maman a homemaker, junior a sports enthusiast, and sis a sharp-tongued would-be journalist. This was a family soap with a strong appeal to women listeners, young and old. Private stations had a precocious grasp of the importance of the women's market to commercial success and programmed accordingly. In 1935, the foreign-based Radio Luxembourg debuted *L'Heure des dames et des demoiselles* (later *Passe-temps des dames et des demoiselles*), a women's advice show that dispensed beauty and homemaking tips. The idea was simple enough and catching. The program enjoyed an uninterrupted run of over thirty years.[79]

Private radio made a show of seeking out listener contact and of tailoring its offerings to suit the public's tastes. Breaking news, the *chanson populaire*, games and soaps: these were the staple fare of the commercial stations, disseminated with an attention to quick-tempo pacing, immediacy of presentation, and naturalness of style. The formula worked to perfection, enabling private radio to outdistance its public-sector rivals.

The expansiveness of commercial radio, however, did not go without response. The state acted first to set its own house in order. Inasmuch as public radio was now funded out of national coffers, the state had a compelling interest in how station management was constituted. In February 1935, PTT Minister Georges Mandel decreed a uniform set of rules governing selection of station management boards (*conseils de gérance*), applicable to most public stations, although not all. Under the new dispensation, the state arrogated to itself the right to appoint half of all board members, the remaining slots to be filled by election. The first radio ballot was held later that year. The franchise was generous—all radio-license payers were entitled to vote—but the turnout was abysmal. Just over two hundred thousand took part, a mere one in nine of all eligible voters. In the event, the same listener-association representatives who had dominated the management boards of old were called on to continue to serve.[80]

The Popular Front's PTT minister, Robert Jardillier, ran a second series of elections in 1937, though this time the number of elected positions was cut from one-half to one-third. Nonetheless, voter interest in these elections was intense, an estimated 1.6 million taking part. The explanation is not far to seek. These elections were politicized to a degree the previous round had not been. A Popular Front affiliate, Radio-Liberté, fielded slates of candidates. The Paris list was headed by Paul Langevin, Victor Basch, and Paul Vaillant-Couturier, the first an antifascist intellectual, the second a senior figure in the Ligue des droits de l'homme, and the third a Communist. Radio-Liberté, however, found itself confronted with a formidable opponent, Radio-Famille. Radio-Famille was an offshoot of the conservative, not to say reactionary, Fédération nationale catholique, a lay confessional ginger group led by General Edouard de Castelnau, which had gotten its start in the midtwenties rousing Catholic opinion against the secularizing policies of Edouard Herriot's Cartel des Gauches. It pitched itself as the paladin of above-party, family programming and, in the name of nonpartisanship, sought out alliances with listener-association old-timers. The strategy paid off, as Radio-Famille candidates outpolled their Popular Front opponents by a considerable margin.[81]

The radio elections of February 1937 are significant on several counts. They were an arresting demonstration of the muscle of Catholic opinion when mobilized, but not just that. The franchise was opened to all *redevance* payers, regardless of gender. These then were the first large-scale contests in which a substantial number of women voters took part, an early indication of the conservative potential of a female electorate. Not least of all, the elections mattered for what they did not do. They did not fill the majority of posts on station management boards, just one-third. It was the state now, through appointment, that exercised the controlling influence on *conseils de gérance*. The once-dominant listener associations had been elbowed aside, and they never again played a decisive role in the medium's history.

Nor was it just in matters of management that the state made its intrusive presence felt. In radio, as in many other domains, policy makers turned for advice to a state-appointed consultative council composed of public and private individuals with a claim to expertise in the field. In October 1936, Jardillier revamped the existing board, henceforth known as the Conseil supérieur des émissions de la radiodifussion. The new body was authorized to exercise general supervision over public-radio programming, a gesture signaling the state's desire to exert a measure of quality control in program selection. The composition of the board is revelatory of what the state took quality to be. It has been argued that the Conseil was left-wing in orientation, and, indeed, it was chaired by a reliable Radical politician, Albert Sarraut. Board members included intellectual stalwarts of the Popular Front like Jean Guéhenno and André Gide, but their number included as well Georges Duhamel, Paul Morand, and Paul Valéry, who were less leftist in conviction.[82] What is most striking in fact is the literary bent of the Conseil. Sarraut apart, these were all writers, and even Sarraut was a veteran journalist. The state wanted quality, and quality still meant belles lettres.

Public radio was subjected to ever tighter state supervision. As for commercial radio, it too was placed under increasing pressure by the state, although not by the state alone. In early 1936, a tax (with some exemptions) was imposed on radio advertising. The Popular Front victory later that year stoked private-sector anxieties of an imminent nationalization. Blum did not move to take over commercial radio, but his successor Camille Chautemps, still working with a Popular Front majority, more than doubled the advertising tax rate.[83] A handful of newspapers were implicated in the radio business, but much of the press looked on radio reporting, not as a complement to its own operations, but as competition. The printed media mounted a campaign in the fall of 1937 to impose limitations on broadcast news, and commercial station owners found themselves compelled to make concessions. A standard feature of radio news was the so-called *revue de presse*, a summing up of major newspaper stories and opinion. The private stations agreed to restrict such summings-up to afternoons and evenings, easing the competitive strain on the morning editions. Private radio further agreed to confine its own news programming to regular, specified hours.

The issue, however, still did not go away, and the state found itself drawn into the conflict in mid-1938. The Daladier administration at first took the side of the press, stiffening restrictions on private-radio news programming and then extending them to public radio as well. But the government relented somewhat in subsequent months. Rising international tensions stoked the public's appetite for news, and Daladier in response loosened the reins on news reporting hours. Even so, the general principle remained in effect: radio, whether private or public, could not report the news when and how it pleased.[84]

Two processes then were at work in the mid-to-late thirties, the *étatisation* of the public sector and a nibbling away at the commercial competition's room for maneuver. The approach of war accelerated both processes, the first in particular, resulting in a seismic and enduring shift in how public radio operated.

It was the Daladier administration of 1938–1940 that rang in the new order. National defense had now become top priority, and Daladier understood that effective news management was critical to the purpose. In December 1938, he decreed formation of a new government bureau, the Service de contrôle de la Radio. The Service, attached to the prime minister's office, was made responsible for supervision of all radio news programming, private as well as public. Emile Lohner, a former journalist at *Le Temps*, was placed in charge.[85] In February the following year, a second organ was created, the Centre permanent de l'Information générale. This body too was lodged in the prime minister's office, and, like the Service, it was run by Lohner. Oversight of the news was the Service's mandate. Getting out the government's story was the Centre's, and to this end it put together a news show or *Radio Journal*, aired on both public and private stations, which functioned in effect as a mouthpiece for state policy.[86]

The real transformation, however, came in the summer months. In July 1939, on the war's very eve, Daladier revolutionized the institutional landscape with a pair of decrees. The first stripped the PTT of its radio management responsibilities, turning them over to a new organ, the Administration de la Radiodiffusion nationale. The Administration ran public radio outright and was invested with nominal authority over the private sector as well. This was not quite a nationalization, but it did signal a further reduction of private-sector autonomy. In most matters, the Administration answered directly to Daladier, who nominated Collège de France physicist Léon Brillouin as the agency's first director.[87] The second decree centralized all state communications in a cabinet-level post, the Commissariat-général à l'Information (CGI). And whom did Daladier pick as France's first information czar? None other than the playwright Jean Giraudoux. So far as news was concerned, Brillouin's Administration de la Radiodiffusion was subordinate to the new Commissariat but not when it came to technical questions or cultural issues. The place of Lohner's various agencies in the new hierarchy was not at all clear. For radio news, he answered to Brillouin (who answered to Giraudoux), but he was also a prime ministerial appointee, already ensconced in the prime minister's office, a position that allowed him a measure of independent decision-making.[88]

In institutional terms, this package of decrees overturned the radio order France had known in the thirties. The public sector was no longer assigned to a minor ministry but now functioned under the direct authority of the prime minister. The Administration de la Radiodiffusion broke down into three departments—two technical, the third cultural—which had final say on such matters for all public stations. Local *conseils de gérance* ceased to play a role, bringing to a definitive end the already waning day of the listeners' association. Radio news was centralized in the SGI, though various subauthorities, responsible also to the prime minister's office, still had a hand in news affairs. As for private radio, it was reduced to second-class status. It could not broadcast news when and how it wanted; it was obligated to retransmit the state's *Radio Journal* unedited. It now operated, in a word, under the general tutelary authority of the state.

It was not just in institutional terms that radio changed. New men were in charge, and they brought with them a new style. The choice of Giraudoux for the Commissariat might appear puzzling at first glance, but he brought an attractive package of qualities to the post. Giraudoux was a reputable man of letters, known for his grace of expression and manner. Here was a veritable "Ariel," a quick and effervescent intelligence who, it was hoped, would make a fair representative of *la pensée française* to the world.[89] Giraudoux was also a member of the diplomatic corps who styled himself a man of action with an understanding of France's current predicament. He had laid out his views in a text published in early 1939, *Pleins pouvoirs*. The nation's energies were flagging, he acknowledged in the book; what was needed was new leadership, take-charge men with the requisite vitality and confidence. Encourage immigration but with an eye to quality, redesign and beautify the nation's cities, summon France's young to the playing fields (the author was himself an accomplished tennis player): these were Giraudoux's prescriptions, which in their particulars did not go much beyond the common wisdom of the day. But they made the playwright sound a most modern-minded man of letters, able to talk demography and urbanism with a good deal more flair than the run-of-the-mill policy maker.[90] Giraudoux's combination of literary style and practical substance made him, at least on the surface, an ideal choice for the new Commissariat, and he brought with him a stellar team of advisers, which caught something of the double-sidedness of his nature. There was his old friend Louis Jouvet, now sporting a monocle, and alongside him a promising young conseiller d'état, Guillaume de Tarde, who had spent much of the preceding decade agitating in nonconformist, technocratic circles.[91]

In the event, Giraudoux's tenure was not a success. The proliferation of agencies involved in news management would have made the job difficult for anyone, and Giraudoux was not much of an administrator to start with. Worse, he spoke with a polished, poetic diction that made him well-nigh incomprehensible to many listeners. Remember that his German counterpart was Joseph Goebbels, who knew the radio game far better than Giraudoux did. Giraudoux talked of the peaceful nature of the average Frenchman, a petit bourgeois whose horizons were bounded by the walls of his "little garden." Goebbels had a skewering reply, demanding to know how it was that the nonexpansionist French had come into possession of such a sprawling empire. As one contemporary remarked, Giraudoux played the "flute" to Goebbels' "trombone."[92] Still, the propaganda battle was not altogether one-sided. The French prime minister, Daladier, made repeated appearances in front of the microphone, and he went over well.[93] He was a war veteran like so many listeners, and he spoke in the unpretentious accents of his native region, the Midi. Giraudoux came across as a litterateur, Daladier as a plain-speaking Frenchman.

Public radio in the run-up to the war and the months that followed tried its hand at a new kind of news programming: centralized and state-run, designed to make contact with the broadest possible public. The effort yielded at best mixed results, hampered by problems of overlapping authority, uncertain leadership, and a high-toned literary sensibility, Daladier excepted, which left more down-to-earth listeners in a state of bewilderment.[94]

Some of the same difficulties plagued state radio's entertainment programming. The man placed in charge was Georges Duhamel, and in point of view he bore more than a passing resemblance to Giraudoux (the two were in fact friends). Duhamel is perhaps best remembered for a work of cultural criticism, *Scènes de la vie future*, published in 1930. The book recounts a visit to the United States, taking aim at the gamut of standard targets: soul-crushing skyscrapers, vulgar picture-palaces, and so on. All these indecencies—portents of a dread future that might yet befall Europe—Duhamel declared himself happy to cast aside for the simpler and more honest pleasures of a meal enjoyed in the garden of his country home.[95]

So what kind of programming did the garden-minded Duhamel come up with? Jouvet, for one, had a clear idea what he hoped the state's new chief programmer would do: "we must have items that raise morale—cheerful, easily understood things like Claudel's *Le Soulier de Satin* or Péguy's *La Jeanne d'Arc*. No foreign authors."[96] It is hard to imagine Claudel a popular favorite. Duhamel in fact showed a little more sensitivity to public tastes, leavening the usual quality offerings with sketches and light music. It was still not enough for listeners, though, the troops in particular, who clamored for Chevalier and the swing sound of Ray Ventura's big-band orchestra. *Le*

Temps, no vulgarizing panderer by any stretch, was to complain of Duhamel's penchant for improvement over diversion: "Enough! too much Corneille, too much religious music."[97] As the state moved in on radio programming, it brought literature—indeed, for some, too much literature—with it.

The 1930s had its culture wars. The Blum regime's efforts to expand popular leisure time and to champion democratized cultural forms to fill it have been chronicled by others in detail. The battle, however, unfolded across a second, less well-documented front. Commercial forms—boulevard theater, Hollywood-style cinema, private-sector radio—came under fire from critics worried about the fate of national traditions of quality in a money-mad era. Their complaints at times came couched in a xenophobic idiom with anti-American or anti-Semitic overtones. The most extreme denunciations originated on the Far Right, but more mainstream voices were to be heard as well. Theater, cinema, radio: these were not just business operations governed by the exigencies of profit making. The Cartel directors dreamed of a theater of enchantment and spiritual communion. Film directors like L'Herbier and Autant-Lara wanted a director's cinema organized along craft, not industrial, lines. Giraudoux and Duhamel, as radio men, brought a note of genuine literary distinction to broadcasting. The media were about money, no doubt, but they were about art as well, and art was understood to encompass not just original works but classics made new again. Is there ever too much Corneille? It dawned on some that the state might be a helpmate in this enterprise, enforcing standards of professionalism and artistic merit. Indeed, in radio, the government had already begun in the prewar years to take action along just these lines.

Then came the war, the defeat of 1940, and the advent of Vichy. The new regime did not hesitate to stake out a position of its own in the culture wars, and in some respects that position was a simple one. Everywhere, Vichy took measures to reinforce the state's hand. But to what end? To back up art or commerce, quality or the bottom line? The answer to this more particular question still remains to be sorted out.

CHAPTER 5

Culture in Wartime

The culture wars of the thirties did not let up under Vichy, although now the terms of struggle had altered. The state intervened in all domains. It could not act, of course, with a free hand, hemmed in as it was by the Occupier's own designs. There was also the urgent need to placate an entertainment-hungry public in an era of shortage and hardship. But Vichy sought to find a path of its own, weighing in where it felt able, positioning itself as the guardian of a national culture of quality beset on all sides by foreigners and moneymen, who were often one and the same.

Robert Paxton has labeled the Pétainist regime "the revenge of the minorities," and so it was in the world of theater. The denigration of the boulevard stage took on an open, anti-Semitic tone. Both German and Vichy authorities sought to fashion a new, more corporatist theatrical order, turning to the Cartel directors to effect, in the name of professionalism and quality, a top-to-bottom overhaul of the French stage. And it was under Vichy that France's first serious experiments in theater decentralization were undertaken, thanks in large measure to the efforts of the state-sponsored arts association Jeune France (JF).

The transformation was yet more thoroughgoing in the movie industry. Vichy constructed an institutional apparatus designed to promote a *cinéma de qualité*, and it got what it wanted. The apparatus was destined to survive the war almost intact, and it helped to model a film industry that, however unsympathetic in political terms to the regime's goals, shared many of its aesthetic objectives. During the war years, Hollywood products were excluded from the French market, opening a space for a French-style quality cinema to entrench itself, which it did to great effect with the assistance of generous helpings of state aid.

Radio presents a more mixed picture. Private radio did not disappear altogether in wartime, but the ever-tightening grip of state management squeezed out its prewar vitality. As for the public sector, it is best remembered for its propagandistic shrillness, which grew all the more insistent and noxious as the war dragged on. Propaganda, however, was not the whole story. The public airwaves remained committed as before 1940 to a high-minded literariness, but the belles lettres were now tempered by increased doses of popular music. These were somber years. Private radio had lost its dynamism. Under the circumstances, it fell to state programmers to address the entertainment needs of radio audiences. In a setting of increased state control, the problem posed was this: how to strike a balance between quality and diversion. The dilemma would become all the more pressing in the postwar era when all radio in France was nationalized.

Vichy made the state a central player in cultural politics as never before, and the state used its newfound powers to drive back commercial forms. Quality was often, though not always, the winner, which explains in part the nostalgia of so many movie men and theater directors for the Vichy era. They may not have liked the regime (although, for a time, many did), but it created an environment in which the arts they were devoted to enjoyed a new flowering. In the process, a complicated legacy was prepared. Vichy's initiatives created a new institutional setting for the arts. They afforded opportunities to a rising cadre of administrators, directors, and programmers. Vichy's quality-minded statism at the same time came steeped in the poisons of authoritarianism and prejudice. Cultural policy makers at the Liberation would have to think long and hard before deciding what, if any, of this spiked brew they wanted to preserve.

Theater

The war years marked a moment of rupture in the performing arts. Well-established figures like Claudel and Giraudoux continued to turn out dramas, which, as in the past, won public acclaim. The former's *Soulier de Satin*, a long-winded extravaganza staged at the Comédie française in 1943, was a major event. The latter capped a long career with *La Folle de Chaillot*, to this day a much-beloved play, which opened to the public at the Théâtre de l'Athénée in 1945 (Giraudoux himself had died the year preceding). But the Vichy era was just as memorable for the new talents it revealed: Anouilh, Camus, Montherlant, Sartre. Montherlant already enjoyed a reputation as a writer, though not as a playwright. Anouilh had begun crafting plays in the thirties, but it was during the war that he made his breakthrough. Camus and Sartre on the other hand were rank newcomers to the stage. But all four were destined for noted and sparkling futures, whether in theater or letters, which would play out well into the fifties and beyond. The relay of generations was matched by a shift no less significant in institutions. The German occupiers, concerned about good order and racial purification, took measures to remold the Parisian stage accordingly. Vichy would not allow itself to be outdone. It imposed an order of its own on the theater, corporatist in design; it funded directors who met National Revolution standards; and it extended patronage to independent bodies, like Jeune France, that promised a general renovation of the arts. The precipitate of such influences was a new deal for the French stage, a revamped institutional and aesthetic landscape that altered the relations of power in the theater world in enduring ways.

The Germans marched into Paris in the summer of 1940. The Occupation agency in charge of the performing arts, the Propaganda Abteilung, sought out local contacts who might mediate in its dealings with the theater world. It turned first to Roger Capgras. The choice was an odd one, as Capgras was more an entrepreneur than a genuine man of the stage. He is best remembered as the deal maker who took over Henry Bernstein's theater, the Ambassadeurs, when Bernstein, consequent on the Germany victory, beat a well-timed retreat to the United States. In the event, Capgras's lack of experience was telling, and he was soon pushed aside in favor of a more representative figure, Robert Trébor, onetime head of a major theatrical trade association. The Germans went to work buttressing Trébor's authority. In October, with German sanction, an altogether new organ was created, the Association des directeurs de théâtre de Paris (ADTP). All theater owners in Paris were required to belong (they could not run their businesses otherwise); a percentage of box-office receipts was set aside to fund the association's operation; and Trébor himself was placed in charge.[1]

The Germans wanted two things from the ADTP. New plays had to earn the Occupier's imprimatur prior to staging, and it fell to the ADTP to act as intermediary in this regard. Of equal importance, the Germans were intent on an aryanization of the French theater, on a cleaning out of Jewish influence at all levels. ADTP statutes, in accordance with German wishes (and also Vichy legislation), excluded Jews from membership and by that token excluded Jews from theater management. In the event, Trébor showed insufficient zeal in pursuing the Germans' aryanization agenda, and they unceremoniously elbowed him out in the spring of 1941.

He was replaced by a three-man presidium, composed of Gaston Baty, Charles Dullin, and Pierre Renoir. Baty and Dullin were veteran Cartel directors. Renoir, the brother of filmmaker Jean Renoir, was not a formal member of the group, but he may be counted among its heirs. Louis Jouvet was unwilling to bend to the constraints of theater work under the Occupation, leaving France to tour abroad. It was Renoir who took over management of Jouvet's theater, the Athénée, one of the great centers of Cartel activity. The Cartel had felt beleaguered in the thirties, but with the Occupation it found itself in a position of unprecedented influence.

What goals then did the now-empowered Cartel set about pursuing? The presidium members were all on record favoring a general reorganization of "the corporation." The problem was to figure out how to translate such a commitment into practice.[2] The trio wrote up a statement of principle that articulated their common determination "to purify" the profession. This signified at a minimum driving out the moneymen who bought and sold theaters on speculation, who fiddled with rents and ticket prices in pursuit of profit. The issue was a particular preoccupation of Dullin's, who had a clear idea just how such a cleansing might be accomplished. He lobbied hard during the war years for a thorough purge of the theatrical profession, favoring a licensing system that would bar undesirables from theater directing.[3]

Speculators and nonprofessionals were counted among that number, and so too were Jews. Dullin was not immune to the anti-Semitic currents of the day. A signature piece in Dullin's repertoire was Ben Jonson's *Volpone*, which he first created at L'Atelier for the 1928 season. He cast himself in the title role, playing Volpone, who was a Venetian nobleman, as an anti-Semitic stereotype, a Shylock figure complete with pointed beard, earrings, and a yarmulke.[4] Now, perhaps it should not be held against Dullin that the theater he ran during the war years had to undergo a name change, from the Théâtre Sarah-Bernhardt (Bernhardt was of Jewish descent) to the Théâtre de la Cité. Yet Dullin did publish material in Alphonse de Chateaubriant's collaborationist and anti-Semitic review, *La Gerbe*. True, the articles were not overtly racist, Dullin contenting himself with rants against the "merchants" and "dishonest schemes" that had brought ruin to "the spirit of our corporation."[5] But what is to be made of the fact that he figured on the list of VIPs invited to attend the August 1941 opening of Le Juif et la France, a vile, racist exposition purporting to document the Jews' corrupting influence in French life? Did Dullin in fact attend, and if he did, what must he have felt, self-styled enemy of boulevard theater that he was, when on entering the exposition he was greeted by a giant-size bust of Henry Bernstein himself, with exaggerated Semitic features?[6]

Dullin figured on the list of invitees. So too, it might be added, did Baty, and of Baty's anti-Semitism there can be no doubt. Baty made a personal appearance before the Propaganda Abteilung in June 1941 to warn German authorities against the "half-Jew Lehmann," director of the Châtelet, whom Baty accused of speculation. French Jews, he wrote to Jewish litterateur Edmond Fleg, were no friends to France. They worried more about their own safety than the well-being of their country, sacrificing its interests in the service of "a malevolent English propaganda and Gaullist treason." Nor were Baty's expressions of prejudice confined to behind-the-scenes accusations and private correspondence. The Germans wanted "Jewish theater" banned, sparking a debate about how to define just what Jewish theater was. Baty did not hesitate to weigh in on the point: a play was Jewish, he argued, in the event half or more of its royalties were paid out to non-Aryans.[7]

The Cartel had a long-standing animus against commercialization and the boulevard theater. In the interwar years, it staked out a position for itself as a purifying counterforce. Under the Occupation, that cleansing, reorganizing impulse was recast in exclusionary, corporatist terms. The Cartel's re-formed wartime agenda fit in well with German plans. The Occupation authorities in fact okayed in all particulars the triumvirate's program of theater reform. But it was not just the Occupier's approval that the Cartel in power courted. They pledged themselves to create a renovated theater worthy of a place in the "new Europe," yes, but they also wanted a theater that would be worthy of a "regenerated France." And in making the connection between their project and a wider project of national renewal, they addressed themselves, not so much to the Germans, as to Vichy.[8]

Vichy, however, proved less supportive than might be expected. It sanctioned the ADTP's formation and approved the triumvirate's appointment, but it rejected the ADTP's corporatist pretensions to speak for the theatrical profession as a whole. If there was to be a theater corporation, the regime felt, it should be of French and not German devising. In the face of such resistance, the presidium attempted to resign; it was persuaded to stay on a while but gave way to the one-man presidency of Baty in November 1942, who was succeeded by Renoir in February of the following year. The ADTP did not cease to exist—it was after all still useful to the Germans—but it had failed in its own project of theater reform.

If French theater was to be revamped, Vichy itself would have to take the initiative, and so it did. On one level, the regime just picked up where the ADTP had left off, continuing on the same exclusionary and corporatist path marked out by Baty and Dullin. Yet it did so with an unmistakable statist bias. Vichy's secretary-general of fine arts, Louis Hautecoeur, shared the Cartel's partiality toward "un théâtre de qualité."[9] A study group was formed under the secretariat's auspices in early 1941 to vet projects for a reorganization of the theater. Jacques Rouché, director of the Réunion des théâtres lyriques nationaux, was placed in charge. Baty and Dullin were asked to collaborate. With such a team in place, it is small wonder that the Rouché committee debates took a Cartelist turn. The group ended up recommending a formal classification system that distinguished art theaters from more commercial establishments. It wanted the state to get into the business of regulating theater property, monitoring rents and sublets, and, "in the interests of theater and of art," regulating theater sales. Not least of all, it took up a proposal dear to Dullin: the licensing of directors. Dullin urged Rouché, as he had urged the ADTP, to adopt a discriminatory scheme. Licenses were not to be handed out to all comers just for the asking. The authorities had a duty to make distinctions, to favor art-house directors over their more commercial-minded brethren.[10]

In July 1941, Vichy theater policy began to take institutional form. The regime replaced Rouché's discussion group with a more formal body, the Comité d'organisation des entreprises du spectacle (COES), funded like the ADTP by a percentage of box-office receipts. The Germans wanted Baty to run the new show; Vichy wanted Rouché; and the nomination went in the end to a third man, René Rocher, sometime director of Copeau's old theater the Vieux-Colombier and current director of the Odéon. Rocher was a man of the Right, someone willing to salute the collaborationist hard-liner Marcel Déat as "notre chef." The film actor Marcel Dalio remembered him in later years, the very image of the well-mannered anti-Semite: "Good old Rocher! He was one of those men who never spoke of Jews but always of Israelites, that's more correct isn't it, he never had to utter the fatal word but one could always tell what his true feelings were." As for the stage, Rocher made no secret of his ambitions. He wanted a theater "transparent, clean and respected," purged of "parasites" and "undesirables."[11]

The COES managed a double achievement under Rocher's leadership. First of all, it shunted aside the old ADTP. From the outset, the Comité insisted on a role in the screening of would-be theater owners, once the ADTP's exclusive domain; and, over time, the new body took over from the ADTP altogether the vetting of plays. The Germans, who did not at first welcome the COES, came around to recognizing its primacy by the spring of 1943.[12] Second, the COES played a key part in drafting a framework law for the theater industry as a whole. Such a law was in fact enacted in December 1943 (though it never went into effect). In many respects, the legislation represented a realization of Cartelist ambitions as relayed through the Rouché commission and then the COES. Under the law's terms, the state arrogated to itself the power to regulate theater leases and sublets; all theater owners were required to obtain a license; and the law extended the licensing system to encompass, not just owners, but technical personnel as well. Actors, composers, and stage directors, as creative people, were exempted from this latter provision. The law's objectives were twofold: to bring commercial interests to heel through state monitoring of theater operations and to contour, through licensing, a theater profession with little room for the amateur and the incompetent. In both respects it spoke to Cartel concerns. But the law also placed a check on the COES's corporatist ambitions. It was to the state that the business of theater monitoring fell, and it was the state that meant to run the new licensing system.[13]

Vichy wanted a corporatism but a corporatism under the state's firm control, and when tensions between the two principles arose, it came down in favor of the latter. The regime's overriding commitment to state prerogative was very much in evidence in its reluctance to apply a generalized system of "professional cards" (*cartes professionnelles*) to the theater world. The idea was a simple one—to require all theater personnel, creative as well as technical, to obtain a card, attesting to their professional status—and Vichy authorities had no principled objection to the arrangement. As we shall see, such a system had been in operation in the film business since 1940. But in theater, unlike in cinema, it was the Germans who had originated the idea. They did so in March 1943, the month after the imposition of the STO. What the Germans were after was a full census of theater personnel in order to simplify the task of calling up recruits for the labor draft. The Occupier asked the COES to draw up just such a census and to begin issuing professional cards in accordance. The system, however, did not take root (at least during the war), in part because of refractory theater professionals who would not play along, but also because of foot-dragging on the part of the Fine Arts secretariat, which saw little interest in a German-inspired, COES-run scheme that sidelined ministerial authorities.[14]

Vichy statism set an upper limit on Cartelist corporatism. When it came to direct financial grants to theaters, however, the regime felt less inhibited. The Third Republic had never been overgenerous in this domain. In 1939, it disbursed a meager sixty thousand francs to nonstate theaters. By 1943, that figure had shot up to six million, a reversal of course in no small part owing to the exertions of a second-rank but energetic Fine Arts official, Jeanne Laurent.[15] Laurent, a Breton of Catholic background, joined the civil service in 1939 in the Third Republic's waning moments. It was a regime whose policies she execrated and would continue to execrate all her life. The Republic's passivity in matters of artistic policy, she later wrote, had allowed an "invasion" of "ugliness and mediocrity" that threatened the moral health of humanity itself. It had failed at every turn to arrest the advance of "new feudalities avid for private gain and often opposed to the interests of the nation as a whole."[16] Laurent, a Pétainist by reflex, felt more in her element at Vichy, at least at first. She meant to use her official powers to set things right, to bring aid to avant-garde theaters, which, as she phrased it in a wartime article, made "an artistic effort" and by that effort, often at the cost of personal advantage, had served the general interest.[17] And what art-house theaters proved in practice worthy of the state's newfound munificence? The list is not hard to predict: Baty's Montparnasse theater; Renoir's Athénée; the Théâtre de l'Atelier, which Dullin in 1940 passed on to André Barsacq and the Quatre Saisons troupe (Barsacq still took the troupe on the road during the summer season); and, of course, Dullin's new theater enterprise, Les Spectacles Charles Dullin.[18] The Cartel directors moved into positions of power during the war years, and their theaters, thanks to Laurent, who was a devotee, enjoyed an exceptional measure of public recognition.

But it was not just the Cartel that flourished in the Vichy era. Regional theater too enjoyed a new birth, and in this domain the principal actor was Pierre Schaeffer, founder of Jeune France and a fascinating character who makes a first appearance now but who will resurface many times again.

Schaeffer was an engineer, a practicing Catholic, and a lover of theater. He graduated the Ecole Polytechnique in the early thirties and joined state radio late in the decade as an electroacoustical technician. The intervening years were spent in part in the service of what must be counted Schaeffer's first love, scouting. At the Polytechnique, he had joined an elite Rover unit of the Catholic Scouts de France. Schaeffer later wrote an evocation of the troop, the Clan des Rois Mages, and of its animating personality Clotaire Nicole, who was killed in a tragic climbing accident as a young man. *Clotaire Nicole*, as the book was called, was in part a meditation on the scouting experience, on the exhilaration both physical and spiritual of an outdoor life spent hiking, cycling, and mountaineering, but it was above all a paean to the charismatic Nicole, the very model of the scout chef de troupe who exemplified "the plenitude, the virility, the joy of a life consecrated to Christ."[19] Extracts first appeared in the pages of *La Revue des jeunes* in 1934. The volume in its final version (with a preface by the Rover scout chaplain-general, Father Marcel Forestier) did not come out until 1938 under the imprimatur of Le Seuil, a fledgling publishing house of nonconformist orientation run by Paul Flamand and Jean Bardet.[20] As for theater, Schaeffer had firsthand knowledge of the doings of Léon Chancerel's Comédiens-Routiers and even tried his hand at a play of his own, *Le Mystère des Rois Mages*, which was staged with an all-scout cast at the Saint-Etienne du Mont cloister in 1934.[21]

Schaeffer's involvement in the Catholic youth movement provided him a critical contact at Vichy in the person of Georges Lamirand, some years older than Schaeffer but otherwise not so different in profile and belief. Lamirand, like Schaeffer, was an engineer. In the interwar decades, he combined a career in business with an ongoing commitment to Catholic youth affairs. Larmirand's growing reputation as a youth spokesman owed more than a little to the patronage of Robert Garric. Lamirand joined Garric's Equipes sociales, rising to become the organization's vice president. It was through Garric, it

seems, that Lamirand first met Maréchal Lyautey, who proved a helpful benefactor to the young engineer.[22] Lyautey encouraged Lamirand to put down on paper his reflections on the engineer's mission
in the management of factory personnel. The result was *Le Rôle social
de l'ingénieur* (an allusion to Lyautey's celebrated article of 1891, "Le
rôle social de l'officier"), published in 1932 with a preface by Lyautey.
Lamirand presented himself in the book as a crusader for social
peace, a *chef* who purified himself through moral and physical discipline, placing the men before himself all the better to command
them.[23] In the 1930s, Lamirand became a regular collaborator at *La
Revue des jeunes*, edited by Father Forestier and Garric, and the journal may have been the vehicle that first brought Schaeffer and Lamirand together.

In 1940, Lamirand's high reputation in certain right-wing circles
drew the attention of Vichy authorities who, in September, appointed
him to run the newly formed Secrétariat-général à la Jeunesse (SGJ).
Lamirand's chance proved to be Schaeffer's as well. Schaeffer had
spent the summer and fall of 1940 working for Vichy radio, but he
saw an opportunity in Lamirand's newfound power, seeking out the
youth administrator's backing for creation of a multipurpose arts organization. Lamirand agreed to supply the funding, and so Jeune
France got off the ground.

Schaeffer was joined at Jeune France by most of the team he had
worked with at Vichy radio, among them Pierre Barbier, Paul Flamand, Maurice Jacquemont, Daniel Lesur, Albert Ollivier, and Claude
Roy, all of whom attended the JF start-up meeting.[24] Who were these
men? Barbier and Jacquemont have been encountered before, Jacquemont as a breakaway from Chancerel's Comédiens-Routiers, Barbier as his partner in the itinerant theater group, the Quatre Saisons.
Theirs was a theater striving for professionalism, yet still rooted in the
confessional universe of Catholic militancy. Roy had been a member
of the ultra-right Action française. Flamand and Ollivier were veterans of the nonconformist *Ordre nouveau* group. Nonconformists came
in many hues, but the *Ordre nouveau* variety harbored a particular
animus against democratic institutions. The group's press organ ran
the headline "Don't Vote" on the eve of the Popular Front elections

of 1936, elaborating on the exhortation in the article that followed: "It is forbidden to vote, just as it is forbidden to spit."[25]

Lesur is in some ways the most difficult to situate. He was a member of a musical current that included André Jolivet and Olivier Messiaen. The trio sought a middle way between academic and avant-garde styles, aiming to fashion a musical idiom that was recognizably modern but at the same time timeless in its meditative spirituality. Lesur remained fairly conventional in his musical means, but not so Messiaen and Jolivet, who turned to non-Western sources, Hindu and African, for rhythmic inspiration. The cultural rock on which the three chose to build, however, was as much religious as aesthetic. All were committed Catholics. Lesur was himself a skilled organist with an appointment to the Benedictines, and he and his partners all looked to medieval forms—the canticle, Gregorian chant—for models. The group did indeed enter into a formal partnership, constituting a musical association in June 1936 under the name Jeune France. This first Jeune France, like its successor, imagined a France gripped by a "crisis of civilization." What the nation needed was a new, spiritual art that, hovering above the earthbound musical partisanship of the day, would uplift and regenerate. From this angle, the Jeune France of 1936 looks much like a musical homologue to the neither-right-nor-left nonconformism espoused by the likes of Emmanuel Mounier, and so it has been argued by the best-informed scholar in the field.[26]

The ex-scout Schaeffer, ever the manager of men, took care with the structuring of his new organization. JF was divided into two branches, one headquartered in Lyon of which he himself took charge, a second based in Paris and directed by Flamand.[27] Around each branch orbited smaller satellite offices: regional delegations or so-called Maisons Jeune France. Chancerel ran one such establishment in Toulouse. An attempt was made to set up a branch office in French North Africa under the leadership of Roger Leenhardt. The North African section never amounted to much, but Leenhardt proved a high-quality recruit. In the thirties, he had been a regular at Mounier's *Esprit*, though he was too much the pacifist to follow the review's anti-Munich line in 1938. It was, nonetheless, via Mounier, who knew Schaeffer, that Leenhardt first came Schaeffer's way, serving with him at Vichy radio before moving on to JF.[28]

Schaeffer's initial team was very much anchored in the various Catholic, nonconformist, not to say ultra-right currents that had roiled the political waters of the 1930s. This was JF's world, and as the organization expanded its range of action, its ties to this exalted, often obstreperous milieu only deepened. The Action française link furnished JF with a second round of recruits in Jean de Fabrègues (active in Lyon) and Maurice Blanchot, who joined the literature section of the Paris branch. From *Ordre nouveau* came the Sciences Po graduate Xavier de Lignac, alias Jean Chauveau. Lesur recruited Jolivet and Maurice Martenot, the latter a pioneer of electronic music and the inventor of the so-called Martenot waves. Schaeffer's Catholic connections brought on board Olivier Hussenot and André Clavé, both theater men. Clavé in turn recruited his friend Maurice Delarue and in due course Jean Vilar. Mounier himself was attracted to the enterprise, working alongside Schaeffer as JF's cultural adviser.[29]

These were all young talents, but Schaeffer took care to seek out the patronage and protection of more established figures as well. He constituted a twelve-man Comité directeur, in effect a board of trustees, composed in equal parts of artistic personalities and Vichy officials of varying degrees of seniority. The body in fact played little role in JF's actual functioning, but its composition gives a fair indication of the organization's aesthetic and political lines of descent. The aesthetic side was represented by Claudel, Copeau, Giraudoux, the pianist Alfred Cortot, architect Auguste Perret (a pioneer in the application of reinforced concrete to church architecture), and Georges Desvallières, a founder of the Sacred Art movement; the political cum administrative side by Lamirand, Garric, Hautecoeur, Louis Garonne (an SGJ administrator), François Valentin (a Catholic youth militant turned veterans administration official), and the former neosocialist, soon to become secretary-general of information, Paul Marion.[30]

Schaeffer's was a disparate crew in some respects, but on one point there was general agreement: French culture in the interwar decades had fallen into decadence, a victim of official neglect but above all of rampant commercialism. Boulevard theater demoralized the stage. Public taste had degenerated, ruined by "the laxities of cinema and radio." As for music, how could one expect listeners, reared on a diet of May Milton and Tino Rossi, to resonate to the healthy simplicities of a farandole or bourrée? What France needed was "a powerful ear-rinsing," a cultural housecleaning that would revitalize taste and prepare a new renaissance of French civilization.[31]

Differences cropped up in JF ranks, however, when it came to figuring out how this was to be achieved. Flamand's branch looked to the regenerative power of individual artistic creation. In May 1941, it sponsored an exhibition of paintings at the Braun Gallery in Paris under the title "Les jeunes peintres de tradition française." The show was organized by Jean Bazaine, chief of JF's plastic arts section in the northern zone. Bazaine selected figurative work executed with a cubist-style abstraction. This was modern, avant-garde art, no doubt, but why then the insistence on "French tradition" in the exhibit's title?

The question admits of two answers that are not incompatible but emphasize different aspects of the JF project. In the interwar years, the Paris art scene had been dominated by the so-called Ecole de Paris, a loose grouping of Montparnasse-based painters (Lipchitz, Soutine, and Zadkine among them) who were often of foreign or Jewish extraction.[32] Such painters were not represented in the Bazaine exhibit. The Germans would not have allowed it to be sure, but would Jeune France, which by statute excluded foreigners and Jews from membership,[33] have wanted it otherwise? The "Frenchness" of the exhibit may have been enhanced by the presence of a number of artists of Catholic background, not least Bazaine, but also Alfred Manessier and Lucien Lautrec (both JF members themselves). The Catholic connection was not just incidental, for it left an imprint on the work the artists did, canvases of a "primitivizing" and spiritual simplicity. The exhibit's modernism, then, was a conservative one, French and Catholic in its identity politics, "cubo-abstract" in its aesthetics. Little wonder then that Jeanne Laurent was so taken with the show, with the work of Bazaine in particular, whose oeuvre she began to collect. But the supposed Frenchness of the Braun Gallery exhibition was a marker in a second sense, not just of an exclusionary rootedness, but of a nationalism that was meant as a provocation to the Occupier: French art still lived, the German presence notwithstanding. It is worth mentioning in this connection that the score of artists on display included at least one communist, Edouard Pignon.[34]

Set before the public work of challenging composition and rigorous spirituality: such was the Braun Gallery's agenda, and it represented one way, as a JF document put it, to regenerate "a popular taste... perverted by mercantile productions."[35] In Schaeffer's southern zone, however, a different set of strategies was pursued. The individual artist might still have a preeminent role to play but not in isolation from the wider culture that nurtured him.

Along these lines, JF in collaboration with Mounier's *Esprit* sponsored a colloquium, "Poésie et chanson," which met at Lourmarin in September 1941. The meeting brought together the young stars of French poetry: Pierre Emmanuel, Loÿs Masson, Pierre Seghers. Leenhardt, one of the organizers, made a point of inviting Henri-Irénée Marrou to participate. Marrou is best known as a groundbreaking historian of late antiquity, but in this context what mattered was his status as a music critic (he wrote for *Esprit*) with a profound passion for popular song. Marrou in fact went on to compile an "admirable miscellany," published in 1944, of French *chansons populaires*.[36]

The Marrou link is interesting on both aesthetic and political grounds. Marrou's volume, *Le Livre des chansons*, argued the case that French lettered culture across the ages had drawn its strength in dynamic exchange with more plebeian currents. German folklorists might vaunt the self-sufficient creativity of the *Volk*. Highbrow pundits, like Thierry Maulnier, might argue the opposite, that it was the elite, not the people, who were the wellsprings of national creativity. Both points of view, Marrou believed, were wrong. Yet in modern times, he lamented, that vitalizing connection between high and low culture had been broken as literate elites turned in on themselves and grew overrefined, and as the humble, in vain pursuit of self-improving embourgeoisement, forsook their cultural roots. The "unity" of French culture, however, might yet be resurrected, and Marrou's anthology was meant to contribute to this end, restoring to the folk their musical birthright while awakening the poets and troubadours of the present day to the inspirational power of popular song.[37] This was the emergent perspective Marrou brought to the Lourmarin conference, deepening its commitment to cultural community understood in part as the artistic fellowship of the poets present but also as the imagined community of a national culture, once sundered but made whole again by artists in touch with vernacular traditions. The quest for wholeness in a community of culture: it might be thought that there was little of the political in such a project, but for Marrou there was. His 1944 volume critiqued German *völkisch*-ness; it refused the snobbery of Maulnier, a fascist intellectual close to Vichy. There was, indeed, a Resistance impulse at work in such a double rejection, an impulse Marrou did his best to make explicit in dedicating *Le Livre des chansons* to Jean-Marie Soutou, by then an active résistant (as was Marrou himself). There is even some evidence, slim to be sure, that such attitudes were already stirring among the poets who gathered at the Lourmarin colloquium in 1941. At the end of a day's session, as the poet Max Pol-Fouchet later recollected, a number of participants (unidentified) descended into the streets to raise their voices in shouts of "Vive de Gaulle."[38]

Marrou did not like the word "folklore," because it suggested something dead, and he wanted a tradition not so much preserved as renewed. Schaeffer, however, did not shy away from the term. He was an unabashed partisan of traditional arts and crafts, of peasant dance and French country music. His was not the Lourmarin style, however, which sought to reconnect the lettered to a rooted Frenchness they had forgotten. It was rather the activist's, which reawakened through hands-on work and animation. JF opened in northern and southern zones alike teaching workshops or *maîtrises* that apprenticed young aspirants in the techniques of their chosen craft, from ceramics to the plastic arts to theater. There was an artisanal dimension to the enterprise, keeping alive and passing on the knowledge of master craftsmen to a new generation, but it also had a scouting flavor. *Maîtrises* organized campfires that mixed uplift—readings from Péguy and Claudel—with scout-style sing-alongs and folkloric dancing.

The idea was to create a new culture, "a culture for the total man," that would shunt aside the moviegoing, newspaper-reading superficialities of the present day.[39] Mounier in fact gave some serious thought to JF curriculum development, and from the texts he thought appropriate for teaching purposes it is possible to discern the outlines of the totalistic humanism he and his JF colleagues dreamed of. Mounier recommended biographical readings above all, proposing a list that began with Roland and the crusading Saint Louis and ended with "Père de Foucault, Péguy, [and] one or two colonizers."[40] The exemplary man was a man of action: a hero who risked all in the service of France and its Catholic faith. These lessons once learned, the graduates of JF teaching were meant to bring them to the nation as a whole.

Performance, indeed, was very much at the heart of the Jeune France project. In 1940, under the auspices of Lamirand's SGJ, a youth labor service corps was set up, the Chantiers de la Jeunesse, run by an old scout, General Paul de La Porte du Theil (seconded by Father Forestier, who served as chaplain). JF turned more than once to the Chantiers for assistance. It recruited several score Chantiers kids for a theater-training course that culminated in a month-long practicum with Hussenot's theatrical *maîtrise* headquartered at Uriage, also the site of a Vichy-sponsored leadership school. Vichy, as might be expected, celebrated the May fete of Jeanne d'Arc with great fanfare. For the first such occasion, Jeune France staged a series of productions across the south, including a recitation by a chorus of JF-trained Chantiers youth. Some of this, of course, was done to impress Lamirand himself. When the minister spoke in the southern zone, he could count on JF to organize accompanying youth performances: folkloric dances, choirs, and the like.[41]

Schaeffer and company's emphasis on performance extended well beyond youth theatricals. It has been estimated that in 1941 Jeune France organized or funded up to half of all theater productions in France. Over the course of its brief year-and-a-half existence, Schaeffer's group involved itself in a staggering 770 plays and performances of all kinds.[42] Indeed, what is remarkable is not just the extent but also the variety of JF's activities. A veteran Copiau, Emile Ducroux, asked Schaeffer for funding to set up a school of mime in Paris; Schaeffer helped out and had reason to congratulate himself in later years, for among Ducroux's first students was a young Marcel Marceau, who went out to elevate French mime to international renown.[43] JF was no less generous to itinerant theater. Clavé's La Roulotte was a beneficiary of such largesse, so too Jean Dasté's La Saison nouvelle.[44]

On the whole, Jeune France favored revivals, with a particular emphasis on the classics, from the ever-accessible Molière to the "violent heroics" (the phrase is Lignac's) of Lope de Vega.[45] But there were original productions as well: Barbier and Schaeffer's ten-tableaux celebration of the life of Jeanne d'Arc, *Portique pour une jeune fille de France* (with music by Messiaen among others), which played throughout the southern zone in May 1941. In July, the first French production of Claudel's *Jeanne au bûcher* (an oratorio with music by Arthur Honegger) premiered at the Lyon opera house under JF auspices. And in August, Vilar's adaptation of Hesiod's *Les Travaux et les jours* opened at Melun, an event memorable for its opening procession, a cavalcade of rural folk sorted by métier, wearing the clothes and shouldering the tools of their various trades.[46] The Germans and the Vichy regime, sometimes working in parallel, sometimes in competition, constructed the institutional framework for theater renewal in Paris, but for the provincial stage, it was Jeune France that took the lead.

Such lavish attentions, both official and semiofficial, were not wasted on appreciative theater professionals, who in later years came to look on the Vichy era as a golden age. It is reasonable to ask, though, whether Vichy officialdom achieved what it was after. French theater flourished, but was it a theater in consonance with the values of the National Revolution?

In the case of Jeune France, the answer must be yes. Its two most celebrated presentations—Barbier and Schaeffer's *Portique* and Claudel and Honegger's *Jeanne*—dealt with a Vichy icon, Jeanne d'Arc, and the treatment in both cases was worshipful and patriotic. France had never seen anything like the *Portique* before. On 11 May 1941, JF organized simultaneous stagings of the pageant across unoccupied France. The audiences were huge—twenty thousand in Toulouse, twenty-five thousand in Marseille, thirty-five thousand in Lyon—and the settings were appropriate to the crowds: a public square in Toulouse (where Chancerel was in charge), a bicycle arena in Marseille. These were France's "first experiences with stadium theater," or at least that is how JF, in a bragging mood, characterized its efforts in a government report.[47] They were plein air extravaganzas played out under the stars and, in the case of the Lyon production, under the maréchal's stars, for to the tricolors decorating the local mise-en-scène were pinned the seven *étoiles* of a maréchal de France. The regime's involvement in the productions, moreover, was substantive as well as symbolic. The army contributed logistical support, and additional performances were organized for Chantiers de la Jeunesse audiences.[48]

Claudel's *Jeanne*, unlike the *Portique*, was no pageant. It accented less the spectacle of Jeanne's life than her martyrdom and agony at the stake as she gave up a life that had been consecrated to the unity of France. But in other respects, Claudel's effort bears some comparison to Schaeffer's. The Lyon presentation boasted a huge cast of several hundred plus a full orchestra. The show, after its July opening, then went on tour, and the chosen venues were large outdoor locales like the Roman amphitheater at Arles or the arena, also Roman, at Nîmes (the show was also presented at Vichy's leadership school at Uriage). As with the *Portique*, the Vichy state lent a hand. *Jeanne au bûcher* was mounted in collaboration with the Commissariat à la lutte contre le Chômage, which, it seems, supplied a number of the cast members involved.[49]

These were not propaganda plays. No mention was made of contemporary events in either production. But both relied on the collaboration of Vichy institutions. Both memorialized the life of a Catholic maiden who sacrificed for the nation. And both, grand in scale, staged out of doors in often antique settings, aspired to a new kind of theater, a theater of mass communion that would bind and transform through spectacle, whether festive or tragic. This was just the sort of theater that Copeau and his disciples, so numerous in Jeune France ranks, had long hungered for; it was also a theater that Vichy might well be pleased to claim as its own.

But how about Paris theater? Was the new order's imprint so evident here? A pair of examples, the production of Claudel's *Soulier de*

Satin at the Comédie française in 1943 and of Anouilh's *Antigone* at the Atelier theater a year later, will show that an unmixed verdict is not easy to render. Jean-Louis Barrault directed the *Soulier de Satin*. In his memoirs, he describes the occasion as an "uprising of the French soul," a virtual "national insurrection." The Vichy press, he explains, was gunning for the play, all the more so as everyone knew of Claudel's supposed Gaullist sympathies.[50] This will not quite do as a characterization of events. Claudel did indeed pen an ode to de Gaulle, but that was in 1944. More pertinent in the present context is that he also wrote an ode to Pétain, recited in 1941 at a Vichy presentation of Claudel's play *L'Annonce faite à Marie*.[51] Circa 1943, it might be fairer to say, it was Claudel's Pétainism everyone knew of. As for Barrault, he was, true enough, no man of the Right. In the thirties, he had been a Popular Front sympathizer with avant-garde tastes, keeping the company of surrealist painters and theater mavericks like Antonin Artaud. But Barrault also trained at Dullin's drama school and there learned to play Claudel from a master who taught how to regulate breathing to capture the rhythms of the playwright's poetry. Come 1940, Barrault was confronted with a critical decision. In May, Copeau was appointed to direct the Comédie française, and Copeau in turn invited Barrault to join the troupe. The invitation came in August when Vichy was firmly in power. To the chagrin of his friends, Barrault accepted. He moved to Paris, and while in the capital, it might be added, joined the theater workshop of Jeune France's Paris branch.[52]

A Barrault/Claudel collaboration, then, did not conjure shades of Gaullism. Nor did the material at hand, Claudel's *Soulier de Satin*. Set in Golden Age Spain, the play resonated with the hispanism of the Vichy moment, a hispanism that shaped the repertoire of the Comédie française as much as if not more than that of Jeune France. In November 1940, Copeau staged a production of Corneille's *Le Cid*, casting Barrault in the title role. The young in the audience loved the production, both for the sober rigor of the staging and for Barrault's own evident youthfulness (so different from the adult gravitas of the standard-issue Rodrigue).[53] Copeau's successor Jean-Louis Vaudoyer commissioned Henry de Montherlant, who had never written for the theater before, to create a play based on Golden Age antecedents. The result was *La Reine Morte,* which debuted at the Comédie française in 1942—an austere, at times agonizing drama of a Portuguese king's single-minded pursuit of *raison d'état,* even at the expense of his son's happiness and, in the end, even at the cost of his own life. The concentrated emotion and high sacrifice of heroic action: such was the stuff of *espagnolisme,* and Claudel's work fit the mold but, as might be expected, with a heavier emphasis on religious themes.

The *Soulier de Satin* takes the story of Le Cid and resets it in late-sixteenth- to early-seventeenth-century Spain. There are infidels to fight; the hero must sacrifice love for duty. But Claudel, who had his reservations about classic French drama, shattered the hallowed unities of the genre. The action of the play is not compressed into a single day but unfolds across four so-called *journées*; and the Rodrigue of *Soulier de Satin,* unlike the Rodrigue of Le Cid, operates on a planetary scale, the scene shifting from Spain to the New World to North Africa. Not least of all, Claudel's hero is a visionary who imagines a globe made Christian, united in a higher love and submission to the divine scheme. Barrault's staging—the spare set designs, the use of mime and body movement to frame Claudel's poetry—heightened the play's prophetic atmosphere. Clergymen in the audience were bowled over by the sense of mystic wholeness that the play conjured and came away wondering how such effects might be applied to liturgical ends.[54]

Here was a theater a nation might take pride in: a theater of high ideals and genuine spirituality that breathed fresh life into the classics even as it transfigured audiences through the magic of staging and poetry. There is nothing of necessity Vichyite in all this; and yet were not the values of the new theater, at least as embodied in the *Soulier de Satin,* values that the regime itself subscribed to: heroic action, Catholic faith, and a tradition renewed? And indeed, contra Barrault, the Vichy press did not savage the play, at least not *La Gerbe,* which praised Barrault's mise-en-scène as fully "worthy of Paul Claudel's oeuvre."[55]

Anouilh, by contrast, was neither a traditionalist nor a believer, and the Antigone story, if it lends itself to a political reading at all, is more associated with resistance to power than with power's justification. Anouilh's *Antigone* opened, it might be added, in February 1944 and continued in production well after the Liberation, not the kind of run that might be expected of a drama altogether out of tune with Resistance values. And yet.

Anouilh's sympathies lay with the individual—the artist, the loner of principle—who was much put upon in a world where money ruled. It was a position that won him friends on the Far Right. The rebarbative Rebatet, who so execrated the corruptions of the boulevard theater, was a particular fan. "[T]he delicious Anouilh," the journalist called him, and there was something of the "anarchist of the Right" about Anouilh that might appeal to the likes of Rebatet.[56] The dramatist wrote for *La Gerbe* and *Je suis partout* during the war; and not more than a decade later, in 1956, he staged a play, *Pauvre Bitos* (directed by Baty), that likened the purge commissions of the Liberation to the Robespierrist Terror tribunals of 1793, all the while skewering the imbecilic mediocrity of parliamentary institutions.[57] There are echoes of such attitudes in *Antigone*. The guards who keep watch on Antigone are as dull witted as they can be. Polyneices, Oedipus's son and successor to the throne of Thebes, is described as "un petit fêtard imbécile,"[58] just the kind of tag polemicists of the Right had applied in the not so distant past to the aperitif-sipping pols of the Third Republic.

But what of Creon and Antigone? Here, all is ambiguity. Creon is a sympathetic figure, an older man, worn out by the cares of state he has felt duty-bound to shoulder in the wake of the civil war that left Oedipus's two sons, the king Polyneices and his rebellious brother Eteocles, both dead. Creon's job? To think of the well-being of all, to make the order of things a little less absurd. Antigone, by contrast, is self-involved, even morbid. *La Gerbe* wrote of her overweening "pride."[59] Happiness is within her reach in the figure of a young suitor, Hémon, but she defies Creon nonetheless, embracing a death she seems to welcome. All the same, Antigone's repeated *nons* to Creon's repeated entreaties transmute the willful maiden into an unbending individual of the sort dear to Anouilh. Between Creon's Pétain and Antigone's résistant, the choice is not evident.

The play's director, André Barsacq, claimed in later years that the choice was in fact loaded to Antigone's side, in favor of "revolt" and against "the ugliness and hypocrisy" of Creon, but that is an after-the-fact judgment.[60] Barsacq, a veteran of the itinerant theater, had taken over Dullin's Théâtre de l'Atelier in 1940, and the younger, up-and-coming director very much wanted to cast himself as a worthy heir to the Cartel's theatrical legacy. In January 1941, he had occasion to deliver himself of a press conference in Paris in which he lashed out at the commercial stage, at the same time expressing his sincere wish that "the repercussions of the National Revolution make themselves felt in the theater world." Barsacq's attack on commercial theater may have had an anti-Semitic edge. The sources differ on the point but not on the fact that he appeared before reporters in the company of a Propaganda Abteilung official who did make anti-Semitic remarks.[61]

Barsacq knew about equivocal circumstances, and something of this knowledge informed his direction of *Antigone*. The actors were costumed in contemporary evening dress, all in blacks and whites,[62] creating a starkness of effect that was one of the hallmarks of Cartel theater. But in a world in which light and dark are fixed on the bodies of all, in which truth sways back and forth between characters as the argument unfolds, where resides the true moral center? This kind of studied ambiguity was not exceptional for the period, and it will be encountered again. It was an ambiguity, moreover, that played to many audiences, garnering praise from collaborationist reviewers in 1944 and then from Liberation audiences after that.[63]

From the vantage point of 1944, Vichy authorities might well look back with satisfaction on what had been accomplished. Commercial theater no longer ruled the boulevards; its interwar embodiment Henry Bernstein had taken the path of exile; and Jews in general were driven off the stage. A concerted effort had been made to professionalize the theater, to wrap it in the protective casing of corporate organization, and to subsidize quality productions. Vichy (and the Germans) had turned to the Cartel, its allies, and heirs to bring about this new deal for theater. They responded to the call, taking up positions of power in the institutional hierarchies erected by Vichy. But more than that, they reinvented the medium. Classics were revived and updated. New creations were imagined: pageants, dramatic oratorios, epic tragedies. And the provincial stage, once the poor relation of legitimate theater, had gotten a sprucing up, thanks to the exertions of itinerant groups like La Roulotte and to the outdoor spectaculars of Jeune France.[64] In the end, there was much in all this, not just in form but in content, to comfort Vichy. The heroes of the Vichy-era stage, whether Rodrigue or Jeanne d'Arc, were heroes the regime could warm to. So too the themes: from the ruralism of Vilar's *Les Travaux et les jours,* to the cosmic Christianity of Claudel, to Montherlant's and Anouilh's anguished meditations on *raison d'état.*

Vichy Cinema

Vichy's success in remaking the movie industry was no less spectacular. The regime set about imposing a new institutional order, centralized and corporate. This order was exclusionary: its administrators justified the purging of Jews and foreigners in the name of professionalism and quality, but pursuit of such principles was not only an excuse for racism. It also defined a positive agenda, a concerted effort to bring order to an industry notorious for its turbulence and to promote filmmaking of distinction. As in theater, the regime in large part achieved its goals. Two hundred and twenty films were made in the Vichy years, a number of them masterpieces. A new generation of directors came to maturity destined for long postwar careers, Claude Autant-Lara, Jacques Becker, Robert Bresson, Henri-Georges Clouzot among them. And audiences responded to such offerings, film attendance shooting up from 220 million in 1938 to over 300 million in 1943.[65] Film historians have written of the paradox of Vichy cinema, of an industry that prospered in straitened circumstances, of an art form that blossomed in the hard soil of Occupation-era France. The paradox is all the greater because so many in the film industry (Becker and Louis Daquin are prime examples) were themselves hostile to the Pétainist regime's authoritarian agenda.

But perhaps the paradox is not so great after all. Vichy lavished attention on movies as the Third Republic had not. Hollywood, which had siphoned away a large chunk of box-office receipts in the thirties, was out of the picture in the war years,[66] and the quality cinema that Vichy authorities did so much to promote was often congenial in content as well as in style to movie professionals, whether or not they were in sympathy with the regime's wider political goals.

Vichy's ambitions for the movie industry were at once centralizing and corporatist, and the two objectives were not always easy to reconcile. On the centralizing end, the regime in its first months created a single agency in charge of all cinematic affairs. The Service du cinéma, as it was called, was placed under the tutelage of the Sécrétariat-général à l'Information (SGI). This was a break from the practice of Third Republic days, when responsibility for movie affairs had been divvied up between multiple ministries and bureaus.[67] The regime's vice premier, Pierre Laval, conscious of the power of the medium, took care to appoint a cinema administrator with whom he had good working relations. Guy de Carmoy was the first to head the Service du cinéma. It will be remembered that Carmoy, a career civil servant, had collaborated with Laval before, as the author of a report on the movie industry drafted at the behest of the Laval administration of 1935.

Carmoy lasted in the post until the fall of 1941 and then was replaced by Louis-Emile Galey, who would serve until the Liberation. Galey was all in all a more political figure. He had been an early member of the *Esprit* collective. But pacifist militancy, more than critical reflection, was Galey's predilection, and he soon spun out of Mounier's orbit into that of Bergery's pro-appeasement *La Flèche*. Vichy once in place, Galey cast about for new opportunities. He joined first the Compagnons de France, a youth-training and service organization, founded by the conseiller d'état and Catholic scouting official Henry Dhavernas. It may be that Galey did not feel altogether at home in confessional and scouting circles, for he soon quit the Compagnons and moved over to Schaeffer's Jeune France, where he enlisted in its Architecture section (Galey was an architect by training). Then, in October 1941, he was tapped to direct the Service du cinéma by the new secretary-general of information, Paul Marion. Marion picked Galey for the post in preference to Robert Brasillach, who also coveted the position.[68]

But Vichy, centralizing as it was in practice, liked to keep up corporatist appearances. In theater, this impulse had found expression in the COES, and the film industry too got its equivalent, the Comité d'organisation des industries cinématographiques (COIC), created by decree in November 1940. An industry professional, Raoul Ploquin, was placed in charge, assisted by a twenty-member consultative commission. Ploquin is best remembered as producer of two Vichy-era masterworks, Jean Grémillon's *Le Ciel est à vous* (1943) and Robert Bresson's *Les Dames du bois de Boulogne* (1944). Marcel L'Herbier, drawing a contrast between Ploquin and the well-known leftist Louis Daquin, described Ploquin as "of less progressive tendencies."[69] He was not a man of the Left, to be sure, but neither, it seems, was he a right-wing doctrinaire, and his lack of ideological zeal did not sit well with Occupation authorities. Alfred Greven, for one, head of the Paris-based German movie consortium Continental Films, disliked him.[70]

Ploquin's relative political moderation was made up for by the more partisan enthusiasms of his secretary-general, Robert Buron. In 1930, Buron had signed a manifesto, circulated by the ultra-right review *Réaction*, heralding monarchy and Christianity as the building blocks of a future French renaissance. His militancy toned down in subsequent years, and by decade's end he had thrown in his lot with the christian-democratic Parti démocrate populaire. The defeat of 1940, however, caused Buron's old prejudices to bubble up once more. At the COIC, it is said, he was among the more resolute partisans of Vichy's policies of aryanization.[71]

The COIC, like the Service du cinéma, was run by a mixed team of conservative professionals and right-wing zealots. That did not mean, however, that the two institutional hierarchies were destined to get along. For all its corporatist rhetoric, the Vichy state was just not able to rein in its domineering ambitions. Laval's return to power in April 1942 was prelude to a shake-up of the movie administration. Starting in May, the Service, now renamed the Direction générale du cinéma, no longer answered to the SGI but directly to Laval himself. Galey was kept on as director-general. On the COIC end, Ploquin was fired and replaced by a three-man Comité directeur headed by film producer Roger Richebé. The highest echelons of state were now positioned to exercise a tightening control over movie affairs, even as the industry's corporate voice was splintered. Just the same, Richebé proclaimed himself content with the arrangement. The Comité directeur, of which he was the senior member, had the right to pronounce first on all professional matters, a source of satisfaction to Richebé who, as a film producer, was a firm believer in industry self-governance. On all other questions, however, the state had priority, and the state, it might be added, did not respect this division of labor for long, ever encroaching on COIC terrain. Richebé and company at first protested and then, in August 1943, resigned. Galey, still director-general, now took over as COIC chief as well, seconded in this position by the immovable Buron.[72]

For all such institutional wranglings, there was considerable unanimity in movie-industry ranks on questions of policy. L'Herbier published an essay in *Cinémonde* in February 1940 complaining about "the growing anarchy of a scattered industry," which left the French screen vulnerable to invasion by an enemy he would not designate by name. Carmoy had a solution to the problem. The freewheeling ways of old had brought ruin, but a new age was dawning. As he told the COIC consultative commission in December: "To the era of liberalism succeeds that of organization." Ploquin also had a message for the commission, lecturing it the year following on the urgency of a "general cleansing of the profession," an exhortation that must have gone down well with the aryanizer Buron. Galey rounded out the agenda with a third item. Organization, yes; cleansing, yes; but these tasks once completed, he wrote in 1940, the movie-industry administration had still to confront a yet more fundamental problem: "restor[ing] to French production the quality which in former times had made its reputation."[73]

There was little that was unheard of in all this. Movie professionals had been agitating for just such an industry overhaul since the 1930s. What was new in 1940, however, was the state's willingness to take action, and it was a state that, although constrained by the Occupier's priorities, otherwise confronted few obstacles to the implementation of its will.

On the matter of organization, Vichy acted at all levels of the profession and did so with dispatch. At the movie-house level, the regime imposed legislation in October 1940 prohibiting the double bill. This may seem a minor gesture, but it eased the pressure on theater managers to multiply offerings in the hope of drawing in larger audiences, and the measure had an unanticipated side benefit as well. Theater owners were not allowed to program B movies, but they might show all the documentaries they liked. This was a boon to the short-subject genre. Four hundred such films would be made during the Vichy years. France's first congress of documentary film was in fact convened in April 1943 at the Palais de Chaillot, with Minister of National Education Abel Bonnard delivering the inaugural address. The event was remarkable in itself but also for the new talent it introduced. Jacques Cousteau screened a documentary on shipwrecks, a pioneering work of underwater photography entitled *Epaves*.[74]

Theater owners no doubt welcomed the state's efforts to manage competition. They may have been more ambivalent, however, about official meddling in movie-house finances. Vichy required theater managers to sell only numbered tickets bearing the COIC stamp. The arrangement was meant to simplify the monitoring of box-office intake for purposes of taxation. In compensation, the regime simplified the movie-industry tax structure, in 1941 abolishing the burdensome triple tax of old in favor of a single graduated levy calculated on the basis of weekly gross receipts.[75]

The state was no less attentive to cleaning up the murky business of movie financing. Film-industry critics had long complained about unscrupulous producers who manipulated and cheated, making it difficult for well-meaning professionals to turn out the quality films they wanted to. Vichy made a modest effort to bring a measure of transparency to the movie deal-making process. A law of February 1944 created a state-kept public registry of cinematography. The registry recorded the titles of movies in production and the contracts signed by the parties involved. The idea was simple: the more information about moviemaking in the public domain, the smaller the likelihood of crooked behavior. No one, however, was obliged to register contracts with the state, although in the event of a bankruptcy it was the registered who were entitled to first reimbursement.[76]

Of more immediate consequence, the Vichy state itself got into the business of movie finance. In May 1941, the regime set up a Comité d'attribution des avances au cinéma. On application, the Comité was prepared to advance up to two-thirds of film production costs, provided certain conditions were met. Producers had to furnish up front a minimum one-third of the financing; they were pledged to pay back the state's advance, at a modest rate of interest to be sure, within three years; and all laboratories and studios involved in the filmmaking process had to be paid in cash and on time. In case of producer default, the state undertook to reimburse banks before individual investors. The money for all this came from the Crédit National, and to make sure that the bank did not end up saddled with a heavy burden of bad debt, Vichy assembled a compensation fund, drawn in part from the tax on box-office receipts, in part from a levy on producers' profits.[77]

The system was remarkable on several counts. First, for the extent of its operations. In the three years of its functioning, a full quarter of all French-made films received financing in some form from the Comité des avances. And not just any film got funding. The official who ran the committee, Henri Clerc, an ex–Radical deputy and zealous proponent of Franco-German rapprochement (a position that drew him into the orbit of Chateaubriant's collaborationist La Gerbe), had long remonstrated against financial improprieties in the moviemaking business. He wanted his committee to exercise first and foremost "a cleansing influence." That accomplished, the committee might then apply its resources to more substantive ends: the promotion of films that gave evidence of "an effort toward artistic improvement." In practice, this meant a bias against films too locked into the star system of old. The committee did not want to discourage commercial films altogether (after all, producers had to earn enough to reimburse their advances), but it did want to boost projects with artistic promise, a preference that benefited both established directors like Marcel Carné (his Les Visiteurs du soir was awarded an advance in 1942) and newcomers like Bresson, whose Anges du péché got funding the year following.[78]

Vichy's plans to restore order to the film industry targeted theater owners and producers first and foremost. There is no surprise here. They had long been the butt of anticommercial rhetoric that cast them as hucksters and finaglers all too happy to sell out the industry they served in pursuit of profit. But organization was not just a good for particular sectors of the moviemaking business. It was something the industry in its entirety stood in need of. Hence the creation of the COIC, of a corporate body that was supposed to represent the interests of the industry as a whole. Hence also the creation in October 1940 of the COIC-administered *carte professionnelle*. Everyone in the movies was required to carry such a card; it had to be renewed on a regular basis; and it was the COIC that was charged with vetting applicants. Theater, in the late stages of the regime, had tried out such a system without much success. In the movie world, by contrast, the professional card was instituted early on, and it stuck. A professionalizing impetus lay behind the scheme. Would-be movie hands had to establish their moral character and professional credentials. But more than that, they had to give evidence of their "nonmembership in the Jewish race."[79]

This is a reminder, if reminder is needed, that Vichy's organizing impulses came inseparable from an exclusionary agenda. It was plenty clear, moreover, at least in the movie business, who needed to be excluded. In February 1940, L'Herbier had not wanted to identify the occult force that threatened French cinema. Such hesitations dissolved in the wake of the defeat. In a piece published in *La Gerbe* in January 1941, he at last gave a name to France's public enemy "number 1": "the imperialism of American film."[80] For Rebatet, however, France's public enemy had another face. In 1941, he wrote approvingly of Paul Morand's midthirties exposé of film-industry immoralism, *France la doulce*, venturing just one reproach. Morand had lambasted the unscrupulous wheeler-dealers with foreign-sounding names who ruled the cinema roost, but he had not had the courage to call them what they were, "to write in plain French the four letters of the word 'juif.'"[81]

Now, there was an actual and not just imagined invasion of the French screen during the Occupation years, but it was one the French were in no position to complain about. Joseph Goebbels dispatched

Alfred Greven, an enterprising and flexible-minded film executive, to Paris to set up a German-funded production studio, Continental Films. The studio had an important, though not overpowering, impact on the French movie scene. It signed up major talent from Carné (not the likeliest choice) to Clouzot, from Jouvet to Fernandel. Carné never in fact made a movie with Greven; Jouvet left France before he had to live up to the terms of his contract. Fernandel, however, made a couple of comedies with Continental.[82] As for Clouzot, he was a house favorite and for good reason. Clouzot's love interest at the time, Suzy Delair, was an actress of collaborationist views who was heard to gripe on return from a trip to Berlin that she had not had a chance to meet Goebbels. Clouzot himself acknowledged at the Liberation that he had felt a certain attraction to Nazism, to National Socialism's "anticapitalism" in particular, which promised a "possible solution" to social problems. Delair and Clouzot hobnobbed with Greven and his mistress; Delair starred in Continental productions; and Clouzot made for the studio one of the Occupation era's most gripping (and perverse) films, *Le Corbeau* (1944).[83] Clouzot was perhaps the most accomplished director employed by Continental, but he was not the only one. The studio turned out thirty films during its brief existence, roughly one movie in seven made under the Occupation.[84] Nor was Continental content just to produce. Greven, a man of imperial ambitions, coveted control of distribution as well and to this end snapped up two major movie-house chains, the Circuit Siritsky and the Jacques Haïk chain.[85]

The Germans could not be kept out of France, but what about the film industry's imagined bugbears, Hollywood and the Jews? The Germans did the dirty work when it came to American film. The Occupier banned Anglo-American films in the northern zone right from the very beginning and pressured Vichy into adopting the ban in the southern zone in October 1942. These measures worked a revolution in the film market. In 1938, American-made movies accounted for over a third of French box-office receipts; from 1942, that figure plummeted to nil. It was "French" films that now dominated French movie houses, raking in a full 90 percent of ticket sales.[86] In the Vichy era, of course, a "French" movie meant a movie sans Jewish input.

Vichy created the professional card in October 1940, applied first just in the occupied zone but from 1941 in the south too. Cards were refused to Jewish professionals, who were, as such, driven out of the industry. All levels of the profession were affected by Vichy's dictates. It was under the shadow of Vichy discrimination that the chain owners Siritsky and Haïk, both Jews, cut their deals with Greven. The largest film studios outside Paris were Marcel Pagnol's in Marseille and the famed Victorine studios at Nice, managed by the partnership of Schwob and Schlosberg. Pagnol, of course, was not Jewish, but Schwob and Schlosberg were, and as Vichy rule settled in, they had recourse to front men to run their enterprise. Greven, however, made noises about a takeover, and Carmoy took preemptive action, requisitioning the firm first before turning it over to a "French" group.[87] As for actors and directors, any number were driven into exile: Marcel Dalio and Jean-Pierre Aumont among the former, Jean Renoir and Max Ophuls[88] among the latter. All four, by varying routes, found their way to the United States.[89]

This is not to say that such measures were always applied with thoroughgoing zeal. US movies continued to get the occasional showing in the southern zone. Continental films assigned screenwriting work to Jean-Paul Le Chanois, the pseudonym of Jean-Paul Dreyfuss, a director of Jewish ancestry. The opportunistic Greven, it is reported, was well aware of the situation but chose to look the other way. There is also the celebrated example of Carné, who employed designer Alexandre Trauner and composer Joseph Kosma, both Jews, on the sets of *Les Visiteurs du soir* and the marvelous *Les Enfants du paradis* (1945). But these were exceptions. For all practical purposes, Hollywood had ceased to be a player on the French film scene, and the number of US films unshown in France piled up with consequences that would be meaningful when the French market was again opened up after the war. As for Jews, German authorities, already in the summer of 1941, were in a position to boast that the French film industry had in effect been made *judenrein*.[90]

From Vichy's perspective, organization and cleansing were paired goals intended to serve a common end: the creation of a new school of French cinema, a school purified of vulgar commercialism that understood the moral and aesthetic potential of film. There should be no mistaking that the regime took with utmost seriousness its commitment to foster a *cinéma de qualité*.

Censorship, to be sure, was one instrument to the purpose. An arrêté of December 1941 created a film censorship board attached to the SGI. New movies required the board's authorization prior to release, and the board's official brief was straightforward: to protect "good morals" and ensure a proper "respect for national traditions."[91] Laval's return to power in 1942 was prelude to a revamping of the censorship apparatus. From the summer of 1942, it was placed under the immediate authority of the Direction générale du cinéma, headed by Galey. The new board, working with Galey, was invested with the authority to review all movies, not just completed productions but even projects still in the scenario stage, which it proceeded to do with a busybody's niggling attention to detail. A Pétain loyalist, Moulin de Labarthète, was appointed first chair of the board but was soon succeeded by Paul Morand. Morand had first gained notoriety in the twenties as author of a series of novelistic exposés of the Parisian demimonde, but, with success, he had modulated the raciness of his prose, becoming a littérateur of more respectable reputation, appreciated for the poesy and subtle aperçus of his travel writing. In 1942, however, it was Morand's status as xenophobe and moralist critic of cinema mores that counted.[92]

The stick of censorship was not, however, the sole or even most important weapon in Vichy's arsenal. A whole battery of more positive measures was deployed, each of them designed to preserve or raise the standards of film production. In the domain of film preservation, no institution in France is more renowned than the Cinémathèque française. Founded in 1936 by the young film buff Henri Langlois, the Cinémathèque was at first very much a one-man affair, Langlois collecting old movie stock and keeping it as best he could in the apartment he shared with his parents. The film journalist Paul Auguste Harlé aided Langlois in finding supplementary space at Orly in the near suburbs. A subsequent bargain with French public authorities provided a home for the film archive at the Palais de Chaillot, which seemed to solve Langlois's perennial storage problems once and for all.

Then came the Occupation. The Cinémathèque's integrity was threatened time and again during the war years, but in the end it came through the period in better shape than ever. It owed its relative good fortune to a trio of benefactors. The first was Major Frank Hensel, who was head of the Reichsfilmarchiv in Paris and shared Langlois's pack rat instincts. Hensel made repeated gestures to protect the Cinémathèque's collections from less sympathetic German authorities who wanted to pillage them for political reasons or to get their hands on the chemicals in the film stock. It is estimated that tens of thousands of movies were saved in this way.[93] The occupying power continued to worry, nonetheless, about the subversive potential of Langlois's archive, and in the spring of 1942 adopted a menacing tone. Here is where Marcel L'Herbier stepped in, the Cinémathèque's second benefactor. L'Herbier acted in his capacity as president of the Cinémathèque, a post he had occupied on and off since 1940. In the company of Langlois and three officers from the German Propaganda Staffel, L'Herbier attended a dinner, taking full advantage of the evening's relaxed social circumstances to persuade the Occupier to back off.[94] The Cinémathèque's third guardian angel was Galey, who took an increasing interest in the fledgling institution's fortunes, furnishing it from 1943 with much-needed subsidies and no less coveted office space. The Cinémathèque moved the bulk of its operations in 1943 to a building, once owned by Jews but confiscated by Vichy, on the avenue de Messine. It was the same building that housed Galey's Direction générale and, for that matter, the Reichsfilmarchiv. The state, it should be said, got something in return for its largesse. Galey's second in command at the COIC, Buron, was named the Cinémathèque's treasurer, and the Cinémathèque's governing board in due course voted Galey himself an "honorary member."[95]

Galey committed the French state's prestige not just to the rescue of the nation's cinematic patrimony but also to the encouragement of filmmakers who might add to it. In 1942, he established the Grand Prix du film d'art français or as he called it in a later interview, "le prix à la qualité."[96] A seven-member commission was constituted to hand out the award; it included Galey, the president of the censorship board, and film critics Rebatet and Robert Régent. Régent would have liked a more aggressive measure, say, a system of tax breaks for "works of quality," but the Galey prize was at least a step in the right direction. And what films were judged worthy of the state's special recognition? The 1942 award went to Carné's *Les Visiteurs du soir*, the next year's to Bresson's *Anges du péché*.[97]

Nor was Vichy's solicitude confined to current filmmakers alone. The regime also took an interest in training the up-and-comers in the next generation of cineasts, who would maintain and renew France's reputation for quality filmmaking into the future. This is the impulse that lay behind creation of the Institut des hautes études ciné-matographiques (IDHEC) in September 1943. Régent described the institution in glowing terms as a "veritable Ecole normale supérieure of Cinema," and IDHEC's first director, the ubiquitous L'Herbier, spoke of it in much the same language. IDHEC opened its Paris head-quarters in January 1944. L'Herbier delivered the inaugural speech and in it referred to IDHEC as "this University of film," the very first of its kind in the world. Moviemakers, he went on, raising the tone, were the "spokesmen of the nation," the expression of its culture and taste, of "the purest French quality." IDHEC's job was to "create cre-ators" who would practice cinema as an art form and through their art defend and illustrate "la France de toujours."[98]

From October 1943, the Institut was placed under the authority of the SGI. Galey, of course, had done much to bring the school into ex-istence, but he was not at the origins of the initiative, which may be traced back to 1941. Not long after the June 1940 armistice, a band of young cinema enthusiasts—Jean Lods and Henri Alekan, among oth-ers—gathered in the southern zone, intent on finding a way to hone their moviemaking skills through workshop-based technical training. They organized a Centre artistique et technique des jeunes du cinéma (CATJC), which set up operations in Nice in March 1941. Lods was a man of left-wing views (though not an active resister). Alekan, in a later interview, talked of the "antifascist" convictions of most of the center's faculty and student body.[99] It is important, however, to recognize the complex mix of ideological currents that fed into the Centre's begin-nings. CATJC was not an independent body but worked under the aus-pices of Lamirand's Secrétariat-général à la Jeunesse. Its filmmaking section did contract work for the Vichy government.[100] The accent on youth and workshop training, the SGJ patronage, the dealings with Vichy—all this calls to mind Schaeffer's Jeune France, and, indeed, Schaeffer claimed the CATJC was a Jeune France spin-off that grew out of the Lourmarin poets' conference. Schaeffer was wrong in this (CATJC got started in March 1941; the Lourmarin meeting took place the following fall). On the other hand, Leenhardt credits Schaeffer with helping him get a position on the CATJC administrative board, and a number of Jeune France disciples, among them Lucien Lautrec and Maurice Jacquemont, ended up working at the school.

A Catholic nonconformism, idealist and restive, had its part in CATJC's brief history, and the connection was sustained even after CATJC was transformed into the IDHEC. In September 1943, Vichy elevated the Centre to institute status and then transplanted the new Institut des hautes études cinématographiques to Paris, all the while keeping it under SGI supervision. But the film school, like the Centre that preceded it, remained hospitable to Catholic nonconformism, Lautrec serving a number of years on the faculty and a young Mounier acolyte, the film critic André Bazin, even taking up a brief appointment there at the Liberation as director of cultural services.[101]

The movies may have begun as a fairgrounds diversion. They may have evolved over time into a profit-generating industry. Yet Vichy wanted a different kind of cinema: an art cinema, purified of foreign and commercial influences, that would be national in both form and content. Did it have success? Autant-Lara thought so. Under the Occupation, he recounted to an interviewer in later years, "the French worked for the French, [and] from there was born a French school of cinema." Of course, when these words were uttered, Autant-Lara, the onetime nonconformist, had become a right-wing crank. Well he might wax nostalgic about the Vichy era. Yet a very similar sentiment was expressed by Louis Daquin, a committed communist. The war had cut off French cinema, he wrote, forcing it back on its own resources, an experience of isolation that afforded it the unexpected but welcome chance "to find again an authentic source of inspiration, truly national."[102] Vichy seems to have gotten the national cinema it desired, but what did that mean?

It did not mean a proliferation of propaganda movies, which were a rarity. Rare too were films with racist themes, although a handful did get playing time. On the whole, the National Revolution was not a direct presence on the screen, save in the newsreels.

France's literary and cultural patrimony, however, was a major source of inspiration to filmmakers. A third of all movies made during the Occupation years were adaptations. Seven Balzac stories were translated onto the screen and nine Simenons.[103] Still-living authors, playwrights in particular, tried their hand at the cinema. Jean Cocteau, of course, had been making movies since the early thirties, and he made one more during the war, *L'Eternel retour*, a stylized and bizarre reworking of the Tristan and Isolde legend with Jean Marais and Madeleine Sologne, both looking stunning, in the lead roles. Giraudoux contented himself with script work, writing the minimalist, at times studied dialogue for Bresson's *Anges du péché*. It was not just literature but the past that filmmakers plundered for material, sometimes with exceptional results. Christian-Jaque's bravura biopic, *La Symphonie fantastique*, was based on the life of Berlioz; Carné's fairy tale of obstructed love, *Les Visiteurs du soir*, is set in a medieval French court. Does all this add up to a *cinéma d'évasion*, as is sometimes suggested, French filmmakers losing themselves in the legends and amours of bygone ages, recycling already published material, or packaging new material with a stylized theatricality? What is certain is that French film, in an era of isolation and scarcity, turned to French sources for strength: to the national past, sometimes historical, sometimes mythic, and to established authors, both living and dead.[104]

The present too had its place in the filmmaker's repertoire, but it was a very particular present. Fernandel made eleven movies during the war years, becoming something of a national institution in the process.[105] His comic persona, that of the good-natured meridional, resourceful but much put upon, was no doubt appealing to audiences who did not want to have to look too hard at painful realities. But Fernandel played serious roles as well. Pagnol in fact made use of him on more than one occasion, including a supporting part in *La Fille du puisatier* (1940).

The picture featured the great Raimu in the lead, an actor of exceptional physical presence with a stout build and a distinctive regional accent. Raimu played a tradition-bound *père de famille* who sends away a daughter impregnated out of wedlock by an aviator called off to the front, where the young man is believed killed. The picture was set just before and during the *drôle de guerre* and includes a scene of townsfolk listening to a Pétain radio broadcast announcing the armistice of June 1940. Papa is at last persuaded to relent; the daughter returns; and so too, mirabile dictu, does the aviator, not dead after all, who marries the girl, constituting a proper family in the end. It is a too sentimental tale but one that presents a sympathetic and, to many, appealing portrayal of a provincial of modest means, cast this time not in the Fernandelian mold but in that of the bighearted and forgiving paterfamilias.

For echt Frenchness, however, none surpassed the lead couple in Grémillon's *Le Ciel est à vous*: such, in any event, was the film critic Robert Régent's judgment.[106] The husband, a modest *garagiste* (and veteran of the Great War), has a dream—to soup up an old monoplane and compete in a high-speed air race—but he breaks an arm. His wife, a woman of abilities, steps in, competes instead and, against all odds, sets a record. The couple's joint effort is testimony to the valor and tenacity of even the most modest of French families.

So there was a present: it was populated by French men and women—provincials, fathers, *garagistes*, humble souls all—who exemplified the heroism of everyday life. Together, they constituted a gallery of national types in which filmgoers might recognize themselves and find strength and reassurance in difficult times.

No doubt, much of this resonated with the values of the National Revolution. The family was the bedrock of social life, and the movies showed just how true this was. *La Fille du puisatier* conveyed the pain of losing a father's love and the joy of finding it again in forgiveness. *Le Ciel est à vous* dramatized the wonders that could be accomplished by families, even the most unassuming, when they pulled together. Gaby Morlay, who in the thirties had attained stardom as a seductress, placed her talent in the Occupation years "in the service of motherhood," reworking her image from *grande amoureuse* to dutiful angel on the hearth.[107]

Vichy-era cinema taught the virtues of family life, and it taught the virtues of effort as well. There was, it seemed, no corner of nature, however secluded, inaccessible to those with a self-surpassing determination. Grémillon's artisan couple took possession of the sky; Cousteau claimed the silent world under the seas. In Louis Daquin's *Premier de Cordée* (1944), it was the daunting Alpine reaches overtowering Chamonix that provided the challenge. The movie, based on a novel by Roger Frison-Roche, tells the story of Pierre, the young son of an Alpine guide, who develops vertigo as a result of a climbing accident. Pierre is forced in consequence to forswear the guide's life he had dreamed of and to settle for the humdrum of a hotelier's career. His father's death in a climbing accident, however, propels him to join the recovery party, indeed, at a critical moment to lead it. It is this feat of self-overcoming, motivated by filial piety, which at once rekindles the hero's Alpine vocation and establishes him as a worthy, manly heir to his father's moral legacy.

There is an irony here, for directors like Daquin and Grémillon were résistants. Both belonged to the principal film-industry resistance organization, the Comité de libération du cinéma français. *Premier de Cordée* was filmed on location in the French Alps, and Daquin opened the set to dissidents looking for an escape route into Switzerland. The Resistance press had the highest praise for Grémillon's *Le Ciel est à vous* (in contrast to the detested *Le Corbeau*), applauding its celebration of the health and vigor of the common man. Yet Vichy was able to see itself in both movies as well, and well it might. Daquin's film after all had gotten backing from the SGJ. Apropos *Premier de Cordée*, Daquin himself conceded in a later interview:

> The boy-scoutish angle, the return to the earth—all that was no doubt inspired by Pétainist ideology. And here I was a communist and a resister. One should not forget that this was a time of contradictions and confusions. And one can never escape the times.[108]

As for *Le Ciel est à vous*, it was appreciated as much by Vichy as by the Resistance press. A special screening was arranged for Maréchal Pétain, and Régent, a member of Galey's art-film prize committee, saluted the picture as "a chef d'oeuvre of French style."[109]

Régent's comment raises an interesting question. Vichy-era cinema mined the national patrimony for themes and creative energy; it peopled the screens with reassuring folk types; it championed the elemental virtues of family and effort. All this was very French, but was it carried off in a *style* that might be called French?

Italian filmmakers, after the war, took a neorealist turn. Daquin acknowledged with some regret that their French counterparts did not follow suit: they had accustomed themselves and the public to a cinema of fantasy and legend. All was not legend in Vichy-era cinema, as we have seen, but Daquin's observation about the shunning of realism is fair enough.[110] What was preferred to the real, it has been suggested, was not so much myth or dream (though that is part of the story) as carefully composed worlds, observed with a detached, at times chilly reserve.[111] Think of the scene early on in Carné's *Les Visiteurs du soir*. The devil has sent two emissaries, a man and a woman, to disrupt the affairs of the court of the baron Hugh. The camera watches them from a distance as they approach the ramp to a white-walled city, the whole captured in a panoramic shot that conveys both the magnificence of the scene and a sense of its remove from the historic present. Bresson's *Anges du péché* takes place in a nunnery dedicated to the reform of fallen girls. Anne-Marie, a young acolyte from a well-to-do background, has committed herself to the rescue of a hardcase character, a rebellious soul who is in fact wanted by the law. Bresson makes the most of the setting, composing a series of shots, remarkable for their visual rhythm, that show the nuns assembled as a body in hall or chapel, the blacks and whites of their habits picked up by the black-and-white diamond patterns on the floor. Clouzot's *Le Corbeau* has a church scene of its own, more creepy than hieratic. The movie is set in a fictional but contemporary French town whose peace of mind, if it ever had any, is shattered by a poison-pen campaign. The Crow of the title is circulating letters of denunciation, exposing the supposed moral failings of various townspeople. One such missive arrives as the townsfolk are gathered in church, the letter fluttering down as though dropped from the rafters. Clouzot's camera, aloft on a crane, observes its earthward trajectory, a high-angle shot that allows the viewer to take in the agitated and apprehensive congregation at the same time.

These three movies may be taken as fair examples of the prestige cinema of the Vichy era. *Les Visiteurs du soir* and *Anges du péché* won Galey prizes for quality; *Le Corbeau* was not a Vichy favorite, but it was the best picture that Continental ever made. Each looks at the world from far away, and the worlds so encompassed are enclosed, frozen or claustrophobic places. The freezing is literal in Carné's movie. Satan's minions are able to stop time, to arrest human motion even as they go about the devil's business. In the end, the male emissary falls in love with the baron's daughter, and the devil, confronting defeat, petrifies the lovers caught in an eternal embrace. Bresson reminds the viewer time and again that convent and prison are not so far removed. It is not just that the delinquent girls pass right from one to the other but also that there are uniforms and cells in both. In *Le Corbeau*, the townspeople come to believe they know who the letter writer is (they are mistaken), and the suspect flees through a cramped maze of narrow village streets, the flight captured in a series of disorienting, off-angle shots.

The painstaking craftsmanship of the movies, the choreographed shots, the alternating effects of distance and confinement: do all these add up to an aesthetic? Enough so as to distinguish a generation of French cineasts from their Italian, neorealist contemporaries; enough so as to serve as a foil to a postwar New Wave in search of a more spontaneous, more personal mode of filmmaking. But not so much as to stifle the creativity of individual expression. The hearts of Carné's frozen lovers continue to beat. Love, art, France endure even in the confining grip of evil enchantment. Bresson promises transcendence of a more spiritual sort. Anne-Marie's motives may be complicated. There is some question whether it is genuine *misericordia* or egoism fueled by class pretension that motivates her to action. In the end, she pushes herself too hard, sacrificing health and then life in an effort to turn around the tough young criminal she has taken in her care. Anne-Marie's renunciation, however, is redemptive, for it gives the sinner the strength at last to confront her guilt, Christian sacrifice thus unbinding and raising up souls caught in the toils of self and sin. Clouzot's resolution, by contrast, is not so uplifting. The protagonist of Le Corbeau is a doctor, an appealing but complicated character whom the Crow has denounced as an abortionist and womanizer (the latter accusation is not off the mark). The doctor, in pursuit of the culprit, enters into conversation with a fellow scientist, a psychiatrist who has been a source of telling, disabused advice about the Crow's modus operandi. A hanging lamp separates the two men, and the psychiatrist gives it a push. The lamp swings back and forth, by turns illuminating the face of one man and leaving the other in darkness. Where, he asks, do good and evil lie in a murky world of oscillating light and shadow? It is a powerful and unsettling moment that makes a pitch for moral ambiguity (this is a movie in which there are no true innocents), and, in this regard, Le Corbeau bears more than a passing resemblance to Anouilh's Antigone.[112] It is this very same psychiatrist who is in the end unmasked as the Crow.

The Third Republic in its waning years had begun to worry about the well-being of the cinema. The occasional reform was undertaken, but a complete revamping had to await a more authoritarian moment, which came with the arrival of Vichy.[113] The regime took the movie industry in hand. It endowed it with corporate institutions (subject of course, and more so over time, to state oversight); it acted to discipline the film market, to ease cutthroat competition, to police shady practices, to censor what was un-French; and it undertook a multifront campaign to encourage quality productions that would do credit to the nation's reputation. Sure enough, the film industry responded, churning out well-crafted movies, commercial material to be sure but also productions that had a legitimate claim to art-film status. It is little wonder these years were looked back on by so many with such fondness. Who was against professionalism and art, after all? Yet such achievements came at a price. The racism and censoriousness of Vichy policy do not need underlining. As for the quality-film aesthetic, it did not squash creativity, far from it. But it advanced a set of national values that, even while bringing reassurance to filmgoers, heartened the regime in the righteousness of its cause.

The War of the Airwaves

The story of Occupation-era radio is in certain critical respects *sui generis*, which complicates comparisons with theater and film. First and foremost, Vichy was not the sole player in the field. In theater, the Germans were content to regulate the Paris stage; in film, they organized a Paris-based film production company; but when it came to radio the Occupier would not settle for an ancillary role. The medium was too useful a propaganda vehicle, and the Germans were determined to take full advantage of it, turning occupied-zone radio into a creature of their will. The Resistance too understood the power of the airwaves. Free French radio, broadcasting from BBC studios in London, matched the Germans blow for blow in a propaganda battle that came to be known as *la guerre des ondes.*

Vichy radio, then, operated in a crowded, ideology-charged context that placed special pressures on it. The impulse to centralized control, always great, was more powerful in this than in other domains. The regime battened down on radio, at least so far as its reach extended, squelching the commercial sector in the process (without altogether abolishing it). In theater and film, Vichy's centralizing ambitions were tempered by a corporate, professionalizing rhetoric. Not so in radio, where state command was the overwhelming imperative. One final point of difference: Vichy boosted popular programming on state stations, reaching out to diversion-minded audiences in a way Third Republic state radio had been slow to do. What a contrast to theater policy, which favored the artistic stagings of the Cartel directors, or to film policy, so heavily oriented toward quality-film production.

The distinctiveness of the radio experience, however, should not be exaggerated. The boundaries between radio, theater, and film were porous, personalities moving between the various media with relative ease. Pierre Schaeffer, for example, was a radio man before Jeune France and would be so again afterward. In radio, as elsewhere, the state took a hands-on stance in the management of culture, rolling back private commercial interests even if not extinguishing them outright. As for the culture purveyed over the airwaves, yes, it had an

entertainment component. The state, now the principal programmer, yielded to the public on this score, but how could it be otherwise
in grim times? Yet however much it yielded, the state still retained an
unflagging commitment to quality programming. In radio as in theater and cinema, culture understood in Arnoldian terms as "the best
that has been thought and said" was too important a good to be left
to vulgarizing market forces.

The great Paris-based stations, both public and private, ceased to
broadcast in the aftermath of the 1940 defeat. The Occupier replaced
them with a station of its own, Radio Paris, which functioned under
the watchful eye of a German administrator, Dr. Alfred Bofinger. The
new station was remarkable on two counts.

First, official though it was, Radio Paris took the business of entertainment to heart. This meant extensive music programming, accounting for up to half of all airtime. There was the expected dose of
the classics, but popular music constituted the dominant mode.
Radio Paris maintained not just a symphonic orchestra but several
variety ensembles as well, which performed with vocal accompaniment from the singing sensations of the day: Chevalier, Rossi, Trenet.
Jazz with too "negro" a flavoring was avoided but not swing. Listeners
could tune in to Django Reinhardt's Hot-Club de France (minus the
jazz violinist Stéphane Grappelli, who spent the war in England). The
station's popular touch made itself felt in other domains as well. Sunday nights were reserved for serious theater, but Radio Paris also featured a Sunday afternoon show for women, *Cette heure est à vous*,
hosted by crooner André Claveau.[114] Symphonic music and swing,
Sunday nights at the theater and the women's hour: the range of offerings balanced the standard (i.e., quality) fare of public programming with a novel leavening of more diverting material.

When it came to commentary, however, there was no interest at all
in balance. This was the Occupier's station, and Radio Paris spoke
with an unmatched ultra-right viciousness. Bofinger recruited French
journalists to the task, journalists with a particular slanging skill when
it came to denunciation: Jean Azéma from *Je suis partout* and Jean
Hérold-Paquis, a former contributor to *Choisir*, the Catholic periodical that had played such a mobilizing role in the radio election

campaigns of the midthirties, rousing listeners in support of the anti–Popular Front Radio-Famille. The tone set by such commentators was anti-Semitic in the extreme and collaborationist. Even Vichy, deemed too softhearted in its commitment to the new European order, was not spared criticism.[115] In the domain of news delivery, Radio Paris abandoned any pretense of high-minded neutrality in favor of a more rabble-rousing style (still very much in vogue today on talk radio).

There was a Resistance answer to Bofinger's operation, and it came in the shape of Radio Londres. On 18 June 1940, the BBC placed its microphones at General de Gaulle's disposal for a radio appeal—a call to ongoing struggle—which was as galvanizing as it was brief. That following July, a team of French broadcasters, still using BBC facilities, began a regular five-minute information program, *Honneur et Patrie*. It was followed by a less formal half-hour program of commentary and sketches, which was broadcast first under the title *Ici, la France*, and then, from September, under its better-remembered name *Les Français parlent aux français*.[116]

Radio Londres, however small its scale of operations, intended to take on its cross-channel adversary on all fronts. On critical occasions, *Honneur et Patrie* featured de Gaulle speeches, but regular broadcasting was handled by Maurice Schumann, spelled for a period in the spring and summer of 1943 by Pierre Brossolette. The team was in certain respects diverse. Schumann had been a member of Jeune République, a splinter group of christian-democratic persuasion; Brossolette was a veteran of socialist politics. But they marched shoulder to shoulder for Free France, propagandizing on behalf of the Gaullist cause with verve and energy. The tone was somewhat different at *Les Français parlent aux français*. Pierre Bourdan and Michel Saint-Denis, who ran the program, were not Gaullists.[117] It was not just that the political tonality of the show was more independent but also that the format had greater variety, the usual commentary enlivened by sketches, songs, and playful routines. Saint-Denis, though a theater man himself (he was in fact Copeau's son-in-law), did not hesitate to borrow a page from commercial radio when it came to quickness of pace or informality of manner. Indeed, in October 1943, he recruited a veteran of interwar private radio, the inimitable Pierre Dac, to add sparkle to the program's carryings-on. Dac was a humorist without peer, a patriot who had lost a brother in the Great War, and also a Jew who had been driven into exile by Vichy anti-Semitism.[118]

Both Radio Paris and Radio Londres spoke with unmistakable voices. Hérold-Paquis and associates hectored in the accents of the demagogue; Schumann answered back with a sober-minded eloquence. At the same time, however, both stations took care to lighten the propagandistic tone with more popular programming, delivered in the fast-paced, familiar style pioneered by interwar commercial radio. The "war of the airwaves" was a war of words, but it was also a war for listenership.

How would Vichy position itself in this struggle? First, it would clarify the chain of command in the radio world, pruning the plethora of centers and agencies that had grown up in the waning years of the Third Republic. Léon Brillouin was kept on for a short period as director of radio administration, rechristened the Radiodiffusion nationale (RN). He answered to the secretary-general of information, a position occupied at the armistice by the press baron Jean Prouvost. And that was all there was to it. The RN and SGI were now the dominant players when it came to radio decision-making.

The structure bears some resemblance to that set up in the film industry but with two important differences. Vichy did not endow radio with a corporate organ. There was no equivalent here to the COIC (or to the COES for that matter). Second, the RN management never enjoyed the same independence of action that Galey's Service du cinéma did. This had something to do with the personalities in charge of the RN, men without the kind of militant past that made of Galey such a formidable figure. Brillouin was an academic. He was succeeded in February 1941 by Commandant Duvivier, a naval officer who was a protégé of then Vichy vice premier Admiral Darlan. Laval's return to power in 1942 led to Duvivier's ouster and replacement by the writer and radio journalist André Demaison. In an administrative reshuffling later in the year, a new post senior to Demaison's was created, that of administrator-general. That job, now the top position at the RN, was awarded to a career civil servant, Hubert Devillez.[119]

The real power in radio, then, lay not with the RN but higher up the bureaucratic hierarchy—first of all, with the SGI. From 1941, the Secrétariat-général was headed by Paul Marion, a high-profile figure with a checkered political past. Marion had been a Communist until breaking with the party in 1929; the early thirties found him a prominent neosocialist, active alongside Jules Romains in drafting the "Plan du 9 juillet"; and then in 1936 he executed a sharp rightward turn, joining the ranks of Jacques Doriot's fascist Parti populaire français. Marion, however, fell out of favor as the war wore on.[120] He was replaced as head of the SGI in January 1944 by Philippe Henriot, a lifelong right-winger who had first made a name for himself as General de Castelnau's vice president at the Fédération nationale catholique. What made Henriot a standout was not so much administrative ability as an unusual oratorical talent. He had proven himself a gifted public speaker at the FNC, but it was during the Occupation that he came into his own. The RN put him on the radio for the first time in March 1942; he began airing daily editorials from February of the following year; and soon, Henriot's flair for verbal jousting won him an expanding audience. He became Vichy's star contribution to the "war of the airwaves," compelling the attention even of listeners who were not true believers. The filmmaker Autant-Lara acknowledged that London had justice on its side but that, when it came to oratorical pyrotechnics, Henriot was hard to beat.[121] He was beaten though in the end, not by Radio Londres, but by a Resistance commando that assassinated him in June 1944.

The SGI was led by strong personalities, but standing over them, from 1942, was a personality stronger still, Pierre Laval. It was Laval who cooled toward Marion, undercutting his authority; it was Laval who found a replacement in Henriot. The vice premier's interest in radio was overdetermined. He was a first-class intriguer who appreciated the shaping power of propaganda, and he was a radio man himself, the proprietor of a major southern zone station, Radio Lyon. This was ultimately to have a meaningful influence on the evolution of relations between the state and the private sector.

For it looked as though the state, just as it had consolidated control of the public airwaves, meant to do the same in the private sector, to the point even of a de facto nationalization. Six private stations survived in the south, including Laval's own, and the state bore down on them with a regulatory zeal. From July 1940, private broadcasters were forbidden to advertise. The regime did make some effort to organize relief in the form of subsidies, but this was little compensation for what amounted to a loss of financial independence. This was done on Laval's first watch.[122]

Laval's successor, Pierre-Etienne Flandin, took matters a major step further. In December 1940, the Flandin administration, no more than days old, requisitioned the private airwaves altogether. But then, in a matter of weeks, it reconsidered the move. A series of negotiations followed between the state and commercial interests, the latter represented by Jacques Trémoulet, vice president of the Fédération française des postes privés. The Trémoulet group had been a major player in interwar radio, owning a piece, if not more, of five stations in France and an interest in the peripheral station Radio Andorre. The war, of course, had stripped the group of its northern-zone possessions, but it still retained several stations in the south.[123] Trémoulet's substantial business assets translated into bargaining leverage, though of a limited sort. Vichy agreed to return requisitioned stations to private management, but there were certain constraints. Although commercials were now allowed, it was on a restricted basis. Private stations, moreover, were required to broadcast up to sixty hours per week of state-dictated programming (the state providing some financial compensation), and what programming still remained "independent" was subjected to review by state officials who exercised veto powers. Commercial radio survived, but it was on a tight leash that threatened to get tighter still. Vichy administrators hinted that the new order in radio might be no more than provisional, pending realization of the regime's ultimate aim: a buyout of the private sector altogether.[124]

The threat resurfaced from time to time but was never acted on. In fact, on the financial front, it did not take long before the state's grip began to slacken. Advertising revenues crept back up (though never attaining prewar levels), and it was an added boon that commercials now went untaxed. One private station in fact, Radio Toulouse, managed to become financially self-supporting and from October 1941 was in a position to dispense with state subsidies altogether.[125] More than that, state and private interests, which not so long ago had confronted one another across the bargaining table, soon found themselves entering into a business partnership. Laval played a material role in bringing this about.

In November 1942, a radio investment company, the Société financière de radiodiffusion (SOFIRA), was founded. The president of the board of directors, General Denain, had been a minister in Laval's 1935 cabinet, and the general persuaded his old boss to get the state to buy up the bulk of SOFIRA shares. SOFIRA's first major business venture was purchase of a 50 percent interest in a peripheral station just then starting out, Radio Monte-Carlo. The balance of the shares went to German, Italian, and private French interests. The new station began broadcasting in 1943; it sold commercials and hired an advertising agent for that purpose, none other than Jacques Trémoulet. The connection is not at all surprising. In the thirties, Trémoulet had cozied up to the right wing of the Parti Radical, making friends along the way, Pierre Laval among them, who turned out to be useful contacts in wartime.[126]

In 1941, it looked as though Vichy might finish off commercial radio. In the end, the regime backpedaled, ceding the private sector financial breathing room and then, with Laval back in power, buoying it with lucrative business contracts. The regime's anticommercial animus, so powerful in theater and cinema, made itself felt in radio as well, but it was blunted in the end by the deal-making cronyism of Laval. Blunted but not parried, for though the private sector survived, it was more as a moneymaking operation than as a cultural pacesetter. In the thirties, the commercial sector had taken the lead in programming. Its energies now depleted, this role fell to RN decision makers.

When it came to news, as we have seen, Vichy radio struck out on a new path, abandoning the sententious ways of old in favor of a more haranguing style. There was innovation as well (though less repellent in character) when it came to regular programming. The man in charge in Vichy's first years was Jean Antoine, a veteran of commercial radio who brought new men on board and, with them, a breath of fresh air to the public airwaves. From 1941, Jean Nohain, like Antoine a transplant from the private sector, hosted a variety show, *Bonjour la France*, which offered up a fast-moving collage of poetry, exercise tips, and culinary recipes. The variety show was, indeed, the order of the day, accounting in June 1941 for more programming hours than the news and state business combined, and the percentage of light fare would increase as the war went on. The airtime devoted to music jumped from 45 percent in 1942 to 60 percent the year following, and of the music on offer, two-fifths was light, a proportion unprecedented on the public airwaves.[127]

Public radio under Vichy relaxed its style, but it did not for all that jettison its long-standing commitment to quality programming. In 1942, the RN set aside four evenings to broadcast Claudel's *Soulier de Satin* (this was a year prior to the Comédie française staging). Then, in 1942, it rebroadcast from the Paris Opéra Charles Munch's interpretation of Berlioz's *Requiem* as performed by an orchestra of six hundred.[128] Not all highbrow productions, however, were so grandiose.

Literary programming in Vichy's first years was assigned to a man of many talents, Paul Gilson. Gilson was a film buff who had done movie reviewing in the early thirties. It was he, in fact, who burnished Georges Méliès's reputation as a founding father of world cinema. Gilson came upon the director in 1929, now down and out, running a kiosk at the Gare Montparnasse. Gilson brought him back to public attention, organizing a screening of the artist's works and, in the process, rescuing him from obscurity. From movie reviewing, Gilson moved on to journalism tout court, but his first love always remained writing. He was a poet himself, a walker in the streets who relished the marvelous and the fantastic, from the freak shows at Luna Park to the abandoned *passages* of central Paris.[129]

This was the sensibility he brought to public radio, and it led to a sprucing up of the RN's cultural offerings. In December 1941, Gilson canceled the fusty *Au service des lettres françaises* and cast about for something a little more interesting. He turned to Claude Roy, who assembled a "literary team" that included some familiar figures—Pierre Barbier, Roger Leenhardt, Albert Ollivier—as well as new faces like songwriter Pierre Asso. These were Jeune France folk. Vichy had soured on Schaeffer's enterprise, judged too churchy for the tastes of the more fascist-leaning in the maréchal's entourage. The regime began to bear down on JF in the fall of 1941 (it would in fact shut the organization down the following March), prompting a number to seek refuge elsewhere, in the case of Roy and company under Gilson's wing. Roy's radio team concocted a series of programs evoking the life and work of France's great writers, enlivened by readings from the texts of the artists themselves. These experiments in radiophonic biography were spiced with the occasional dissident aside— invocations of out-of-favor writers, criticisms of Pierre Drieu la Rochelle (collaborationist editor of the *Nouvelle revue française*)—or so Roy claimed in later years. What is certain is that he quit the show in the spring of 1942, when Laval returned to power.[130]

Vichy radio's efforts to loosen up did not dethrone highbrow programming, which, from great performances to literary bios, continued to occupy a prominent place. Nor did loosening up mean getting off message. Vichy radio innovated in a number of domains, but even as it did, it never wandered far from the regime's ideological agenda.

Vichy prided itself on its special concern for youth. The regime, as we have seen, created a separate secretariat for youth affairs. And it created a special radio program too, Radio-Jeunesse, pitched exclusively to a youth audience. Planning for the program got started in July 1940 even as the Pétainist regime was still settling into office. The first broadcast was aired in August, and the show went daily in September. The whole enterprise was the brainchild of Pierre Schaeffer, and it was a remarkable project indeed. Schaeffer put together a working team composed in the main of future Jeune France stalwarts, and the team set itself the task of packaging the maréchal's message for a young listenership. *Réponse des jeunes*, an eight-show series dedicated to this purpose, was launched in October. Pétain had delivered a speech to the youth of the nation. Radio-Jeunesse enlisted Alfred Cortot to read the address for its series. Pierre Barbier, Albert Ollivier, and Maurice Jacquemont wrote the commentary, which purported to be the voice of French youth, and the commentary was in turn declaimed by scout performers or recruits from Dhavernas's

Compagnons de France.[131] What was unusual about Radio-Jeunesse was its mix of inspirational content and innovative presentation. For uplift, there were Pétain speeches, readings from Péguy, poetic interludes organized by Claude Roy, and updates on youth initiatives, whether in the arts or elsewhere. Jean Desailly got his start on the program with a brief spot on the itinerant theater group La Roulotte, which included an interview with the troupe's director André Clavé.[132] But such material was not always delivered by standard-issue announcers. Radio-Jeunesse featured choral singing, spoken choirs, various forms of collective address. There should be no surprise here. These were modes of expression that scout theatricals had experimented with in the thirties, and Schaeffer's team counted several onetime Comédiens-Routiers among its number, not the least of them Olivier Hussenot, the program's choir director.[133]

Schaeffer was proud of what he achieved at Radio-Jeunesse and boasted, in later years, of the favorable buzz the program had stirred among media professionals. Jean Antoine took an interest. Jean Masson, who covered the maréchal for RN, was intrigued. Schaeffer himself stopped broadcasting in May 1941 (he was taken up by his new Jeune France duties), but he passed the show on to a kindred spirit, Jean Thévenot, a former activist in Garric's Equipes sociales who was, like Schaeffer himself, a "militant catholic."[134]

Youth found a voice on Vichy radio, and so also did the family. Indeed, the most popular program on the RN was a family show, *L'Alphabet de la famille*. Vichy was ever on the lookout for vehicles to promote its family agenda. On the whole, it contented itself with sponsoring programs like *France famille*, which retailed a rather conventional Catholic moralism.[135] In 1942, however, the regime had a stroke of luck. Emilien Amaury, the Vichy official in charge of family propaganda, approached Louis Merlin about putting together a show. The choice turned out to be inspired. Merlin was a public-relations man with wide experience in radio advertising; he was an aficionado of popular entertainments (with a particular fondness for the Cirque Fernando); and, not least of all, he was a man of reliable political views. Merlin had a long-standing connection to Jean Luchaire, president of the Paris press association during the Occupation years and a sometime go-between in Laval's dealings with the German ambassador, Otto Abetz. Merlin was tempted by Amaury's offer but would not accept until assured of a free hand in the show's production.[136]

L'Alphabet de la famille was a modest affair when it began broadcasting in 1942. A mother and her three children gathered around the dining-room table for general discussion and, dictionary in hand, for talk about words. The littlest was too young to do more than burble. Father, a prisoner of war, was absent. The cast was expanded over time to include a "flag-waving" grandfather and an uncle, played by Charpin, an actor celebrated for the warmth of his performances opposite Raimu in the Marius-Fanny-César film trilogy. The emotional intimacy of the show, at a moment of national difficulty, made it a hit. The program's increasing willingness to strike patriotic chords did not hurt either. In a 1943 show, the uncle and two eldest children, Georges and Françoise, paid a visit to Montmartre, the uncle pointing out from the heights of the butte the Arc de Triomphe below and evoking the Bastille Day victory parade of 1919 in which he, as a veteran, had taken part. The success of the episode prompted further outdoor expeditions: to Notre Dame, Versailles, and the Invalides. The Invalides trip, complete with a visit to Napoleon's tomb, was recorded on the spot, a minor technical feat in its own right. Here then was an unusual soap that depicted a French family in trying times, making an effort at self-improvement, getting on amidst difficulties, without ever forgetting the grander moments of the nation's past. *L'Alphabet de la famille* offered up a distinctive mix of family feeling and nationalist sentiment, and it was no less searching in the technical domain, as attested by its experiments with outdoor recording.[137]

Vichy radio, indeed, made technical research a priority, enough so to launch an experimental studio, the Studio d'essai, in January 1943.[138] Here is the point to evoke Pierre Schaeffer's name yet once more, for it was he who was named director. The closing of Jeune France had left Schaeffer at loose ends. He spent time in Marseille writing, but ever the radio man, ended up in the fall of 1942 running an RN-backed project in sound experimentation based at Beaune. This was Copeau country (Beaune is in Burgundy), and Copeau was in fact signed on to the project as a technical adviser. Together with a team of actors and engineers (including JF veterans Hussenot and Ol-livier), Schaeffer and Copeau explored the possibilities of voice repro-duction, recording both individual voices and choral groups, includ-ing a recitation of Péguy's "Présentation de Notre-Dame de Beaune." Radio officialdom got wind of such efforts and took an interest, Dev-illez in particular, in whom Schaeffer recognized a soul mate, an artist like himself who had wandered into an administrative career. Such attention translated into creation of an experimental studio in Paris, rue de l'Université, with Schaeffer himself placed in charge.[139]

Schaeffer's Studio d'essai is remembered on two accounts. First, for its dissident activities: Schaeffer changed sides in 1943, abandon-ing Vichy for the Resistance. The precise timing of the about-face is not clear. The onetime Radio-Cité newsman Jean Guignebert headed the principal broadcasting-industry Resistance organ, the Comité de libération de la radio (CLR). It is certain that Schaeffer had become an active member of the CLR no later than January of 1944, although the association may have begun as early as the August before.[140] What-ever the exact moment of affiliation, Schaeffer had been seeking out Resistance contacts for some months preceding. Prior to the Guigne-bert connection, it seems, he had begun using the Studio d'essai fa-cilities to record readings by Louis Aragon, Paul Eluard, and Jean Tardieu—Resistance poets all, who had contributed to the Editions de Minuit volume L'Honneur des poètes, published in July of 1943.[141] The dating of Schaeffer's switch—sometime in the latter half of 1943—does not provide many clues as to why he made it. The Allied invasion of North Africa and the subsequent German occupation of the southern zone had taken place in November 1942; the STO was imposed in February 1943; and yet Schaeffer still had not turned. Why then, so late in the game, did he at last give up on Vichy? Schaef-fer wrote a wartime letter to Guignebert that hints at a possible mo-tive. He made a clean breast of his Vichy past; it was Guignebert's right to know. But Schaeffer was now with the Resistance, and so too was his entire crew at the Studio d'essai. They had no personal ambi-tions, just a common commitment "to make the voice of the French nation, a viewpoint of artistic quality and probity, resound to the four corners of the earth."[142] The nation, quality, probity: these had always been Schaeffer's lodestones, and by mid-1943 it was no longer Vichy but the Resistance that seemed to him their surest guarantor.

What this line of interpretation implies is that Schaeffer, even as he changed camps, remained constant in his aesthetic choices, and this is evident in his running of the Studio d'essai. He was as always on the lookout for a "a radio style," for speaking modes and program genres suitable to the medium. In this connection, Schaeffer is credited with inventing the literary interview, a one-on-one intimate chat between host and artist, which went on to become such a staple of cultural programming in France as elsewhere. This is the Studio d'essai's second claim to fame. And who was the artist chosen to illustrate the potential of the new format? Paul Claudel.[143]

No, Vichy radio, whatever the evolving loyalties of some of its personnel, never strayed far in cultural terms from the official line. The regime had adopted the slogan "Travail, Famille, Patrie" as its device. The RN, it might be said, made the triptych its own, reworking it just a little to read: "Jeunesse, Famille, Claudel."

The Vichy era transformed the dynamics in the radio industry. In the thirties, public radio had specialized in quality programming, high-toned and often ponderous in its presentation. The private sector had set a faster pace with a snappy mix of breaking news and popular entertainment, the sticky glue of publicity holding the amalgam together. The approach of the war had eroded commercial radio's preeminence as the state insisted on the primacy of its interests, in the news domain above all. With the Occupation, the private sector went into eclipse, its stars migrating elsewhere: to London in the cases of Pierre Brossolette and Pierre Dac, to the RN in the case of Jean Antoine. Competing state or would-be state interests (Vichy, Free France, the Third Reich) now ruled the airwaves.

What would happen to the private sector's programming legacy in such circumstances: the news, the entertainment, the commercials? Advertising, for a little while, almost vanished from the airwaves. It was in bad odor. Schaeffer, in his final broadcast for Radio-Jeunesse, extended a thanks to his various collaborators, singling them out by name. They had remained anonymous until this time, just unidentified voices, as Schaeffer put it: "in reaction against individualism and publicity."[144] As for the news, Radio Paris's lies and the RN's diatribes were the antitheses of the reporter-on-the-spot style that had been the prewar private sector's stock-in-trade. Radio Londres did better: it spoke truth to Vichy falsehood, but it was also truth in the service of a political cause, however noble. The question of how news and politics mixed on the official airwaves was not one the war resolved. Nor did it settle the state programmer's ever-pressing dilemma: how to strike the right balance between quality and diversion. In the thirties, diversion was assigned a backup role on the public airwaves. During the war, on the other hand, with the private sector handicapped, more room was made for entertainment: for sketches on Radio Londres, for swing on Radio Paris, for soaps on the RN. On the RN, though, programming innovations were kept well within ideological bounds, and state radio's originary commitment to France's literary culture was never abrogated.

In radio, as in other domains, the war strengthened the state's hand, dealing a body blow to commercial interests. Quality remained, as before the defeat, a watchword of the public airwaves, but what makes the case of radio distinct is that, here, the ongoing concern with quality had to make measured concessions to the imperatives of mere diversion.

The Vichy regime built a "cultural state" of its own. The commercial forms of the Third Republic—boulevard theater, Hollywood-inflected cinema, the radio jingle—were spurned. To be sure, a defeated and occupied France hungered for diversion, and the regime felt dutybound to supply it, but Vichy wanted to enshrine other principles—principles of heroism, family, youth. It wanted to supplant the degraded, foreign-tainted culture of the defunct Republic with a healthy, "national" culture, anchored in France's past achievements in art, music, and literature. The concern for rootedness did not preclude formal experimentation. But whatever experiments were tried, it was essential to maintain throughout the highest standards of quality and professionalism. New institutions, some corporate, some statist, were created to achieve these ends; and new personnel were brought on board to bring the project to fruition. The enterprise was more innovative and more successful than it is pleasant to admit. Perhaps the most disturbing proof of this observation lies in how much of the Vichy cultural apparatus was kept on in the aftermath of the war.

CHAPTER 6

The Culture State

The urge to make a clean break with the past was powerful and pervasive at the Liberation. The lax public mores of the Third Republic had led France to defeat. Vichy had plunged the nation into a degrading moral squalor. Now was the time for a thoroughgoing purge, both spiritual and literal, that would restore the nation to itself. It remains to be seen, however, whether France got the new start the men and women of the Resistance hankered for with such a purifying zeal.

In the cultural domain, as elsewhere, the question does not admit of a simple yes-or-no answer. The Liberation moment did mark a turning away from the laissez-aller policies of the Third Republic. Travail et Culture and Peuple et Culture, grassroots organizations with exemplary Resistance credentials, seconded the decentralizing impulses of a Jeanne Laurent, a collaboration that resulted in the creation of five new state-sponsored regional theaters. In cinema, it was Communists who seemed to have the upper hand at the Liberation. A commando of the Comité de libération du cinéma français (CLCF) took over the offices of the COIC in August 1944, installing Jean Painlevé, a party member and veteran résistant, in Galey's old post as director of motion picture services. Painlevé and the CLCF envisioned a new order for cinema managed, not by capital, but by the corporation itself: by movie technicians and professionals organized in strong and recognized trade unions. As for radio, the Gaullist government in Algiers had made known its intentions to nationalize the industry, and such in fact was the medium's immediate fate.

The state-run Radiodiffusion française (RDF, later Radiotélévision française) was created in 1945, bringing to an end the era of private radio, which would not reopen again until the 1980s when the state, after much debate, gave up its monopoly on the airwaves. Culture was to be organized at the Liberation in ways it had not been under the prewar Republic. Vichy, to be sure, had wanted to organize culture too, but Vichy's Kulturpolitik was authoritarian and racist in conception; not so that of the Resistance, which understood its mission in democratizing terms. A French culture was every citizen's birthright, regardless of race or creed, and public authorities had an obligation to make it available to all; culture was, in a word, a *service public* "just like gas, water, electricity."

The author of this celebrated phrase is, of course, Jean Vilar,[1] from 1951 director of the Théâtre national populaire. Vilar, it will be remembered, had worked for Jeune France in the early Vichy years, which raises the question whether the rupture with the recent past at the Liberation was so complete as all that, and indeed it was not. Jeanne Laurent remained on the job at the Ministry of Fine Arts into the 1950s. Marcel L'Herbier was kept on as director of IDHEC, the state film school. Paul Gilson, onetime official at Vichy national radio, was named in 1946 by the still-fledgling RDF to take charge of its cultural programming. As IDHEC's survival attests, it was not just individuals but institutions that made the transition from one regime to the next. Policies too persisted, none more so than the public commitment to quality culture. The well-worn opposition between commercial forms, tainted by the profit motive and lowbrow pandering, and art forms, understood in Arnoldian terms as "the best that has been thought and said" (with special preference to French creations), remained as much in force in the postwar era as under Vichy.

The new cultural order established at the Liberation was neither revolution nor restoration but an amalgam of breaks and continuities. The balance between the two was not quite the same from one medium to the next, more continuity than break in theater, more break than continuity in radio. Yet whatever the particular variations, the essential point still remains: the postwar *état culturel*, formidable creation that it was, was no ad hoc construction but the offspring of a mixed marriage, part résistant, part Vichyite, and it was not always easy to distinguish which parent bequeathed the more dominant legacy.

Theater Decentralization

The team that took charge of theater reform at the Liberation was Catholic and nonconformist in background. At the top was Jeanne Laurent, who stayed on in her post at the Direction des spectacles et de la musique. She was assisted by Raymond Cogniat, a former Jeune France official, and by the new inspector-general of theater, Pierre-Aimé Touchard, who had been associated with Mounier's *Esprit* circle since the 1930s.

But background does not tell the entire story, for the Occupation years had prompted a reordering of commitments. Laurent and Touchard are cases in point. Laurent, a Pétainist in 1940, had by the war's end joined the Resistance. She had important connections in the Church hierarchy. The ethnologist Germaine Tillion, a member of the Musée de l'Homme Resistance network, approached Laurent in early 1941, hoping to persuade her to intervene on behalf of network members arrested earlier in the year. Tillion, found Laurent "open but hesitant." Such hesitations, however, had evaporated by the war's end. In May 1944, Laurent can be found helping to relocate the Resistance archives of Henri Frenay's Mouvement de libération nationale (MLN), and in the months following she deepened her involvement, opening her apartment to MLN meetings.[2]

Touchard's trajectory was not so different. Vichy from the very beginning ran into opposition from the substantial student population of Paris. On the first Armistice Day after the defeat, 11 November 1940, protesting high schoolers and *universitaires* clashed with German forces on the Champs-Elysées. Vichy authorities, anxious to dampen student political volatility, set up a chain of youth centers, one for each of the University's four faculties. The direction of the Maison des lettres, founded in 1941, was confided to Touchard. The year 1943 seems to have been a turning point for the Maison des lettres, as for Touchard himself. In the spring, he brought in a new crowd, many of them colleagues from *Esprit*—André Clavé, Maurice Delarue, Jean-Marie Serreau, Edmond Humeau. The first three, it will be noted, were all Jeune France graduates, but of greater signifi-cance in the present context, a number of the newcomers were active résistants: Serreau, Clavé (soon to be deported), and Humeau, an employee at the Commissariat à la lutte contre le Chômage who, from December 1942, had launched into a double life as a clandes-tine operative. This is not to say that the Maison des lettres was trans-formed at a stroke into a Resistance stronghold, but it did become "a democratic space," a venue for underground plottings, whether artis-tic or political in nature.[3]

Laurent and Touchard had moved away from a Vichy past, but this did not mean a jettisoning of long-held cultural priorities. De Gaulle's Provisional Government issued an ordonnance in October 1945 that in most essentials, racial exclusion apart, confirmed the framing prin-ciples of the 1943 Rocher law. The preamble in fact made explicit and approving reference to the Rocher law's cleansing ambitions, which the present legislation meant to pursue. In particular, the 1945 ordonnance called for preserving the state licensing of theater direc-tors, Dullin's hobbyhorse in the Vichy years. Laurent, ever the parti-san of art theater, applauded the provision as a necessary protection against "special interests foreign to the profession."[4]

In the postwar era, as in bygone days, anticommercial animus went hand in hand with a partiality to youthful innovation. In May 1946, Cogniat launched a competition to reveal up-and-coming talents to the public, the so-called Concours des jeunes compagnies. That year's top award went to Michel Sarrazin of the Grenier de Toulouse. The Jeunes Comédiens de Rennes figured in the list of prizewinners the first three years running. Both troupes had connections to Léon Chancerel. Chancerel had spent a portion of the war in Toulouse working for Jeune France and there struck up acquaintance with the core group that went on to found the Grenier in 1945. As for the Rennes company, its success in the Jeunes compagnies competition of 1948 had brought it to Paris, where it crossed paths with Hubert Gignoux, a veteran Comédien-Routier who had gone on to become

director of the Compagnie des marionettes des Champs-Elysées. Gignoux was the son of Claude-Joseph Gignoux, the formidable right-
wing business journalist who had seen service under Vichy. The
younger Gignoux, by contrast, spent the war years in a German POW
camp, an experience that had a widening effect on the horizons of
the onetime Catholic scout.

Cogniat's Concours project was followed in short order by a second youth-oriented initiative, the Aide à la première pièce. In July
1947, the Ministère de la Jeunesse, des arts et des lettres set up a
panel of judges to award production funding to promising playwrights
just getting started. The commission was chaired by that old Cartel
stalwart Charles Dullin.[5]

But the most enduring commitment of all was that to decentralization. At Laurent's behest, Touchard drafted a series of reports on the
subject. The arts administration was primed to act, but the opportunity to follow through waited on initiatives from below.

The Third Reich had annexed Alsace in 1940, siphoning off its men
and wealth for the Nazi war effort. At the Liberation, local officials felt
an urgent need to reassert a French cultural presence in the region. In
October 1946, municipal officials from Colmar, Mulhouse, and Stras-
bourg pooled resources to create a regional theater and appealed to
Laurent for additional funding. She was only too happy to comply, and
the theater, in operation already for some months, was rechristened
the Centre dramatique national de l'Est in January 1947.[6]

There were initial difficulties finding a director to run the enterprise. The first nominee, Louis Ducreux, fell sick. He was succeeded
by Roland Piétri, who proved unequal to the task. The next in line
was a less established figure, a young man not much past thirty, André
Clavé. Clavé turned out to be an inspired choice for at least two reasons. He was a genuine Resistance hero who had been arrested by the
Gestapo in December 1943 and then deported. And young though
he was, Clavé had already earned a reputation for himself as an enterprising theatrical innovator. He had managed an itinerant troupe
under Jeune France auspices in the Occupation's early years, but of
greater moment was Clavé's association on return from deportation
with the Paris-based arts alliance Travail et Culture (TEC).

Founded in September 1944, TEC was an immediate spin-off of Touchard's Maison des lettres. Touchard was in fact named TEC's first president, although the association's animating spirit was Maurice Delarue. In the present context, three points bear making about TEC's orientation and activities. The organization was at pains to demonstrate its Resistance bona fides. No sooner had Clavé returned from the camps than he was named TEC's honorary president. Clavé's presence is at the same time a reminder of TEC's Jeune France lineage. The association was directed by a JF alumnus (Delarue), and its senior membership included a number of personalities once active in JF ranks: Paul Flamand, Jean-Marie Serreau, and Jean-Louis Barrault.[7] Such filiations left an imprint on the way TEC went about its business. The organization set itself the task of bringing French culture, a culture of quality, to the people through animation and hands-on instruction. To this end, TEC managed to assemble a quite remarkable teaching corps: André Bazin (a Mounier disciple) for film, Lucien Lautrec for the arts, Marcel Marceau for mime. Serreau and Charles Dullin organized a program they described as "culture through dramatic initiation." Barrault, long a believer in the pedagogic possibilities of improvisational acting, launched a school providing "education through dramatic play." This was not teaching as usual, de haut en bas, but interactive instruction that inspired through participation and exchange. The dynamic experimentalism of TEC's program and the prevailing spirit of democratic camaraderie were very much of the Liberation moment. TEC had a progressive sheen that was buffed by growing communist involvement in the organization.[8] Indeed, Touchard himself went on record in the pages of *Esprit* praising the PCF's discipline, sacrifice, and revolutionary commitment.[9]

Clavé's Resistance past and prominent involvement in an innovative popular arts organization made him a suitable and, in the event, imaginative appointment as director of the first Centre dramatique national (CDN). There was a *gauchisant* flavoring to the enterprise, but Clavé's antecedents were in fact more spiritual than leftist, anchored in the Christian and nonconformist currents that had roiled the theatrical waters of the thirties and which, during the war years, found embodiment in Jeune France.

The origins of the second CDN, inaugurated as the Comédie de Saint-Etienne in the summer of 1947, were not dissimilar. A combination of local activism, inspirational personnel, and state patronage got the operation up and running, and the package of ideological influences—a blend of Jeune France–style theatrics and Resistance idealism—was much the same as well.

The initial activist impulse was supplied, not by the Saint-Etienne town fathers, but by a Grenoble-based arts initiative, Peuple et Culture (PEC). PEC, much like its fraternal twin TEC in Paris, had a direct Resistance connection, but tracking its ancestry a little further back reveals Vichy antecedents as well. Pétain's regime made a cult of leadership just as it did a cult of youth, and to form the elites of tomorrow, it sponsored creation of a leadership-training school, the Ecole d'Uriage, headquartered in France's Alpine region at the château of the renaissance knight Bayard. Pierre Dunoyer de Segonzac, a veteran cavalry officer who went by the nickname "Vieux Chef," was placed in charge. His director of studies was Hubert Beuve-Méry, an accomplished journalist and Mounier acolyte. The curriculum on offer at Uriage was designed to cultivate the "total man," mixing strenuous out-of-door activity with high-minded lectures by visiting *conférenciers* (Mounier prominent among them) and earnest, often intense group dialogue. A fallen France needed the firm guiding hand of a rough-and-ready elite, men hardened in the physical and moral discipline of team command, and Uriage meant to hammer out that cadre. The hard Right at Vichy had it in for Mounier, and as its star ascended, Mounier's fell, and with him the associations he was involved in, Uriage not least of all. Mounier was forbidden to take part in Uriage activities from July 1941; Uriage itself was shut down in December of the following year.[10]

A number of Uriage loyalists, however, would not be deterred from the course they had set themselves. One of them, Gilbert Gadoffre, formed a clandestine study group—a team that included Bénigno Cacérès and Joffre Dumazedier—which dedicated itself to joint reflection on the "crisis of the twentieth century" and the possible ways out of it. A collective manuscript was drafted, destroyed in December 1943 by marauding German troops, and then reconstituted in 1944 in Paris, where it was serialized the following year in *Esprit* before appearing in book form under Le Seuil's imprimatur with the title *Vers le Style du XXe siècle.*[11]

Reflection, however, did not mean inaction. Contact was made with the Resistance. From the fall of 1943, Gadoffre's group dispatched small bands, "flying squads," to maquis units in the Vercors, which initiated the Resistance in Uriage-style cultural and spiritual animation. The fraternal ties established proved enduring. The Comité départemental de la libération de l'Isère (the department where Grenoble was situated) selected Dumazedier to run its Education commission in September 1944. Dumazedier's pedagogic ambitions soon overflowed the confines of a simple commission, coursing into an altogether new organization, Peuple et Culture, which was launched at year's end.[12]

PEC was an astonishing institution for more than one reason. It was in many ways, for all its Resistance origins, an Uriage spin-off. Dumazedier enlisted in the enterprise a half-dozen Uriage comrades, Cacérès, Gadoffre, Paul-Henry Chombart de Lauwe among them. From a certain angle, very little had changed since Uriage days in how these men conceived the drama of France's condition. As ever, bourgeois individualism and money power remained the villains of the piece. Salvation lay with "new elites," no surprise here either. But that left unanswered the perennial question of how these new elites were to be formed. The Resistance had begun the task; indeed, it was in Resistance work, a PEC document acknowledged, that France's military men had at last begun to learn what Lyautey meant when invoking "the social role of the officer."[13] The admiring reference to Lyautey, it should be underlined, was not a throwaway line. *Vers le Style du XXe siècle,* though a Liberation text, cited Vichy-era institutions, from the Fondation Carrel to Uriage itself, as intellectual models. An *école des cadres* designed to fashion a new order of men, an order monastic in the rigor of its physical and moral discipline: such had been the aspiration of Gadoffre and his cohort in 1940, and so it remained at the Liberation.[14]

Yet in the event, PEC differed from Uriage in critical respects. Uriage was for the few. PEC styled itself a popular organization, catering to a broad public of ex-résistants, trade unionists, and political militants. Indeed, the communist sympathies of the rank-and-file membership were strong enough to inflect the organization's leadership, and for a brief period Cacérès and Dumazedier themselves were moved to join the party.[15] The prevailing climate at PEC, however, was not so much *communisant* as it was communitarian and productivist. The people had a need for culture, and PEC was there to supply it. As Dumazedier put it with lapidary succinctness: "the final objective of our action remains the creation of a *service public* to promote the leisure and culture of workers."[16]

The PEC ethos then was an amalgam, an Uriage core encased in the public-service ethos of the Liberation. A similar observation may be made apropos its cultural practice. In the spring of 1945, PEC set up a Maison de la Culture in Grenoble under the direction of Georges Blanchon, an architect and sometime collaborator of Le Corbusier. The Maison in turn organized a range of services: a workers' education program, a speakers series, movie festivals, a motorized library or bibliobus, and, of course, a theater program.[17] Blanchon called in Jean Dasté to head the theater project, and Dasté went at the task with a youthful enthusiasm. He assembled a troupe of a dozen or so actors, small enough to squeeze into a single truck. Dasté was not content to play to Grenoble audiences but wanted in a literal sense to be able to take the show on the road. "We were doing boy-scoutism," recollected one trouper with amusement, remembering the gung ho ways of the company's first theatrical forays. Dasté's troupe assembled a repertoire to match: no boulevard sophistication for them, but dramas with strong characters, "capable of evoking a present moment that was by turns exalting, anguished or impassioned."[18]

The buses, movies, and trucks, the exaltation of committed action, the workerist rhetoric (tickets for Dasté's theater program were sold in local factories[19]) all resonated with the heroic and modernizing temper of the Liberation moment. But the boy-scoutish strains of Jeune France, though fainter, are still discernible, and little wonder, as Dasté had run an itinerant troupe under JF auspices during the war.

Such was the mixed pedigree of the second CDN, for it was from Dasté's Grenoble troupe that the Comédie de Saint-Etienne evolved.

Blanchon had great ambitions for Dasté's troupe, but funding was in short supply. Dasté and he approached Jeanne Laurent for a subvention; she expressed a willingness to help, provided the Grenoble municipal authorities made a contribution; and they balked. Dasté then turned elsewhere and in the end found the backing he needed from Saint-Etienne. His troupe relocated there, setting up shop in a former movie house. CDN status was conferred on the Comédie de Saint-Etienne in July 1947; Dasté stayed on as director until 1970.[20]

By 1952, the network of CDNs had expanded to five. The origins of the three newcomers, however, owed much less to independent local energies, whether municipal or PEC-style, than was the case with the two pioneers (although, as will be seen, the decision making was not altogether top-down). Laurent picked the locales—Toulouse, Rennes, Aix—selecting towns that had preexisting theatrical assets. In the case of Toulouse, that asset was Sarrazin's Grenier, which, though young, had made a name for itself in the Jeunes compagnies competition of 1946. Laurent compensated for the troupe's relative inexperience by designating a codirector, more titular than hands-on, of undoubted seniority. He was Charles Dullin. The Grenier de Toulouse was elevated to CDN status in January 1949.[21] The Rennes story was much the same. A promising young company was on hand, the Jeunes Comédiens; the company stood in want of more seasoned leadership; and that leadership was provided by Hubert Gignoux, named the company's director, and Maurice Jacquemont (late of Jeune France), who was appointed Gignoux's artistic counselor. In May of 1949, with the new team in place, the Jeunes Comédiens de Rennes was rechristened the CDN de l'Ouest.[22]

In the case of Aix, the local asset was not a troupe but a powerful personality, that of Gaston Baty. How, it might well be asked, was Baty, the onetime monarchist and anti-Semite, in any position at all to matter in postwar theater affairs? During the Occupation, he had embraced Pétain as "a lesser evil."[23] Into 1943, he had played a starring part in the corporatization and cleansing of Parisian theater. But there was more to Baty's wartime career than such compromising associations. Over the course of 1943, Baty withdrew from the limelight, devoting himself to an art form he called "the most beautiful creation of French comic genius since Molière": puppetry.[24] Indeed, he is credited with sparking a hand-puppet renaissance, aimed not just at a children's audience but also at adults with a susceptibility for romantic fantasy and the *funambulesque*. This was the Baty who emerged from *les années sombres*, a Cartel great who had taken a timeworn art form, minor but charming, and breathed fresh life into it. He was also not a well man, which explains in part why Baty relocated to the warmer climes of the south after the war, taking up residence in Aix in 1949.[25] It was from there that he approached Laurent about setting up a CDN, and Baty's stature made a refusal impossible, even though the city was not well prepared for the endeavor. So it was that, in March 1952, the last of the new CDNs, the Centre dramatique national de Provence, came into being with Baty in the post of director.[26]

Laurent's experiments in decentralization, it turns out, were a triumph not just for a Resistance credo that placed a premium on cultural democratization but also for the antiboulevard opposition of the thirties: onetime Copiaus, Cartel veterans, and graduates of Chancerel's Comédiens-Routiers. That opposition had become Vichy insiders in 1940, wielding power in the ADTP or basking in the patronage of l'Etat français via Jeune France subsidies. Many, but not all by any means, had later veered into the Resistance, and the group resurfaced in force at the Liberation, now recast as impresarios of theater decentralization.

The list of Laurent's postwar achievements is impressive. The professionalizing intent of Vichy-era legislation was confirmed, young artists were singled out for special recognition, and a long-standing dream, *la décentralisation théâtrale*, was brought at last to realization. There was a fourth and final piece to Laurent's new deal for theater: the resuscitation of the Théâtre national populaire (TNP). The TNP had been created in 1920, just after the Great War. Its charge: to produce shows that would draw in, not just the *mondain* types who flocked to the boulevards, but a broad Parisian public. A lack of adequate funding and theatrical imagination, however, had led to disappointing results. The TNP sank into an uninspiring routine, offering a conventional mix of the serious and the lighthearted, of classics and comic opera.[27] This was the institution Laurent meant to rejuvenate, and she found just the man for the job in Jean Vilar. Vilar was a Dullin student, trained in the physical, expressive style of the Cartel. He was a partisan of the ensemble, a road-hardened trouper who had tramped with Clavé's La Roulotte during the war years. And he was a man of purifying principle, revolted by the "putrid," boudoir atmosphere of the Parisian scene.[28] It was Vilar who, in 1947, founded the Avignon theater festival, playing to outdoor audiences at the Palais des Papes on a rough-and-ready stage. Such were the qualities Vilar brought to the TNP, whose direction he assumed in September 1951. Such, moreover, was the theater he created there, a coming to life of the theatrical revelations of Copeau and the Cartel, but now on an altogether grander scale. For the TNP's base of operations, the Palais de Chaillot, held space for 2,600, and to draw in audiences in such numbers, Vilar had to be inventive. Tickets were sold at a fraction of the cost of private theater seats; there were special rates for group subscriptions; and the show got started at an earlier hour than on the boulevards to make it easier for an after-work crowd to attend. The crowds did come: young people in large part, a generation who to this day harbor appreciative memories of the quality repertoire and public-spiritedness of the Palais de Chaillot experience.[29]

By all accounts, it was indeed "a repertory of quality"[30] that the TNP, and the new CDNs too for that matter, tended to favor, and quality in the postwar era meant much the same thing it had in the decades preceding. Vilar and the CDNs shunned the boulevard tradition;[31] the glory days of Henry Bernstein were now but a passing memory (Bernstein himself died in 1953), and it was a good thing too. Yet Laurent's "boys" (the characterization, a little pointed, is Schaeffer's[32]) were not for all that partisans of the theatrical avant-garde. Not for them Ionesco and Genêt or even Camus and Montherlant, who were judged too "literary" and "philosophical" for the audiences the TNP and CDNs catered to. From the mid-1950s, Dasté took a growing interest in Brecht, but it was the playwright's poetic humanism, more than his politics, that Dasté found appealing, a predilection which drew critical fire from one young Marxist critic, Roland Barthes.[33]

No, quality meant above all the classics. The classics might, of course, be foreign. Which foreigners merited inclusion may well be guessed from the Cartel antecedents of Vilar and the CDN directors: the ancient Greeks, Shakespeare, the dramatists of Spain's Golden Age. But first preference went to homegrown authors, to Molière foremost, followed by Corneille and Racine. More than half the dramas staged by the TNP in its early years were classics, and no production played to greater enthusiasm than Corneille's *Le Cid* with Gérard Philipe, handsome and intense, in the title role. The new, state-backed theater of the postwar era understood that it had a national vocation, a duty to defend and illustrate "that French culture" which drew its vitality from roots plunged deep in the native soil.[34]

The emphasis on the classics and the rooted virtues of the nation's cultural patrimony might suggest a musty traditionalism, but this was not at all the case. These were, first of all, classics made new. The physicality of the acting, the ensemble casts, the austerity of the staging all made for an experience of exceptional communal intensity. Vilar got rid of the front-stage curtain, constructing instead a proscenium that jutted into the theater. This allowed actors to approach the parterre, "like officiating clergy." The drama now played out in the audience's very midst, taking on "the aspect of a ceremony," as Dasté recollected it.[35] And though prime emphasis was placed on a canon of time-honored greats, this did not entail the total exclusion of more contemporary work. Among foreign modernists, Chekhov, Gogol, and Pirandello all passed muster, as did, among the French, Anouilh, Copeau, Giraudoux, and François Mauriac.[36]

These lists are not just compilations of names but suggest a set of programmatic ambitions. As already observed, this new theater was meant to be national, a cultural expression of France's aspiration to reconstruction. But French culture, as the new, "national" theater conceived it, was not multiform or protean but had a unitary character. It constituted "a single" whole.[37] We have seen how the new canon first began to take shape in the prewar era. It had been hammered out by Copeau, the Cartel directors, and Chancerel and his scout acolytes, men who understood themselves as artists disdainful of money. The animus against the money changers, whether in the audience, in the wings, or onstage, was redoubled for many—Baty, Copeau, and Chancerel's disciples—by serious commitment to a purifying Catholicism. But what they all wanted, believers or not, was a theater of poetic communion, and that is the criterion they applied in refining the postwar repertoire of quality theater. Clavé, looking back at his CDN years, acknowledged with a hint of surprise his "taste" for "texts of strong spirituality": Shaw's *Saint Joan,* Claudel's *L'Otage,* the stage adaptation of Graham Greene's *The Power and the Glory.* Yet are such tastes so astonishing from a onetime JECiste who had come up through the ranks of itinerant theater under Jeune France auspices?[38]

Laurent's oeuvre, from Vilar's TNP to the new CDNs, came under political assault from all sides. Communists criticized its lack of proletarian class-consciousness. The Right execrated Laurent's elitist pretensions to know what was best for the public. A retired arts official, André Cornu, assailed Laurent's new theater for its boy-scoutish nationalism.[39] Schaeffer, who had been a scout himself, took a different but in its way no less malicious line, likening Laurent to the Holy Virgin keening for "her Theater on the Cross, her Jesus of the sacred Culture, whose decentralized limbs were stretched across the hexagon."[40] Each critique has its moment of truth but misses the whole.

The new, state-backed theater has been described by its most knowledgeable historian as pacifist and anti-American, progressive yet non-Marxist.[41] It took an aggressive and risky anticolonial stand as the Algerian war heated up. The very same mix of views was to be found in the editorial pages of France's newspaper of record *Le Monde,* much disliked by the American establishment in Cold War days for its neutralism, much disliked again in decolonizing days by France's establishment for its anti-imperialism. Need it be added that *Le Monde*'s editor in chief was a ferocious partisan of a clean press with a deep, personal distaste for advertising in any form? That editor, of course, was Hubert Beuve-Méry, Mounier loyalist and Uriage veteran. Laurent's oeuvre, like *Le Monde* itself, had its roots in a nonconformist, *ni droite ni gauche* past. In the thirties and early war years, the *ni droite ni gauche* stance tended to be more Right than Left; by the late forties and beyond, it had become more Left than Right.

A Cinema of Quality

The Communists had a clear understanding of how they wanted the cinema reorganized at the Liberation. They envisioned an industry funded by the state but run by itself. This was corporatism, but a corporatism of the Left, which aimed to place unionized professionals on an equal footing, if not more, with the movie bosses, the producers and theater-chain owners who had ruled the industry in laissez-faire days. For a moment in the early postwar years, it seemed that the Communists had the clout to realize their ambitions, and yet in the end they fell short. It is reasonable to ask why this should have been so.

The answer is in large part political. Gaullists blocked or tempered the Communist advance, trumping the party's corporatist plans with a more state-centered scheme. The result was a new deal for cinema, statist in design, which owed more than a little to Vichy precedents. It was not just that certain institutions, like the IDHEC, were held over, but so too the project embedded in them, that of nurturing a quality cinema. The rhetoric of quality had always had an anti-American dimension. Its remobilization in the postwar era had a peculiar rallying effect, reconciling a left-leaning film world to a new institutional order that was not so leftist in inspiration and design.

The PCF was indeed a formidable presence in the postwar cinema world. In 1943, the party began publication of its own underground film magazine, *L'Ecran français*. A half-dozen movie-industry Resistance cells fused in early 1944 to form the CLCF, which became at a stroke the dominant Resistance organ in the trade. It was presided over by the actor Pierre Blanchar, a member of the editorial board at *L'Ecran français*. In August, at the Liberation of Paris, CLCF militiamen seized the Champs-Elysées offices of the COIC, arresting in the process the Comité's senior staff, the secretary-general Robert Buron and his right-hand man, Philippe Acoulon. Galey himself was divested of all responsibilities, leaving the COIC for the moment leaderless. Not so, however, the Direction générale du cinéma, which was placed under the command of Jean Painlevé, a party member and engineer turned moviemaker. Roger Richebé, not so long ago a senior COIC official, had little doubt what was happening: "The Communist Party wants the cinema."[42]

It is worth asking, though, what the party wanted the cinema for. The CLCF's first order of business was a thorough housecleaning. Louis Daquin for one had a clear idea what the movie business stood in need of—"clean hands"[43]—and Daquin was a man of parts on the postwar scene, a member of the staff at *L'Ecran français* and secretary-general of the CLCF. To this end, the CLCF set up a series of purge commissions. It was before one such body that Henri-Georges Clouzot first appeared in October 1945 to answer for his Occupation-era activities. Clouzot was forbidden to direct, and he did not make another film until *Le Quai des Orfèvres* was released in 1947, a conventional murder mystery enlivened by Clouzot's characteristic perversity (one of the suspects likes to take photos of nude young ladies) and a riveting performance by Louis Jouvet as the crime-solving detective.

But a purge was just the first step in remaking a profession that had been corroded by collaborators and moneymen. The CLCF wanted to hold on to the Vichy-era system of *cartes professionnelles*, now as before to keep out the incompetent and undesirable (a category, it should be added, that no longer included Jews). It was the COIC that had handed out the cards under the Occupation. The CLCF took over the task at the Liberation, an interim measure pending formation of a more formal, professional body. The problem was how this new body, the expression of the movie industry's corporate identity, was to be constituted. The CLCF, backed by the ever more powerful industry unions (membership in the CGT's Fédération nationale du spectacle shot up from eighteen thousand in 1938 to forty thousand in 1945), favored a joint worker-management commission, each side with equal representation. The commission was not meant to be a mere talking shop but a genuine deliberative body with the cash resources (furnished by state subsidies and professional dues) to ensure its effective functioning. The unions had yet one more interventionist item on their agenda, hoping to see Greven's old empire at Continental nationalized and its studios turned into a state-owned cinema city.[44]

Powerful as they were, though, the party and the unions did not have their hands on all the levers of command. Under Vichy, the Direction générale du cinéma had answered at first to the minister of information and then later straight to Laval. The old chain of command was restored at the Liberation, and the first postwar minister of information was Pierre-Henri Teitgen, a first-hour résistant and veteran member of the Resistance think tank the Comité général d'études. He was also a christian democrat (he had been to Catholic school with Schaeffer) and not one to be outmaneuvered by Communists. Teitgen got support from an unlikely quarter.

Unknown to the domestic Resistance, a number of Vichy movie officials had been in touch with de Gaulle's Provisional Government in Algiers. They constituted themselves as a Resistance network, taking the code name OPERA. The timing of the event is murky, but the network seems to have been up and running by the spring of 1944 at the latest. Acoulon and Buron belonged, an affiliation that saved them both at the Liberation. No sooner were they arrested in August 1944 than more senior men in the Gaullist administration got them released. It was to OPERA agents that Teitgen turned for allies. He appointed Pierre Riedinger, a Vichy official turned OPERA operative, as Painlevé's second in command at the Direction générale. Buron did not stay on in the cinema administration. It may be that he had been too compromised, but not so Acoulon, who was made head of the not yet defunct COIC in October. At the top, Painlevé was hemmed in between Riedinger, who was undermining, and Acoulon, who had direct and regular access to the christian-democratic minister in charge.[45]

In due course, Painlevé himself was eliminated. He was sacked in May 1945 to be replaced by a career civil servant, Michel Fourré-Cormeray. Fourré-Cormeray had worked at the Cour des comptes under Vichy but early on joined a Resistance network that organized the rescue of downed British aviators. His administrative skills and impeccable Resistance credentials prompted de Gaulle's Provisional Government to appoint him to the prefectoral corps at the Liberation. It helped no doubt that he was a christian democrat who also happened to be "close to Michel Debré."[46] It was from here that

Fourré-Cormeray was reassigned to the Direction générale, an appointment, as might be imagined, that had a "bombshell effect" on the movie-world rank and file. The Fédération nationale du spectacle declared a protest strike on 23 May but to no avail.[47]

In August 1944, the Communists had taken command of the film industry. Not a year later, they had been shunted aside. Résistants were still in charge, but they were now résistants with christian-democratic or Gaullist connections. In a couple of instances, the new men were not so new at all but came encumbered with recent Vichy pasts. And in all cases they were servants of the state, more bureaucrats than filmmaking professionals.

The Gaullist state's counteroffensive put an immediate damper on the cleansing impulses so powerful at the movie industry's leftist grassroots. In the months after the Liberation, purging procedures were formalized and CLCF commissions made answerable to more official and moderating bodies. In the end, a mere 171 movie personnel were cleaned out, and in almost all cases the ostracism proved no more than provisional. Such in the end was Clouzot's fate. A CLCF commission had banished him sine die, but the sentence was later reduced on appeal to a simple two-year suspension. This then was a limited purge, in the judgment of Robert Aron "the most moderate" in the world of arts and letters.[48]

The "face" of the profession may not have changed at the Liberation,[49] but what about its structure? Vichy's institutional legacy was bicephalic. The Direction générale was an agency of the state; the COIC was supposed to be an emanation of the profession (though, of course, Vichy made no attempt to set up genuine representative procedures). In the end, the regime finessed the inevitable tensions between the two bodies by appointing the same man, Galey, to head them both. In the immediate aftermath of the Liberation, this organizational schema was held over, the Direction générale now in Fourré-Cormeray's hands, the COIC in Acoulon's.

This arrangement, however, could not and did not last. It was inevitable that the COIC, tarnished in name and design by its Vichy origins, would have to go. No one, however, desired to revert to the free-market ways of the thirties. Not the Communists who agitated for a unitary, corporatist system based on worker/management parity. Nor the ex-Vichy administrator Acoulon who, in the words of one film historian, wanted no part of a "return to unfettered prewar liberalism."[50]

In 1945, the *rapports de force* between a left-leaning profession and Gaullist higher-ups dictated that a compromise be sought. Acoulon came up with the terms. In August, the COIC was dissolved, replaced by an Office professionnel du cinéma (OPC). The Office, as first conceived, was to consist of a forty-member parity board, appointed by the state and chaired by a board-elected director. The state had little initial difficulty making its nominations, working in consultation with the principal trade unions and management associations in the industry. Problems arose, however, when the parity board met in October to choose a director. The vote split down the middle, twenty ballots cast for management's man, Acoulon, and nineteen for labor's candidate with one abstention. A subsequent ballot did not render a more decisive majority, and a deal was then struck, confirmed by ministerial decree in January 1946: the job of senior administrator was assigned to Acoulon, but a new post was also cooked up, a second in command, reserved for a personality more to labor's liking. In the event, the adjunct's slot was filled by Claude Jaeger, a veteran of the military wing of the Resistance, known for his "communist ideas." None of this boded well for the future functioning of the OPC, and, indeed, the Office's operations were hampered by persistent labor/management tussling.[51] Nor was it ever settled just how the Office professionnel and the still-functioning Direction générale would divide film administration responsibilities.

A more permanent solution was worked out in the months ahead. De Gaulle left office in January 1946. The general now gone, France was governed by a series of tripartite coalitions composed of Communists, Socialists, and christian democrats. In the matter of film administration, it was the MRP that took the lead. The diumvirate of Fourré-Cormeray's Direction générale and Acoulon's internally divided OPC was not working, and the MRP minister of information Robert Bichet, counseled by Fourré-Cormeray, came up with a scheme that adopted a new approach. Bichet proposed creating a Centre national de la cinématographie (CNC) to replace both the Direction générale and the OPC. The state would appoint a candidate of its own choosing as the CNC director; the director in turn would be assisted by a parity board of sixteen members designated by the state after discussion with the relative labor and management unions. The board's powers, however, were to be circumscribed, consultative in nature rather than deliberative. In the event, Bichet's proposition did not meet substantial opposition and was enacted into law in October 1946. Fourré-Cormeray himself was named the first CNC director, a post he would occupy into the 1950s.[52]

The Cold War was not yet on, but already in the domain of cinema a successful policy of containment had been applied, blocking a too thorough purge and the institutionalization of Communist influence via a left-based corporatism. It was not that the Communists had lost out altogether. They wanted parity representation on the movie industry's governing board, and they got it; they wanted film interests handled by a single professional body, and they got that too in the shape of the CNC. That said, the parity board did not have policy-making power. And more than that, it was subordinate to a director-general who was the real decision maker, and he was the state's man. The upwelling of communist sentiment, so powerful at the Liberation, was capped at the top, and the men who did the capping were an odd assortment of christian democrats, Gaullists, and ex-Vichyites. Long gone were the freewheeling ways of the old Third Republic, yet the Vichy past was not so distant. Pétain's regime had touted its corporatist intentions vis-à-vis the film industry but hesitated to follow through on them. Indeed, the decision to appoint Galey, already head of the Direction générale, to run the COIC as well signaled an unmistakable statist turn in Vichy policy. The creation of the CNC in 1946 did not reverse this trend. To be sure, there was now a parity board, but its authority was limited, and it was the state and its agents who held the real upper hand.

The continuity with the past in matters of policy was no less great. The double bill, prohibited by Vichy, remained so in the postwar era. Vichy's Direction générale had monitored box-office receipts. The CNC took over the task. It also took over the distribution of *cartes professionnelles,* which in Vichy days had been the COIC's prerogative. Vichy-style censorship was now a thing of the past, but that did not mean the French state had adopted an anything-goes attitude. All new films required a visa issued by the Ministère de l'Information. Visas might be denied pictures judged contrary to "good morals"; or an adults-only visa might be granted, which green-lighted distribution but prohibited ticket sales to customers sixteen and under.[53] The impulse so potent at Vichy to discipline the movie industry—to curb sharp business practices, to exclude the "unprofessional," to moralize audiences—did not disappear at the Liberation, although now it came cloaked in less authoritarian and racist garb.

The same may be said of the impulse to enshrine quality as the defining trait of French film. The IDHEC had been founded with that objective in mind, which helps to explain its survival at the Liberation. It also made a difference that the political climate at the Institut had evolved with the times. The Left was always well represented at IDHEC. It was students from the school who, during the making of René Clément's wartime film *Ceux du rail,* gathered clandestine footage of Italian coastal defenses, which was then spirited out of the country to England. Clément himself went on to make another and yet more celebrated railroad movie, *La Bataille du rail* (1945), which was a stirring chronicle, unique of its kind, documenting Resistance activity among railwaymen. With the Liberation, moreover, the leftist presence at IDHEC grew more public and assertive. Jean Lods, now a party member, continued on as a director of studies. Georges Sadoul, the dean of communist film critics, was hired to teach a course on the history of cinema, screening movies at the Cinémathèque in conjunction. A direction of cultural services was attached to the Institut at the Liberation, and the first man placed in charge was a Communist, Claude Roy.[54]

But the surfacing of Roy's name in this context should give pause. Last encountered in the spring of 1942, he had just quit Vichy radio. Laval's return to power brought out the dissident in him, prompting a reconsideration of commitments in the months that followed. At the urging of friends, Roy drew closer to communism, joining the party itself the ensuing winter. Roy's stunning about-face did not, however, betoken a total abandonment of former belief. Whether as Action française militant or party member, he was repelled by what he called "this abject world of almighty money." As a Communist, moreover, Roy remained no less staunch a nationalist than before. Indeed, he encountered in party ranks a number of "former Maurrasian 'nationalists,'" much like himself, who had embraced wartime communism as a saving creed that allowed them "to *breathe* at last, free to be at one and the same time socialists and 'patriots.'"[55]

Perhaps Roy's association with IDHEC evidences less the Institut's ideological rebirth at the Liberation than its subterranean connection to an older project of cultural renewal, nationalist and anticommercial in thrust. Nor was the connection always subterranean. IDHEC's Vichy-era director, Marcel L'Herbier, was kept on at the Liberation: L'Herbier of the anti-Hollywood diatribes retailed in the collaborationist press. The "quality" project had always had a certain ambiguity to it, mixing aesthetic seriousness of purpose with a patriotism that at times spilled over into out-and-out xenophobia.

The whole range of such impulses was on broad display in the movie-industry campaign against the Blum-Byrnes agreement of May 1946. France at the Liberation stood in desperate need of investment capital to finance its reconstruction. In 1946, former prime minister Léon Blum led a delegation to Washington to solicit a loan, which was negotiated in due course. The sum involved, however, was less generous than the French had hoped for, and it came with a proviso attached that had serious repercussions for France's movie business. During the war, Hollywood had been excluded from the French market, but now it wanted back in. France's movie administration had a different idea. The Direction générale did not want to resurrect the old *contingentement* system, but it did have plans to fix screen-time quotas that would oblige movie houses to reserve six weeks per quarter for French-made films. The Blum-Byrnes accord addressed the issue, proposing a solution that was part compromise, part French capitulation. The United States agreed to screen-time quotas for French films, but the actual quota established was minimal, just four weeks in thirteen.

The film industry was incensed and made its sentiments known. Daquin called a press conference at IDHEC in June 1946 to protest the accord. In the months following, the PCF newspaper, *L'Humanité*, pounded out a steady drumbeat of anti–Blum-Byrnes articles, and cinema trade associations, both labor and management, convened meetings that echoed the party's expressions of outrage. These various efforts converged in the formation of a Comité de défense du cinéma français in December 1947, which in turn called for massive out-of-doors action. That very next January the *grands boulevards* of Paris were witness to a huge, star-studded demonstration of cinema professionals, which marched to chants of "Cinéma français libre."[56]

The Communists, to be sure, were very much in the forefront of the anti–Blum-Byrnes campaign.[57] Sadoul disdained the American movie industry, run as he saw it by a cartel of millionaires and Hays Code moralists. Not ten decent movies, he claimed, had been made in the United States during the war years, so who wanted a flood of such trash inundating the French market? For sure not Daquin, who spurned Blum-Byrnes as a "death warrant" for the French movie industry. France had to stand up for itself: "We must defend quality for it is the only way we have of saving our cinema."[58]

But the Communists were not alone in their repudiation of Blum-Byrnes. *Le Monde* published a broadside by the Thomist scholar Etienne Gilson (uncle of Paul), which likened the American cinema to a drug and worried about its stupefying effect on the moral health of the French people. The most memorable line of the anti–Blum-Byrnes campaign was no doubt coined by the old Cartel director and actor Louis Jouvet. At Daquin's IDHEC press conference, he compared US movies, not so much to drugs, as to a stomach-rotting soft drink. He wondered how palates, cultured by the fine wines of Burgundy and Bordeaux, could ever be made to adapt to the Coca-Cola vulgarities dispensed by Hollywood.[59] Nor was Jouvet the only old hand of 1930s nonconformism to join in the general hue and cry. The moving force behind the launching of the Comité de défense was none other than Claude Autant-Lara. And it will come as no surprise that the Comité's founding meeting, held on IDHEC premises, was presided over by that veteran anti-American Marcel L'Herbier.[60]

A veritable "union sacrée" of interests arrayed itself against the Blum-Byrnes accord, and its exertions did not go without result.[61] In parliament, a majority crystallized endorsing ratification of Blum-Byrnes, but there was mounting sentiment, even within the majority itself, in favor of a reopening of talks with Washington on the accord's film provisions. This position was articulated by, of all people, Robert Buron, now recycled as a christian-democratic deputy with general expertise in media matters. This is in fact what happened. Blum-Byrnes was revised in September 1948, the Americans conceding a rise in the screen-time quota for French-made movies from four to five weeks per quarter.[62] Of perhaps greater moment, the Blum-Byrnes controversy was backdrop to the creation in June 1946 of the Commission de modernisation du cinéma, which operated under the auspices of Jean Monnet's Commissariat-général au Plan. The Commission was not an important institution in itself, but it came up with a proposal that would help to sustain French cinema for decades to come.

The idea was to impose a levy on movie-ticket prices, the proceeds going to a state-managed subvention fund for the French movie industry. The proposal was in fact made into law in 1948, the so-called *loi d'aide*. The measure created a tax on all new releases, foreign and domestic. The resulting revenue, which turned out to be substantial, was handed over to the CNC with the explicit proviso that the CNC disburse the money to advance the interests of *French* film alone. This meant in practice meting out subsidies to film institutions like the IDHEC and Cinémathèque, but the CNC also invested important sums in new productions. In due course, a special jury was set up to hand out additional cash awards to films deemed of exceptional artistic or thematic merit, in effect *primes à la qualité*.[63]

There is much in all this reminiscent of Vichy days. The COIC had vanished from the scene but come back in more statist guise as the CNC. The IDHEC did not even have to bother with a name change. The rhetoric of professionalism and quality remained as insistent as ever, and what was intended by the terms did not alter much either. The directors who had risen to prominence during the war years—Autant-Lara, Clouzot, Daquin—continued to dominate the postwar industry. There was the occasional newcomer (Jacques Tati is the most notable example), but there were few carryovers from the classic cinema of the thirties. Carné's career had peaked with *Les Enfants du Paradis* (1945); Renoir was slow to return to France and did not in fact come back until the 1950s.

To the New Wave filmmakers of the next generation, the directorial cadre who dominated the French movie scene in the postwar era were a dismal lot, purveyors of a quality cinema that lacked immediacy and individuality. Exceptions were made to the general denunciation: for the austere spirituality of Bresson's work, for the evocative atmospherics of Becker's.[64] These directors had asserted a distinctive personal style, but the others? New Wave critics, François Truffaut in the lead, taxed them for a lack of originality. They worked with well-plotted scripts, often adaptations, written not by themselves but by professional scenarists. They made well-constructed films, but the storytelling was stilted and conventional. They had a moral to convey, but it was a worn-out moral, seasoned with antibourgeois sentiments that might have been piquant in Flaubert's time but which had lost much of their freshness since.[65]

There was much that was unfair in Truffaut's polemic. The postwar system was organized, professional, unionized, all of which kept production standards high, if perhaps at the cost of a certain routinization of filmmaking practice. The system was also well funded, and without the state funds now available to movie-makers the New Wave itself might never have taken off. In critical respects, moreover, the postwar order was not so routine-minded as all that. Better sound and lighting equipment, lighter cameras, and faster film speeds now made it easier to film out of doors, and mainstream filmmakers had already begun to shift to location shooting, paving the way for the New Wave, which made such a fetish of authentic, true-to-life settings.[66]

That said, the New Wave's aesthetic critique had enough bite to enrage its targets, Claude Autant-Lara for one, who was much disliked by the New Wave young and returned the favor, branding the likes of "True-Faux" and Godard as "Yankee flunkies" (*larbins amerlos*).[67] Now, the postwar moment had not been altogether easy for Autant-Lara. It seems that he had distinguished himself under Vichy as an anti-Semite. At the Liberation, Pierre Braunberger, a producer of Jewish origin, had attempted a boycott campaign against Autant-

Lara but to no lasting effect.[68] Autant-Lara's prominent role in the
anti–Blum-Byrnes effort may have helped get him past such difficulties. What is certain is that he returned to filmmaking with gusto,
churning out a series of movies, good and not so good, that may be
taken as a fair embodiment of the postwar quality aesthetic.

Take *Le Diable au corps* (1946) and *Le Rouge et le Noir* (1954) as examples. Both were adaptations, the first based on Raymond Radiguet's
1923 novel by the same name, the second on Stendahl's masterpiece;
both were written by Jean Aurenche and Pierre Bost, frequent collaborators of Autant-Lara's and at the time among the very best in the
scriptwriting trade;[69] and both featured a rather standard use of flash-
back construction. *Le Diable au corps* tells the story of a forbidden love
affair, set in provincial France during the Great War, between a young
woman whose husband is off at the front and an ardent sixteen-year-
old. The novel's narrative is linear, but the film version opens with the
burial of the adulterous wife who has died just at the war's end because of complications due to a pregnancy (it is the teenage adulterer
who has impregnated her). A similar setup is used in *Le Rouge et le Noir*.
The film begins, not with Julien Sorel's rustic youth as in the novel,
but with a courtroom scene. Sorel has made a failed attempt on the
life of his inamorata, Mme de Rênal, and is on trial for his life.

As for the productions themselves, they were put together with
real professional care. Autant-Lara had a flair for pans and tracking
shots. He was also a stickler for costume and decor. *Le Rouge et le Noir*,
even if ponderous at well over two hours in running time, is a handsome film (it was shot in color), and the handsomeness of it is not
confined to the mise en scène. Autant-Lara assigned the male lead to
an actor of still youthful good looks, Gérard Philipe. This was not the
director's first recourse to Philipe. Autant-Lara had used him in 1946,
then an actor not much into his twenties, in the starring role of *Le
Diable au corps.*

And the message both films conveyed had all the nonconformist
animus that the most conventional antibourgeois could want. The
adulterous lovers in *Le Diable au corps* have a right to their passion,
whatever the dictates of middle-class morality; that the cuckolded
husband is a frontline soldier does not in the end alter the equation,

even if it is the source of some soul-searching. As for Autant-Lara's Julien Sorel, he is a *révolté* against the bourgeois social order, by turns ambitious and ardent, but ardent above all, in the end sacrificing worldly success on the altar of passion.

Film critics have classified Autant-Lara's work as a species of neo-classicism.[70] The New Wave preferred to see him as a standard-bearer of France's "tradition of quality." Whatever the label, it was a formula that worked. It was "quality" pictures—adaptations, costume dramas, historical romances—that enjoyed greatest public esteem in the French 1950s. Add in the genre movies, the *policiers*, the Fernandel comedies, and the picture grows rosier still. To be sure, American movies poured onto the reopened French market after the war. Yet, once the initial onslaught had been absorbed, it was French productions that got the larger market share, taking in half of all box-office receipts in the fifties to the less than one-third garnered by US-made films.[71] The French film industry's formula for success in the 1950s, a mix of quality pictures and Fernandelleries, was not, it will be recognized, a pure postwar invention. It had a demonstrated track record that dated back to the Vichy years.[72]

Still, care must be taken not to exaggerate the continuities between the war and postwar eras. There was trade-union representation on the CNC, which Vichy would never have allowed. The communist presence was public and assertive at institutions like the IDHEC. Vichy's insistence on sound professional ethics had come tainted with anti-Americanism and anti-Semitism. After the war, screen-time quotas and public criticism notwithstanding, US films returned to the French market in force. Jews, however, were not quite so fortunate, never recovering in the postwar era the film-world prominence they had enjoyed in the 1930s. The Siritsky and Haïk chains, which Continental had taken over during the war, did not return to private hands afterward but were nationalized and rolled into a single state-run firm, the Union générale du cinéma.[73] The formal discriminations of the Vichy era, of course, were gone, but less institutionalized obstacles remained. Marcel Dalio, who spent the war years in Hollywood, recollected how hard it was to reintegrate into the French scene afterward:

The producers who ruled the roost at Le Fouquet's were the same ones as under the Occupation. They welcomed me with sympathy.... But as for working with me on a picture, that was another matter.... Did they see me as some kind of guilt-inspiring revenant who was going to reproach them for having worked at Continental during the war?[74]

The line from Vichy to the postwar order was not straight, but Dalio's experience is a reminder that Vichy did indeed cast a long shadow. The film industry was no longer structured to serve authoritarian and racist ends. It was now home to a militant, leftist rank and file. All the same, the movie Left worked within an institutional and aesthetic framework not altogether of its own making, a framework that owed much in personnel, policy, and design to war-years antecedents.

National Radio

Since the Daladier administration of the late Third Republic, radio had been moving in a statist direction. The Liberation era consummated the process. De Gaulle's Provisional Government in Algiers decreed a series of measures in late spring and early summer of 1944 making plain its intention to take over the airwaves. No one wanted the mercantile interests of the prewar era to come back, a resolution reinforced by the private sector's dubious dealings under Vichy. The unsavory relationship Laval had maintained with the Trémoulet group was confirming proof of private radio's unworthiness, if additional proof was needed.[75] But who was to run the new state radio; how was it to be organized; and what policies was it to follow? These questions gave rise to years of acrimonious debate and political infighting.

What resulted was a system that represented less of a break with past practice than might have been anticipated. The team that, after much wrangling, was put in charge of managing public radio's fortunes included a new face, that of Vital Gayman (responsible for radio news), but some familiar ones as well, those of Wladimir Porché and Paul Gilson. They did not have the kind of autonomy enjoyed by their BBC counterparts in Great Britain but answered to political superiors, to the minister of information and, in the final instance, to the prime minister himself. This setup had a stifling effect on radio news, though less so, of course, than under the authoritarian Vichy regime. As for cultural programming, public radio, as in the past, excelled at quality production, indeed, was better at it than ever, but the more humble genres—variety entertainment, quiz shows—continued to get short shrift and began to emigrate to the peripheral stations in search of a more congenial home. The postwar order, in a word, looked a lot like the old Daladier system, but now on a monopolistic scale and with a high-quality specialization that owed more than a little to radio personnel, like Gilson, inherited from the Vichy past.

Control of the airwaves generated a political tug-of-war at the Liberation, the Comité de libération de la radio (CLR), the Gaullists, and a renascent SFIO all pulling in different directions. Round one of the match—the CLR versus de Gaulle's Provisional Government—went hands down to the latter.

Jean Guignebert, a Socialist, was the principal figure at the CLR. The organization contained a strong communist contingent, but one of its critical contacts in the radio world, Pierre Schaeffer, was no leftist at all. Whatever the peculiarities of Schaeffer's political past, he was an enormous asset, the director of a Vichy radio facility, the Studio d'essai, which he had placed at the disposal of the Resistance cause. Indeed, on 20 August 1944, as Paris rose in insurrection against the German occupiers, Schaeffer's Studio d'essai began broadcasting Resistance news, issuing a general call to arms on the twenty-second and then on the night of the twenty-fourth summoning the city's priests to ring the church bells in celebration of Paris's refound freedom. It was Schaeffer, the veteran Catholic scout, who issued the appeal.[76] The CLR had in the meantime seized the offices of Radio Paris, rechristened Radio National. The capital's airwaves were now in the hands of the CLR, and its first priority, as had been the CLCF's in the movie industry, was a thorough housecleaning. A purge commission was set up. For the moment, Guignebert occupied the most senior rank in the radio world. In principle, he answered to de Gaulle's minister of information, Teitgen, but Teitgen had been captured by the Germans in June and did not return from captivity until September after a daring escape.

Guignebert, however, was gone before the year was out. He had difficulties first of all with Schaeffer, never an easy man to get on with. Schaeffer emerged from the Liberation as vice president of the CLR and, as such, Guignebert's second in command. In that capacity, he had powers of appointment, and he used them to designate an old Resistance comrade—"my co-conspirator from days in the underground"—as administrative director of the public airwaves. That buddy turned out to be Robert Buron, late of the Vichy cinema administration and soon to be MRP deputy (Buron lasted in the job until the middle of 1945, when he was replaced by Jack Francès, a senior civil servant and an altogether less partisan figure).[77] How Guignebert felt about Schaeffer's predilections in personnel is not clear, but the two men for a certainty clashed on the question of radio nationalization. Guignebert was a strong advocate; Schaeffer, troubled about potential state dominance of the medium, was not.[78] Then, of course, there was Schaeffer's record of Vichy service. He became the target of public criticism and, in short order, was demoted back to the Studio d'essai. Schaeffer, conscious of the awkwardness of the situation, resigned from the CLR and then in early 1945 headed off *en mission* to the United States, still on the radio payroll but no longer a senior official.[79]

Guignebert's most serious disputes, however, arose not with Schaeffer but with Teitgen and, in the end, with de Gaulle himself. Guignebert imagined a French national radio on the model of the BBC, but Teitgen for one wanted a system less autonomous vis-à-vis the state.[80] Teitgen wanted as well a managed purge of the medium. In radio, as in cinema, he contrived to stymie the bottom-up cleansing undertaken by Resistance forces. In October 1944, Teitgen short-circuited the CLR's purge apparatus, setting up an official state commission. It had limited, advisory powers, final decision-making in all cases resting with the minister himself. The result was a mild purge, which was lightest for artistic personnel. Schaeffer, for a period, was obliged to keep a low profile, but not so many of his less compromised Jeune

France confreres. Pierre Barbier went into radio producing. Roger Leenhardt, solicited first by Schaeffer and then Guignebert, returned to the airwaves in 1945. With Claude Roy and Nicole Védrès, both big talkers, Leenhardt put together a movie-review show, *Le Tribunal des ondes*, which featured spirited exchanges on the most recent releases. The biggest success story, however, was Albert Ollivier, who, back into radio at the Liberation and then recycled through Gaullist politics, rose in 1959 to become program director at the RTF.[81]

Teitgen maneuvered to contain Guignebert and the CLR, but de Gaulle wanted to do more. He did not like Guignebert's militant leftism and, in December 1945, had him sacked and replaced by Claude Bourdet, a résistant of sterling credentials, a "progressive Christian" as one colleague called him, and no crypto-communist.[82]

As 1945 wound down, the radio Resistance, at least in the person of Guignebert, had been sidelined, but what or who was to replace it? De Gaulle's departure from the public scene in January 1946 complicated the situation. The first post-Gaullist minister of information, Gaston Defferre, had a definite understanding of the direction he wanted to take radio. Defferre was a former résistant, a socialist stalwart, and a tough institutional infighter. He intended to put a socialist stamp on radio and set about the task with characteristic bluntness of purpose. Bourdet was called in and instructed to liquidate "all the Gaullists and all the communists."[83] A man of principle, Bourdet balked, but he paid for his insubordination by getting fired himself. The pretext was a radio scandal, a French variant on Orson Welles's celebrated 1938 "War of the Worlds" broadcast. In this instance, the provocateur's part was played by Jean Nocher, a journalist and inveterate practical joker. Nocher went on the air in February 1946 in the part of a certain Professor Helium, alerting an unwitting radio public, not to an alien invasion, but to an atomic disaster of earthshaking proportions. The "gag" earned Nocher a suspension, and Defferre profited from the occasion to get rid of Bourdet outright. Defferre cast about for a right-thinking replacement, but the SFIO's partners in government at the time, the christian-democratic MRP and the PCF, were alert to Defferre's machinations and insisted on an above-party appointment. The candidate settled on was Wladimir Porché, who took over national radio from March 1946.[84]

The setback did not deter Defferre, however. He created a new position at national radio, that of news chief, and selected a loyal party man for the job, Henri Noguères, a distinguished résistant and journalist who also happened to be principal editor of the socialist daily *Le Populaire*. Such naked partisanship caused a stink; Defferre himself left office in the summer of 1946; and Noguères was in due course pushed aside in favor of a new man, Vital Gayman, appointed in November.[85] The Gaullists had shut down the Resistance Left. Now it was Defferre who had been outmaneuvered.

What remained behind was a leadership of less evident political commitments: Porché in charge overall and Gayman responsible for the newsroom. A third figure rounded out the team: Paul Gilson, the poet and devotee of the fantastic. Porché named him head of public radio's artistic services in the fall of 1946. None of the trio was a party man, which helps explain why they were able to weather so many changes of government, even of regime. Porché lasted in office until 1956, Gayman until 1958, and Gilson, most durable of all, until 1963. Yet it would not be quite right to say that the three were altogether apolitical.

Porché is the most elusive of the three. He came from a literary family with theatrical connections. As a young man, Porché considered a civil-service career but failed the entry exam for the Conseil d'état. It was at this juncture that his father intervened, contriving an interview for his son with then minister of posts Georges Mandel, a well-disposed family friend. The connection landed Porché a job as director of dramatic programming in 1935, a position in which he remained for some time. Porché's wartime years, however, remain something of a blank. He retreated into the private sector; that much appears certain.[86] It seems too that he had friends on the Left, enough so as to be well regarded by the CLR, which backed his appointment in 1946 as director of a reviving national radio. Porché, then, got to be a servant of the state after all, and he had the qualities to match, a middle-of-the-road nonpartisanship and suppleness of intellect that allowed him to cultivate friendships on both sides of the aisle: among center-right politicians like Mandel, who provided initial protection, and among leftist résistants whose endorsement opened the path to promotion.[87]

Gayman, on the other hand, was not such a neutralist. He had been a Communist in the 1930s and a loyalist volunteer in the Spanish Civil War. The Nazi-Soviet pact of 1939 prompted a rupture with the party but not an abandonment of militancy. Gayman entered the Resistance. He got in, on his own account, via the good offices of fellow Spanish Civil War veteran André Malraux. Gayman's Resistance activities were cut short in 1943 when he was arrested, impressed into labor service on Hitler's Atlantic Wall, and then, in the wake of the Allied invasion at Normandy, placed on a deportation train to Germany, a terrifying prospect to anyone but above all to an ex-Communist like Gayman who was also of Jewish ancestry. Gayman managed an escape and survived, toughened by his experiences and warier, as a result, of political enthusiasms. He remained, however, a staunch anticommunist. The party had it in for him as a renegade and turncoat; he had occasion to return the favor in Cold War days when the time came to purge Communists from public radio's news services.[88]

Gayman had a communist past to live down; Gilson's was Vichyite. He was last encountered in 1941, employed as a programmer at Vichy radio, helping Jeune France types like Barbier, Ollivier, and Roy get on the air. The headquarters of the RN relocated to Paris in 1943, but Gilson did not follow. He took a job instead at Radio Monte-Carlo, where he worked under the veteran radio man Jean Antoine. This was still a Vichy posting, though, since the principal owner at Radio Monte-Carlo was SOFIRA, the Vichy regime's radio holding company. Gilson disappears from view at this point, not to resurface until after the war when, still a radio employee, he was sent off to the United States. It is not unreasonable to suppose that more senior policy makers felt that he, like Schaeffer, had a past that needed forgetting, a process that a stay abroad might well advance. Gilson still had friends at home, however, not least of them Barbier, who, not long after the Liberation, published a pseudonymous article in the pages of *Esprit* urging the radio administration to make better use of seasoned programmers like Gilson. It was indeed from the United

States that, within the year, Porché plucked Gilson, calling him back to take the job of public radio's chief programmer.[89]

This then was the team that would manage radio's fortunes into the fifties. Its political profile was modulated enough to allow it leeway in navigating the treacherous shoals of post-Liberation public life, but it had certain guiding principles nonetheless: an anticommunism born of hard experience and a Jeune France–inflected appreciation of quality culture and its redemptive potential.

The team, however, did not have a completely free hand but operated within an institutional framework devised by political superiors. At the Liberation, radio policy makers made it a priority to insulate the public airwaves against outside pressures. This meant, first of all, freezing out commercial interests. By ordonnance of March 1945, all private stations were nationalized. There was to be a single radio network in France, publicly owned and run and, as such, immune to the manipulations of trusts and bosses. The March 1945 ordonnance settled the matter of radio advertising as well. Commercials were not banned outright, but they might just as well have been, the tone of the document was so disparaging. In principle, it was possible to air jingles and plugs on the public airwaves, but in practice it was not, and such would remain the case for decades to come. What to do about listeners' associations, however, turned out to be a more complicated problem. The CLR favored some form of user representation, but not so the old-line Left, which harbored unhappy memories of the role listeners' groups had played in the radio elections of 1937. In the end, the old-line Left got its way. Listeners' associations, once such central players in radio management, were sidelined in a postwar order designed to give the state full control.[90]

But the state's reach was not unbounded. There were private networks located just across France's frontiers that broadcast to all-too-eager French audiences. These stations might be reined in up to a point. SOFIRA was a useful institution in this regard, holding a controlling interest in extraterritorial stations like Radio Monte-Carlo. This explains in good part why the Société was preserved at the Liberation, albeit with a minor change in name, SOFIRA departing the scene to reenter as SOFIRAD.[91] SOFIRAD's investment activities, however, did not alter the fundamental dynamics of the situation. French state radio faced competition from private operations on the periphery, from Radio Luxembourg in particular, which brought to the airwaves the same mix of innovative zeal and commercial savvy that had made the fortunes of French private radio in the 1930s. Such stations would be formidable rivals, indeed, which all the French state's efforts and resources would not be able to keep at bay.

Commerce, banished from the airwaves in the French heartland, threatened to reenter via the margins. Politics too ate away at the system, but here the threat came not from the outside but from within. Guignebert's dream of a BBC-like broadcasting system in France, state owned yet autonomous, was never realized. There was to be sure much talk about setting up an independent Office national de la radio whose status and resources would be defined in law. But when the matter came up for one final round of public debate in the summer of 1947, insuperable differences arose. Communists and Socialists backed enactment of a formal *statut de la radio.* Opposing voices advocated at least some modest role for private interests, Jean Antoine's, for example, and Marcel Bleustein-Blanchet's. Bleustein-Blanchet, a station owner from prewar days, had compiled an exemplary record of service in the Resistance, but such credentials did not carry sufficient weight to tip the discussion. Swashbuckling entrepreneurs of Bleustein-Blanchet's ilk had had their day, unless they found a way to reinsert themselves into the medium through the peripheral stations (which in the long run is what Bleustein-Blanchet did). The most consequential opposition, however, came not from liberal-minded partisans of the private sector but from the MRP. It is not that the christian democrats were against a state system. Teitgen and Buron in the lead, they had denounced commercial interests, the so-called "trusts," with as much zeal as anyone. But in mid-1947, the Cold War had begun to heat up (the PCF, which after de Gaulle's departure had governed in coalition with the SFIO and MRP, was booted out of government in April; the Marshall Plan was announced June 5), and the christian democrats fretted that a self-managed radio industry might prove all too susceptible to Communist manipulation. In the face of christian-democratic opposition, the proposal to create a *statut de la radio* died.[92]

In the meantime, the Socialist prime minister Paul Ramadier had attached the RDF to his own office. This happened in February 1947, part of a general scaling back of the powers of the Information portfolio. The measure was meant to be provisional, pending legislation of a *statut*, but that legislation never materialized, and the provisional ended up lasting a period of years. Until the Fourth Republic's demise, radio answered to a minister or secretary of state who in turn answered to the prime minister, an arrangement bound to politicize the medium, all the more so in an era of deepening Cold War. It was not long in fact before Communist radio professionals began to feel the chill. Francis Crémieux, a journalist and Communist, lost his job at the news show *Ce Soir en France* in November 1948. A year and a half later, it was the turn of fellow party member Lucien Barnier, who had once been a central figure in youth programming.[93]

The Porché-Gayman-Gilson team did not work in a vacuum, then. Politics, anticommunist politics above all, impinged from above and commercial pressures from without. How then did the team perform under the circumstances?

Porché and Gilson, veterans that they were, understood the central dilemma of public programming: how to balance quality fare and solid news-reporting with lighter material that would appeal to a popular listenership. It was with this problem in mind that they set about a top-to-bottom reorganization of the RDF in October 1948 (it would become Radiotélévision française or RTF the following year). Three stations were developed. To the first, the Chaîne nationale, fell the task of maintaining standards, of airing programs, both musical and literary, that would illustrate the vigor and distinction of French culture. This was the high-status station, "destined," in the words of its director, "for the elite."[94] The Chaîne Parisienne, by contrast, was intended for a more modest public, to that end offering lighter, diverting fare, variety shows and the like. The third station, Paris-Inter, had a less well-defined profile. Its offerings were musical in the main, but the music in question was an eclectic mix, running the gamut from light classics to jazz. The division of labor, although never so neat in practice, was systematic enough to promise a way out of the old quality-versus-entertainment predicament.

On the quality front, postwar state radio had ample reason for self-congratulation. Music had always been the strong suit of the public airwaves, and it remained so now more than ever. In the classical domain, this meant, of course, airing prestige performances. It meant playing the standards of the classical repertoire: Bach, Mozart, Beethoven. But there was room for more adventuresome selections as well: for Stravinsky, for the compositions of Les Six (Auric, Durey, Honegger, Milhaud, Poulenc, Tailleferre), for the dissonances of the Viennese school, even for jazz.[95]

Schaeffer's Studio d'essai, after its moment of glory at the Liberation, was shut down in 1945... and then, the following year, it was reopened, though now under a new name, the Club d'essai. The Resistance poet Jean Tardieu was placed in charge, an artist of varied tastes who, like Gilson himself, had a liking for jazz. The Club d'essai was in part a gathering place for Saint-Germain-des-Prés hangers-on like the rising jazzman Boris Vian. But it was also a radio studio that introduced jazz to not always receptive French audiences, broadcasting programs like *Aimer le jazz* over the Paris-Inter airwaves. It brought live jazz too: André Francis, state radio's great jazz specialist, hosted a much-remembered concert at the Pigalle Music-Hall in 1950. Aired on Francis's program *Jeunnesse de jazz*, the event featured saxophonist Coleman Hawkins, a bridge figure between swing and bebop, and a rising nightclub chanteuse with a remarkable, sultry voice, Eartha Kitt. This was not the conventional "hot" big band sound, so popular during the war but something cooler, more avant-garde.[96]

Nor was jazz the sole avant-garde form the Club d'essai experimented with. Jean Tardieu's chance at the Club d'essai turned out to be Pierre Schaeffer's as well. Schaeffer had recorded Tardieu during the war, and Tardieu returned the favor, inviting the old radio hand back to the medium in 1949, this time to organize a sound research laboratory under the Club d'essai's aegis. Schaeffer worked with found sounds, recordings of door creaks and cats' meows, to assemble what he called a *musique concrète*. This was intended to be a human music, not machine generated but resonant of actual aural experience; yet at the same time it was supposed to be avant-garde, rejecting conventions that placed a premium on performance and, as Schaeffer put it, the canonical "DoReMi" of Western tonality. Schaeffer's lab matured into a Groupe de recherches de musique concrète, equipped with its own training studio, which welcomed eager-to-learn newcomers. Among the first was a Messiaen student, Pierre Boulez, at the beginning of a career that would establish him as France's most celebrated music personality in the postwar era.[97]

In the music department, the state airwaves broadcast first-rate material, quality sounds with appeal to discriminating listeners of all kinds, from longhairs to hipsters to avant-gardists. This represented an advance compared with the thirties, a step up from good to excellent.

In the literary department, the change was more dramatic still. The pretentious mediocrity of prewar days gave way to something far more remarkable: cultural programming that placed the best writers and poets center stage, that elevated the "author" to virtual icon status. For literary chatter, listeners could tune in to Barbier's book-review show, *Lu et approuvé*, or to *Belles lettres*, and it was not always radio intellectuals who did the chattering but oftentimes the genuine article. In 1947, Sartre's *Les Temps Modernes* got a show of its own, featuring the master philosopher himself. During the war, Schaeffer had begun experimenting with the literary interview format. Gilson set to work perfecting the genre, airing a series of in-depth conversations from 1949 with the literary luminaries of the day—Cocteau, Gide, Montherlant, and the like. In the 1930s, public radio had been the preserve of not so great talents; now, it was a venue that brought the cream of the French literary world to a truly national listenership.[98]

And it was not just the content of public radio's cultural programming that was first-rate but often the mode of presentation itself. The RTF set up a blind audition process to screen speakers, the better to ensure voice quality. The man placed in charge was Maurice Martenot, assisted by a jury that included yet a second Jeune France old-timer, André Clavé. Live broadcasting, however, auditioned or not, remained a risky enterprise, prone to false notes of all kinds. The Chaîne Parisienne, recognizing the difficulties, made the move over time to prerecordings, which by the 1950s accounted for a full 70 percent of its programming.[99]

It is possible, of course, to exaggerate the cultural achievement of postwar public radio. The presentation and intellectual pretense could still be heavy-handed. There were definite limits as well on how freewheeling the programming was allowed to be. Sartre's *Temps Modernes* show was canceled before 1947 was out, following a broadcast that proposed a comparison between de Gaulle and Adolph Hitler. A recording for radio was made of an Artaud play, *Pour en finir avec le jugement de Dieu*. The piece's militant atheism, advertised in its very title, caused such a stir that Porché yanked the show before it was broadcast. This was February 1948, and not long thereafter the director in charge of dramatic and literary programming, Fernand Pouey, himself stepped down. He did not specify the reason in his memoirs, but undoubtedly professional chagrin played a part.[100]

State radio then was under obligation to respect certain boundaries, which it did. Yet even so, it still came in for criticism: from listeners who grumbled about an excess of jazz, what one called "Tom-Tom nightclub music";[101] or from critics like Pierre Scize of the conservative *Le Figaro*, who found the programming altogether too elitist. Why, he wondered, should a "plow-pushing peasant from the Beauce" care in the least about the existentialist carryings-on at the Deux Magots?[102] That said, public radio's achievement remains impressive. When it came to disseminating high culture—and by this is meant the work not just of consecrated authors and composers but of experimentalists as well—state radio had no reason to be ashamed of itself. Little wonder that radio professionals, looking back on the postwar era, regarded it as a "golden age."[103]

When it came to handling more demotic forms, however, state radio ran into greater difficulties, which is not to say that no effort was made in this area. But postwar policy makers, within the radio world and without, harbored serious reservations about programming that smacked even a little of vulgarity and commercialism, and in this bias they were abetted by intellectual elites. The result was that state radio's entertainment programming lost energy over time, yielding ground to the more dynamic offerings of Radio Luxembourg.

State radio did make an effort, at least at first. Porché promised, as he took office, a radio that would "satisfy the greatest number." This meant embracing the variety-show format, and the RTF did not balk at the prospect. It aired shows from the Moulin de la Galette and Théâtre de l'Empire, music-hall spectaculars hosted by outsize radio personalities like the irrepressible Jean Nohain. Paris-Inter made a veritable cult of the accordion, the staple instrument of Parisian popular music. And it was not just a Parisian face that state radio showed to France.[104] *On chante dans mon quartier* got its start on the public airwaves. The show toured the nation, recording in front of live audiences. Local talent was invited onstage to perform familiar tunes, and the audience itself was invited to join in the chorus, a sing-along format that engendered a climate of convivial fellow feeling with deep appeal to a nation just emerging from war and occupation. The variety format was taken in a somewhat different direction by radio producer Jean-Jacques Vital. Vital concocted a double-barreled show, *Pêle-Mêle*, that opened with the usual variety fare hosted by comedian Bourvil (de Gaulle's favorite comic) but then topped off the proceedings with a quiz competition. Now, the quiz show in question, the *Coupe interscolaire*, was a high-minded affair, pitting teams of school students against one another, but it was a quiz show nonetheless, and as such a phenomenon all too rare on the public airwaves.[105]

Public radio's tentative embrace of demotic forms did not, however, dissipate deep-seated suspicions associating them with a degraded commercialism. State radio in 1944 created a public-relations service, hiring the young philosopher Roger Veillé to handle listener correspondence. Veillé execrated the variety format, the "June-moon-spoon" songs in particular, which exploited genuine human yearnings in the service of what he called a "bargain-basement aesthetic." He had no more liking for soap operas, a genre, he noted, that almost never represented the lives of real people—peasants and factory workers—but blathered on instead about the superficialities, romantic, psychological, or otherwise, of the bourgeoisie.[106] Jean Thévenot's criticisms were similar in tone. Thévenot was a regular on the public airwaves in the postwar era as critic, *animateur*, and journalist, and to him soaps were the very antithesis of what state radio ought to be all about. They bred a mediocrity of taste, appealing to a "certain public" whose capacity for discernment had been dulled by too many pasta and tea ads. Thévenot was a Communist at the time, and it is tempting to chalk up his anticommercial animus to his Marxist sympathies, which were real enough. It was, indeed, for political reasons that he was sacked from the RTF in 1953.[107] Yet it should also be remembered that Thévenot had a less than left-wing past. When Pierre Schaeffer left Vichy's Radio-Jeunesse to devote himself full-time to Jeune France, Thévenot—a graduate of Garric's Equipes sociales—was the man who took over the direction. Anticommercialism was the common coin of anticapitalist critics of all kinds, whether Marxist or Christian, as likely to crop up in the pages of *Esprit* as in those of *L'Humanité*.[108]

Radio historians concur that game shows, soap operas, and the like had a bad press among public authorities who cherished instead "a certain conception of quality," who understood the medium's principal task, not in terms of entertainment or diversion, but in terms of moral reconstruction and uplift.[109] Under the circumstances, state radio's opening to what were deemed commercial genres did not last long. The trouble began almost from the beginning. In 1946, the government banned from the airwaves a trio of popular songs, judged too risqué in content, and called on variety-show directors to clear all future program scripts with the appropriate state officials. Then in 1950 Teitgen, once more in charge of the Information portfolio, canceled four variety shows outright. A firm believer in quality standards, he found the programs just too vulgar. A state-sponsored competition was then organized to come up with variety-show ideas more wholesome in nature, but the results were disappointing.[110] The problem was clear enough: the variety format, as heir to the music hall, had a Rabelaisian aspect that troubled men of moral rigor, whatever their party of origin. The solution was clear enough too: develop a toned-down variety repertoire with the songs and sketches people wanted but absent the undesirable high jinks and double entendres.

The strategy might have worked well enough had public radio not faced such a formidable competitor in the shape of Radio Luxembourg. The peripheral station's management had the good sense in the immediate postwar era to appoint Louis Merlin its chief programmer, not an easy choice in certain respects: Merlin had served under Vichy as a member of the Comité d'organisation de la publicité. But Merlin was a brilliant choice just the same, for he was an adman who knew how to line up sponsors—L'Oréal's chief executive Eugène Schueller not least among them—and who knew even better how to sell, not just product lines, but program formats.[111] State radio treated the variety show as a poor relation, but Merlin felt otherwise, and he succeeded in luring both *On chante dans mon quartier* and *Pêle-Mêle* over from the RTF. He raided the old private stations as well, picking up the long-running soap *La Famille Duraton* and the amateur-hour hit *Le crochet radiophonique*, time-tested favorites that had done so much to make Radio-Cité's fortunes back in the 1930s. And for better or worse, Merlin made Radio Luxembourg home to the most listened-to game shows. He imported *Reine d'un jour* from the United States, a French version of *Queen for a Day* that made its Radio Luxembourg debut in 1952 with Jean Nohain hosting; and he introduced to the general public *Quitte ou double*, a quiz show on the *$64,000 Question* model presided over by a radio personality every bit as memorable as Nohain. He was Zappy Max, who delivered his emcee's patter in the slangy accents of the Paris faubourgs, a style many found lacking in distinction but whose natural verve, to Merlin's ear, rang a thousand times truer than "the accent of Marie-Chantal from the *Seizième.*"[112]

Such competition drained listenership from the public stations, and RTF management knew it. It solicited a series of polls—an IFOP poll in 1949, one by INSEE in 1952—and they all pointed to the same conclusion. Radio Luxembourg was the public's preferred station, its programs the most listened to.[113] Porché put pressure on Gilson to spice up RTF's programming. Some adjustments were made, but on the whole Gilson dragged his feet, devoted as he was (in his own words) to "the illustration of national quality." He would not, as a fellow radio professional later recalled, bow to "the Diktat of listeners or poll results."[114] Public radio's entertainment programming, off to such a promising start at the Liberation, foundered in the end on its own high-minded misgivings about lowbrow forms and commercial influence.

At RTF news, the problems were of a different order. Competition from the peripheral stations in this instance was a source of difficulty, but what most bedeviled the news services was the heavy-handed interference of politicians. Government ministers regarded radio news as a handmaiden of policy, an attitude that provoked a series of run-ins with radio journalists. It is not that the state got its way in every instance, but most of the time it did. The result was a domesticated news service, professional but lackluster in style, factual (on the whole) but prudent in content.

Right from the outset, the state kept a close watch on radio news. In September 1945, Jacques Soustelle, Teitgen's successor at the Ministry of Information, laid down the law to the radio news services: it answered straight to him and not to anyone else in between.[115] In the years that followed, it was not at all unusual for unhappy ministers to call Gayman on the phone with complaints about unwelcome reporting. Postwar ministers dreaded the "regrettable surprises" that too independent-minded radio reporters sometimes served up, enough so that in 1947 the Ramadier administration took action. On its instigation, Porché established a review procedure to screen news materials prior to broadcasting, a measure that applied not just to straight news but to features and commentary as well.[116] The government looked on radio news, not as an independent watchdog free to report stories as it saw them, but as the voice of the nation and, as such, censorable in the name of the national interest.[117]

Perhaps the picture is too dark. However canned the regular news, there were still news talk shows that generated unscripted moments when points of view not always approved by the state got articulated. The old Resistance radio program *Les Français parlent aux français* was repatriated at the Liberation, first under the title *Paris vous parle* and then from 1946 as *La Tribune de Paris*. It was a hosted event with multiple guests invited round to talk over the issues of the day. That same year, the RDF launched *La Tribune des journalistes parlementaires*, which brought together newsmen from across the political spectrum, Communists included, for open-ended discussion.[118] Radio news, though leashed, still had some life in it.

The margin for maneuver narrowed a good deal, however, with

the intensification of the Cold War. De Gaulle, disillusioned with the new Republic—its parliamentarism and all too leftist tilt (as he saw it)—founded the oppositional Rassemblement du peuple français in April 1947. That very same month, the Communists entered into opposition as well, ejected from the governing coalition by Prime Minister Ramadier. The general's voice and that of PCF chief Maurice Thorez were not to be heard on the public airwaves thereafter.[119] In November and December, the CGT conducted a series of strikes that led to confrontations, sometimes lethal, with the forces of order. Gayman warned his staff against words and phrases that might abet or encourage the strikers. Yet more formal prohibitions were handed down by the minister of information. A set-to in Valence between a strike cortege and the police had resulted in two deaths. The minister was explicit in his instructions to the RTF news bureau: be brief; describe the workers, not as strikers, but as "demonstrators"; mention the presence of Communist officials in their ranks; and make reference to fatalities if need be, but do not, under any circumstances, indicate how the fatalities came about.[120] A second strike wave in the fall of 1948 ratcheted up the censorship. The official in charge of Information, now François Mitterrand, was moved to step in again, prohibiting discussion of the strikes on the news talk shows. *La Tribune des journalistes parlementaires* was canceled in the wake of the order and would not start up again until late in 1949 (although now minus the participation of Communist journalists). It was in this context that Crémieux got into a public spat with Gayman that ended in Crémieux's firing. So it went, public radio over time casting aside its putative nonpartisanship to align itself with the anticommunist struggle.[121]

It would not be right to say that the radio news was muzzled, but it had to work in constrained circumstances, with the government at its very elbow in a near-literal sense. Old-timers, looking back on the fifties, remembered that a "black notebook" had been kept in the RTF newsroom, attached by cord to a desk. It listed off-limit subjects and spelled out appropriate language for the handling of topics, not out-of-bounds, but judged of a sensitive political nature. The book's contents were dictated by the responsible minister and kept up-to-date by regular communications from members of the minister's cabinet.[122]

State radio's balance sheet in the postwar era was a mixed one. It bequeathed a sparkling legacy of quality programming, but in the domains of entertainment and news its performance was not so stellar. The Cold War provides a partial explanation for this uneven outcome. Policy makers kept a tight rein on radio, the better to express the state's point of view, the better to keep disruptive elements out. The RTF might aspire to BBC status, but given the tense political conjuncture, such hopes were in vain. The explanation for the RTF's uneven showing on the cultural front, however, is a little more complex. Resistance officialdom, from the Communists to the christian democrats, wanted a high-minded radio that would edify and instruct. This was a noble ambition, and they found the man in Paul Gilson to make it happen. Gilson in turn recruited a host of talents to help out, many of them ex–Jeune France. It may seem an odd partnership, this alliance of résistants and former Vichy servants (most of them much chastened to be sure), but it is not odd in this sense: both parties to the deal shared an appetite for quality and a disdain for its antithesis, commercialism, which stood condemned on so many grounds—for hucksterism, for base vulgarity, for pandering to capital. The result was a programming bias that placed a premium on high culture, whether canonical or experimental, to the detriment of mass entertainment.

The radio story then is in its own way a story of continuity. The push for state control and quality programming did not originate at the Liberation but got its start earlier, beginning already under the Third Republic and gathering steam under Vichy. Statism, of course, did not mean the same thing from one regime to the next. Vichy's version—authoritarian and racist—was a far cry from the Fourth Republic's, however politicized radio may have become in Cold War days. The difference, however, was less dramatic when it came to non-news programming. It was a step from Schaeffer's Studio d'essai to Tardieu's, from Schaeffer's taped literary interviews for RN to Gilson's for the RTF, but the step was not a giant one. Here, as in cinema, a quality aesthetic embedded itself during the war that had a postwar life ahead of it. Here too, that aesthetic generated a reflex of resistance, which in cinema expressed itself in the New Wave and which in radio took initial form in Radio Luxembourg.

The culture state erected at the Liberation was a formidable enterprise that endowed French theater, cinema, and radio with a framework of institutions and policies that would remain in place for decades to come. The Popular Front's Kulturpolitik had been in the end more promise than delivery. Malraux's achievement, impressive as it was, was less of a breakthrough than Malraux, the relentless self-dramatizer, pretended. The groundwork had been laid for him in the immediate postwar years by men and women who, however accomplished in their particular domains, could not pretend to Malraux's notoriety as an impresario of national culture, and yet what they accomplished, if less publicized, was not the less remarkable: a cultural "golden age" that left an enduring mark on generations who thrilled to TNP productions or the quality cinema. Today still, that mark is visible. Tune in to France-Culture and listen for the echoes of Gilson's belle-lettristic programming; watch a Bertrand Tavernier film and note the homages, explicit in *Laissez-passer* (2002), to Aurenche and Bost, even to Clouzot.

It is tempting to chalk up this achievement to the Resistance, to an idealist Left committed to a public-service ethic and the moral reconstruction of the nation. This line of interpretation is not wrong. Jeanne Laurent, TEC, and PEC were all, at war's end, on the Resistance side, and they were the principals in the remaking of the theater world. The CFLC was a Resistance organ, and its agitations ensured that there would be trade-union representation in a reconfigured film industry. As for radio, the Resistance targeted it early on for nationalization, which was in fact the medium's ultimate fate.

But the story is a good deal more complicated than this. First of all, a number of the résistants, so central to the culture reform projects of the postwar era, had not always been so. Laurent, Schaeffer, and Buron for a time had been sincere Pétainists. And it was not just ex-résistants who were active in the postwar reconstruction but various

Vichy fellow travelers as well, graduates of Jeune France, men like L'Herbier and Gilson, who had served the maréchal's regime, not always with enthusiasm, but without ever sliding into demonstrative opposition either. They had occupied positions of a low-level or "non-partisan" character, enough so at least to escape the full rigors of a formal purge.

It is curious how many such survivors came out of a Catholic, often Catholic Action background. But perhaps this should be less of a surprise than appears at first glance. Catholic France was stirred by powerful renovative currents in the interwar decades that aspired to a spiritual reawakening, to the reconquest and purification of a national culture that many felt under mortal threat from an unchecked materialism.[123] It was hard for such militants of the spirit—JECistes, JOCistes, editorialists at *Esprit* or at one of its nonconformist confreres—to feel at home in the Third Republic. The Resistance, however, was another matter, and a handful, Teitgen for example, joined its ranks right from the start. More were drawn, however, to the Catholic wing at Vichy, gravitating to institutions like Uriage and Jeune France, which promised them room to act without, it was hoped, excessive supervision from above. But Vichy proved too authoritarian, too subservient to the Nazis, and such would-be redeemers settled into *attentisme* or, in a number of cases, made the break into outright Resistance. But whatever the path, they were there at the Liberation, poised to take part in a cultural reconstruction that they did as much as anyone to shape.

Their participation in the reconstruction enterprise, moreover, stands as a reminder that the postwar moment did not in all respects represent a break with the past. Personnel were held over at the Liberation. So too were institutions and policies. IDHEC, a Vichy creation, went on as before. SOFIRA became SOFIRAD, the Studio d'essai the Club d'essai. Numbered movie tickets, *cartes professionnelles* in the film industry, state-issued licenses for theater directors: all such practices, every one a Vichy innovation, were kept on after Vichy's demise.

Why this should be so admits of a simple enough explanation. The cultural administrators of the postwar era, like their Vichy predecessors, shared a common commitment to quality, French quality. The term, of course, is a diffuse one, multiple in its meanings. It encompassed phenomena as varied as a Corneille drama, an Autant-Lara film, a radio interview with Cocteau, all very different from each other in form and content. Corneille was a classic, Autant-Lara a nonconformist, Cocteau a self-styled avant-gardist. What sense can it make to lump them together? And yet it does make a certain sense. *Le Cid* was not boulevard; *Le Diable au corps* was not Hollywood; Gilson's Chaîne Nationale was not Radio Luxembourg. Quality did not denote a specific set of characteristics but a particular location in a field of possibilities whose twin poles were quality and its opposite, commerce.

This way of looking at the matter helps to bring out of the shadows the sometimes unappealing underside of the discourse on quality. For what or who embodies the monied interest? It may be the Republic, all too susceptible to the occult manipulations of the self-serving and greedy. It may be America, a nation unsurpassed in its worship of lucre and subservience to capital. And, of course, it may be the Jews—the Bernsteins, Bleustein-Blanchets, and Dalios, who deal wholesale in junk culture, squeezing out profit from degradation and vulgarity.

In the story told here, such biases were in the main a property of the Right, their articulation gaining in volume as the Right itself advanced, reaching a crescendo under Vichy. The Right's eclipse at the Liberation did not put paid to the discourse on quality, however. Quite the contrary, it was made into the stuff of state policy, enshrined even as the legitimating principle of a new *état culturel.* But quality in the postwar era had been cleaned up, its inner demons laid to rest by a public-spirited Resistance elite that reconceived the good, the true, and the beautiful in democratic terms as the cultural birthright of all.

This happy ending is correct in its broad outlines, but two caveats bear keeping in mind. The form taken by the new cultural state was inflected by politics at every turn. Gaullists, christian democrats, Socialists all, to varying degrees, were alarmed about the Communist presence in the media. This is why they opposed or hemmed in the corporate organization of film and radio in favor of more statist solutions. This too is why they were willing to hold over or recycle so many former Vichy administrators—nonconformists and Catholics in the main—who might be counted on to keep the Communists at arm's length. The cultural state showed a neutral public-service face to the nation, but such neutrality was in part a mask, concealing (and not always well) intense and at times violent political battles.

The second caveat touches on the exclusionary character of the quality aesthetic, even in its more open-ended postwar incarnation. For there still were exclusions: Radio Luxembourg operated from the periphery; Hollywood remained as ever a symbol, at once alluring and repellent, of all that was not French. Nor, it may be ventured, did the quality aesthetic do full justice to French culture itself, conferring second-class status on forms and faces, whether popular song or the high-decibel radio emcee, that to the unsuspecting foreigner seem plenty French enough.

And one last point: it is easy to understand why Liberation France might have anguished over the steamroller impact of the American cultural juggernaut, but that is not the whole story. Henry Bernstein never made a comeback in the postwar era; Dalio felt cold-shouldered; Bleustein-Blanchet got involved again in radio, but it took time, and he managed it as a publicity man through deal making with the peripheral stations, not the RTF. The Liberation quieted the inner demons of the quality aesthetic, but perhaps it did not silence them altogether.[124]

Conclusion

In April 1955, *L'Express* published a list of best-selling books, not the first of its kind in France, but the first compiled since the decade of the fifties had begun.[1] In order of popularity, the top eight titles ran as follows: Giovanni Guareschi, *Le Petit Monde de don Camillo* (Italian, 1948; French, 1952); Pierre Clostermann, *Le Grand Cirque* (1948); Victor Kravchenko, *J'ai choisi la liberté* (English, 1946; French, 1947); Arthur Koestler, *Le Zéro et l'infini* (1947); Vercors, *Le Silence de la mer* (1942); Antoine de Saint-Exupéry, *Le Petit Prince* (1943); Albert Camus, *La Peste* (1947); Roger Frison-Roche, *La Grande Crevasse* (1948).

The Anglo-American reader will pick out two thematic clusters right away: anticommunism and the Resistance. Kravchenko's volume is known in English under the title *I Chose Freedom*, Koestler's as *Darkness at Noon*. The former is an exposé, penned by a Soviet defector, of communist doublethink and brutality. It is cast in the autobiographical mode, recounting the author's political odyssey from communist true believer to disillusioned apparatchik. Koestler's work, on the other hand, is a fiction, more philosophic parable than narrative, that tells of an interrogation conducted by a communist commissar, the time and place unspecified. The prisoner is an innocent man but also a fervent Marxist, caught up in an ideological labyrinth that leads him to deny truth and to condemn himself (the commissar abetting) in the name of History and the Party. Guareschi's work, though now less well remembered, was celebrated in its time, and it too has an anticommunist leitmotif. Don Camillo is a priest in a northern Italian town, and his archnemesis is the local Communist mayor, Peppone. The temporal setting is immediately postwar, a moment of high political tension, but the tone of the novel is humane and good-humored. Don Camillo and Peppone are both creatures of the fallen world with all the attendant foibles, and despite obvious differences they have a grudging respect for one another (it helps that they were both in the Italian Resistance). Yet the novel's moral anchor is the curate, who, though sometimes overhasty and ham-handed, is a man of conscience. Over the altar in Don Camillo's church hangs a crucifix, and the crucified Christ enters into regular conversation with the priest, admonishing him in firm but understanding tones to act, not out of temper, but in a spirit of Christian forgiveness.

In the Clostermann, Vercors, and Camus books, the Resistance theme is not just leitmotif but the very heart of the matter. Clostermann's memoir is a harrowing account of his combat exploits as Free France's most-decorated air ace. It is the real-life story of a Resistance hero who, in the war's aftermath, would remain in the public eye both as a sportsman (he was a devoted fisherman) and as a Gaullist loyalist. Vercors's novella is set in occupied France; a German officer has been billeted in the country home of a carpenter and his niece; the officer is handsome, polite, the model of the "good German." How are the French to respond? With silence. The officer's charm attracts the niece, but it is made clear that however appealing a particular German might be, he is part of a larger project whose ultimate objective is the extinction of the French soul. *Le Silence de la mer* was written during the war. It appeared in 1942 in clandestine edition, the first major venture of the underground publishing house Editions de Minuit. The book then, not just in theme but in the very circumstances of its production, constituted an act of resistance. Camus's *La Peste* was not a Resistance novel in quite the same, self-evident way. It was published after the war in 1947, and the story it tells does not have an explicit political message. The mise en scène is the town of Oran in French Algeria sometime in the 1940s. Bubonic plague has crept into the city. It spreads with devastating effect and then fades away. The question, as in *Le Silence de la mer*, is how the residents of Oran are to react. The narrative center is Dr. Rieux, a world-weary medical man detained in Oran away from his family. In the event, Rieux's individual concerns do not deter him from connecting to others and working to mobilize a collective response to the misfortune visited upon the city. The moral then is a straightforward one: the answer to catastrophe lies not in withdrawal or self-seeking but in the practice of an ethic of social responsibility that tightens the bonds of human solidarity. Abstract as such a conclusion is, it is hard not to think of it as growing out of Camus's own particular wartime experience. In the face of the Nazi plague, he joined a Resistance movement, Combat, working with others to salvage what of honor and dignity could be salvaged out of the calamity of the Occupation.

What then of *La Grande Crevasse* and *Le Petit Prince*? What do they tell us about France in the aftermath of the war? Well, the Frison-Roche novel makes plain that effort and adventure still matter. The hero is an Alpine guide, Zian, the exemplar of an uncomplicated masculinity that thrives in the silence and pure air of the mountains. A girl "from below," worldly but not unsympathetic, takes an interest in Zian. She riffles through the scrapbook he keeps of his life and learns what makes him tick: "mountains, skiing: effort, always effort."[2] From this angle, the 1955 best-seller list takes on a different light. There is Clostermann the aviator and fisherman and Saint-Exupéry the "knight of the air" who made a literary reputation in the thirties fictionalizing his experiences as a mail-delivery pilot. Indeed, it was on a reconnaissance mission for Free France that Saint-Exupéry died in 1944. Indeed again, *Le Petit Prince* begins with a plane accident, a flyer crashing in the desert where he will meet an extraterrestrial visitor, the eponymous little prince. Even Guareschi's Don Camillo is a man's man, a heavy-fisted fighter who can trade punches with Peppone when called upon. There was talk in Hollywood of making an English-language version of Guareschi's novel, and Spencer Tracy was mentioned as a likely candidate for the title role, Tracy the former seminarian who in *Boy's Town* (1938) had played a tough but loving priest, inaugurating the role of the so-called superpadre, which would become such a stock figure in the Hollywood cinema of the postwar era.[3]

The man of effort appeared in many guises—pilot, priest, mountain climber. In political terms too, he was a multivalent figure. He might be a Gaullist like Clostermann or the head of the local section of Catholic Action as was Don Camillo. And Zian? The guide and his girlfriend find refuge in a hut during a mountain storm; the moment to express what they feel for each other has come. Zian opens with an avowal: "one never lies in the high mountains [on ne ment jamais en haute montagne]."[4] The reader is pulled up short, having heard a variation on these words before from the mouth of Maréchal Pétain: "the earth, it does not lie [la terre, elle, ne ment pas]." As it happens, Frison-Roche had had a Pétainist period. He was a skier and journalist first and foremost, of course, but also by his own description a "flag-waving patriot" who in the thirties had joined the Volontaires nationaux, a branch of de La Rocque's Croix de feu. The defeat of 1940 found him employed as a newspaperman in Algiers, working for *La Dépêche algérienne*, once a Croix de feu organ and now pro-Vichy in its editorial line. It was in the pages of the paper's evening edition that Frison-Roche first published in serial form *Le Premier de cordée*, which in its later movie version, as we have seen, was not without its ambiguities. But Pétainism does not tell the whole story of Frison-Roche's political commitments. A visit to Paris in the spring of 1942 and the Allied invasion of North Africa later in the year reoriented his loyalties, turning him into a war correspondent and, before the Occupation was over, into a soldier himself, fighting for Free France.[5] The gospel of effort then led in more than one direction, and in Frison-Roche's case the itinerary was a complicated one. It took him first into Vichy and then into the Resistance, a change of destinations, however, that did not erase all traces of a former Pétainism.

That leaves for last *Le Petit Prince*. It is, like a number of the others, a wartime story written by a résistant. Saint-Exupéry drafted the text and drew the accompanying pictures while in New York exile, trying to sort out how he might contribute to the cause of Free France. It was not such an easy deliberation, as Saint-Exupéry had little liking for the Gaullists, nor did they much care for him and, from the Gaullist point of view, for good reason. Saint-Exupéry had endorsed Pétain's decision in the summer of 1940 to sign an armistice with the Germans. The aviator viewed the maréchal as the least of three evils, not a welcome choice to govern an occupied France but better than a quisling, let alone the Nazis themselves. Then, in January 1941, a grateful Pétainist regime had extended Saint-Exupéry a measure of recognition, appointing him in absentia to Vichy's Conseil national, a position the writer had neither solicited nor desired.[6] Yet it was all enough to make Saint-Exupéry a suspect figure in New York's Gaullist enclave. None of this, however, finds its way into the pages of *Le Petit Prince*. True, the book is dedicated to the author's friend Léon Werth, "a grown-up," who is stuck in France where he "is hungry and cold," but that is the sole topical referent.

This is after all a children's tale, as poetic and melancholy in tone as the little prince himself, who has fallen to earth from a star, landing in the Sahara where he meets the narrator, himself a crash-landed pilot. The pilot is charmed by the prince, who recounts stories of his interplanetary travels and run-ins along the way with various "grown-ups," each one more vain and foolish than the last. But there is more at stake here than a gentle send-up of adult ways. The prince is sad, pining for a self-centered flower back home with whom he is in love; and he is wise in a way only the pure of heart can be, understanding that what matters most in the world is not the surface of things, the shell of life, but the life within. The narrator begins to comprehend the full gravity of the little prince's message toward the story's end. The prince has discovered a well in the desert, complete with pulley and bucket, such as might be found in a French country village. The water, once tasted, is refreshing, good not just for the body but for the soul or, as the narrator puts it, "good for the heart, like a gift." And the little prince's gift of life-giving water summons up in the narrator a memory from childhood: "When I was a little boy, the light of the Christmas tree, the music of the midnight mass, the sweetness of the smiles made up, just so, the radiance of the Christmas gift I received."[7] The Christian imagery in the passage is overpowering. It is not just that the little prince performs a miracle, finding water in the desert; it is the quality of the water he finds, which, like a Christmas gift, like the infant Jesus himself, brings light, music, sweetness, radiance. At the story's conclusion, moreover, the little prince's fate turns out to be much like Christ's own. The boy wants to return home to

the flower he loves, and the way back lies through death and resur-
rection. He encounters a poisonous serpent and allows the snake to
bite him. The little prince reassures the narrator that he, the prince,
will appear to be dead but in fact will not be. He will rather have rejoined his flower, his own loving sacrifice having made possible new
life in the stars above.

Guareschi's tale also ends on a redemptive note. The text unfolds
in a series of almost forty vignettes. Most are lighthearted. A French-
language movie of *Le Petit Monde* was in fact made in 1951, starring
the inevitable Fernandel in the title role. Guareschi did not much
like it. The film was lighthearted all right, but its ending struck a false
note. Fernandel's Don Camillo has gotten into a fight at a fair, and
his bishop sends him on a restorative mountain retreat. As the priest
boards his train to leave, his parishioners come to wish him farewell,
and then, a little farther down the track, Peppone and his Communist comrades also turn out for a last good-bye. The town's hostilities,
it seems, do not run very deep after all. The two sides, a voice-over
narrator concludes, seek a better world, each in its own way. But for
Guareschi the path to a better world was not so ecumenical; he had a
serious message to convey, however wrapped up in good humor, and
that message was religious.[8] *Le Petit Monde*, upbeat in tone on the
whole, takes a darker turn in the final suite of stories. A political murder is committed. One of Peppone's band—it is not known who—
guns down an innocent man, and a climate of fear seizes the village.
The victim's little son knows the identity of the culprit, and it is assumed that Don Camillo does too, placing the lives of the two in
jeopardy. An evening not long thereafter, Don Camillo is repairing
the crucifix above the altar of his church when the killer takes a shot
at him. The killer's aim is on target, but don Camillo's head snaps
back and out of the bullet's path at the last moment; the hand of the
crucified Christ, however, is pierced. Did Jesus reach out, push Don
Camillo out of harm's way, and take the bullet instead? Then there is
the final tale: Peppone has been watching over Don Camillo, trying
to protect him from the unknown assassin; the Communist mayor, a
normally fearless man, comes to don Camillo and confesses that he

feels the weight of fear, an oppression as though he were in prison; it is Christmas season and Don Camillo is arranging a manger scene before the altar, touching up the figures with a paintbrush; Peppone joins in the work, and—"no one knows how"—the figure of the infant Jesus finds its way into the Communist's hands. The weight of fear is lifted from his soul as he paints, and he then announces with pride to Don Camillo that his son has been memorizing a Christmas poem. Guareschi finishes the story and the book with these lines:

> On leaving [the church], Peppone found himself once more in the dark Paduan night. But now he was at peace because he had held in his hand the warmth of the rose-colored Child and because the poetry of Christmas still resonated in his heart.
> —It will be essential, he mused, for proletarian democracy to make poetry obligatory![9]

The humor cuts through the sentimentalism of the scene; the battle between priest and Communist will go on. Guareschi has nonetheless made his point. The material world is a world of partisanship, murder, and fear, but there is a higher order of being, ruled over by a loving God whose sacrifice and warmth bring peace to all men of goodwill, whether priest or Communist.

A best-seller list offers at best a rough approximation of what is on the reading public's mind. What then, more or less, were French readers thinking about in the midfifties? They were still moved by stories of the Resistance. They worried about communist intentions. They thrilled to the heroics of masculine adventure. They were touched by expressions of an abiding Catholic faith. As for the politics of the best-seller list, the authors covered a wide but not unbounded terrain. Camus and Koestler came out of the non- and soon to be anticommunist Left. Clostermann, on the other hand, was a Gaullist, Guareschi a christian democrat (of a maverick sort to be sure), and Saint-Exupéry neither Right nor Left. It is possible even to pick up the occasional Pétainist echo, as in Frison-Roche's *La Grande Crevasse*. None of this, it is hoped, will come as a revelation to readers of the present volume. Such is the portrait of France sketched in the preceding chapters, which brings us back to the questions posed in the introduction: where did this France come from, and how is it to be characterized?

There was once a simple answer to the first question. Postwar France was, of course, born in the postwar era. The Resistance coalition that acceded to office in 1944 empowered a cadre of institution builders who redesigned France's state apparatus top to bottom. The Fourth Republic was still a parliamentary regime, and in this respect it resembled its much-despised predecessor, the Third Republic, but it was equipped with something its predecessor never had, a leadership cadre who understood what industrial civilization was all about and how state power might be applied to enable a too-backward France to meet the challenges of modernity. The institution builders themselves—from Monnet on down—were quite partial to this modernization story. A number of them, Sauvy for example, taught at Sciences Po, and so it is not surprising that Sciences Po too attached itself with such élan to the modernization thesis, recasting it to be sure in a social-science idiom that emphasized less individual heroics than the concerted action of a new policy elite.

There is an edited essay collection, now almost fifty years old, that gives classic expression to this point of view: *In Search of France* (1963). It is the fruit of a transatlantic collaboration that brought together Harvard and Sciences Po faculty: first at a Harvard-based seminar that met over the course of the 1959/1960 academic year, then in a follow-up colloquium that gathered in Paris in July 1961 under the auspices of the FNSP. In a series of papers and essays, the participants elaborated what was to become the dominant interpretive paradigm in modern French history for many decades to come. Prewar France was individualist, stalemated, backward. The Third Republic itself, "plenty of brakes and not much of a motor" in the still-famous phrase, was in large measure responsible for this state of affairs, for France's descent into decadence.[10] But the shocks of defeat and occupation had generated a "new state of mind"[11] that made it possible for a postwar order, better adapted to the exigencies of modern life, to take shape under the auspices of an enlightened, interventionist state. To be sure, the French remained attached to old habits in many, many ways, and as for de Gaulle's Fifth Republic, it was still an unknown quantity. No one lamented the passing of the party-ridden, factionalized Fourth Republic, but was the Fifth the efficient, yet still democratic alternative so much hoped for? De Gaulle's all too patent authoritarian tendencies gave good reason to harbor second thoughts. The modernization story, which was the implicit plotline of *In Search of France*, raised the possibility of a happy ending to France's contemporary history, but in the final analysis the volume was too critical-minded to make any promises.

It was critical-minded in a second major respect as well. Stanley Hoffmann's contribution takes a moment to talk about the role of politics in the modernizing process. The Third Republic had enemies in the thirties, and Hoffmann details who they were, a list that includes not just the usual suspects like de La Rocque but "former *planistes*" and Christian personalists, the editorial boards of *L'Ordre nouveau* and *Esprit*. Such dissenters found their way into the Resistance, commingling there with representatives of the classic Left, the amalgam constituting an updated reworking of the old Popular Front. Yet, Hoffmann notes, a number of the 1930s nonconformists also gave Vichy a try. There were nonconformists then on both sides, and so it is not surprising that Vichy and the Resistance, however antipathetic in most respects, wound up sharing certain character traits in common: a revulsion against the moral decay of French public life, a deep-seated anti-individualism, and a ferocious rejection of parliamentary forms. On the Vichy end, such commitments fueled a corporatist revolution that, reactionary though it was in intent, had its creative dimensions. Vichy set up a peasant corporation; it organized doctors and architects into professional orders. These proved to be useful institutions, and they were kept on at the Liberation, the latter more or less intact, the former metamorphosing first into the CGA and then into the Fédération nationale des syndicats d'exploitants agricoles. Hoffmann's reflections here are startling on more than one count: for their novel insistence on the dissident minorities of the thirties as the source of so much history to come, for their illumination of the hidden commonalities between the Resistance and elements at Vichy, for their evocation of continuities between Vichy and the postwar era.

What is important to note in the present context is how much this line of analysis undercuts the understanding of the postwar era as a moment of modernizing rupture. *In Search of France* instantiates the modernizing paradigm, but it at the same time points the way past it. That way past was first explored in depth by one of Hoffmann's own students, Robert Paxton, who contextualized Vichy both front and back. At the front end, Paxton interpreted the regime as in part the creation of dissident minorities who had been frozen out in the 1930s and then got a chance with Vichy to make their mark. At the back end, he saw Vichy as a moment of opportunity for a technocratic managerialism that would get a second and more lasting opportunity after the war.[12] Paxton's principal concern, of course, was to work out Vichy's fit into the ongoing flow of French history. The regime was not a parenthetical aside but the expression of enduring currents in the nation's public life.

The principal concern in the present volume, however, has been the Liberation moment, not Vichy, but in many respects the conclusions are the same. The dissidents of the 1930s—technocrats and nonconformists—occupy a central place in the story, with an addition, however, that is often overlooked in the existing literature: Catholic Action and related confessional movements. It has further been argued that the dissident agenda was more ambitious than sometimes supposed. Its determination to remake France's political and economic policy-making apparatus is well known, much less so its hopes for an overhaul of France's cultural institutions.

And here, as in the Paxton story, the dissidents meet with a measure of success. On the cultural front, success awaited the arrival of Vichy, which cleared space for arts organizations like Jeune France.[13] On the technocratic side, success came even sooner. It was the late Third Republic, the Daladier administration in particular, that created openings for the likes of a Debré or a Sauvy to begin reshaping policy.[14] They were, of course, just the vanguard of a technocratic army that would get yet wider deployment under the command of Maréchal Philippe Pétain.

The Resistance modernizers who came to power at the Liberation, then, did not find an empty playing field but a crowded institutional landscape with a built-in policy-making logic of its own. As we have seen, that landscape was pruned but not cleared. A portion of what Vichy planted was preserved. This might have been, of course, just a practical matter, Vichy having undertaken useful things that it would have been shortsighted to set aside. The line of argument pursued here, however, is somewhat different, and once again a longer-term perspective that scrolls back to the thirties and encompasses the war as well has proven useful.

Who after all were the Resistance modernizers? The Resistance did not arise out of nothing, nor, once born, did it remain unchanging. So how might the Resistance story read, on the understanding that it is a story in many chapters? It might begin with the Popular Front, jump to the CNR action program, and then wind up with the founding of the modern welfare state. This narrative has a lot to recommend it, but it leaves out important details. First, the Popular Front never had a major confessional component. Not so, of course, the Resistance, which was a critical seedbed for the maturation of postwar christian democracy. Whatever might be said of de Gaulle, moreover, he was no man of the Left. He had come of age in the climate of National Revival that crystallized on the eve of the Great War, and the Great War itself had sharpened his understanding of the kind of leadership needed in a modern army, indeed, in a modern nation. He distrusted political parties and did not care for parliaments much more, all of which drew him closer to interwar nonconformity than to any partisan formation. Last of all, there were the ex-Vichyites who rallied to Resistance ranks as the war wore on. This is not to say that such ci-devants were ever numerous, but they were more influential than their numbers might suggest, as the examples of Couve de Murville, Pierre Schaeffer, Robert Prigent, and Aimé Lepercq attest.

This is a long way to go to make a simple point: that the Resistance was a complex amalgam that generated more than one vision of what postwar France might become. There were many who wanted to raze what Vichy had erected, but there were others who looked for compromise solutions, wanting to build on what was already in place. The motives for such practicality were many: simple pragmatism, to be sure; an antipathy to radical solutions that might empower the Communists; but also in some cases sympathies, declared or not, for portions of what Vichy had achieved. And in the political battles that ensued at the Liberation, it was the compromisers most often who gained the advantage.

Of course, this is not how things looked on the surface. The CNR program did indeed speak in the accents of social democracy. It called for nationalizations and a comprehensive program of social security, and these reforms and much else besides were in due course enacted. Not only that: the rhetoric of the postwar era was all about public service and cultural democratization, about making the economy and the media work for one and all. This was a rhetoric with a left-wing buzz that in fact grew louder over time.

But on closer inspection, the Liberation was at best a partial victory for the social democratic Left. Mendès France and Philip got outmaneuvered by Monnet when it came to the organization of planning; the welfare system was cast in a corporatist, pronatalist mold; as for the new IEP/FNSP/ENA complex, it went on to do what it had been programmed to do, educating generations of progressive-minded public servants, but that elite was more technocratic in outlook than socialist. The Resistance Left might well have set the terms of the postwar debate, but it then went on to lose many of the institutional arguments that followed. Even on the rhetorical front, victory was less total than might at first appear. From the thirties on (if not before), the chorus of voices pleading for a new kind of elite had swelled. France's elites—its officers, engineers, business executives—needed to rethink what it meant to be leaders of men. Lyautey, de Gaulle, Lamirand, Schaeffer, Coutrot: all of them had joined in the argument, attempting to define a model of the selfless, above-party, public-service-minded *chef*. Soldiers, Catholic Action veterans, and technocrats were just as comfortable with the rhetoric of "public service" as social democrats.[15] The same may be said of the rhetoric of cultural democratization. The Popular Front had its "houses of culture," but so too did Jeune France. Schaeffer's band understood

themselves as the standard-bearers of French quality. They were determined to bring the best in the national patrimony to as wide a
public as possible, and they meant to do so with a hands-on animation and formal experimentalism that would make the classics live
again. Did the Liberation era proclaim culture a social good destined
not just for an elite but for the nation as a whole? It was not difficult
for Schaeffer's allies and associates to see themselves in such a project. Indeed, they positioned themselves in the postwar era to play a
key role not only in how that project was conceptualized but in how
it was turned into policy.

This way of looking at things reorients in critical ways how the Liberation moment is to be understood. It was first of all less a moment
of rupture than often portrayed. The postwar order had roots deep
in the 1930s—in the imaginings of nonconformist dissidents as in the
reformist practice of Daladier-era administrators. The Popular Front
plays a part in this drama, but it is assigned a smaller role than in
much of the current historiography. As for Vichy, it was not just a
detour en route to the new order but an important way station. It
would have been a provocation and a distortion to title the present
volume the Vichy origins of the modern French state, and yet Pétain's
regime did accelerate the process of state remaking, in so many areas
laying the foundations on which the institutional entrepreneurs of
the postwar era would later build.

Such a conclusion mutes the importance of debates among the
Free French abroad in configuring how the postwar order would
look. To be sure, the Great Exiles, none more than de Gaulle himself,
played a key part articulating principles that would guide state reconstruction. Grandeur mattered. More comprehensive social security
was promised. It was evident to all that laissez-faire economics had
had its day. But how were these principles to be translated into concrete institutional form? The answer to this question was not a simple
one. There were the on-the-ground legacies of the past to deal with—
initiatives undertaken by Daladier or by Vichy—and these were in
many instances retained, minus, it must be insisted, the racism and
authoritarianism of Vichy days. The Resistance itself, moreover, had
generated competing projects, the choice among them settled by a

series of intense postwar battles. Victory went to the best infighters, to institution builders like Monnet and Sauvy who in some cases had been exiles, in some cases not. But either way, it was in France, on French soil, that the nation's future was decided.[16]

As for the institutional entrepreneurs themselves, they were a hodgepodge. The emphasis has been less on the new elite's social democratic contingent than on the Gaullists, technocrats, and one-time nonconformists so numerous in their ranks. Not least of all, and the point bears repeating because it has not always gotten the attention it merits, Catholics—Catholic Action militants, christian democrats, Mounier acolytes—stood front and center in shaping the way the postwar story played out.

It is, of course, possible to imagine any number of counterarguments to this line of interpretation. Two will be addressed here. The first touches on the top-down character of the analysis, which, it may be objected, does not give sufficient weight to the contributions of ordinary French men and women.[17] It is true that the focus has been on institution builders, a perspective bound to emphasize the role of elites. It is hoped, though, that due attention has been paid to the constraints under which the institution builders labored. Some of these constraints—US arm-twisting to open up French markets— were external, but many more were domestic in origin, welling up from the French body politic. Unions were a force to contend with in multiple domains, and policy makers had to make room for them, whether in the management of social-insurance *caisses*, on modernization commissions, or in the running of the film industry. The pronatalist lobby left a deep imprint on the familist design of welfare institutions. And business interests contrived to insinuate themselves into every instance of the new machinery of economic administration. Nor was it just from interests that policy makers felt pressure. The Assemblée provisoire consultative, while not an elected body, still had a quasi-representative character, made up as it was of representatives from major Resistance movements and old-line political parties not too compromised by Vichyite associations. The postwar legislation that defined the profile of elite education would no doubt have taken a less interventionist form had policy makers like Debré not had to wrestle with critical voices coming from the legislature's Left. Then there were the massive electoral interventions of October 1945 and June 1946. On the former occasion, voters returned a Left majority to parliament, and on the latter they cast more ballots for the fledgling MRP than for either of its left-wing competitors. There is no doubt that these elections made a substantial difference in my story, ensuring Socialists a determinative role in shaping the new order in radio, reinforcing christian-democratic leverage on the construction of the welfare state. Then, of course, there was the onset of the Cold War, an international phenomenon that found potent domestic expression in increased PCF militancy. This particular manifestation of opinion, however, proved less an obstacle to the institution builders' designs than a boon. The near-insurrectionary climate of 1947–1948 opened the door to a repressive backlash that drove the Communists out and circumscribed trade-union power, whether communist or not, into the bargain.

So, yes, interests and parties made a difference in how the postwar order came to be defined. The French public wanted change, and change it got, but it mattered just as much that the state's executive apparatus was in the hands of men and women who had plans of their own. In pursuit of them, the institution builders came to terms with public opinion when they felt they had to or deflected it to advantage when they saw the opportunity. They were not puppet masters but self-styled "leaders" skilled at operating in close quarters, and they used their exceptional skills to fashion an elite-managed public order of the sort many of them had been advocating since the thirties.

It might be countered yet again, though, that such a conclusion has at best a limited validity. It might well make sense where the origins of INED or INSEE are concerned but has much less purchase in other areas of public life. This book has covered a wide stretch of institutional territory, but lots has been left out, and it is possible such selectivity has led to distortions.

This second line of counterargument has its merits. Organized labor has figured in the narrative in a variety of capacities, and it might have played a yet weightier role had more attention been paid to the nationalized sector, where the trade unions were such important players. The story would also have been different, though not for the same reasons, if the military had been added into the equation. This book has made the case for a revolution in statecraft at the Liberation, but no such revolution occurred in France's armed forces. There was a purge to be sure, but Cold War in Europe and hot war in Indochina generated a heightened demand for experienced officers, and to meet it, much of what the purge accomplished was later undone. Throughout, moreover, the army brass remained wedded to the colonial adventure. Indeed, now that so much else had been lost, the empire may have loomed larger in the military imagination than ever before as a necessary buttress to French greatness.[18] These are important correctives. The first helps to explain why labor in the long run came to embrace the postwar settlement, the second why decolonization turned out to be such a painful, indeed, fatal process to the Fourth Republic.

On the other hand, it is possible to come up with institutional examples that confirm, rather than complicate, the general interpretive line laid out here. Take housing and reconstruction as a case in point. De Gaulle's Provisional Government created the Ministère de la Reconstruction et de l'Urbanisme in November 1944, placing a familiar figure in charge, Raoul Dautry. Dautry, though no Pétainist himself, turned in part to Vichy institutions to staff his new ministry. He recruited personnel from Vichy's Commissariat technique à la Reconstruction immobilière and hired the urbanism team that had worked at Frédéric Surleau's DGEN (remember that Surleau was himself a onetime Dautry disciple). In the policy domain too, Dautry built on past initiatives. Vichy enacted a Code de l'urbanisme in June 1943; the code was not repealed at the Liberation but, with minor adjustments, held over. Postwar urbanists, taking to heart the often-repeated criticism that France was overcentralized, committed themselves to the material and cultural development of the provinces, *l'aménagement du territoire* in the French phrase. No text was more influential in shaping the new mind-set than Jean-François Gravier's *Paris et le désert français*, first published in 1947 with a preface by Dautry. Gravier had signed on to Monnet's planning team after the war, but in the Vichy years, it will be recalled, he had been a research

associate at the Fondation Carrel and a fervent supporter of Maréchal
Pétain's regime.[19] Vichy, in the domain of regional planning as in so
many others, served as a bridge moment that enabled men of the
Right like Gravier to cross over from an antiparliamentary past into a
modernizing, developmental future.

There is much indeed that the pages above do not include. Filling
in the lacunae would no doubt nuance the analysis in useful ways, but
I am not convinced that it would require a full-scale recalibration of
the book's center of gravity. The French state got an overhaul at the
Liberation. The Resistance Left had a hand in the undertaking, but
the story was good deal more complex than that. Gaullists, technocrats, christian democrats, ex-Vichyites (repentant or otherwise),
even revenants from the Daladier years all joined in the enterprise.
The new state apparatus that was born of such combined and con-
flicting efforts was not so new as it appeared, built as it was on dreams
and experiments that harked back to the more troubled years of the
depression and Occupation.

Such a conclusion is not meant to belittle what was accomplished
at the Liberation. That achievement was spectacular and enduring. I
do want to suggest, though, that it was harder than sometimes thought
for the institution builders who did so much to shape the postwar
order to shake free of the past that had formed them. There is, of
course, no reason to think that France was in any way exceptional in
this regard. A look at state elites in postwar Germany and Italy might
well reveal stories far more unsettling than those recounted here, but
in the current state of research this must remain more a hypothesis
than a conclusive judgment.[20]

Let us now revisit the postwar stories sketched out in the introduction
and reflect on how well they stand up. The restorationist thesis is the
weakest of the lot, but it must be given its due. Capitalism made a
comeback and then some after the war. The constitutional structures
of the Fourth Republic looked a lot like those of the Third. And the
austere and purifying Resistance mystique, which meant so much to
battle-hardened veterans like Bourdet, dissipated as petty partisanship and the jockeying for power became once again the common

practice of public life. Still, capitalism in the postwar era was not what it had been in prewar days. France now had a Plan, a vast public sector, a national statistical service, a Social Security apparatus, none of which it had had before. Deputies and senators might still strut the parliamentary boards, but more and more it was behind the scenes—in the offices of bureaucrats and in ministerial boardrooms—that the real drama of public life was played out. Here, the nation's stage managers had erected the scaffolding of an administrative and cultural state whose operations were less noisy than those of parliament but not less consequential. As for the stage managers themselves, the institutional entrepreneurs of the postwar era, they were a new breed. They appear in photos from the era as serious-minded men—lean, often athletic, with close-cropped hair and dressed in sober-toned suits that bespeak a deliberate unpretentiousness. They may not have been the *maquisard* elite dreamed of by Bourdet (although many of them were Resistance veterans), but they were something different from the aperitif-sipping, potbellied politicos of Third Republic caricature.

So, Third Republic old hands they were not, but does that mean they were Americans or, at least, Frenchmen of Americanized tastes and habits? There is something to this, but not much. Monnet, it is true, had spent a portion of the war in Washington. The practice of the working lunch, a Yankee practice indeed, enjoyed a certain vogue among France's postwar decision-making elite. Then, there were the Blum-Byrnes accord and the Marshall Plan. The former opened the cultural floodgates to American film; the latter locked France into an Atlantic economy that came mantled in the rhetoric of open markets and productivity. US hegemony in the postwar era was constraining and weighed in favor of French interests who were willing to find a place for France in what was now an Atlantic world. But two additional points need to be made. These interests were French first, and it was French experience that had turned them to lines of thinking congenial or, in any case, congenial enough to American schemes. The can-do decision maker of France's postwar era was not an American clone but a graduate of the Resistance, of a Vichy youth camp, or in some cases of both. The French had been meditating on leadership and what it entailed for decades and did not need American encouragement to do so. It was, moreover, the depression and defeat of 1940, more than any American example, that had prompted a serious rethinking of France's economic destiny. And what were the critical lessons that the nation's own recent past had to teach? A Malthusian France, all too set in its relaxed but backward ways, had sleepwalked through the thirties and, as such, had proven itself an easy mark for Germany's industrial war machine. On this understanding, the way forward was clear enough: a France reborn needed a new economy—organized, industrial, modernized. If the United States stepped forward to help, so much the better. Second, within the parameters set by American hegemony, the French proceeded to build a world that was very much their own. The postwar state made sure that French culture enjoyed institutional protections. The Hollywood invasion ran up against a state-supported cinema of quality, not to mention that bulwark of gallicism Fernandel. As for economic management, France opened itself to US investment, but the biggest investor in the postwar years was the French state itself, and it worked according to plan, pushing a statist model of growth that Americans to this day have a hard time even imagining. The United States set ground rules after the war, but within that framework France built a model tailored to its needs and values, one that in critical ways was in fact defined against America's own.

Was that model social democratic? Once more, it is hard to render an unmixed verdict. The CNR program *was* cast in the language of social democracy, and it set the pattern for much of what was accomplished after the war. And it is worth mentioning once again in the present context the groundswell of Left opinion at the Liberation. Resistance committees and commandos, often left-wing in composition, inaugurated the process of change from the ground up, seizing local businesses and municipalities as Vichy authority collapsed. The first nationalizations were not the work of policy makers but of the workers themselves. Not least of all, Communists and Socialists triumphed at the polls.

Nonetheless, such schemes of transformation, whether sponsored from above or below, ran into opposition as soon as they had gotten started. De Gaulle wanted the armed Resistance disbanded and its remnants integrated into the regular army, and he was successful in getting his way on both points. The Provisional Government put a stop to the "savage purge," imposing a discipline on the purging process that in due course wound down. There was a national housecleaning, but it was in the end a state-managed one. As for nationalizations, they began at the grass roots, but then the legislators took over. It is true that in practice nationalized industries did not operate like profit-minded private enterprises. On the other hand, management did come to insist on its prerogatives over time, and it bears recalling at this juncture the discussion of Electricité de France in the introduction. Executives there, Pierre Massé in the lead, made clear their determination to run the company according to principles of efficiency and productivity, working out a "technocorporatist" approach that was on the whole top-down in its management style. As for Communists, they ran into nonstop efforts to rein them in, to make certain that they were never in a position to take over entire sectors, the movie industry for example. The heating up of the Cold War, of course, pushed them out altogether, but the process of marginalization had begun earlier over the course of a series of tough institutional battles that the Communists lost more often than they won. France's Socialists also experienced defeats, though not so many. Postwar radio was nationalized; its new managers made sure that listeners were entertained with quality programming; and the broadcast news kept Communists and Gaullists alike at arm's length. What more could a social democrat hope for? On the other hand, christian democrats also had an impact on the radio scene, adding in a moralizing note that was not altogether helpful when it came to attracting mass audiences. Indeed, in almost every area, there is an "on the other hand." France got a Plan, but it was Monnet's indicative plan that won out, not Mendès France's more dirigiste variant. It got its ENA, but Sciences Po lived on, reinventing itself as ENA's principal feeder school.

In time, as the new state apparatus settled into place, as the constituencies it served bought in, it began to look more workerist in design. In no domain was this more true than in that of Social Security, where trade-union representatives came to play such a major role in managing the system's actual machinery. Then add in the experiences of the 1980s and 1990s, when France's center-Right parties began to think about scaling back benefits, and now the welfare state did indeed begin to look like a Left conquest under siege from Reaganite liberalizers. But this retrospective vision obscures the complexities of the system's actual origins. Of course there was a social democratic component, but the system's father, Pierre Laroque, was more technocrat than socialist, a problem solver who in the thirties had thought hard about the fascist model of labor relations and then in 1940 signed on, if just for a few months, to work for a self-styled corporatist regime. In the course of negotiating Social Security into existence, moreover, Laroque had had to make sometimes major concessions, watching a system he had wanted to be unitary fragment along corporatist and familist lines. Social democracy was a major force at the Liberation, but it was not the sole or in the end even the dominant force.

Who then was? Was it the technocrats like Laroque who got the upper hand after all? There is no minimizing what the postwar institution builders achieved, constructing a dense network of agencies, foundations, and institutes, most of them still around today. But three additional points need to be kept in mind. The institution builders were not mere rational calculators. They had childhoods and pasts that oriented them in the world. Marjolin, the postwar planner, was a lifelong believer in Enlightenment principles, a belief that had led him back in Popular Front days to join the Blum government. It would be a mistake, however, to imagine that every technocrat, once scratched, turned out to be a closet social democrat. There are the counterexamples of Bloch-Lainé, the ex–Catholic scout, of Delouvrier and Gaillard, both graduates of Vichy's youth movement, or of the Protestant Claude Gruson, who understood the planning process not just in technical terms but in spiritual ones, as a device to program France for a better, more hope-filled future. It is perhaps worth recollecting in this connection the reading habits of the ENA student body. In spare moments, the nation's future technocrats picked up *Le Monde*, edited by a Mounier acolyte, Hubert Beuve-Méry, or turned to

Mounier's own magazine, *Esprit*. The point is this: France's postwar technocratic elite was not just a value-neutral modernizing agent but was value laden. It was enlightened and progressive to be sure, but that did not preclude in many cases a serious commitment to Christian values. Point two: technocrats, important as they were, operated in a wider political field that hemmed them in. Laroque is a case in point. He did not get the welfare scheme he wanted but was obliged to make concessions to christian democrats and pronatalists. Last of all, in the domain of culture, technocrats did not play much of a role at all. There is Fourré-Cormeray, who was critical to keeping Communists at bay in the film industry. And there is Jeanne Laurent, but she seems less a technocrat than the visionary of a stage purified and made new. In the service of that vision she rallied to herself a cohort of young directors, men like the former JECiste Clavé who, it turns out, had an almost instinctive predilection for a theater of "strong spirituality." Technocracy does not tell the whole story of the postwar era, and even when it seems to, it keeps opening out onto wider vistas, sometimes socialist in hue, but more often Christian.

That must be the answer, then: the real story of the postwar era is none of the above, but that of an energized christian democracy, staking a surprise but successful claim to continental leadership as it steered Catholic electorates away from the reactionary ways of old toward a modern future: neocorporatist, anticommunist, and European in design. This might make a sensible conclusion for Germany and Italy, where christian democrats did in fact come to hold a dominant position by the fifties, but it will not do for France. On the public stage, the MRP was just one player among many, and over the course of the decade its fortunes waned. And behind the scenes, as has been observed time and again in the preceding pages, christian-democratic policy makers had to jostle for advantage with a host of competitors—Gaullists, pronatalists, technocrats—and they did not always come out on top.

No, there not was a single, clear victor in France's postwar reconstruction battles. The state got a full-dress makeover. The terms of the transformation were set by the Resistance, and at first it appeared that the Resistance Left itself might take charge of things. But that prospect dimmed fast and grew ever dimmer with time. Instead, it was de Gaulle, backed by technocrats, christian democrats, and pronatalists who set the pace with, depending on the sector, the Socialists not far behind. Framing the story in these terms may not get the exact weighting of influence right, but it is a useful perspective in the following regard.

The experience of statist rebirth in the postwar era was not unique to France, but there is a specificity to the French case, at least compared with the Anglo-American world. In the United Kingdom and the United States, the postwar political order came in for a major renegotiation in the 1970s and 1980s. The neoliberal administrations of Prime Minister Thatcher and President Reagan attempted a rollback of welfarist institutions, decrying the corrosive moral effects of an overweening state. There were echoes of this in France to be sure, but they were faint and in comparative terms remain so. The state's job is to educate, to supply welfare services, to make cultural goods available to one and all. On these basic points, most French can still agree, and they do not want to go down the Anglo-American road with its dog-eat-dog capitalism and consumerist kitsch. Liberalism and individualism, words that some Anglo-Americans hold dear, do not have the same positive ring in French ears. The postwar order in France has shown itself more durable than in the United States and Great Britain, and that is because it was more consensual.

Many constituencies, as we have seen, had a hand in state reconstruction in postwar France. Catholics and *la haute fonction publique* had not felt at home in the old Third Republic, but they did in the Fourth. France's working class had an ambivalent relationship to the Third Republic; that ambivalence dissipated under the Fourth. To be sure, the Communist Party was as ever cast in the pariah's role, but after the war it was no longer controversial for a Socialist to become prime minister in the way it had been in Blum's day. The welfare apparatus, moreover, afforded trade unionists an unprecedented stake in the state's smooth functioning.

France's postwar new deal made a pledge to the nation: that the state would undertake to make a better France for every citizen and that it would do so not just by reducing the risks and anxieties of day-to-day existence but by enriching the lives of all through the dissemination of a culture of quality. That pledge elicited a near consensus of support, not right away, to be sure, but over time, and to this degree it is reasonable to think of the postwar era, however riven with political conflict, as a moment of national rebirth. The French, moreover, still believe in the Liberation pledge, and the politician who means to tinker with the state apparatus that stands behind it had better do so with care. It is not that France has not liberalized in recent decades. But liberalization has run into stiff opposition; its partisans have often had to act on the sly, liberalizing "by stealth"[21]; and the public conviction that "tout passe par l'Etat" and that on the whole this is not such a bad thing remains intact.

But perhaps such a conclusion is overhasty. The Fourth Republic, after all, lived a short, fretful life and ended no less unmourned than the Third. It was the Algerian war, of course, that brought about the Republic's demise, and France's postwar elite fractured over the issue. Debré and Bidault remained staunch in support of Algérie française, but many of their colleagues went the other way. The antiwar Club Jean Moulin is a pertinent example. The Club was founded in May 1958 by ex-résistants and pitched its appeal in part to civil servants and opinion makers upset over the course of the war. It is remarkable, running through its list of members, to encounter so many names familiar from the pages above—André Clavé, Paul Flamand, Etienne Hirsch, Simon Nora, Pierre-Aimé Touchard, and so on.[22] It is worth noting, moreover, that the Club Jean Moulin was also anti-Gaullist, in the course of events relaying its anti-Gaullist energies into a resurrected Parti socialiste (although the Club itself did not formally affiliate to the PS when the party was formed in 1969). The postwar state would get a serious constitutional restructuring with the coming of the Gaullist Fifth Republic; and it would get another reworking, much less thorough to be sure, when the Socialists came to power in the 1980s. All this is just a reminder that France's postwar new deal, however enduring in certain respects, still had serious bouts of renegotiation ahead of it.

Notes

Introduction. Postwar Stories

1. Joseph Barsalou has characterized the regime as *mal aimée*, that is, not well loved. See Barsalou, *La Mal-Aimée: Histoire de la IVe République* (Paris, 1964).

2. Claude Bourdet, *L'Aventure incertaine, de la Résistance à la Restauration* (Paris, 1998). The restorationist thesis is given a thorough but critical airing in François Bloch-Lainé and Jean Bouvier, *La France restaurée, 1944–1954: Dialogue sur les choix d'une modernisation* (Paris, 1986).

3. Cited in Robert L. Frost, *Alternating Currents: Nationalized Power in France, 1946–1970* (Ithaca, 1991), 40.

4. Rebecca Boehling, *A Question of Priorities: Democratic Reforms and Economic Recovery in Postwar Germany; Frankfurt, Munich, and Stuttgart under U.S. Occupation 1945–1949* (Providence, 1996); Eberhard Schmidt, *Die verhinderte Neuordnung 1945–1952: Zur Auseinandersetzung um die Demokratisierung der Wirtschaft in den westlichen Besatzungszonen und in der Bundesrepublik Deutschland* (Frankfurt, 1977). For a critique of the restorationist thesis, see James C. Van Hook, *Rebuilding Germany: The Creation of the Social Market Economy, 1945–1957* (Cambridge, 2004).

5. Ralf Dahrendorf, *Society and Democracy in Germany* (Garden City, 1969); Jürgen Kocka, "1945: Neubeginn oder Restauration?" in Carola Stern and Heinrich August Winkler, eds., *Wendepunkte deutscher Geschichte, 1848–1945* (Frankfurt, 1979), 141–168; Volker Berghahn, *The Americanisation of West German Industry, 1945–1973* (Leamington Spa, 1986).

6. Alan Brinkley, *The End of Reform: New Deal Liberalism in Recession and War* (New York, 1996); Elizabeth Fones-Wolf, *Selling Free Enterprise: The Business Assault on Labor and Liberalism, 1945–60* (Urbana, 1994).

7. Lizabeth Cohen, *A Consumer's Republic: The Politics of Mass Consumption in Postwar America* (New York, 2003).

8. Victoria de Grazia, *Irresistible Empire: America's Advance through Twentieth-Century Europe* (Cambridge, MA, 2005).

9. Annie Lacroix-Riz, *Le Choix de Marianne, les relations franco-américaines 1944–1948* (Paris, 1985); idem, "Négociation et signature des accords Blum-Byrnes (octobre 1945–mai 1946) d'après les archives du Ministère des Affaires étrangères," *Revue d'histoire moderne et contemporaine*, 31 (July–September 1984): 417–447.

10. Kenneth O. Morgan, *Britain Since 1945* (Oxford, 2001), ch. 2; David Kynaston, *Austerity Britain, 1945–51* (London, 2007), ch. 2.

11. Correlli Barnett, *The Audit of War: The Illusion and Reality of Britain as a Great Nation* (London, 1986); Steven J. Fielding, Peter Thompson, and Nick Tiratsoo, *England Arise! The Labour Party and Popular Politics in 1940s Britain* (Manchester, 1995).

12. Claire Andrieu, "La France à gauche de l'Europe," *Le Mouvement social,* no. 134 (January–March 1986): 131–153.

13. See Sheri Berman, *The Social Democratic Moment: Ideas and Politics in the Making of Interwar Europe* (Cambridge, MA, 1998); idem, *The Primacy of Politics: Social Democracy and the Making of Europe's Twentieth Century* (Cambridge, 2002), ch. 8; Tony Judt, *Postwar: A History of Europe since 1945* (New York, 2005), ch. 11.

14. Gabrielle Hecht, *The Radiance of France: Nuclear Power and National Identity after World War II* (Cambridge, MA, 1998), 137, 164.

15. Frost, *Alternating Currents,* 2–3, 131–132, 247.

16. David Edgerton, *Warfare State: Britain, 1920–1970* (Cambridge, 2006).

17. John Dower, "The Useful War," in Dower, *Japan in War and Peace: Selected Essays* (New York, 1993), 14.

18. Richard J. Samuels, *"Rich Nation, Strong Army": National Security and the Technological Transformation of Japan* (Ithaca, 1994).

19. For examples of this approach to the period, see Stanley Hoffmann, "Paradoxes of the French Political Community," in Hoffmann et al., *In Search of France: The Economy, Society, and Political System in the Twentieth Century* (New York, 1965); Richard Kuisel, *Capitalism and the State in Modern France: Renovation and Economic Management in the Twentieth Century* (Cambridge, 1981); Herrick Chapman, *State Capitalism and Working-Class Radicalism in the French Aircraft Industry* (Berkeley, 1991); Michel Margairaz, *L'Etat, les finances et l'économie: Histoire d'une conversion, 1932–1952* (Paris, 1991); Paul-André Rosental, *L'Intelligence démographique: Sciences et politiques des populations en France (1930–1960)* (Paris, 2003).

20. Michael Marrus, "Vichy avant Vichy," *Histoire,* no. 3 (November 1979): 77–92; Julian Jackson, *France: The Dark Years, 1940–1944* (Oxford, 2001); Gérard Noiriel, *Les Origines républicaines de Vichy* (Paris, 1999).

21. Claire Andrieu, *Le Programme commun de la Résistance: des idées dans la guerre* (Paris, 1984); Andrew Shennan, *Rethinking France: Plans for Renewal, 1940–1946* (Oxford, 1989).

22. The classic text remains Robert Paxton, *Vichy France: Old Guard and New Order, 1940–1944* (New York, 1972). See also Kuisel, *Capitalism and the State,* and Henry Rousso, *Le Syndrome de Vichy, 1944–198...* (Paris, 1987).

23. Remi Lenoir, *Généalogie de la morale familiale* (Paris, 2003).

24. Sheldon Garon, *Molding Japanese Minds: The State in Everyday Life* (Princeton, 1997), 178.

25. See the remarkable book by Pascal Ory, *La Belle Illusion: Culture et Politique sous le signe du Front populaire, 1935–1938* (Paris, 1994).

26. Herman Lebovics, *Mona Lisa's Escort: André Malraux and the Reinvention*

of French Culture (Ithaca, 1999); Olivier Todd, *André Malraux: une vie* (Paris, 2001).

27. Emmanuelle Loyer, *Le Théâtre citoyen de Jean Vilar: une utopie d'après-guerre* (Paris, 1997); Jean-François Muracciole, *Les Enfants de la défaite: La Résistance, l'éducation et la culture* (Paris, 1998); Philippe Poirrier, *L'Etat et la Culture en France au XXe siècle* (Paris, 2000), ch. 4.; Pascale Goetschel, *Renouveau et décentralisation du théâtre, 1945–1981* (Paris, 2004).

28. See Daniel Lindenberg, *Les Années souterraines, 1937–1947* (Paris, 1990).

29. For a long-term view of state expansion in France that emphasizes moments rather than linearity, see Pierre Rosanvallon, *L'Etat en France de 1789 à nos jours* (Paris, 1990).

PART I. THE FRENCH MODEL

1. Pierre Laroque as cited in Paul-André Rosental, *L'Intelligence démographique, Sciences et politiques des populations en France (1930–1960)* (Paris, 2003), 26.

2. For France as a stalemate society, see Stanley Hoffmann, "Paradoxes of the French Political Community," in Hoffmann et al., *In Search of France: The Economy, Society, and Political System in the Twentieth Century* (New York, 1965), 3–60; Michel Crozier, *La Société bloquée* (Paris, 1970). For the Liberation as a transformational moment, see the discussion and critique in Pierre Bourdieu and Luc Boltanski, "La Production de l'idéologie dominante," *Actes de la Recherche en sciences sociales*, nos. 2/3 (June 1976), 4–73.

3. Tony Judt, *Postwar: A History of Europe since 1945* (New York, 2005), 360–389. Geoff Eley argues that "the Left set the agenda" at the Liberation: *Forging Democracy: The History of the Left in Europe, 1850–2000* (New York, 2002), 295–298. For a different perspective that places greater weight on the christian-democratic contribution to the postwar order, see Martin Conway, "Democracy in Postwar Western Europe: The Triumph of a Political Model," *European History Quarterly* 32 (2002): 59–84; and idem, "The Rise and Fall of Western Europe's Democratic Age, 1945–1973," *Contemporary European History* 13 (2004): 67–88.

4. Jean-Louis Loubet del Bayle, *Les Non-conformistes des années 30* (Paris, 1969).

5. Olivier Dard, *Le Rendez-vous manqué des relèves des années 30* (Paris, 2002), 247–263.

6. Laurent Douzou and Denis Peschanski, "La Résistance française face à l'hypothèque Vichy," in David Bidussa and Denis Peschanski, eds., *La France de Vichy: Archives inédits d'Angelo Tasca* (Milan, 1996), 3–42; Henry Rousso, "Les paradoxes de Vichy et de l'Occupation: Contraintes, archaïsmes et modernités," in Patrick Fridenson and André Straus, eds., *Le Capitalisme français XIXe–XXe siècle, Blocages et dynamismes d'une croissance* (Paris, 1987), 79.

7. Claude Bourdet, *L'Aventure incertaine, De la Résistance à la Restauration* (Paris, 1998 [orig. 1975]); for a more nuanced assessment, see the discussion in Fran-

çois Bloch-Lainé and Jean Bouvier, *La France restaurée, 1944–1954: Dialogue sur les choix d'une modernisation* (Paris, 1986).

8. Andrew Shennan, *Rethinking France: Plans for Renewal, 1940–1946* (Oxford, 1989), 288.

Chapter 1. The Crisis of the Thirties

1. Robert Marjolin, *Le Travail d'une vie: Mémoires, 1911–1986* (Paris, 1986), 28ff.

2. René Belin, *Du Secrétariat de la C.G.T. au gouvernement de Vichy (Mémoires, 1933–1942)* (Paris, 1978), 46. See also Georges Lefranc, *Le Mouvement socialiste sous la Troisième République, 1875–1940* (Paris, 1963), 308–313.

3. Jean-François Biard, *Le Socialisme devant ses choix: La Naissance de l'idée de plan* (Paris, 1985), 121 and 121n.

4. Richard Kuisel, *Capitalism and the State in Modern France: Renovation and Economic Management in the Twentieth Century* (Cambridge, 1981), 109; Michel Margairaz, *L'Etat, les finances et l'économie: Histoire d'une conversion, 1932–1952* (Paris, 1991), I:147.

5. Biard, *Socialisme*, 125–132; and "Conférence de M. Robert Lacoste (12 mars 1937): Le syndicalisme français et le redressement national," as reprinted in *X-Crise, de la récurrence des crises économiques, son cinquantenaire, 1931–1981* (Paris, 1981), 159–163.

6. Philippe Burrin, *La Dérive fasciste: Doriot, Déat, Bergery, 1933–1945* (Paris, 2003), 160.

7. Paul Marion, "L'Equipe France," *L'Homme nouveau* 12 (1 January 1935); for the Bonnard quote, see the inside cover of *L'Homme nouveau* 2 (February 1934); Marcel Déat, "Enfonçons la porte," *L'Homme nouveau* 10 (1 November 1934); Georges Izard, "Rassemblement ou guerre civile," *L'Homme nouveau* 17 (June 1935); Pierre Laroque, "Les conditions nécessaires de l'organisation corporative," *L'Homme nouveau* 18 (July–August 1935).

8. Georges Roditi and Bertrand Varages, "La route des corporations," *L'Homme nouveau* 4 (April 1934).

9. Pierre Laroque, *Au Service de l'homme et du droit. Souvenirs et refléxions* (Paris, 1993), 95, 98–100.

10. Pierre Laroque, "Les conditions nécessaires de l'organisation corporative," *L'Homme nouveau* 18 (July–August 1935). See also by Laroque: "Le mouvement social," *L'Homme nouveau* 1 (January 1934); "Les syndicats ouvriers en régimes autoritaires," *L'Homme nouveau* 5 (May 1934); "Les syndicats ouvriers," *L'Homme nouveau* 12 (1 January 1935).

11. Kuisel, *Capitalism and the State*, 112–119.

12. Bernard Comte, *Une Utopie combattante: L'Ecole des cadres d'Uriage, 1940–1942* (Paris, 1991), 33; Simone de Beauvoir, *Memoirs of a Dutiful Daughter*, tr. James Kirkup (London, 1963), 179–181; Evelyne Cohen, *Paris dans l'imaginaire national de l'entre-deux-guerres* (Paris, 1999), 46.

13. Philippe Laneyrie, *Les Scouts de France: L'évolution du mouvement des origines aux années quatre-vingt* (Paris, 1985), 94, 107, 109, 120.

14. Rémi Baudouï, *Raoul Dautry, 1880–1951: Le technocrate de la République* (Paris, 1992), 131–140.

15. Raoul Dautry, *Métier d'homme* (Paris, 1937), 8, 16, 18, 21, 27, 246.

16. Olivier Feiertag, "Wilfrid Baumgartner, les finances de l'Etat et l'économie de la Nation, 1902–1978" (Thèse de doctorat, University of Paris–X, 1996), I:181.

17. Philippe Lamour, "Jeunesse du monde," *Plans* 4 (April 1931): 9–18; Le Corbusier, "Vers la 'Ville Radieuse,' Descartes est-il américain?" *Plans* 7 (July 1931): 64; Lamour, "Lettre à Aron et Dandieu," *Plans* 8 (October 1931): 34–35.

18. Aron and Dandieu, "U.S.A. Faillite économique du libéralisme," *L'Ordre nouveau* 1 (1933): 21; "Nous Voulons," *L'Ordre nouveau* 9 (1934): 2–16; Xavier de Lignac, "La culture libérale," *L'Ordre nouveau* 18 (1935): 11; Edmond Lipiansky and Bernard Rettenbach, *Ordre et Démocratie: Deux sociétés de pensée, de l'Ordre Nouveau au Club Jean Moulin* (Paris, 1967), 11.

19. René Dupuis, "Destin des régimes," *L'Ordre nouveau* 11 (1934): 13–14; Lipiansky and Rettenbach, *Ordre et Démocratie*, 9; "Nous Voulons," *L'Ordre Nouveau* 9 (1934): 4, 8, 14, 21.

20. Emmanuel Mounier, "Manifeste au service du personnalisme," *Esprit* 49 (1 October 1936): 16–18

21. John Hellman, *Emmanuel Mounier and the New Catholic Left, 1930–1950* (Toronto, 1981), 11–12, 27.

22. Loubet del Bayle, *Non-conformistes*, 136.

23. Michel Winock, *"Esprit": Des intellectuels dans la cité, 1930–1950* (Paris, 1996 [orig. 1975]), 132–134; Emmanuel Mounier, "Apologie pour la République," *Esprit* 78 (1 March 1939): 786–787. It is worth noting, though, that Mounier tempered his praise of the Republic's foreign-policy resolve with swipes against the Radical Party, parliament, and the League of Nations, all of which he counted on the negative side of the regime's balance sheet. On Goguel's pacifism, see Henri Jourdan, "Une lucidité passionnée," 1974, in François Denoël, ed., *François Perroux* (Lausanne, 1990), 243; on Leenhardt's, see Roger Leenhardt, *Les Yeux ouverts: entretiens avec Jean Lacouture* (Paris, 1979).

24. Roger Leenhardt, "Panorama de l'hérésie révolutionnaire," *Esprit* 40 (1 January 1936): 588.

25. Jean Lacroix, "Situation de la France," *Esprit* 70 (1 July 1938): 468. See also Georges Izard, "Rester dans le peuple pour l'élever," *Esprit* 38 (1 November 1935): 289, 301; Roger Leenhardt, "Journal des témoins," *Esprit* 50 (1 November 1936): 367; Bernard Serampuy [François Goguel], "La Flèche, le frontisme," *Esprit* 72 (1 September 1938): 735–740.

26. L. E. Galey, *Esprit* 7 (1 April 1933): 143–144; Emmanuel Mounier, "Manifeste au service du personnalisme," *Esprit* 49 (1 October 1936): 161, 163; idem, "Quelques conclusions," *Esprit* 78 (1 March 1939): 878.

27. Gérard Destanne de Bernis, "La Dynamique de François Perroux, l'homme, la création collective, le projet humain," 1977, in Denoël, ed., *Perroux*, 109–112.

28. François Perroux, *Capitalisme et communauté de travail* (Paris, 1938), 305.

29. See, for example, François Perroux, "La personne ouvrière et le droit au travail," *Esprit* 42 (1 March 1936): 866–897.

30. Perroux, *Capitalisme*, 108, 121, 287, 308, 321. For an informed discussion of the evolution of Perroux's thinking, see Antonin Cohen, "De la Révolution Nationale au *Revenu national*: l'économie politique de François Perroux. Aux origines d'un changement de référentiel dans les politiques publiques en 1945," unpublished ms, presented at the Centre d'histoire sociale du 20éme siècle (Paris, 13 November 2003). On Salazar as a model for Vichy's National Revolution, see Marc Olivier Baruch, *Servir l'Etat français: L'administration en France de 1940 à 1944* (Paris, 1997), 56.

31. Dominique Pestre, "Le renouveau de la recherche à l'Ecole polytechnique et le laboratoire de Louis Leprince-Ringuet, 1936–1965," in Bruno Belhoste, Amy Dahan Dalmedico, and Antoine Picon, eds., *La Formation polytechnicienne, 1794–1994* (Paris, 1994), 339. In the same volume, see also the essays by Antoine Picon, "Les années d'enlisement: L'Ecole polytechnique de 1870 à l'entre-deux-guerres," 175–176, and Vincent Guigeno, "Une figure contestée: l'officier-ingénieur (1920–1943), 405.

32. Gérard Brun, *Technocrates et technocratie en France (1914–1945)* (Paris, 1985), 33–35; Raymond Abellio, *Ma Dernière Mémoire* (Paris, 1975), II:101–102; Coutrot Papers, AN 468 AP 9, dossier 3, Guy Desaunay, "X-Crise: Contribution à l'étude des idéologies économiques d'un groupe de polytechniciens durant la grande crise économique (1931–1939)" (Thèse de 3e cycle, University of Paris, nd), 12.

33. Coutrot Papers, AN 468 AP 9, dossier 2, sdr b, John Nicolétis, "Le Centre polytechnicien d'études économiques: X-Crise," *La Jaune et la Rouge* (August–September 1977): 20.

34. "Conférence de M. A. Detoeuf (1er mai 1936), La fin du libéralisme," reproduced in *X-Crise*, 71–87. See also "Conférence de M. Jacques Branger (22 février 1935), Le Contenu économique des plans…et le planisme," in ibid., 130.

35. "Rélexions sur six mois de travaux" and "Conférence de M. Jacques Branger," in *X-Crise*, 55, 130.

36. "Réflexions sur six mois de travaux," in *X-Crise*, 55.

37. Olivier Dard, *Jean Coutrot, de l'ingénieur au prophète* (Besançon, 1999), 318.

38. Coutrot Papers, AN 468 AP 7, dossier 1, remark by Coutrot in *X-Information* (25 December 1931): 125; "Réflexions sur six mois de travaux" and "Conférence de M. Jean Ullmo (séance du 12 février 1937), Les Problèmes théoriques de l'économie dirigée," in *X-Crise*, 55, 221.

39. Coutrot Papers, AN 468 AP 7, dossier 8, sdr b, letter from Gibrat to Mon Cher Ami (Jean Coutrot), 25 March 1935.

40. "Conférence de François Divisia (21 décembre 1933), Travaux et méthodes de la société d'économétrie," in *X-Crise*, 201–209; "Conférence de M. Jean Ullmo (séance du 12 février 1937), Les Problèmes théoriques de l'économie dirigée," in *X-Crise*, 213–214; Coutrot Papers, AN 468 AP 8, dossier, 4, sdr e, "Assemblée générale du C.P.E.E., Procès-verbal," 7 December 1936; dossier 5, "C.P.E.E. Equipe de conjoncture," 24 January 1936.

41. Dard, *Rendez-vous*, 193–196.

42. Laroque, *Au Service*, 113; Eric Jabbari, "Pierre Laroque and the Origins of French Social Security, 1934–1948" (Ph.D. dissertation, Oxford University, 2000), 130; inside back cover, advertisement for the "Plan du 9 juillet," *L'Homme nouveau* 7 (1 August 1934); Bertrand Varages, "La première réunion publique du Groupe du 9 juillet," *L'Homme nouveau* 11 (1 December 1934). Many thanks to Eric Jabbari for allowing me to read his unpublished thesis.

43. Marjolin, *Travail*, 61.

44. Dard, *Jean Coutrot*, 278ff.; Brun, *Technocrates*, 166.

45. Brun, *Technocrates*, 165; Paul Desrosières, *La Politique des grands nombres: Histoire de la raison statistique* (Paris, 1993), 195.

46. Alain Chatriot, *La Démocratie sociale à la française: l'expérience du Conseil national économique, 1924–1940* (Paris, 2002), 342, 344; Margairaz, *Etat*, I:341.

47. E. Nadaud, "Charles Spinasse," in Jean-François Sirinelli, *Dictionnaire historique de la vie politique française au XXe siècle* (Paris, 1995), 988.

48. Desrosières, *Politique des grands nombres*, 194.

49. Claude Gruson, *Programmer l'espérance: Conversations avec Philippe Dominique* (Paris, 1976), 35.

50. Alfred Sauvy, *La Vie en plus: Souvenirs* (Paris, 1981), 51.

51. Paul V. Dutton, *Origins of the French Welfare State: The Struggle for Social Reform in France, 1914–1947* (Cambridge, 2002), 152; Michel Debré, *Trois Républiques pour une France: Mémoires* (Paris, 1984), 144–145; Sauvy, *Vie*, 74.

52. Sauvy played on the same rugby squad as the filmmaker Jacques Tati. See David Bellos, *Jacques Tati: His Life and Art* (London, 1999), 29.

53. Béatrice Touchelay, "L'INSEE, des origines à 1961: évolution et relation avec la réalité économique et sociale" (Thèse de doctorat, University of Paris–XII, 1993), I:48–49; Michel Volle, *Histoire de la statistique industrielle* (Paris, 1982), 20–22; Margairaz, *L'Etat*, I:480; François Fourquet, *Les Comptes de la puissance: Histoire de la comptabilité nationale et du plan* (Paris, 1980), 29, 34–35.

54. Baudouï, *Dautry*, 194.

55. The real puzzle of the accords is why a trade-union leader like Jouhaux should have appended his name to them at all. But perhaps the answer is not so hard to come by. Here, after all, was a chance, however slim, to bring a wounded union movement back into a position of influence. Of no less importance, the accords helped noncommunist trade unionists like Jouhaux to build themselves up, the better to settle scores with the communist competition in CGT ranks. See Talbot C. Imlay, *Facing the Second World War: Strategy, Politics, and Economics in Britain and France, 1938–1940* (Oxford, 2003), 281–284; Baudouï, *Dautry*, 194–195; Jean-Pierre Le Crom, *Syndicats, nous voilà! Vichy et le corporatisme* (Paris, 1995), 50–51.

56. Brun, *Technocrates*, 167–168; Jean-Louis Crémieux-Brilhac, *Les Français de l'an 40* (Paris, 1990), II:109–110; Baudouï, *Dautry*, 194, 197.

57. It is important, however, not to give the impression that the technocrats Reynaud tapped were that much more right-wing than the technocrats who populated Dautry's ministry. Baudouin did go on to work at Vichy and then quit in 1941. But Dautry's man, Lehideux, who also ended up a Vichyite, stuck by the

regime a good deal longer, serving Pétain in a ministerial capacity from 1941 until Laval's return to office in April 1942.

58. As reported by Gruson in François Bloch-Lainé and Claude Gruson, *Hauts Fonctionnaires sous l'Occupation* (Paris, 1996), 32–33. See also Crémieux-Brilhac, *Les Français,* I:267–269.

59. Michel Lévy, *Alfred Sauvy: compagnon du siècle* (Paris, 1990), 25–27; Jacques Dupâquier, "Le rôle d'Adolphe Landry dans l'élaboration d'une législation familiale," paper presented at the Colloque international. Adolphe Landry, économiste, démographe, législateur: 1874–1956, Université de Corse, 3–6 September 1997, 1–2; Jabbari, "Pierre Laroque," 13n.

60. Alain Girard, "Adolphe Landry et la démographie," *Revue française de sociologie* 23 (January–March 1982): 111–126; idem, *L'Institut national d'études démographiques: histoire et développement* (Paris, 1986), 40.

61. Robert Debré, *L'Honneur de vivre* (Paris, 1974), 398.

62. Paul Haury, "Natalité et Défense Nationale," *Revue de l'Alliance nationale contre la dépopulation* (February 1937): 36–39; idem, "Familles nombreuses," *Revue de l'Alliance nationale contre la dépopulation* (April 1937): 112.

63. "Pour le vote familial," *Revue de l'Alliance nationale contre la dépopulation* (February 1937): 56–57; Paul Haury, "Familles nombreuses," *Revue de l'Alliance nationale contre la dépopulation* (April 1937): 112; idem, "Pour le retour de la mère au foyer," *Revue de l'Alliance nationale contre la dépopulation* (November 1937): 328–330; idem, "Allocations familiales," *Revue de l'Alliance nationale contre la dépopulation* (February 1938): 45–48.

64. This theme is treated in detail in Cheryl Koos, "Gender, Anti-individualism, and Nationalism: The Alliance Nationale and the Pronatalist Backlash against the *Femme moderne,* 1933–1940," *French Historical Studies* 19 (Spring 1996): 699–723.

65. Susan Pedersen, *Family, Dependence, and the Origins of the Welfare State: Britain and France, 1914–1945* (New York, 1993), ch. 5; Dutton, *Origins,* ch. 1.

66. Henri Hatzfeld, *Du Paupérisme à la Sécurité sociale, 1850–1940* (Paris, 1971), 178.

67. *Jocistes dans la tourmente: Histoire des jocistes (JOC-JOCF) de la région parisienne, 1937–1947* (Paris, 1989), 207.

68. Bloch-Lainé and Gruson, *Hauts Fonctionnaires,* 63.

69. *Jocistes dans la tourmente,* 35–36; Pierre Pierrard, Michel Launay, and Rolande Trempé, *La J.O.C., Regards d'historiens* (Paris, 1984), 75. See also Jessica Wardhaugh, *In Pursuit of the People: Political Culture in France, 1934–1939* (Basingstoke, 2009), 177–182.

70. Adrien Dansette, *Destin du catholicisme français, 1926–1956* (Paris, 1957), 425–426.

71. Dansette, *Destin,* 373–375; Cholvy, "Une image de la jeune fille entre les deux guerres: les bulletins diocésains de la jeunesse catholique féminine," in Françoise Mayeur and Jacques Gadille, eds., *Education et images de la femme chrétienne en France au début du XXe siècle* (Lyon, 1980), 190; Jean-Claude Delbreil, *Centrisme et démocratie chrétienne en France: Le Parti démocrate populaire des origines au M.R.P., 1919–1944* (Paris, 1990), 57, 134–135, 240–242, 249–250.

72. "Le Président de l'Alliance Nationale chez S.E. le Cardinal Verdier," *Revue*

de l'Alliance nationale contre la dépopulation (February 1938): 55; "Une lettre pastorale," *Revue de l'Alliance nationale contre la dépopulation* (April 1938): 114; "Un appel des Cardinaux français en faveur de la natalité," *Revue de l'Alliance nationale contre la dépopulation* (June 1939): 188.

73. Coutrot Papers, AN 468 AP 21, dossier 1, sdr a, "Centre d'études des problèmes humains," nd.

74. Coutrot Papers, AN 468 AP 21, dossier 1, sdr a, "Le Centre d'études des problèmes humains, ses objectifs et ses méthodes (E. Rivoire), 3–4; see also in the same subdossier, "Pour un pionnier fatigué (1938)"; and Coutrot's speech in Coutrot Papers, AN 468 AP 23, dossier 6, sdr a, "Institut de Psychologie appliquée. Séance inaugurale, 20 juin 1938," 4, 19.

75. Coutrot Papers, AN 468 AP 23, dossier 6, sdr a, "Institut de Psychologie appliquée. Séance inaugurale, 20 juin 1938," 19. For Coutrot's interest in Montessori, see Dard, *Jean Coutrot*, 360–362. Le Corbusier delivered a talk at CEPH headquarters in June 1938 titled "Commençons à Paris un urbanisme humain." See Coutrot Papers, AN 468 AP 22, "Calendrier Cephéen," *Humanisme économique* (May–June 1938): 7.

76. Coutrot Papers, AN 468 AP 27, dossier 3, "Entretiens de Pontigny, 4 juin 1938," 36.

77. Coutrot Papers, AN 468 AP 23, dossier 6, sdr a, "Institut de Psychologie appliquée. Séance inaugurale, 20 juin 1938," 4.

78. Letter from Coutrot to Saint-Exupéry, 6 October 1938, in Coutrot Papers, AN 468 AP 25, dossier 5. Coutrot expressed similar sentiments in a letter to Albert Bayet, 16 May 1939. See AN 468 AP 25, dossier 6.

79. Alain Drouard, *Alexis Carrel (1873–1944): De la mémoire à l'histoire* (Paris, 1995), 136–138.

80. Alexis Carrel, *L'Homme, cet inconnu* (Paris, 1997 [orig. 1935]), 272.

81. Carrel, *L'Homme*, 347–348.

82. Carrel, *L'Homme*, 197, 311–312, 316–317, 319; Alain Drouard, *Une Inconnue des sciences sociales: la Fondation Alexis Carrel, 1941–1945* (Paris, 1992), 39; Carrel Papers, Georgetown University, box 69, folder 68, "Dr. Carrel's Revision" of a *Reader's Digest* essay titled "Prayer is Power," 1–6.

83. Carrel Papers, Georgetown University, box 43, folder 27, reprint of Carrel's Phi Beta Kappa address, "The Making of Civilized Men," in *Dartmouth Alumni Magazine* (November 1937).

84. See Andrés Horacio Reggiani, "Birthing the French Welfare State: Political Crises, Population and Public Health, 1914–1960" (Ph.D. dissertation, SUNY–Stonybrook, 1998), 287.

85. Coutrot Papers, AN 468 AP 22, "Le Centre d'Etudes des Problèmes Humains," *Humanisme économique* (October 1937): 2; Carrel Papers, Georgetown University, box 64, folder 30, letter from Carrel to Coutrot, 3 November 1937; Coutrot Papers, AN 468 AP 21, dossier 3, sdr d, exchange of letters, Carrel to Coutrot, 26 August 1939, Coutrot to Carrel, 28 August 1939; AN 468 AP 27, dossier 1, letter from Missenard to Coutrot, 30 September 1937, and dossier 6, letter from Missenard to Pierre Aube, CEPH, 17 August 1938; Drouard, *Une Inconnue*, 138, 138n.

86. Carrel Papers, Georgetown University, box 68, folder 21, letter from Carrel to Missenard, 7 February 1939; box 44, folder 26, letter from Carrel to Paul Frank, 31 January 1941.

87. Carrel Papers, Georgetown University, box 40, 14-1, folder 3, letter from Carrel to Guigou, 4 November 1938; box 68, folder 21, letter from Missenard to Carrel, 1 March 1939, and from Carrel to Missenard, 18 March 1939.

88. On the Gap meeting, see Coutrot Papers, AN 468 AP 24, dossier 6, "La reoncontre de Saint-Léger, 27–28 août 1938," and "Le Chemin de l'Union, 25 septembre 1938."

89. Coutrot Papers, AN 468 AP 24, dossier 6, letter from André Boutier to Coutrot, 6 November 1938, and from Marc to Coutrot, 14 December 1938, and from Coutrot to Marc, 16 December 1938.

90. Carrel cited in Robert Soupault, *Alexis Carrel, 1873–1944* (Paris, 1952), 189, 191–192, 196–197; and Carrel Papers, Georgetown University, box 40, 14-1, folder 3, letters from Carrel to Guigou, 4 November 1938, 1 January 1939, and 23 February 1940.

91. Carrel Papers, Georgetown University, box 40, 14-1, folder 3, letter from Carrel to Guigou, 18 December 1940.

92. On Lindbergh, see Carrel Papers, Georgetown University, box 40, 14-1, folder 3, letters from Carrel to Guigou, 16 November 1938 and 9 December 1938; on Munich, letter from Carrel to Guigou, 14 September 1938.

93. Carrel Papers, Georgetown University, box 40, 14-1, folder 3, letter from Carrel to Guigou, 4 January 1940.

94. Carrel Papers, Georgetown University, box 40, 14-1, folder 3, letter from Carrel to Guigou, 25 August 1939. See also letter from Carrel to Guigou, 9 December 1938, and Drouard, *Carrel*, 152.

95. Carrel Papers, Georgetown University, box 40, 14-1, folder 3, Carrel to Guigou, 18 January 1937.

96. Carrel Papers, Georgetown University, box 67, folder 43, letter from Dr. Wilhelm Zipperling to Carrel, 5 February 1938, and Carrel's reply, 7 March 1938.

97. Carrel Papers, Georgetown University, box 40, folder 3, letter from Carrel to Guigou, 20 March 1939.

98. Soupault, *Carrel*, 192; Drouard, *Carrel*, 99; idem, *Une Inconnue*, 30n; Carrel Papers, Georgetown University, box 40, 14-1, folder 3, letter from Carrel to Guigou, 9 December 1938.

99. Carrel Papers, Georgetown University, box 40, 14-1, folder 3, letter from Carrel to Guigou, 4 January 1940. See also letter from Carrel to Guigou, 11 July 1938; Soupault, *Carrel*, 188–189; and Drouard, *Une Inconnue*, 35.

100. See the following articles in *Revue de l'Alliance nationale contre la dépopulation*: "Action de l'Alliance nationale" (August 1938): 236; "Le Gouvernement crée deux timbres 'Natalité' en faveur de l'Alliance Nationale" (February 1939): 33; Adolphe Landry, "La Révolution démographique" (April 1939): 112.

101. Rosental, *L'Intelligence démographique*, 23.

102. Andrés Horacio Reggiani, "Procreating France: The Politics of Demography, 1919–1945," *French Historical Studies* 19 (Spring 1996): 741.

103. The HCP's constitution is discussed in illuminating detail in Rosental, *L'Intelligence démographique*, 21–27; and Reggiani, "Procreating France," 741–742.

104. Shennan, *Rethinking France*, 204.

105. Carrel Papers, Georgetown University, box 40, 14-1, folder 3, Carrel to Guigou, 10 February 1940; see also Carrel to Guigou, 14 January 1940.

106. See, in *Revue de l'Alliance nationale contre la dépopulation*: "Les allocations familiales dans l'agriculture" (July 1938): 208–209; "L'allocation de la mère au foyer" (May 1939): 161.

107. Antoine Prost, "L'évolution de la politique familiale en France de 1938 à 1981," *Le Mouvement social*, no. 129 (October–December 1984), 10.

108. Fernand Boverat, "Le décret-loi du 29 juillet 1939 relatif à la famille et à la natalité française," *Revue de l'Alliance nationale contre la dépopulation* (July 1939): 243–263. Boverat's analysis of the code is followed by the text of the law itself (264–291).

109. Debré, *Trois Républiques*, 166–168.

110. Alexis de Tocqueville, *Souvenirs* (Paris, 1978), 116.

111. Gérard Vincent, *Sciences Po: Histoire d'une réussite* (Paris, 1987), 53, 59–60.

112. Fondation Nationale des Sciences Politiques, Archives d'histoire contemporaine, ELSP, 1 SP 14, dossier 6, tiré à part, d'Eichthal (December 1927), 13, 17.

113. ELSP, 1 SP 30, dossier 4, Procès-verbal des séances du Conseil d'Administration (hereinafter Procès-verbal), 23 November 1934 and 21 November 1935; Vincent, *Sciences Po*, 192; Brun, *Technocrates*, 214.

114. Daniel Guérin, *Autobiographie de jeunesse* (Paris, 1972), 123.

115. Claude Des Portes, *L'Atmosphère des Sciences Po* (Paris, 1935), 48.

116. Olivier Dard, "Economie et économistes des années trente aux années cinquante: un tournant keynésien?" *Historiens et géographes*, no. 361 (March–April 1998): 175, 177.

117. André Siegfried, *Tableau politique de la France de l'Ouest* (Paris, 1995 [orig. 1913]); idem, *Les Etats-Unis d'aujourd'hui* (Paris, 1927); Pierre Birnbaum, "La France aux Français," *Histoire des haines nationalistes* (Paris, 1993), ch. 5.

118. Des Portes, *L'Atmosphère*, 53–54; Vincent, *Sciences Po*, 358–359.

119. ELSP, 4 SI 2, dossier 3, "Conférence de révision de géographie économique."

120. Roselyne Chenu, *Paul Delouvrier ou la passion d'agir* (Paris, 1994), 36. See also ibid., 18, 29, 33, 40.

121. ELSP, 1 SP 30, Procès-verbal, 27 February 1932; 1 SP 15, dossier 3, Présentation de l'Ecole des Sciences Politiques (1949), testimony of Jacques Belin, promotion 1923. See also François Bloch-Lainé, *Profession: fonctionnaire. Entretiens avec Françoise Carrière* (Paris, 1976), 154; Des Portes, *L'Atmosphère*, 74–80; Vincent, *Sciences Po*, 346, 349.

122. Chenu, *Delouvrier*, 48–50.

123. Debré, *Trois Républiques*, 83–85.

124. Jacques Georges-Picot, *Souvenirs d'une longue carrière, de la rue de Rivoli à*

la Compagnie de Suez, 1920–1971 (Paris, 1993), 69–71; Des Portes, *L'Atmosphère*, 91.

125. François Piétri as cited in André Ferrat, *La République à refaire*, 3rd ed. (Paris, 1945), 143. See also Feiertag, "Wilfrid Baumgartner," I:44; Bloch-Lainé, *Profession*, 43.

126. Pierre Uri, *Penser pour l'action, un fondateur de l'Europe* (Paris, 1991), 22–23; Bloch-Lainé and Gruson, *Hauts Fonctionnaires*, 83–84.

127. Guérin, *Autobiographie*, 123; Laroque, *Au Service*, 75; Jacques Le Roy Ladurie, *Mémoires, 1902–1945* (Paris, 1997), 204.

128. Jean Zay, *Souvenirs et solitudes* (Paris, 1945), 315; Marc Bloch, *Strange Defeat: A Statement of Evidence Written in 1940*, tr. Gerard Hopkins (New York, 1968), 159–160; Bloch-Lainé and Gruson, *Hauts Fonctionnaires*, 64–65.

129. Guy Thuillier, "Les projets d'Ecole d'administration de 1936 à 1939," *La Revue administrative* 177 (1977): 240.

130. Thuillier, "Les projets d'Ecole d'administration," 242–243.

131. Debré, *Trois Républiques*, 366.

132. ESLP, 1 SP 52bis, dossier 2, sdr b, "Visite de MM. Lebée et Roger Seydoux à M. Doussain, Député de l'Alliance démocratique," 4 March 1937.

133. Vincent, *Sciences Po*, 96, 105; ELSP 1 SP 30, dossier 4, Procès-verbal, 6 March and 12 November 1936.

134. ELSP, 1 SP 30, Procès-verbal, 5 May 1937. The first scholarships, it appears, were not awarded until 1938. See Marie-Christine Kessler, *La Politique de la haute fonction publique* (Paris, 1978), 25.

135. Christophe Charle has apposite comments to make apropos the school's strategic maneuvers in 1937. Charle, "Savoir durer: la nationalisaton de l'Ecole libre des sciences politiques, 1936/1945," *Actes de la Recherche en sciences sociales*, nos. 86–87 (March 1991): 100. See also ELSP, 1 SP 52bis, dossier 3, sdr b, newspaper clipping, "L'Ecole d'administration," *Le Temps*, 24 November 1937; and sdr c, newspaper clipping, "M. Sébastien Charléty, employé intéressé de la féodalité de l'Argent," *La Lumière*, 20 May 1938.

136. ELSP, 1 SP 52bis, dossier 2, sdr b, letter from Seydoux to Hippolyte Ducos, Président, Commission de l'enseignement, Chambre des députés, 23 February 1937; and in the same file, "Visite de MM. Lebée et Roger Seydoux à M. Doussain," 4 March 1937.

137. ELSP, 1 SP 52bis, dossier 2, sdr b, circular letter from Seydoux to various deputies, November 1937, and letter from François [Piétri] to Mon Cher Ami [Seydoux], 27 November 1937; dossier 1, sdr b, copy of letter from [René Seydoux] to Roger Seydoux, c/o Schlumberger, Houston, Texas, 16 December 1937.

138. ELSP, 1 SP 52, dossier 4, sdr a, typed note, 14 August 1936; see also 1 SP 53, dossier 2, sdr f, "Note de Quatre Pages sur l'Ecole," 1 February 1937.

139. ELSP, 1 SP 52bis, dossier 1, sdr b, letter from Tirard to Zay, 15 November 1937; "Memento," 25 November 1937; 1 SP 52, dossier 3, sdr a, typed note, 21 December 1937.

140. ELSP, 1 SP 53, dossier 1, *Journal officiel, Chambre des députés*, séance du 27

janvier 1938, remarks by Cogniot and Pierre Vaillandet, 112–113, 115–116. The Left press was even more unrestrained in its attacks.

141. ELSP, 1 SP 30, Procès-verbal, 8 March 1938; 1 SP 52, dossier 4, sdr c, "Réponse à M. Zay, le 21 mars 1938," marked confidential; 1 SP 52bis, dossier 1, sdr c, "Entretien," 8 June 1938.

142. For the February meeting, see ELSP, 1 SP 52bis, dossier 2, sdr c, letter from Tirard, Romieu, and Siegfried to M. le Président (of the Senate Commission), 7 February 1938; "L'Ecole d'Administration au Sénat," 17 February 1938. For the June meeting, see dossier 2, sdr c, "Aide-mémoire pour la séance du 16 juin," and dossier 1, sdr c, letter from Tirard to Daniel Serruys, 29 October 1938.

143. ELSP, 1 SP 52bis, dossier 1, sdr c, letter from Maxime Leroy, November 1938; letter from François Goguel to Seydoux, 13 December 1938; dossier 2, sdr a, "Sénateurs ayant été inscrits à l'Ecole."

144. ELSP, 1 SP 52bis, dossier 1, sdr c, letter from Tirard to Serruys, 29 October 1938.

145. Pétain's speech made clear that the course had a double purpose: to stiffen the nation's resolve in the face of foreign enemies and, on the home front, "to block the advance of subversive doctrines and sowers of disorder." ELSP, 1 SP 62, dossier 1, "Cours sur la Défense Nationale." See also 1 SP 52bis, dossier 1, sdr c, letter from Tirard to Serruys, 29 October 1938; 1 SP 30, dossier 4, Procès-verbal, 23 January 1939.

146. ELSP, 1 SP 52bis, dossier 1, sdr c, letter from Zay to Tirard, 16 January 1939, and letter from Tirard to Zay, 23 January 1939; 1 SP 30, dossier 4, Procès-verbal, 23 January 1939.

147. ELSP, 1 SP 52bis, dossier 1, sdr c, letter from Debré to Seydoux, 13 February 1939; letters from Seydoux to Berthod and Mireaux, 7 February 1939; letter from Seydoux to Bardoux, 24 February 1939.

148. ELSP, 1 SP 52, dossier 4, sdr d. "Exposé des discussions au Ministère de l'Education nationale, 10 février 1939"; 1 SP 30, dossier 4, "Projet de procès-verbal, 5 avril 1939."

149. ELSP, 1 SP 52bis, dossier 1, sdr c, letter from Seydoux to Abraham, 5 August 1939.

150. School authorities, looking back from a postwar perspective, felt that an accord had been "very close." ELSP, 1 SP 66, dossier 4, sdr a, "Relations de l'Ecole et de l'Etat, février 1945."

151. ELSP, 1 SP 30, dossier 4, Procès-verbal, 20 December 1939.

152. ELSP, 1 SP 30, dossier 4, Procès-verbal, 26 June 1935; 1 SP 15, dossier 3, clipping from L'Illustration, 19 January 1935.

153. ELSP, 1 SP 53, dossier 2, sdr f, "Confidentiel no. 6, Observations faites depuis 7 ans, janvier 1936." The dating and the title of the document suggest that René Seydoux was the author. See also 1 SP 52bis, dossier 3, sdr a, clipping from La Flèche, 29 August 1936.

154. ELSP, 1 SP 30, dossier 4, Procès-verbal, 11 October 1937 and 24 June 1938; 1 SP 15, dossier 3, pamphlet, Nos Grandes Ecoles (1932), 114–116; François

Perthuis, *Auguste Detoeuf (1883–1947), l'ingénieur de l'impossible paix* (Paris, 1990), 27; Laroque, *Au Service*, 106.

155. Loïc Blondiaux, *La Fabrique de l'opinion: une histoire sociale des sondages* (Paris, 1998), 293–297; Hélène Riffault, "L'Institut français d'opinion publique, 1938–1978," in Raymond Boudon, François Bourricaud, and Alain Girard, eds., *Science et théorie de l'opinion: Hommage à Jean Stoetzel* (Paris, 1981), 232n.

156. See, in *Sondages*: Pierre Henry, "L'Opinion publique française en face des deux crises de septembre 1938 et de mars 1939" (June 1939): 7–8; Henri Paoletti, "L'Opinion et la crise de la natalité" (July 1939): 9–10; "Enquêtes du juin–juillet 1939" (August 1939), supplement, I–II.

157. The check was never cashed. Blondiaux, *La Fabrique*, 291–292, 373, 454–455.

158. Perthuis, *Detoeuf*, 43; Brun, *Technocrates*, 45; Guillaume de Tarde, "Sur les Nouveaux Cahiers," *Nouveaux Cahiers* (1 March 1938): 13.

159. Simone Weil, "Ne recommençons pas la Guerre de Troie," *Nouveaux Cahiers* (1 April 1937) and (15 April 1937): 8–10, 15–19; A. Detoeuf, "Blasphèmes," *Nouveaux Cahiers* (1 April 1938): 1–4. Needless to say, the *Nouveaux Cahiers* editorial line at the time of the Munich crisis was pro-appeasement. Brun, *Technocrates*, 47.

160. Auguste Detoeuf, "Le Rôle social du patron," *Nouveaux Cahiers* (1 June 1938): 2; Bernard Serampuy [François Goguel], "La Réforme de l'Etat," *Nouveaux Cahiers* (1 February 1939): 14–15.

161. "Le Recrutement et la formation des fonctionnaires," *Nouveaux Cahiers* (15 November 1938): 10–12. The Sciences Po archives contain an offprint of the article: see ELSP, 1 SP 52bis, dossier 3, sdr f.

CHAPTER 2. THE WAR YEARS

1. René Belin, *Du Secrétariat de la C.G.T. au gouvernement de Vichy, Mémoires 1933–1942* (Paris, 1978), 195.

2. Belin, *Du Secrétariat*, 133–134; Pierre Laroque, *Au Service de l'homme et du droit, Souvenirs et réflexions* (Paris, 1993), 125. See also François Bloch-Lainé and Claude Gruson, *Hauts Fonctionnaires sous l'Occupation* (Paris, 1996), 34–35.

3. Laroque, *Au Service*, 125.

4. Richard Kuisel, *Capitalism and the State in Modern France: Renovation and Economic Management in the Twentieth Century* (Cambridge, 1981), 132–144; Dominique Barjot, "Introduction," in Hervé Joly, ed., *Les Comités d'organisation et l'économie dirigée du régime de Vichy* (Caen, 2004), 8.

5. Henry W. Ehrmann, *Organized Business in France* (Princeton, 1957), 76–90; Belin, *Du Secrétariat*, 153; François Perthuis, *Auguste Detoeuf (1883–1947), l'ingénieur de l'impossible paix* (Paris, 1990), 120, 137; Gérard Brun, *Technocrates et technocratie en France, 1918–1945* (Paris, 1985), 171; Olivier Dard, "La Technocratie," in Jean-Pierre Rioux and François Sirinelli, eds., *La France, d'un siècle à l'autre, 1914–2000: Dictionnaire critique* (Paris, 1999), 885.

6. Bloch-Lainé and Gruson, *Hauts Fonctionnaires*, 42–43.

7. Bloch-Lainé and Gruson, *Hauts Fonctionnaires*, 23; Béatrice Touchelay, "L'INSEE, des origines à 1961: évolution et relation avec la réalité économique et sociale" (Thèse de doctorat, University of Paris–XII, 1993), I:72–74.

8. Brun, *Technocrates*, 178. Philippe Mioche's list of Conseil members does not include Davezac or Pirou. See Mioche, *Le Plan Monnet: Genèse et élaboration, 1941–1947* (Paris, 1987), 24–25, 32n31.

9. Kuisel, *Capitalism and the State*, 152.

10. G. Brun, "Histoire d'X-Crise," *X-Crise, de la récurrence des crises économiques, son cinquantenaire, 1931–1981* (Paris, 1981), 34.

11. Once discharged from Vichy service, Lepercq threw himself into Resistance activity. He militated in the OCM, of which he became head in February 1944. Not long thereafter, Lepercq was arrested by the Germans but escaped in time to take part in the armed insurrection that liberated Paris in August 1944. "Aimé Lepercq," http://www.ordredelaliberation.fr/fr_compagnon/594.html, 5 March 2009; Jean-Pierre Azéma, *De Munich à la Libération, 1938–1944* (Paris, 1979), 246.

12. Jacques Le Roy Ladurie, *Mémoires, 1902–1945* (Paris, 1997), 263; Michel Margairaz, *L'Etat, les finances et l'économie: Histoire d'une conversion, 1932–1952* (Paris, 1991), I:510.

13. According to Kuisel, it was not until May 1942 that DGEN was prepared to present its plan to the government: *Capitalism and the State*, 148; see also Mioche, *Le Plan Monnet*, 19–23.

14. Alain Desrosières, Jacques Mairesse, and Michel Volle, "Les temps forts de la statistique française depuis un siècle," in Desrosières, Mairesse, Volle, et al., eds. *Pour une Histoire de la Statistique* (Paris, 1976), I:509. Béatrice Touchelay proposes somewhat different figures. On her account, the number of persons employed at the SNS jumped from roughly 4,300 in 1941 to 8,000 in 1944. See Touchelay, "Les Comités d'organisation, des freins au développement de la statistique industrielle?" in Joly, ed., *Les Comités d'organisation*, 303.

15. Jean-Pierre Azéma, Raymond Lévy-Bruhl, and Béatrice Touchelay, "Mission d'analyse historique sur le système de statistique française de 1940 à 1945" (1998), 24, 61. This is an unpublished report, a copy of which can be found in the INED library. See also Touchelay, "L'INSEE," I:107–113. It was in 1961 that the Ecole d'application changed its name, at the same time opening its doors to students not employed in state service.

16. Alfred Sauvy, *La Vie en plus: Souvenirs* (Paris, 1981), 120; Azéma, Lévy-Bruhl, and Touchelay, "Mission d'analyse," 10.

17. François Fourquet, *Les Comptes de la puissance, histoire de la comptabilité nationale et du plan* (Paris, 1980), 35–38; Michel Volle, *Histoire de la statistique industrielle* (Paris, 1982), 39–40.

18. Jean Monnet, *Memoirs*, tr. Richard Mayne (Garden City, 1978), 233, 242–243.

19. Olivier Dard, "Economie et économistes des années trente aux années cinquante: un tournant keynésien?" *Historiens et géographes*, no. 361 (March–April

1998): 180–181. See also Pierre Rosanvallon, "The Development of Keynesianism in France," in Peter A. Hall, ed., *The Political Power of Economic Ideas: Keynesianism across Nations* (Princeton, 1989), 184.

20. Pierre Uri, "Souvenirs sur François Perroux" (1978), in François Denoël, ed., *François Perroux* (Lausanne, 1990), 169; Pierre Uri, *Penser pour l'action, un fondateur de l'Europe* (Paris, 1991), 34–37.

21. François Perroux and Rémy Prieur (Pierre Uri), *Communauté et société* (Paris, 1941), 1, 6–7, 21, 26, 46. See also Uri, *Penser pour l'action*, 35–36.

22. Dard, "Economie et économistes," 180.

23. Fourquet, *Les Comptes*, 42–43; Antonin Cohen, "De la Révolution Nationale au *Revenu national*: l'économie politique de François Perroux. Aux origines d'un changement de référentiel dans les politiques publiques en 1945," unpublished essay presented at the Séminaire du Centre d'histoire sociale du 20ème siècle (Paris, 13 November 2003), 38.

24. Fourquet, *Les Comptes*, 43–44.

25. Kuisel, *Capitalism and the State*, 153–155; Mioche, *Le Plan Monnet*, 25ff.; idem, "Aux origines du Plan Monnet: les discours et les contenus dans les premiers plans français (1941–1947)," *Revue historique* 265 (April–June 1981): 409–413.

26. When it was first created in June 1943, the CFLN was copresided over by de Gaulle and America's favorite at the time, General Henri Giraud. In a matter of months, however, Giraud had been pushed aside.

27. Kuisel, *Capitalism and the State*, 176–177. See in general on the CNR program Claire Andrieu, *Le Programme commun de la Résistance, des idées dans la guerre* (Paris, 1984), 173.

28. Kuisel, *Capitalism and the State*, 177–178.

29. Mioche, *Le Plan Monnet*, 44–45; Kuisel, *Capitalism and the State*, 191–195.

30. "Cahier III," May 1943, and "Cahier IV," September 1943, in Arthur Calmette, *L'"O.C.M."—Organisation civile et militaire: Histoire d'un mouvement de résistance de 1940 à 1946* (Paris, 1961), 60–62, 163–164.

31. "Cahier III," May 1943, in Calmette, *L'"O.C.M.,"* 60–62; Kuisel, *Capitalism and the State*, 165–167. Blocq-Mascart, Lefaucheux, Lepercq, and Rebeyrol were all listed in late 1943 as belonging to OCM's thirteen-member steering committee. See Calmette, *L'"O.C.M.,"* 155–156.

32. "Lutte pour la Libération," *Chroniques* (January 1941), in Calmette, *L'"O.C.M.,"* 25; "Tableau de la Résistance," *Chroniques* (January 1942), in Calmette, *L'"O.C.M.,"* 28; remarks by Jacques Arthuys cited in Calmette, *L'"O.C.M.,"* 23.

33. "Cahier I," June 1942, in Calmette, *L'"O.C.M.,"* 52–54 and 54n. There is evidence, though, that elements of the wider Resistance, while not sharing in Blocq-Mascart's particular prejudices, did share in his general concern about "a Jewish problem." See Renée Poznanski, *Propagandes et persécutions: La Résistance et le "problème juif," 1940–1944* (Paris, 2008).

34. "Forces en présence," *Chroniques* (1 February 1941), in Calmette, *L'"O.C.M.,"* 26.

35. Jean-Louis Loubet del Bayle, *Les Non-conformistes des années 30, une tentative de renouvellement de la pensée politique française* (Paris, 1969), 417.

36. Diane de Bellescize, *Les Neuf Sages de la Résistance: Le Comité Général d'Etudes dans la clandestinité* (Paris, 1979).

37. Bellescize, *Neuf Sages*, 258.

38. Francis Louis Closon, *Le Temps des passions: De Jean Moulin à la Libération, 1943–1944* (Paris, 1998), 55.

39. Bellescize, *Neuf Sages*, 81–82.

40. Lefaucheux was headed toward the socialist camp but did not get there until later.

41. Laroque, *Au Service*, 130–133, 352; Eric Jabbari, "Pierre Laroque and the Origins of French Social Security, 1934–1948" (Ph.D. dissertation, Oxford University, 2000), 188–189.

42. Bellescize, *Neuf Sages*, 256.

43. For this observation and the Courtin report in general, see Kuisel, *Capitalism and the State*, 168–173.

44. It was published in 1945, although even then the authors were identified as Jacquier-Bruère, the hyphenated noms de guerre of Debré and Monick.

45. Jacquier-Bruère, *Refaire la France: l'effort d'une génération* (Paris, 1945), 111, 122.

46. Michel Debré, *Trois Républiques pour une France: Mémoires* (Paris, 1984), 213.

47. Andrew Shennan, *Rethinking France: Plans for Renewal, 1940–1946* (Oxford, 1989), 71–77, 236–239.

48. Jean Planchais, *Une Histoire politique de l'armée, de de Gaulle à de Gaulle, 1940–1967* (Paris, 1967), 35–44; Marc Olivier Baruch, *Servir l'Etat français: L'Administration en France de 1940 à 1944* (Paris, 1997), 442–443, 580.

49. François Bloch-Lainé and Jean Bouvier, *La France restaurée, 1944–1954: Dialogue sur les choix d'une modernisation* (Paris, 1986), 133. See also Bloch-Lainé and Gruson, *Hauts Fonctionnaires*, 78; Jacques Georges-Picot, *Souvenir d'une longue carrière: de la rue de Rivoli à la Compagnie de Suez, 1920–1971* (Paris, 1993), 183n41.

50. Eric Roussel, *Jean Monnet, 1888–1979* (Paris, 1996), 293–357.

51. Monnet, *Memoirs*, 209–210; Etienne Hirsch, *Ainsi va la vie* (Lausanne, 1988), 58–59.

52. Monnet, *Memoirs*, 228.

53. François Le Douarec, *Félix Gaillard, 1919–1970: un destin inachevé* (Paris, 1991), 11–14.

54. Roselyne Chenu, *Paul Delouvrier ou la passion d'agir* (Paris, 1994), 41–43, 74–76, 79.

55. Hirsch, *Ainsi*, 92, See also Monnet, *Memoirs*, 242–243; Margairaz, *L'Etat*, II:815.

56. Fourquet, *Les Comptes*, 45. See also Monnet, *Memoirs*, 243.

57. Gravier as cited in Monnet, *Memoirs*, 241–242; Jean Fourastié, *Jean Fourastié entre deux mondes: mémoires en forme de dialogues avec sa fille Jacqueline* (Paris, 1994), 50; Bloch-Lainé and Bouvier, *La France restaurée*, 139.

58. Olivier Dard, "Fourastié avant Fourastié: la construction d'une légitimité d'expert," *French Politics, Culture & Society* 22 (Spring 2004): 2–3, 5, 8, 11; Bernard

Marchand, "La haine de la ville: Paris et le désert français de Jean-François Gravier," *L'Information géographique*, no. 3 (2001), 244.

59. Mioche, *Le Plan Monnet*, 92–93.

60. Cited in Bruno Valat, "Résistance et Sécurité sociale, 1941–1944," 11, ms communicated by Valat to the author. The text exists in published form in the *Revue historique*, no. 592 (October–December 1994). See also Paul V. Dutton, *Origins of the French Welfare State: The Struggle for Social Reform in France, 1914–1947* (Cambridge, 2002), 208.

61. Valat, "Résistance et Sécurité sociale," 11; Bruno Palier, *Gouverner la Sécurité sociale: les réformes du système français de protection sociale depuis 1945* (Paris, 2002), 71. See also Jabbari, "Pierre Laroque," 9.

62. Cited in Julian Jackson, *France: The Dark Years, 1940–1944* (Oxford, 2001), 327.

63. Jean-Pierre Le Crom, "Les Idées de la Résistance," in Philippe-Jean Hesse and Le Crom, eds., *La Protection sociale sous le régime de Vichy* (Rennes, 2001), 338; Dutton, *Origins*, 192–193. Le Crom makes the case that Laroque's role in the elaboration of the project was peripheral.

64. Dutton, *Origins*, 180–181.

65. Hesse and Le Crom, "Conclusion," in Hesse and Le Crom, eds., *La Protection sociale*, 358–359; Dutton, *Origins*, 199.

66. Paul Haury, "Vers la coordination des forces familiales," *Revue de l'Alliance nationale contre la dépopulation* (November–December 1940): 139.

67. "Principales dispositions," *Revue de l'Alliance nationale contre la dépopulation* (September 1941): 10.

68. Paul-André Rosental, *L'Intelligence démographique: Sciences et politiques des populations en France (1930–1960)* (Paris, 2003), 60–68.

69. "Action de l'alliance nationale," *Revue de l'Alliance nationale contre la dépopulation* (January–February 1941): 203; "Assemblée générale du 18 november 1944," *Revue de l'Alliance nationale contre la dépopulation* (June–December 1944): 38; Rosental, *L'Intelligence démographique*, 60–61.

70. P. Lefebvre-Dibon, "Progrès: Ayons confiance et redoublons d'efforts," *Revue de l'Alliance nationale contre la dépopulation* (July–August 1941): 249–252. See also "La journée des mères (25 mai 1941)," *Revue de l'Alliance nationale contre la dépopulation* (July–August 1941): 261–262; and Miranda Pollard, *Reign of Virtue: Mobilizing Gender in Vichy France* (Chicago, 1998), 48.

71. The name change was significant. Nonworking mothers were no longer the sole recipients of the benefit. Now, certain categories of working mothers—wives of POWs and later of STO conscripts—were also entitled to assistance.

72. "La lutte contre l'alcoolisme," *Revue de l'Alliance nationale contre la dépopulation* (September–October 1940): 124; "Lois relatives à la famille," *Revue de l'Alliance nationale contre la dépopulation* (March–April 1941): 235–236; "L'organisation de l'enseignement démographique et familial," *Revue de l'Alliance nationale contre la dépopulation* (July 1943): 104. See also Rosental, *L'Intelligence démographique*, 65.

73. Paul-Marie Romani, untitled communication, presented at Colloque international: Adolphe Landry. Economiste, démographe, législateur: 1874–1956, Université de Corse, 3–6 septembre 1997, 4.

74. Francine Muel-Dreyfus, *Vichy et l'éternel féminin* (Paris, 1996), chs. 2, 5.

75. See two essays by Cheryl Koos: "Gender, Anti-individualism, and Nationalism: The Alliance Nationale and the Pronatalist Backlash against the *Femme moderne,* 1933–1940," *French Historical Studies* 19 (Spring 1996): 699–723; "'On les aura!' The Gendered Politics of Abortion and the Alliance Nationale contre la Dépopulation, 1938–1944," *Modern and Contemporary France* 7 (February 1999): 21–33.

76. Touchelay, "L'INSEE," I:60–61, 85; Azéma, Lévy-Bruhl, and Touchelay, "Mission d'analyse," 60; Michel Volle, "Naissance," in Desroisières, Mairesse, Volle, et al., *Pour une Histoire,* 347–349.

77. Azéma, Lévy-Bruhl, and Touchelay, "Mission d'analyse," 15–16, 19–20, 50–51, 53–56.

78. Volle, "Naissance," in Desrosières, Mairesse, and Touchelay, *Pour une Histoire,* 348–349; Touchelay, "L'INSEE," I:38; Azéma, Lévy-Bruhl, and Touchelay, "Mission d'analyse," 15, 44–46. For the earliest uses of the term "Vichysto-résistant," see Azéma et al. and also Laurent Douzou and Denis Peschanski, "La Résistance française face à l'hypothèque Vichy," in David Bidussa and Denis Peschanski, eds., *La France de Vichy: Archives inédits d'Angelo Tasca* (Milan, 1996), 27. An entire, rather substantial book has now been devoted to the subject. See Bénédicte Vergez-Chaignon, *Les Vichysto-Résistants, de 1940 à nos jours* (Paris, 2008).

79. Touchelay, "L'INSEE," I:126, 169; Azéma, Lévy-Bruhl, and Touchelay, "Mission d'analyse," 35–36.

80. *Cahiers de la Fondation française pour l'étude des problèmes humains,* I (1943), 44.

81. André Missenard, "Sombres souvenirs: La vérité sur le séjour d'Alexis Carrel en France de 1941 à 1944," *Journal de Médecine de Lyon* (June 1980): 404; Carrel Papers, Georgetown University, box 40, 14-1, folder 3, letter from Carrel to Guigou, 8 June 1941.

82. Alain Drouard, *Une Inconnue des sciences sociales: la Fondation Alexis Carrel, 1941–1945* (Paris, 1992), 146; idem, "Les trois âges de la Fondation française pour l'étude des problèmes humains," *Population* 38 (November–December 1983): 1026.

83. Carrel Papers, Georgetown University, box 43, folder 27, letter from Carrel to Katherine Crutcher, 19 January 1942.

84. Carrel Papers, Georgetown University, box 43, folder 27, letter from Katherine Crutcher to Mr. Coudert, 31 May 1944.

85. Carrel Papers, Georgetown University, box 40, 14-1, folder 3, letters from Carrel to Guigou, 31 August 1943, 12 December 1943, 31 December 1943.

86. Carrel Papers, Georgetown University, box 40, 14-1, folder 3, letter from Carrel to Guigou, 31 December 1943.

87. Robert Soupault, *Alexis Carrel, 1873–1944* (Paris, 1952), 235, 249.

88. Carrel Papers, Georgetown University, box 40, 14-1, folder 3, letter from Carrel to Guigou, 28 April 1944; and Soupault, *Carrel,* 250.

89. Missenard, "Sombres souvenirs," 404.

90. Carrel Papers, Georgetown University, box 40, 14-1, folder 3, letters from Carrel to Guigou, 15 April and 4 May 1944.

91. Drouard, *Une Inconnue*, 223–225; Anne Carol, *Histoire de l'eugénisme en France: Les médecins et la procréation, XIXe–XXe siècle* (Paris, 1995), 347–349.

92. Drouard, *Une Inconnue*, 188–190; 229–231, 232–233. See also Rosental and Isabelle Couzon, "Le Paris dangereux de Louis Chevalier: un projet d'histoire utile. *Classes laborieuses et classes dangereuses* (1958)," in Bernard Lepetit and Christian Topalov, eds., *La Ville des sciences sociales* (Paris, 2001), 197–198.

93. Andrés Horacio Reggiani, "Birthing the French Welfare State: Political Crises, Population and Public Health, 1914–1960" (Ph.D. dissertation, SUNY–Stony Brook, 1998), 300; Drouard, *Une Inconnue*, 225, 238; Rosental, *L'Intelligence démographique*, 201; Jean Bourgeois, "Evolution de la population française de 1939 à la fin de 1944," *Cahiers de la Fondation française pour l'étude des problèmes humains*, IV (November 1945), 118.

94. Drouard, *Une Inconnue*, 257–258; Jean-Jacques Gillon, "La fondation française pour l'étude des problèmes humains," in Raymond Boudon, François Bourricaud, and Alain Girard, eds., *Science et théorie de l'opinion: Hommage à Jean Stoetzel* (Paris, 1981), 257.

95. Jean Stoetzel, *Théorie des opinions* (Paris, 1943), 385, 388–389, 392–394.

96. Reggiani, "Birthing," 292; Drouard, *Une Inconnue*, 248, 251–253; *Cahiers de la Fondation française pour l'étude des problèmes humains*, II (March 1944), 63, 118; Le Crom, *Syndicats, nous voilà! Vichy et le corporatisme* (Paris, 1995), 348–350.

97. Reggiani, "Birthing," 297.

98. ELSP, 1 SP 67, sdr a, "No. 322, Proposition de Résolution," 2, 4, 6, 11, 15.

99. See Philip's preface to André Ferrat's *La République à refaire*, 3rd ed. (Paris, 1945); Olivier Feiertag, "Wilfrid Baumgartner, les finances de l'Etat et l'économie de la Nation, 1902–1978" (Thèse de doctorat, University of Paris–X, 1996), I:259.

100. ELSP, 1 SP 30, dossier 4, Procès-verbal, 15 November 1940.

101. ELSP, 1 SP 66, dossier 1, "Entretien téléphonique de M. Seydoux avec M. Epting," 29 August 1940; "Note pour Monsieur le Maréchal Pétain," 23 August [1940], "non-envoyée"; 1 SP 30, dossier 4, Procès-verbal, 15 November 1940.

102. ELSP, 1 SP 66, dossier 1, "Visite à M. Mireaux, Ministre de l'Education Nationale," 4 September 1940; 1 SP 62, dossier 3, "Bulletin 1940–41," 11.

103. Philippe Burrin, *La France à l'heure allemande, 1940–1944* (Paris, 1995), 313; ELSP, 1 SP 30, dossier 4, Procès-verbal, 15 November 1940; Feiertag, "Wilfrid Baumgartner," I:248; ELSP, 1 SP 67, dossier 1, sdr a, "Note sur la Proposition de Résolution no. 332."

104. ELSP, 1 SP 62, dossier 3, "Bulletin 1940–1941," 11; 1 SP 67, dossier 1, sdr a, "Note sur la Proposition de Résolution no. 322."

105. ELSP, 1 SP 62, dossier 3, "Bulletin 1941–1942," 15; 1 SP 30, dossier 4, Procès-verbal, 10 March 1942 and 17 July 1942; 1 SP 31, Procès-verbal, 26 November 1943. See also Margairaz, *L'Etat*, I:535.

106. ELSP, 1 SP 30, dossier 4, Procès-verbal, 26 December 1940. Seydoux's growing responsibilities were acknowledged in a series of title changes. He had been promoted to sous-directeur in 1938 and then in 1942 to directeur, plain and simple. See 1 SP 30, dossier 4, Procès-verbal, 12 November 1942.

107. ELSP, 1 SP 66, dossier 1, "Note sur la réorganisation de l'Ecole, nd [1940?]; 1 SP 30, dossier 4, Procès-verbal, 15 November and 26 December 1940.

108. ELSP, 1 SP, dossier 4, Procès-verbal, 17 July 1941; 1 SP 66, dossier 4, sdr a, "Note sur les principales transformations apportées à l'Ecole des Sciences Politique depuis 1940," November–December 1943; dossier 6, sdr b, "Convention entre l'Université de Paris et l'Ecole Libre des Sciences Politiques," nd.

109. ELSP, 1 SP 30, dossier 4, Procès-verbal, 15 November and 10 March 1942; 1 SP 62, dossier 2, text of Borotra conference, 23 March 1942; dossier 3, "Bulletin 1941–1942," 15.

110. Gérard Vincent, *Sciences Po: Histoire d'une réussite* (Paris, 1987), 313; ELSP, 1 SP 30, dossier 4, Procès-verbal, 19 March and 4 November 1941.

111. ELSP, 1 SP 30, dossier 4, Procès-verbal, 15 November 1940, 4 November 1941, and 12 November 1942.

112. ELSP, 1 SP 64, dossier 5, polycopy, A. Siegfried, "Les Etats-Unis et la Civilisation Américaine," 1941–1942.

113. Lucette Le Van-Lemesle, *Le Juste ou le Riche: L'Enseignement de l'économie politique, 1815–1950* (Paris, 2004), 637; ELSP 1 SP 63, dossier 4, Gaëtan Pirou, "Economie libérale et économie dirigée," 1942–1943.

114. Roger Seydoux, "L'Ecole des Sciences Politiques" (1976), and Yves Mainguy, "Le création de l'I.S.E.A." (1974), in Denoël, ed., *Perroux*, 174, 175.

115. François Denord, "Genèse et institutionalisation du néo-libéralisme en France (années 1930–années 1950)" (Thèse de doctorat, EHESS, 2003), 288–303; Brun, *Technocrates*, 56–57. The Comité d'études et d'informations had begun as an independent organization but fused with the Comite d'études pour la France in 1943.

116. Denord, "Genèse," 294–295; Brun, *Technocrates*, 178.

117. Pierre Birnbaum, *"La France aux français": histoire des haines nationalistes* (Paris, 1963), 160; Bellescize, *Neuf Sages*, 33; Richard Kuisel, *Ernest Mercier, French Technocrat* (Berkeley and Los Angeles, 1967), 150.

118. Birnbaum, *"La France aux français"*, 165–166; Jean Lacouture, "La Mort de Roger Seydoux," *Le Monde*, 12 July 1985; Jean Chauvel, *Commentaire, de Vienne à Alger, 1938–1944* (Paris, 1971), I:302.

119. ELSP, 1 SP 30, dossier 4, Procès-verbal, 17 July 1942.

120. ELSP, 1 SP 66, dossier 4, sdr a, "Note sur l'attitude politique de l'Ecole depuis 1940." The document, although not dated, was written after the Liberation. See also 1 SP 67, dossier 1, sdr a, "Note sur la Proposition de Résolution no. 322," and 1 SP 66, dossier Affaire Bonnard, "Entretien de M. Abel Bonnard et de M. Roger Seydoux," 18 May 1943.

121. Philippe Viannay, *Du Bon Usage de la France: Résistance, journalisme, glénans* (Paris, 1988), 39, 85. In parliamentary debate in June 1945, Viannay made the claim that the relationship with Seydoux and the forged-papers operation had begun earlier, in 1942. See Jean-François Kesler, *L'ENA, la société, l'Etat* (Paris, 1985), 32.

122. The receipt worked its wonders at the Liberation, keeping the otherwise compromised Prouvost out of trouble. In 1949, he went on to found postwar France's most successful photo magazine, *Paris-Match*.

123. Lacouture, "La Mort de Roger Seydoux," *Le Monde*, 12 July 1985; Debré, *Trois Républiques*, 218–219, 221–223, 248–250.

124. Guy Thuillier, "Les projets d'Ecole d'administration," *La Revue administrative* 177 (1977): 252; ELSP, 1 SP 66, dossier 4, sdr a, "Note sur l'attitude politique de l'Ecole depuis 1940."

125. Claude Bellanger et al., *Histoire générale de la presse française* (Paris, 1975), IV:115; Henri Michel, *Les Courants de pensée de la Résistance* (Paris, 1962), 448; Viannay, *Du Bon Usage*, 50, 82.

126. Robert Tennaille (Robert Salmon), "Vers la Révolution," *Cahiers de Défense de la France* (March 1944), and Ph. Viannay, "Le combat pour une cité libre," *Cahiers de Défense de la France* (January 1944). Both articles are reproduced in Henri Michel and Boris Mirkine-Goutzévich, *Les Idées politiques et sociales de la Résistance* (Paris, 1954), 155–158, 209–211. See also *Défense de la France* (20 May 1943), as cited in Brun, *Technocrates*, 246.

127. ELSP, 1 SP 66, dossier 7, sdr a, "Entretien du 22 septembre 1944 avec MM Joxe, Hoffherr, Ségalat, Chatenet."

128. ELSP, 1 SP 66, dossier 4, sdr c, letter to Louis Joxe, 24 November 1944. The author is not identified, but it was in all likelihood Chapsal. See also 1 SP 67, dossier 1, sdr a, letter from Siegfried to Cogniot, 23 February 1945.

129. ELSP, 1 SP 31, dossier 1, Procès-verbal, 2 January and 6 February 1945, morning and afternoon sessions.

130. On Duhamel at the Académie française, see Gisèle Sapiro, *La Guerre des écrivains, 1940–1953* (Paris, 1999), ch. 4.

131. See Jean Touchard, "L'Esprit des années trente: une tentative de renouvellement de la pensée politique française," *Tendances politiques dans la vie française depuis 1789* (Paris, 1960), 89–118.

Chapter 3. The Liberation Moment

1. See Claire Andrieu, "Comment la nationalisation entra dans le programme du CNR?" in Andrieu, Lucette Le Van, and Antoine Prost, *Les Nationalisations de la Libération* (Paris, 1987), 60–61, and the volume's concluding remarks, 362.

2. Bruno Palier, *Gouverner la Sécurité sociale: les réformes du système français de protection sociale depuis 1945* (Paris, 2002), 88. Palier himself does not subscribe to this line of interpretation.

3. Gøsta Esping-Andersen, *The Three Worlds of Welfare Capitalism* (Princeton, 1990), 27, 112, 122–124; Palier, *Gouverner*, 7.

4. Jean-Luc Bodiguel, *Les Anciens Elèves de l'ENA* (Paris, 1978), 30.

5. Christophe Charle, "Savoir durer: la nationalisation de Sciences-Po, 1936/ 1945," *Actes de la Recherche en sciences sociales*, nos. 86–87 (March 1991): 99–105.

6. Philippe Mioche, *Le Plan Monnet: Genèse et élaboration, 1941–1947* (Paris, 1987), 90.

7. Richard Kuisel, *Capitalism and the State in Modern France: Renovation and Economic Management in the Twentieth Century* (Cambridge, 1981), 196–197.

8. Kuisel, *Capitalism and the State*, 229; Michel Margairaz, *L'Etat, les finances et l'économie: Histoire d'une conversion, 1932–1952* (Paris, 1991), II:826–827.

9. "Décret du 14 juin 1946 organisant l'I.N.S.E.E.," *Economie et Statistique*, no. 24, supplement (June 1971), ii.

10. Francis Louis Closon, *Le Temps des passions: De Jean Moulin à la Libération, 1943–1944* (Paris, 1998), 144.

11. Béatrice Touchelay, "L'INSEE, des origines à 1961: évolution et relation avec la réalité économique et sociale" (Thèse de doctorat, University of Paris–XII, 1993), I:207–208, 299, 303, 332.

12. Michel Volle, *Histoire de la statistique industrielle* (Paris, 1982), 46–48; idem, "Naissance," in Alain Desrosières, Jacques Mairesse, Michel Volle, et al., *Pour une Histoire de la statistique* (Paris, 1977), I:356–361; Touchelay, "INSEE," II:448.

13. Mioche, *Plan Monnet*, 89.

14. Margairaz, *L'Etat*, II:835.

15. Irwin M. Wall, *The United States and the Making of Postwar France, 1945–1954* (Cambridge, 1991), 55; Kuisel, *Capitalism and the State*, 231–232.

16. Hirsch, as cited in Kuisel, *Capitalism and the State*, 226; Isabel Boussard, "L'agriculture française—options et résultats," presented at La France en voie de modernisation, 1944–1952, colloque des 4 et 5 décembre 1981 (Paris, 1981), I:28. The proceedings of this colloquium, held under the auspices of the Fondation nationale des sciences politiques, were never published. The papers presented, including Boussard's, were bound in two typescript volumes that can be found at the library of the Institut d'études politiques de Paris.

17. Jean Monnet, *Memoirs*, tr. Richard Mayne (Garden City, 1978), 258–259.

18. Kuisel, *Capitalism and the State*, 230, 235; Mioche, *Plan Monnet*, 102.

19. Monnet, *Memoirs*, 240, 245; Henry W. Ehrmann, *Organized Business in France* (Princeton, 1957), 285; Mioche, *Plan Monnet*, 103.

20. For Gingembre, see Ehrmann, *Organized Business*, 172.

21. Gérard Brun, *Technocrates et technocratie en France, 1914–1945* (Paris, 1985), 168.

22. Mioche, *Plan Monnet*, 103.

23. Henry Rousso has made the same observation, not so much about the Conseil du Plan as in a more general way about the senior ranks of France's postwar economic administration. See Rousso, "Le Ministère de l'Industrie dans le processus de planification: une adaptation difficile (1940–1969)," in Rousso, ed., *De Monnet à Massé: enjeux politiques et objectifs économiques dans le cadre des quatre premiers plans (1946–1965). Actes de la Table Ronde tenue à l'IHTP les 24 et 25 juin 1983* (Paris, 1986), 28; and idem, "Les paradoxes de Vichy et de l'Occupation. Contraintes, archaïsmes et modernités," in Patrick Fridenson and André Straus, eds., *Le Capitalisme français, 19e–20 siècle: Blocages et dynamismes d'une croissance* (Paris, 1987), 79.

24. Claude Gruson, *Origine et espoirs de la planification française* (Paris, 1968), 39.

25. As of 1941, just 91 COs existed, but the number shot up in the years following, reaching 234 by the Occupation's end. Ehrmann, *Organized Business*, 87.

26. Philippe Mioche, "Planification et industrie du pétrole, 1946–1952: le cas d'une Commission de modernisation," presented at La France en voie de modernisation, I:10–11, 21; Michel Margairaz, "La mise en place de l'appareil de di-

rection économique (1944–1947): des objectifs lointains aux choix du moment," presented at ibid., I:25.

27. Mioche, "Planification et industrie du pétrole," I:11.

28. Henry Rousso, "Les élites économiques dans les années quarante," *Mélanges de l'Ecole française de Rome* 95 (1983-2): 39–40.

29. The seven Commissions in question are those for the six *secteurs de base*, plus the Commission des carburants. Mioche, *Plan Monnet*, 210.

30. Monnet, as cited in François Fourquet, *Les Comptes de la puissance: histoire de la comptabilité nationale et du plan* (Paris, 1980), 57; Etienne Hirsch, *Ainsi va la vie* (Lausanne, 1988), 93.

31. Monnet, *Memoirs*, 225.

32. Mioche, *Plan Monnet*, 210.

33. Margairaz, *Etat*, II:1204–1205; Jean Fourastié, *Jean Fourastié entre deux mondes: mémoires en forme de dialogues avec sa fille Jacqueline* (Paris, 1994), 99; Richard Kuisel, *Seducing the French: The Dilemma of Americanization* (Berkeley and Los Angeles, 1993), 73.

34. Anthony Rowley, "Les missions de productivité aux Etats-Unis," presented at La France en voie de modernisation, I:8; Kuisel, *Seducing the French*, ch. 4. In the period 1950–1953, an estimated 450 missions made the trek across the Atlantic. Luc Boltanski, "America, America…le Plan Marshall et l'importation du 'management,'" *Actes de la Recherche en sciences sociales*, no. 38 (May 1981): 21.

35. Rowley, "Les missions de productivité," 11; Boltanski, "America, America," 21.

36. See Margairaz's magisterial *Etat*; and Fourquet, *Comptes*.

37. Gérard Destanne de Bernis, "La Dynamique de François Perroux" (1977), in François Denoël, ed., *François Perroux* (Lausanne, 1990), 113; Yves Mainguy, "La Création de l'I.S.E.A." (1974), in ibid., 178; Fourquet, *Comptes*, 67, 67n, 68.

38. Monnet, *Memoirs*, 262; Kuisel, *Capitalism and the State*, 238.

39. Bloch-Lainé, cited in Fourquet, *Comptes*, 100.

40. Claude Gruson, *Programmer l'espérance: Conversations avec Philippe Dominique* (Paris, 1976), 66–68; Fourquet, *Comptes*, 100.

41. Gruson, *Programmer*, 87–88; Kuisel, *State and Capitalism*, 240–242.

42. Fourquet, *Comptes*, 78, 105–106, 109, 115–116.

43. Gruson, *Programmer*, 75; Blanc, cited in Fourquet, *Comptes*, 186.

44. Pierre Bitoun, *Les Hommes d'Uriage* (Paris, 1988), 104, 156–158.

45. Fourquet, *Comptes*, 107, 129–133; Gruson, *Programmer*, 147–149.

46. Gruson, *Programmer*, 70.

47. François Bloch-Lainé, *Profession: fonctionnaire. Entretiens avec Françoise Carrière* (Paris, 1976), 75.

48. Palier, *Gouverner*, 90–91, 162.

49. Bruno Valat, *Histoire de la Sécurité sociale (1945–1967): l'Etat, l'institution et la santé* (Paris, 2001), 74.

50. Eric Jabbari, "Pierre Laroque and the Origins of French Social Security, 1934–1948" (Ph.D. dissertation, Oxford University, 2000), 220.

51. François-Xavier Merrien, "Etats-providence: l'empreinte des origines," *Revue française des affaires sociales*, no. 3 (July–September 1990): 52–54.

52. "Assemblée générale du 18 novembre 1944," *Revue de l'Alliance nationale contre la dépopulation* (June–December 1944): 35; "Activité de l'Alliance nationale," *Revue de l'Alliance nationale contre la dépopulation* (April–June 1945): 26.

53. "La Vie de l'Alliance nationale," *Vitalité française* (July–August 1945): 17; "La famille nombreuse, est-elle un risque?" *Vitalité française* (November–December 1945): 56; Pierre Laroque, *Au Service de l'homme et du droit: Souvenirs et réflexions* (Paris, 1993), 214; Valat, *Histoire de la Sécurité sociale*, 77–78.

54. Valat, *Histoire de la Sécurité sociale*, 104, 108; Laroque, *Au Service*, 216.

55. Valat, *Histoire de la Sécurité sociale*, 55, 84, Paul V. Dutton, *Origins of the French Welfare State: The Struggle for Social Reform in France, 1914–1947* (Cambridge, 2002), 213–214.

56. Jean-Marie Mayeur, *Des Partis catholiques à la démocratie chrétienne, XIXe–XXe siècles* (Paris, 1980), 162, 167.

57. Jabbari, "Pierre Laroque," 256–257.

58. Jabbari, "Pierre Laroque," 243; Andrés Horacio Reggiani, "Birthing the French Welfare State: Political Crises, Population, and Public Health, 1914–1960" (Ph.D. dissertation, SUNY–Stony Brook, 1998), 9.

59. Peter Baldwin, *The Politics of Social Solidarity: Class Bases of the European Welfare State, 1875–1975* (Cambridge, 1990), 167–171.

60. Baldwin, *Politics of Social Solidarity*, 175–186: Palier, *Gouverner*, 109.

61. On Bacon and Doublet, see Valat, *Histoire de la Sécurité sociale*, 36, 177–178; Laroque, *Au Service*, 244–245; Alain Girard, *L'Institut national d'études démographiques: histoire et développement* (Paris, 1986), 139–140.

62. Closon, *Le Temps des passions*, 222, 234.

63. Michel Lévy, *Alfred Sauvy: compagnon du siècle* (Paris, 1990), 91; Alfred Sauvy, *La Vie en plus: Souvenirs* (Paris, 1981), 126, 128–129; Paul-André Rosental, *L'Intelligence démographique: sciences et politiques des populations en France (1930–1960)* (Paris, 2003), 89, 91, 113.

64. "Notre cinquantenaire à Paris," *Vitalité française* (November–December 1946): 204–205. The Compagnons de la Musique are known to American audiences under another name, the Compagnons de la Chanson. They accompanied Edith Piaf to the United States when she made her debut there in 1947.

65. "Les Compagnons de la Chanson," http://www.rifmusique.com/siteen/biographie/biographie_6216.asp, 19 October 2007.

66. Robert Debré, *L'Honneur de vivre* (Paris, 1974), 399.

67. "Lu au 'Journal Officiel,'" *Revue de l'Alliance nationale contre la dépopulation* (April–June 1945): 31–32, Rosental, *L'Intelligence démographique*, 95–100.

68. See Patrick Weil, "Georges Mauco: un itinéraire camouflé: ethnoracisme pratique et antisémitisme fielleux," in Pierre-André Taguieff, ed., *L'Antisémitisme de plume, 1940–1944, études et documents* (Paris, 1999), 267–273; K. H. Adler, *Jews and Gender in Liberation France* (Cambridge, 2003), ch. 5.

69. Weil, "Georges Mauco," 274–275.

70. Robert Debré and Alfred Sauvy, *Des Français pour la France* (Paris, 1946), 93, 230.

71. Weil, "Georges Mauco," 273–276; idem, "Racisme et discrimination dans la politique française de l'immigration: 1938–1945/1974–1995," *Vingtième siècle,*

no. 47 (July–September 1995): 77–102; Rosental, *L'Intelligence démographique*, 108.

72. Yvonne Knibiehler, "La Famille," in Jean-Pierre Rioux and Jean-François Sirinelli, eds., *La France, d'un siècle à l'autre, 1914–2000: Dictionnaire critique* (Paris, 1999), 228.

73. "Sombres souvenirs: La vérité sur le séjour d'Alexis Carrel en France de 1941 à 1944," *Journal de Médecine de Lyon* (June 1980): 407.

74. Alain Drouard, *Une Inconnue des sciences sociales: la Fondation Alexis Carrel, 1941–1945* (Paris, 1992), 179–180; Reggiani, "Birthing," 370.

75. Lévy, *Alfred Sauvy*, 80–82, 120; Sauvy, *Vie*, 127, 129; Girard, *L'Institut national d'études démographiques*, 159.

76. For the list of Comité technique members, see *Population: Revue trimestrielle de l'Institut national d'études scientifiques*, 1 (January–March 1946): front matter; see also Rosental, *L'Intelligence démographique*, 144–145.

77. Girard, *L'Institut national d'études démographiques*, 73.

78. See the avant-propos by Henri Leridan, Drouard, *Une Inconnue*, xx; Jacques Dupâquier, *Histoire de la Population française* (Paris, 1988), IV:25.

79. Sauvy, *Vie*, 130.

80. Dupâquier, *Histoire*, IV:25; Hervé Le Bras, *Marianne et les lapins: L'obsession démographique* (Paris, 1991), 235.

81. Rosental, *Intelligence démographique*, 134–135.

82. Girard, *L'Institut national d'études démographiques*, 147–148; Lévy, *Alfred Sauvy*, 154.

83. Sauvy, *De Paul Reynaud à Charles de Gaulle: un économiste face aux hommes politiques, 1934–1967* (Tournai, 1972), 178.

84. Debré and Sauvy, *Français*, 127.

85. Le Corbusier, "Habitation Moderne," *Population* 3 (July–September 1948): 417–418, 423.

86. Rosental, *Intelligence démographique*, 163–164.

87. Alain Girard, "Sondages et démographie," *Population* 1 (April–June 1946): 277–278; Rosental, *Intelligence démographique*, 164; Drouard, "Les trois âges de la Fondation française pour l'étude des problèmes humains," *Population* 38 (November–December): 1032–1033.

88. When the Plozévet findings were at last published in 1975, Gessain penned an introduction in which he cited with approval Carrel's research example. André Burguière, *Bretons de Plozévet* (Paris, 1975), 7, 12.

89. Burguière, *Bretons*, 326.

90. Edgar Morin, *Commune en France: la métamorphose de Plodement* (Paris, 1967), ch. 11. The book was later reprinted under the title *La Métamorphose de Plozévet: une commune en France* (Paris, 1984). Morin's archaism/modernity binary had a long and productive career ahead of it. See the works of Maurice Agulhon, *La République au village: les populations du Var de la Révolution à la Seconde République* (Paris, 1970); and Alain Corbin, *Archaïsme et modernité en Limousin au XIXe siècle, 1845–1880* (Paris, 1975).

91. Burguière, *Bretons*, 312–320.

92. Rosental, *Intelligence démographique*, 200–201; Girard, *L'Institut national*

d'études démographiques, 128, 132, and 132n; Lévy, *Alfred Sauvy*, 112; Hélène Ber-
gues et al., *La Prévention des naissances dans la famille: Ses origines dans les temps
modernes* (Paris, 1960).

93. See Rosental, *Intelligence démographique*, 233–236; and for a discussion
from a global perspective, Matthew Connelly, *Fatal Misconception: The Struggle to
Control World Population* (Cambridge, MA, 2008).

94. Jean Fourastié, *Les Trente glorieuses: ou, la révolution invisible de 1946 à 1975*
(Paris, 1979); Alfred Sauvy, "Trois mondes, une planète," *L'Observateur*, no. 118
(14 August 1952): 14. Sauvy's article was an enlightened man's call to arms. Communists and capitalists were in competition for the allegiance of the developing
world. Overpopulation had made this third world a veritable powder keg, primed
to explode. The *Tiers Monde*, like the *Tiers Etat* of France's own revolutionary
past, now counted for little, but it wanted to count for something. It was up to the
first world, the West, to take heed. Answer the third world's development needs
or face an upheaval that would profit the communists. Sauvy had little faith that
the United States, wrapped up in Cold War paranoia and mesmerized by free-
market shibboleths, would answer the call, but perhaps there were others in the
first world who might step forward.

95. Touchelay, "INSEE," I:276–277.

96. Desrosières, "Eléments pour l'histoire des nomenclatures socio-profession-
nelles," in Desrosières, Mairesse, Volle, et al., *Pour une Histoire*, I:173–174.

97. Desrosières, "Eléments," I:184.

98. Alain Desrosières, Jacques Mairesse, and Michel Volle, "Les temps forts,"
in Desrosières, Mairesse, Volle, et al., *Pour une Histoire*, I:515; and Desrosières,
"Eléments," I: 181–182.

99. See Graham Burchell, Colin Gordon, and Peter Miller, eds., *The Foucault
Effect* (London, 1991), ch. 4.

100. Remi Lenoir, *Généalogie de la morale familiale* (Paris, 2003), 344, 354, 363;
Rosental, *Intelligence démographique*, 68.

101. ELSP, 1 SP 66, dossier 4, sdr a, "Note sur l'attitude politique de l'Ecole
depuis 1940," nd. The document does not identify the eight ministers in question.

102. ELSP, 1 SP 67, dossier 3, sdr a, "Procédure et Marche du Projet, 7 juin
1945." See also Michel Debré, *Trois Républiques pour une France: Mémoires* (Paris,
1984), 346, 376; Marie-Christine Kessler, *La Politique de la haute fonction publique*
(Paris, 1978), 37. The sources disagree about the timing of these events. Kessler
dates Debré's appointment to 28 April. Debré himself is less precise, citing a mid-
March date. According to Sciences Po documentation, the date was 5 April. Kessler and Sciences Po sources agree that the interministerial committee convened
on 4 June, but Debré remembers it as 28 May. As for the general cabinet meeting, Kessler does not mention it. Debré says it took place on 6 June, but a Sciences Po document puts it on 8 June. I have followed the Sciences Po documentation.

103. Jean-Marcel Jeanneney was also an old friend of Debré's. Debré, *Trois
Républiques*, 86; Olivier Feiertag, "Wilfrid Baumgartner, les finances de l'Etat et
l'économie de la Nation, 1902–1978" (Thèse de doctorat, University of Paris–X,

1996) I:146. There was some question that the younger Jeanneney might teach at Sciences Po in 1945–1946, but he turned down the opportunity, explaining that he might be of more use to the school as his father's directeur de cabinet. ELSP 1 SP 67, dossier 2, sdr b, letter from Chapsal to Seydoux, 14 April 1945.

104. ELSP 1 SP 67, dossier 1, sdr a, "Note sur la Proposition de Résolution no. 322," 9, 12.

105. ELSP 1 SP 67, dossier 1, sdr a, "Envoi de la lettre Cogniot," and circular letter from Siegfried dated 16 April 1945. A second round of letters was sent out in mid-June. See 1 SP 67, dossier 4.

106. ELSP 1 SP 67, dossier 2, sdr b, letter from Chapsal to Seydoux, 14 April 1945.

107. Viannay, *Du Bon Usage de la France: Résistance, journalisme, glénans* (Paris, 1988), 183–184; Olivier Wieviorka, *Une Certaine Idée de la Résistance: Défense de la France, 1940–1949* (Paris, 1995), 361–362.

108. ELSP 1 SP 67, dossier 1, sdr a, Siegfried interview to *France-Soir*, 30 March 1945.

109. ELSP 1 SP 67, dossier 1, sdr a, undated typescript of Seydoux interview to *L'Université Libre*.

110. For these various meetings, see ELSP 1 SP 67, dossier 3, sdr c, "Note pour l'audience du Général de Gaulle," and "Note sur l'audience accordée par le Général de Gaulle à MM André Siegfried et Roger Seydoux, le 20 juin."

111. See ELSP 1 SP 67, dossier 4, *Journal officiel, Assemblée consultative*, séance du jeudi, 21 juin 1945, 1167–1177; dossier 4, "La Presse et l'Ecole libre des sciences politiques," 25 June 1945.

112. ELSP 1 SP 67, dossier 3, sdr a, "Note sur le Projet d'Ordonnance relative à l'éducation de certaines catégories de fonctionnaires," 6 June 1945.

113. ELSP 1 SP 68, dossier 1, letter from Seydoux to Chapsal, 26 July 1945.

114. ELSP 1 SP 68, dossier 2, letter from Seydoux to Debré, 7 September 1945.

115. Debré, *Trois Républiques*, 374.

116. For the various proposals re the FNSP's composition, see ELSP 1 SP 68, dossier 1, "Projet de Statut (dernier état)," 30 July 1945; dossier 2, document dated 4 August 1945; and, last, the decree of 9 October , 1 SP 69, dossier 3, *Journal officiel, Ordonnances et Décrets*, 10 October 1945, 6380–6381. See also 1 SP 68, dossier 3, letter from René Capitant, Ministre de l'Education nationale, to M. le Président, 12 September 1945.

117. ELSP 1 SP 68, dossier 3, letter from Capitant to M. le Président, 12 September 1945; 1 SP 69, dossier 3, *Journal officiel, Ordonnances et Décrets*, 10 October 1945, decree of 9 October, 6382–6383; 1 SP 68, dossier 5, "Convention," 27 October 1945.

118. ELSP 1 SP 68, dossier 5, "Convention," 2 November 1945.

119. ELSP 1 SP 68, dossier 1, letter from Seydoux to Chapsal, 26 July 1945.

120. ELSP 1 SP 30, dossier 4, Procès-verbal, 12 September 1945; Debré, *Trois Républiques*, 376.

121. See Kessler, *La Politique de la haute fonction publique*, 46; and ELSP 1 SP 69, dossier 3, arrêté of 7 February 1946, *Journal officiel, Lois et Décrets*, 4–5 March 1946,

187. There was, however, an injection of new blood. The state's contingent of appointees included four trade unionists, Léon Jouhaux among them, as well as prominent academics like Lucien Febvre and Gabriel Le Bras, who had no Sciences Po connections.

122. Gérard Vincent, *Sciences Po: histoire d'une réussite* (Paris, 1987), 115, 188; Kessler, *La Politique de la haute fonction publique,* 115–116.

123. Fourquet, *Comptes,* 240; Laroque, *Au Service,* 243; Olivier Dard, "Economie et économistes des années trente aux années cinquante: un tournant keynésien," *Historiens et géographes,* no. 361 (March–April 1998): 190.

124. Vincent, *Sciences Po,* 379.

125. Fourquet, *Comptes,* 71; Alain Besançon, *Une Génération* (Paris, 1987), 164; Jean-François Kesler, *L'E.N.A., la société, l'Etat* (Paris, 1985), 371.

126. François Goguel, *La Politique des partis sous la IIIe République,* 2 vols. (Paris, 1946); J.-M. Domenach, "François Goguel: la Politique des Partis sous la IIIe République," *Esprit* 128 (December 1946): 921, 924.

127. Loïc Blondiaux, *La Fabrique de l'opinion: une histoire sociale des sondages* (Paris, 1998), 476.

128. Hélène Riffault, "L'Institut français d'opinion publique, 1938–1978," in Raymond Boudon, François Bourricaud, and Alain Girard, eds., *Science et théorie de l'opinion publique: Hommage à Jean Stoetzel* (Paris, 1981), 235–237.

129. Riffault, "L'Institut français d'opinion publique," 238, 243; Jean-Noël Jeanneney, *L'Echo du siècle: Dictionnaire historique de la radio et de la télévision en France* (Paris, 2001), 661.

130. Marie Scot, "L'Influence intellectuelle et idéologique américaine sur la formation des élites en France: Le cas de l'IEP-FNSP, 1945–1960" (Thèse de maîtrise, University of Paris–VIII, 2000–2001), 36, 145–146. I owe a special thanks to Ms. Scot for giving me permission to cite her work.

131. Pierre Bourdieu, *La Noblesse d'Etat: grandes écoles et esprit de corps* (Paris, 1989), 302–303; Scot, "Influence intellectuelle," 28.

132. Pierre Favre, "La science politique en France depuis 1945," *International Review of Political Science* 2 (1981): 105–106; Jacques Lautman, "Chronique de la sociologie française après 1945," in Boudon, Bourricaud, and Girard, eds., *Science et théorie de l'opinion,* 275. In 1951, the RFSP editorial board included Aron, Chapsal, Chevallier, Maurice Duverger, Goguel, Stoetzel, and Georges Vedel. See Blondiaux, *La Fabrique,* 456.

133. Or Uriage acolyte. Besançon, *Une Génération,* 162; Bloch-Lainé, *Profession,* 154.

134. Besançon, *Une Génération,* 162, 165; Favre, "La science politique en France depuis 1945," 98; Pierre Elliot Trudeau, *Memoirs* (Toronto, 1993), 40. Many thanks to Seth Armus for the Trudeau reference.

135. Jean-Michel Gaillard, *L'ENA, miroir de l'Etat: de 1945 à nos jours* (Brussels, 1995), 41–42.

136. Cited in Gaillard, *ENA,* 47, 54, 64.

137. Gaillard, *ENA,* 60; Kesler, *E.N.A.,* 393.

138. Fourquet, *Comptes,* 104; Pierre Uri, *Penser pour l'action: un fondateur de l'Europe* (Paris, 1991), 67.

139. Feiertag, "Wilfrid Baumgartner," I:263; Dard, "Economie et économistes," 190.

140. Vincent, *Sciences Po*, 188.

141. Kesler, *E.N.A.*, 88, 91; Kessler, *La Politique de la haute fonction publique*, 118; Luc Boltanski and Pierre Bourdieu, "Les aventures d'une avant-garde," *Actes de la Recherche en sciences sociales*, nos. 2–3 (June 1976): 53.

142. Bourdieu, *Noblesse d'Etat*, 247; Kesler, *E.N.A.*, 301–302.

143. Fourquet, *Comptes*, 121–122.

144. Gaillard, *ENA*, 73.

145. Kesler, *E.N.A.*, 131.

146. Debré, *Trois Républiques*, 373; Bodiguel, *Les Anciens Elèves de l'ENA*, 33; Kesler, *E.N.A.*, 119.

147. Kesler, *E.N.A.*, 392.

148. See *Le Fil de l'épée* in Charles de Gaulle, *Le Fil de l'épée et autres écrits* (Paris, 1999), 141–225.

149. Jean-Louis Crémieux-Brilhac, *La France libre: De l'appel du 18 juin à la Libération* (Paris, 1996), 195–197, 210, 336–337.

Part II. A Culture of Quality

1. Bernard Dort, "Un âge d'or: Sur la mise en scène des classiques en France entre 1945 et 1960," *Revue d'histoire littéraire de la France* (November–December 1977): 1002–1015.

2. Pierre Sorlin, "Tradition and Social Change in the French and Italian Cinemas of the Reconstruction," in Nicholas Hewitt, ed., *The Culture of Reconstruction: European Literature, Thought and Film, 1945–50* (London, 1989), 89.

3. Pascal Ory, *L'Aventure culturelle française, 1945–1989* (Paris, 1989), 16.

4. Robert Prot, "Avec Jean Tardieu et Paul Gilson," *Cahiers d'histoire de la radiodiffusion*, no. 36 (March–May 1993): 81.

5. Pascal Ory, *La Belle Illusion: Culture et Politique sous le signe du Front populaire, 1935–1938* (Paris, 1994), 826; idem, *L'Aventure culturelle*, 127–128.

6. For Laurent as Lenin of the culture state, see Marc Fumaroli, *L'Etat culturel, essai sur une religion moderne* (Paris, 1992), 105.

Chapter 4. Art and Commerce in the Interwar Decades

1. Dorothy Knowles, *French Drama of the Inter-War Years, 1918–1939* (London, 1967), 260, 262; Jacqueline de Jomaron, "Le boulevard en question," in Jomaron, ed., *Le Théâtre en France* (Paris, 1989), II:350; Charles Dullin, "1934," in Dullin, *Ce sont les dieux qu'il nous faut* (Paris, 1969), 139–140; see also Hubert Gignoux, *Histoire d'une famille théâtrale* (Lausanne, 1984), 17; and Chantal Meyer-Plantureux, *Les Enfants de Shylock, ou, l'antisémitisme sur scène* (Brussels, 2005), 22.

2. Charles Dullin, "Saison 1928–1929," in Dullin, *Ce sont les dieux*, 73, 75; and "Conférence" (28 May 1932), in ibid., 109, 112.

3. See Robert Brasillach, *Animateurs du théâtre* (Paris, 1954 [orig. 1936]), 15; Gaston Baty, *Le Masque et l'encensoir* (Paris, 1926), 317; Dullin, "1934," 142.

4. Gignoux, *Histoire d'une famille théâtrale*, 34, 36, 51.

5. David Bradby, *Modern French Drama, 1940–1990*, 2nd ed. (Cambridge, 1991), 2; Jean Dasté, *Voyage d'un comédien* (Paris, 1977), 24–25; Gignoux, *Histoire d'une famille théâtrale*, 36–37, 45–46.

6. According to Dullin. See Jean Hort, *Les Théâtres du Cartel* (Geneva, 1944), 186.

7. Denis Gontard, ed., *Le Journal de bord des Copiaus, 1924–1929* (Paris, 1974), 38–39.

8. Gignoux, *Histoire d'une famille théâtrale*, 50, 90.

9. Bradby, *Modern French Drama*, 3; Jacqueline de Jomaron, "Ils étaient quatre…," in Jomaron, ed., *Théâtre en France*, II:228; Charles Dullin, "Radio causerie" (November 1946), in Dullin, *Ce sont les dieux*, 240. See also Brasillach, *Animateurs du théâtre*, 99.

10. See the following by Charles Dullin in Dullin, *Ce sont les dieux*: speech (21 May 1927), 44, 48; "Conférence" (5 January 1929), 57, 61, 68–69; "Conférence" (28 May 1932), 117; "Radio causerie" (November 1946), 242, 246. See also Jean-Claude Bardot, *Jean Vilar* (Paris, 1991), 39ff.

11. Hort, *Théâtres du Cartel*, 154, 166; Knowles, *French Drama*, 195, 204, 211; Pierre-Marie Dioudonnat, *Je suis partout, 1930–1944: Les Maurrassiens devant la tentation fasciste* (Paris, 1973), 226–230.

12. Hort, *Théâtres du Cartel*, 30, 77, 110–111; Brasillach, *Animateurs du théâtre*, 52–53; idem, *Notre avant-guerre* (Paris, 1992 [orig. 1941]), passim.

13. Baty, *Le Masque*, 304 and see also 251–260.

14. Baty, *Le Masque*, 323 and see also 292–293; Hort, *Théâtres du Cartel*, 140; Gérard Lieber, "Gaston Baty et ses auteurs: le théâtre de l'évasion" (Thèse d'Etat, University of Paris–X, 1987) I:101, 106; Brasillach, *Animateurs du théâtre*, 87.

15. Gignoux, *Histoire d'une famille théâtrale*, 133. For Chancerel's career and oeuvre, see Maryline Romain, *Léon Chancerel: portrait d'un réformateur du théâtre français, 1886–1965* (Paris, 2005).

16. Denis Gontard, *La Décentralisation théâtrale en France, 1895–1952* (Paris, 1973), 86; Bradby, *Modern French Drama*, 13; François Bloch-Lainé, *Profession: fonctionnaire. Entretiens avec Françoise Carrière* (Paris, 1976), 24.

17. Gignoux, *Histoire d'une famille théâtrale*, 146, 181, 183, 191–193, 225.

18. Jacques Copeau, "La représentation sacrée," *Art Sacré* 18 (April 1937): 109–110.

19. Romain, *Chancerel*, 195.

20. Gignoux, *Histoire d'une famille théâtrale*, 152–153, 173.

21. Gignoux, *Histoire d'une famille théâtrale*, 111–112.

22. Gignoux, *Histoire d'une famille théâtrale*, 241, 247; Dasté, *Voyage*, 28; Knowles, *French Drama*, 313.

23. Gontard, *Décentralisation*, 101ff.; Francine Gaillard-Risler, *André Clavé: théâtre et résistances, utopies et réalités* (Paris, 1998), 33.

24. Dasté, *Voyage*, 28; Romain, *Chancerel*, 287–288; Gignoux, *Histoire d'une famille théâtrale*, 250.

25. Gignoux, *Histoire d'une famille théâtrale*, 111.

26. Pascal Ory, *La Belle Illusion: Culture et Politique sous le signe du Front populaire, 1935–1938* (Paris, 1994), 385, 918n300; Eugen Weber, *Action française, Royalism and Reaction in Twentieth-Century France* (Stanford, 1962), 389–390, 390n.

27. Gaillard-Risler, *André Clavé*, 34.

28. Ory, *La Belle Illusion*, 98, 100, 866n223; Gaillard-Risler, *André Clavé*, 38.

29. Charles Dullin, "Rapport" (Autumn 1938), in Dullin, *Ce sont le dieux*, 164.

30. Jens Ulff-Moller, *Hollywood's Film Wars with France: Film-Trade Diplomacy and the Emergence of the French Film Quota Policy* (Rochester, 2001), 118.

31. Jean Bertin-Maghit, *Le Cinéma français sous l'Occupation* (Paris, 2002), 13–15; idem, *Le Cinéma français sous l'Occupation* (Paris, 1994), 4–5; Louis Daquin, *Le Cinéma notre métier* (Paris, 1960), 33; Paul Léglise, *Histoire de la politique du cinéma français* (Paris, 1970), I:55–56, 99; Jean-Pierre Jeancolas, "From the Blum-Byrnes Agreement to the GATT Affair," in Geoffrey Nowell-Smith and Steven Ricci, eds., *Hollywood and Europe: Economics, Culture, National Identity, 1945–95* (London, 1998), 48; Ulff-Moller, *Hollywood's Film Wars*, 128–129.

32. Jean-Pierre Jeancolas, *15 Ans d'années trente: le cinéma des français, 1929–1944* (Paris, 1983), 99.

33. Colin Crisp, *The Classic French Cinema, 1930–1960* (Bloomington, 1997), 22.

34. Crisp, *Classic French Cinema*, 116, 274–275.

35. This characterization may be a satisfactory starting point for an understanding of Gabin's appeal, but as Ginette Vincendeau's analysis makes clear, the Gabin story is on closer inspection a good deal more complicated than that. See Claude Gauteur and Ginette Vincendeau, *Jean Gabin: Anatomie d'un mythe* (Paris, 2006), chs. 5–6.

36. Crisp, *Classic French Cinema*, 364–366; Bertin-Maghit, *Le Cinéma français* (2002), 15–16.

37. Maurice Bardèche and Robert Brasillach, *Histoire du cinéma: le parlant* (Paris, 1964), II:9–14.

38. Marcel L'Herbier, *La Tête qui tourne* (Paris, 1979), 244–245; and L'Herbier's testimony to the Chamber of Deputies as cited in Jean-Michel Renaitour, *Où va la Cinéma français?* (Paris, 1937), 149.

39. Daquin, *Le Cinéma*, 33, 41; Georges Sadoul, *Histoire générale du cinéma, l'époque contemporaine: Le Cinéma pendant la guerre, 1939–1945* (Paris, 1954), VI:3.

40. L'Herbier, *La Tête qui tourne*, 245.

41. The anti-Semite in question is Claude Autant-Lara, who cited these exaggerated figures in an Occupation-era interview with the collaborationist *Je suis partout*. See François Garçon, *De Blum à Pétain: cinéma et société française, (1936–1944)* (Paris, 1984), 35; and Bertin-Maghit, *Le Cinéma français* (2002), 74.

42. Bardèche and Brasillach, *Histoire du cinéma*, 1935 edition, as cited in Evelyn Ehrlich, *Cinema of Paradox: French Filmmaking under the German Occupation* (New York, 1985), 60; Paul Morand, *France la doulce* (Paris, 1934), 10.

43. Louis-Ferdinand Céline, *Bagatelles pour un massacre* (Paris, 1937), 185, 222; Lucien Rebatet, *Les Tribus du cinéma et du théâtre* (Paris, 1941), 86 and see also 26–27, 66, 81.

44. Rebatet, *Les Tribus*, 81.

45. Céline, *Bagatelles*, 268.

46. L'Herbier, as cited in Bertin-Maghit, *Le Cinéma français* (1994), 31.

47. Dioudonnat, *Je suis partout*, 141.

48. Claude Autant-Lara, *Les Fourgons du malheur: Chronique cinématographique du XXe siècle* (Paris, 1987), 145. Autant-Lara writes of a "German flood" that followed on Hitler's seizure of power in 1933.

49. Autant-Lara, *Les Fourgons*, 15, 145, 536.

50. John Hellman, *Emmanuel Mounier and the New Catholic Left, 1930–1950* (Toronto, 1981), 57; Edmond Lipiansky and Bernard Rettenbach, *Ordre et démocratie. Deux sociétés de pensée: de l'Ordre Nouveau au Club Jean-Moulin* (Paris, 1967), 15; Jacques Siclier, *La France de Pétain et son cinéma* (Paris, 1981), 229. Autant-Lara also collaborated with a Popular Front theater group, Octobre.

51. Jeancolas, *15 Ans*, 130.

52. Roy Armes, *French Cinema* (New York, 1985), 95; Eugen Weber, *The Hollow Years: France in the 1930s* (New York, 1994), 93.

53. Roger Richebé, *Au delà de l'Écran* (Monte Carlo, 1977), 130; Léglise, *Histoire de la politique du cinéma*, I:122ff.; Ory, *La Belle Illusion*, 417–418.

54. Léglise, *Histoire de la politique du cinéma*, I:163, 176, 181.

55. Bertin-Maghit, *Le Cinéma français* (2002), 17; Ory, *La Belle Illusion*, 435–437.

56. Léglise, *Histoire de la politique du cinéma*, I:250; idem, *Histoire de la politique du cinéma français* (Paris, 1977), II:5.

57. Cécile Méadel, *Histoire de la radio des années trente* (Paris, 1994), 198.

58. Jean-Noël Jeanneney, ed., *L'Echo du siècle: Dictionnaire historique de la radio et de la télévision en France* (Paris, 2001), 27, 102–103.

59. Méadel, *Histoire de la radio*, 29. Méadel states that fourteen private stations were authorized. The entry in Jeanneney (*L'Echo du siècle*, 108) puts the number at thirteen. There was one less as of 1933, when the state took over the once-private Radio Paris.

60. Jeanneney, ed., *L'Echo du siècle*, 103–104; Méadel, *Histoire de la radio*, 39.

61. Méadel, *Histoire de la radio*, 198.

62. Marcel Bleustein-Blanchet, *Les Ondes de la liberté, sur mon antenne, 1934–1984* (Paris, 1984), 11; Fernand Pouey, *Un Ingénu à la radio* (Paris, 1949), 34; Christian Brochand, *Histoire générale de la radio et de la télévision en France* (Paris, 1994), I:412.

63. Méadel, *Histoire de la radio*, 284.

64. Prot, "Le Club d'essai," *Cahiers d'histoire de la radiodiffusion*, nos. 13–14 (April 1986): 15.

65. Hélène Eck, *La Guerre des ondes: Histoire des radios de langue française pendant la Deuxième Guerre mondiale* (Paris, 1985), 24, 26; Brochand, *Histoire générale*, I:304, 407–409; Méadel, *Histoire de la radio*, 252–254, 310.

66. Meyer-Plantureux, *Les Enfants de Shylock*, 83, 109.

67. Bleustein-Blanchet, *Les Ondes*, 11, 109, 152; Brochand, *Histoire générale*, I:467.

68. Jacques Meyer, "Les Souvenirs de Jacques Meyer sur la naissance de Radio

Cité," *Cahiers d'histoire de la radiodiffusion*, no. 23 (July 1989): 9–11; Bleustein-Blanchet, *Les Ondes*, 81–82; Jeanneney, ed., *L'Echo du siècle*, 109; Ory, *La Belle Illusion*, 30.

69. Pouey, *Un Ingénu*, 34; Bleustein-Blanchet, *Les Ondes*, 151, 155; Brochand, *Histoire générale*, I:417.

70. Pouey, *Un Ingénu*, 74–75.

71. Pouey, *Un Ingénu*, 164–167; Jeanneney, ed., *L'Echo du siècle*, 658.

72. René Duval, *Histoire de la radio en France* (Paris, 1979), 274; Bleustein-Blanchet, *Les Ondes*, 113–114.

73. Pouey, *Un Ingénu*, 70–71; Duval, *Histoire de la radio*, 286.

74. In fact, begun on the streets in Piaf's case.

75. Bleustein-Blanchet, *Les Ondes*, 115.

76. Bleustein-Blanchet, *Les Ondes*, 109–110; Duval, *Histoire de la radio*, 274; Brochand, *Histoire générale*, I:419.

77. Méadel, *Histoire de la radio*, 344; Duval, *Histoire de la radio*, 302.

78. Duval, *Histoire de la radio*, 275–276.

79. Duval, *Histoire de la radio*, 265.

80. Jeanneney, ed., *L'Echo du siècle*, 644; Brochand, *Histoire générale*, I:295, 298; Méadel, *Histoire de la radio*, 80–87.

81. Radio-Liberté and Radio-Famille had gotten involved in the 1935 elections as well but did not play a decisive role. For the 1937 elections, see André-Jean Tudesq and Elisabeth Cazenave, "Radiodiffusion et politique: les élections radiophoniques de 1937," *Revue d'histoire moderne et contemporaine* 23 (October–December 1976): 529–555. See also Brochand, *Histoire générale*, I:296, 301–303; Ory, *La Belle Illusion*, 586–588.

82. Ory, *La Belle Illusion*, 583–585; but see also Méadel, *Histoire de la radio*, 134–136.

83. Brochand, *Histoire générale*, I:261; Méadel, *Histoire de la radio*, 77; Bleustein-Blanchet, *Les Ondes*, 135.

84. Duval, *Histoire de la radio*, 278; Pouey, *Un Ingénu*, 114–115; Brochand, *Histoire générale*, I:444–447.

85. Philippe Amaury, *Les Deux Premières Expériences d'un 'Ministère de l'Information' en France (1939–1940, 1940–1944)* (Paris, 1969), 399; Ory, *La Belle Illusion*, 592.

86. Amaury, *Les Deux Premières Expériences*, 399–400, 405; Jeanneney, *Histoire des médias: des origines à nos jours* (Paris, 1996), 181.

87. Jeanneney, *Histoire des médias*, 182; Méadel, *Histoire de la radio*, 183–184; Jeanneney, ed., *L'Echo du siècle*, 110; Eck, *La Guerre des ondes*, 19–20.

88. Amaury, *Les Deux Premières Expériences*, 27, 56.

89. Amaury, *Les Deux Premières Expériences*, 28.

90. Jean Giraudoux, *Pleins pouvoirs*, 33rd ed. (Paris, 1939), passim.

91. Amaury, *Les Deux Premières Expériences*, 51.

92. Amaury, *Les Deux Premières Expériences*, 45; Brochand, *Histoire générale*, I: 187n.

93. Jeanneney, *Histoire des médias*, 181.

94. Louis Merlin, an adman and future radio producer, was serving in the

military during the opening months of the war. He remembered the "understandable stupefaction" of his fellow soldiers on hearing Giraudoux's broadcasts. From the radio set came "a language entirely different from their own." Yes, it was French, but they did not understand at all what was being said. Merlin, *C'était formidable!* (Paris, 1966), 25.

95. Duhamel, *Scènes de la vie future* (Paris, 1930), passim.

96. Jouvet made the statement to Dullin, who repeated it, with irritation at Jouvet's pretensions, to Simone de Beauvoir. See Beauvoir, *The Prime of Life*, tr. Peter Green (New York, 1976), 313.

97. *Le Temps*, as cited in Jeanneney, *Histoire des médias*, 183. See also Eck, *La Guerre des ondes*, 23, 26–27.

Chapter 5. Culture in Wartime

1. For the preceding and much of what follows, see Serge Added's very informative *Le Théâtre dans les années Vichy* (Paris, 1992), 115.

2. Baty, Dullin, and Renoir had worked together at the ADTP under Trébor, drafting a study on the "general organization of the corporation." See Added, *Le Théâtre dans les années Vichy*, 145.

3. Added, *Le Théâtre dans les années Vichy*, 145, 151–154.

4. Chantal Meyer-Plantureux, *Les Enfants de Shylock, ou, l'anti-sémitisme sur scène* (Brussels, 2005), 71–72 and photo collection following page 96.

5. Charles Dullin, "Les maux dont nous souffrons," *La Gerbe*, 25 July 1940; idem, "Sous le règne de la combinaison," *La Gerbe*, 22 August 1940. See also Catherine Brice, "Le Groupe 'Collaboration'" (Mémoire de maîtrise, University of Paris–I, 1978), 114.

6. Added, *Le Théâtre dans les années Vichy*, 150, 319; Meyer-Plantureux, *Les Enfants de Shylock*, 90 and photo collection following page 96.

7. Added, *Le Théâtre dans les années Vichy*, 147, 149, 160n13.

8. Added, *Le Théâtre dans les années Vichy*, 143, 151–153.

9. Added, *Le Théâtre dans les années Vichy*, 33.

10. Added, *Le Théâtre dans les années Vichy*, 63–65, 183–184.

11. Jean Laurent, "Le théâtre et la Révolution nationale, vus par René Rocher," *La Gerbe*, 13 January 1944; Marcel Dalio, *Mes Années folles* (Paris, 1976), 98–99.

12. Added, *Le Théâtre dans les années Vichy*, 167, 171ff.

13. Added, *Le Théâtre dans les années Vichy*, 66, 183–184, 249.

14. Added, *Le Théâtre dans les années Vichy*, 185ff.

15. Added, *Le Théâtre dans les années Vichy*, 77–78.

16. Jeanne Laurent, *La République et les Beaux-Arts* (Paris, 1955), 80–82.

17. Marion Denizot-Foulquier, *Jeanne Laurent, le théâtre et les arts* (Paris, 1997), 20, 36; Jeanne Laurent, "L'administration des Beaux-Arts et le théâtre parisien en 1941–1942," *La Revue des Beaux-Arts de France*, no. 4 (April–May 1943): 225.

18. Laurent, "L'administration des Beaux-Arts et le théâtre parisien," 225; Added, *Le Théâtre dans les années Vichy*, 78–79.

19. Pierre Schaeffer, *Clotaire Nicole*, Edition définitive (Paris, 1943), 40.

20. Véronique Chabrol, "Jeune France—une expérience de recherche et de décentralisation culturelle, novembre 1940–mars 1942" (Thèse de Troisième cycle, University of Paris–III, 1974), 16; Sylvie Dallet, *Bibliographie commentée de l'oeuvre éditée de Pierre Schaeffer* (Paris, nd), 26, 31; [Paul Flamand], *Sur le Seuil, 1935–1979* (Paris, 1979), 7–8. Le Seuil's first best-seller was in fact a scouting novel, Guy de Larigaudie's posthumous *Etoile au grand large* (1943).

21. Roger Leenhardt, *Les Yeux ouverts: entretiens avec Jean Lacouture* (Paris, 1979), 121; Dallet, *Bibliographie commentée*, 26.

22. See Lyautey's introduction to Georges Lamirand, *Le Rôle social de l'ingénieur* (Paris, 1937), v.

23. Lamirand, *Le Rôle social*, 49, 211, 232.

24. Chabrol, "Jeune France, un 'maillon manquant' pour l'histoire de la décentralisation théâtrale," *Les Cahiers de l'animation*, no. 53 (December 1985): 88.

25. Edmond Lipiansky and Bernard Rettenbach, *Ordre et Démocratie, deux sociétés de pensée: de l'Ordre Nouveau au Club Jean-Moulin* (Paris, 1967), 36.

26. See Jane Fulcher, "The Politics of Transcendence: Ideology in the Music of Messiaen in the 1930s," *Musical Quarterly* 86 (Fall 2002): 449–471. Many thanks to Jane Fulcher for help with the preceding paragraph.

27. Chabrol, "Jeune France—une expérience," 29.

28. Leenhardt, *Les Yeux ouverts*, 107, 119; Chabrol, "Jeune France—une expérience," 20; Dallet, *Bibliographie commentée*, 34.

29. Chabrol, "Jeune France—une expérience," 27–29; Lipiansky and Rettenbach, *Ordre et Démocratie*, 77; Francine Gaillard-Risler, *André Clavé: Théâtre et résistances, utopies et réalités* (Paris, 1998), 62.

30. Chabrol, "Jeune France—une expérience," 180.

31. On theater, see Centre d'études et de recherche Pierre Schaeffer, Montreuil-sous-Bois (hereinafter CERPS), carton Libération, Radio Paris, 1944–1945, Jeune France, dossier Jeune France, "Réalisations et projets," 1941, 1; on radio and cinema, see the JF brochure *Principes, directions, esprit* (Lyon, 1941), cited in Chabrol, "Jeune France—une expérience," 43; on music, CERPS, carton Libération, dossier Jeune France, "Animateurs de la Jeune France," August 1941, 8. See also Added, *Le Théâtre dans les années Vichy*, 208. The CERPS archive contains two boxes labeled Libération, Radio Paris, 1944–1945. The archive was closed down some years ago. Its holdings have now been relocated to the Institut Mémoires de l'Edition contemporaine (IMEC), which is headquartered at the abbaye d'Ardenne just outside of Caen.

32. Romy Golan, *Modernity and Nostalgia: Art and Politics in France between the Wars* (New Haven, 1995), ch. 6.

33. Michel Bergès, *Vichy contre Mounier: les non-conformistes face aux années 40* (Paris, 1997), 55–56.

34. Denizot-Foulquier, *Jeanne Laurent*, 90–91. On the exhibition in general, see Michèle C. Cone, *French Modernisms: Perspectives on Art, before, during, and after Vichy* (Cambridge, 2001), 85–88.

35. CERPS, carton Libération, dossier Jeune France, "Réalisations et projets," 1941, 6.

36. Chabrol, "Jeune France—une expérience," 174; Leenhardt, *Les Yeux ouverts*, 123–124.

37. Henri Davenson (Henri-Irénée Marrou), *Le Livre des chansons* (Neuchâtel, 1946 [orig. 1944]).

38. Michel Winock, *"Esprit," des intellectuels dans la cité (1930–1950)* (Paris, 1996), 231.

39. CERPS, carton Libération, dossier Jeune France, sdr "Organisation des activités culturelles générales à Jeune France," rapport d'Emmanuel Mounier, 3. See also Chabrol, "Jeune France—une expérience," 96, 119.

40. CERPS, carton Libération, dossier Jeune France, sdr "Organisation des activités culturelles générales à Jeune France," rapport d'Emmanuel Mounier, 11.

41. CERPS, carton Libération, dossier Jeune France, "Animateurs de la Jeune France," August 1941, 11, 13; Chabrol, "Jeune France—une expérience," 92–93, 161–163.

42. Chabrol, "Jeune France—une expérience," 142; idem, "Jeune France, 'un maillon manquant,'" 92.

43. Pierre Schaeffer, *Les Antennes de Jéricho* (Paris, 1978), 274.

44. Chabrol, "Jeune France—une expérience," 144; Added, *Le Théâtre dans les années Vichy*, 207.

45. Lignac as cited in Chabrol, "Jeune France—une expérience," 153.

46. Chabrol, "Jeune France—une expérience," 169; Added, *Le Théâtre dans les années Vichy*, 213.

47. CERPS, carton Libération, dossier Jeune France, sdr "Réalisations de Jeune France, compte-rendu," nd, 8. The *Portique* just beat by a couple of months Jean-Louis Barrault's production of a double bill (Aeschylus's *The Suppliant Women* and André Obie's *800 mètres*) at the Roland-Garros stadium in July. The Obie play, a dramatization of a celebrated race from the 1924 Olympic games, was a natural for Barrault, ever preoccupied with the expressive possibilities of the body. The Vichy regime, a firm believer in the power of sport to reinvigorate the nation, saw its own interest in Barrault's venture and agreed to provide funding. See Added, *Le Théâtre dans les années Vichy*, 83–84; David Bradby, *Modern French Drama, 1940–1990*, 2nd ed. (Cambridge, 1991), 24–25.

48. Added, *Le Théâtre dans les années Vichy*, 215; Chabrol, "Jeune France—une expérience," 166.

49. CERPS, carton Libération, dossier Jeune France, sdr "Réalisations de Jeune France, compte-rendu," nd, 9; Chabrol, "Jeune France—une expérience," 168–169; Bergès, *Vichy contre Mounier*, 127.

50. Jean-Louis Barrault, *Souvenirs pour demain* (Paris, 1972), 164.

51. Added, *Le Théâtre dans les années Vichy*, 134n12.

52. Barrault, *Souvenirs*, 69–70, 144–146; Chabrol, "Jeune France—une expérience," 88.

53. This was a breath of fresh air in the stuffy confines of the house of Molière; and the occasion was all the more bracing given the date of the play's opening, 11 November, Armistice Day. The crowd, in a patriotic mood, was rambunctious. German authorities had never much liked Copeau (he was too much the nation-

alist) and profited from the disturbances to have him sacked. While Copeau was no friend of the Germans, it should not be thought he was any the less sympathetic to Vichy. He published a text during the war years, Vichyite in tone, that spelled out his ongoing commitment to a "theater of the Nation," "a theater of union and regeneration." Jacques Copeau, *Le Théâtre populaire* (Paris, 1941), 32. See also Marie-Agnès Joubert, *La Comédie-Française sous l'Occupation* (Paris, 1998), 40–41; Barrault, *Souvenirs*, 149.

54. Sabine de Lavergne, *Art sacré et modernité: Les grandes années de la revue 'l'Art Sacré'* (Namur, 1992), 189–191.

55. André Castelot, "'Le Soulier de Satin' à la Comédie française," *La Gerbe*, 9 December 1943. Barrault was not just reviewed in *La Gerbe* but, according to Catherine Brice, published in it himself. See Brice, "Le Groupe 'Collaboration,'" 114.

56. Lucien Rebatet, *Les Tribus du cinéma et du théâtre* (Paris, 1941), 99–101, 120. It was the avant-garde playwright Adamov who called Anouilh an "anarchist of the Right." Adamov, cited in Dorothy Knowles, *French Drama of the Inter-War Years, 1918–39* (London, 1967), 179.

57. Brice, "Le Groupe 'Collaboration,'" 114; Pierre-Marie Dioudonnat, *Je suis partout, 1930–1944: Les maurrassiens devant la tentation fasciste* (Paris, 1973), 349; Knowles, *French Drama*, 177. *Je suis partout* was very well disposed to Anouilh. Rebatet's sympathies have been mentioned; they were shared by the journal's theater columnist, the notorious Alain Laubreaux. Dioudonnat, *Je suis partout*, 382n38. Daxiat, the sinister and repellent theater critic in Truffaut's *Le Dernier Métro*, is modeled on Laubreaux.

58. Anouilh, *Antigone* (Paris, 1946), 86.

59. André Castelot, "Antigone, de Jean Anouilh," *La Gerbe*, 24 February 1944.

60. André Barsacq, "A l'Atelier pendant près de quinze ans," *Cahiers de la Compagnie Renaud-Barrault*, no. 26 (May 1959): 34.

61. Barsacq cited in Patrick Marsh, "The Theatre: Compromise or Collaboration?" in Gerhard Hirschfeld and Patrick Marsh, eds., *Collaboration in France: Politics and Culture during the Nazi Occupation, 1940–1944* (Oxford, 1989), 145; see also Emile Copfermann, "L'Etat intervient," in Jacqueline de Jomaron, ed., *Le Théâtre en France* (Paris, 1989), II:387; and Added, *Le Théâtre dans les années Vichy*, 112–113.

62. Barsacq, "A l'Atelier," 35.

63. Knowles, *French Drama*, 174–175.

64. On this point, see Christian Faure, *Le Projet culturel de Vichy: Folklore et révolution nationale, 1940–1944* (Lyon, 1989), 136–138.

65. Jean-Pierre Bertin-Maghit, *Le Cinéma français sous l'Occupation: Le monde du cinéma français de 1940 à 1946* (Paris, 2002), 9; Evelyn Ehrlich, *Cinema of Paradox: French Filmmaking under the German Occupation* (New York, 1985), 83. See also François Garçon, "Ce curieux âge d'or des cinéastes français," in Jean-Pierre Rioux, ed., *La Vie culturelle sous Vichy* (Paris, 1990), 293–313.

66. Georges Sadoul, *Histoire générale du cinéma, L'Epoque contemporaine: Le Cinéma pendant la guerre, 1939–1945* (Paris, 1954), VI:45.

67. Jean-Pierre Bertin-Maghit, *Le Cinéma français* (2002), 34.

68. On Galey's career, see Bertin-Maghit, *Le Cinéma français* (2002), 55–56;

Philippe Burrin, *La Dérive fasciste: Doriot, Déat, Bergery, 1933–1945* (Paris, 2003), 399; Bergès, *Vichy contre Mounier*, 75; Philippe Amaury, *Les Deux Premières Expériences d'un 'Ministère de l'Information' en France (1939–1940, 1940–1944)* (Paris, 1969), 226, 423.

69. Marcel L'Herbier, *La Tête qui tourne* (Paris, 1979), 265.

70. Bertin-Maghit, *Le Cinéma français* (2002), 57.

71. Jean-Louis Loubet del Bayle, *Les Non-conformistes des années 30* (Paris, 1969), 460; Jean-Pierre Bertin-Maghit, *Le Cinéma français sous l'Occupation* (Paris, 1994), 112n.

72. For these changes, see Paul Léglise, *Histoire de la politique du cinéma français* (Paris, 1977), II:67–69; Roger Richebé, *Au delà de l'Ecran* (Paris, 1977), 141–143; Bertin-Maghit, *Le Cinéma français* (2002), 58–59.

73. L'Herbier, *La Tête qui tourne*, 314; Carmoy, cited in Bertin-Maghit, *Le Cinéma français* (2002), 52; Ploquin and Galey, cited in Léglise, *Histoire de la politique du cinéma*, II:48, 66.

74. André Robert, "Après la bataille," *La Gerbe*, 6 May 1943; Léglise, *Histoire de la politique du cinéma*, II:33; Jacques Siclier, *La France de Pétain et son cinéma* (Paris, 1981), 29; Amaury, *Les Deux Premières Expériences*, 431; Steve Wharton, *Screening Reality: French Documentary Film during the German Occupation* (Bern, 2006), 34–35, 119. Wharton's book provides a detailed listing of all the documentary films produced in France from 1940 to 1944. According to Wharton's documentation, Cousteau's short was not released until 1944.

75. Pierre Darmon, *Le Monde du cinéma sous l'Occupation* (Paris, 1997), 153; Léglise, *Histoire de la politique du cinéma*, II:60.

76. Léglise, *Histoire de la politique du cinéma*, II:71.

77. Bertin-Maghit, *Le Cinéma français* (1994), 32; Léglise, *Histoire de la politique du cinéma*, II:55–56.

78. On Clerc, see Bertin-Maghit, *Le Cinéma français* (1994), 32–33; and the brief entry in *Dictionnaire des parlementaires français*, III:155. In the thirties, Clerc had militated alongside Marcel Déat in neosocialist planning circles. Jean-François Biard, *Le Socialisme devant ses choix: La naissance de l'idée de plan* (Paris, 1985), 180. The Clerc Committee's work is discussed in Léglise, *Histoire de la politique du cinéma*, II:21–23; Bertin-Maghit, *Le Cinéma français* (1994), 35; and idem, *Le Cinéma français* (2002), 78–80.

79. Bertin-Maghit, *Le Cinéma français* (2002), 71; Léglise, *Histoire de la politique du cinéma*, II:52.

80. "L'ennemi cinématographique numéro 1," *La Gerbe*, 9 January 1941. Reproduced in L'Herbier, *La Tête qui tourne*, 315–319.

81. Rebatet, *Les Tribus* (Paris, 1941), 70.

82. Léglise, *Histoire de la politique du cinéma*, II:208.

83. Bertin-Maghit, *Le Cinéma français* (2002), 226; Clouzot's testimony, 17 October 1945, before the film industry Commission d'épuration, as cited by Bertin-Maghit, "1945, l'épuration du cinéma français: mythe ou réalité," in Marc Ferro, ed., *Film et histoire* (Paris, 1984), 137; Darmon, *Le Monde du cinéma*, 95.

84. Darmon, *Le Monde du cinéma*, 97.

85. Sadoul, *Histoire générale*, VI:40.

86. Sadoul, *Histoire générale*, VI:45.

87. Bertin-Maghit, *Le Cinéma français* (2002), 40ff.

88. Ophuls was not native-born but an immigrant working in France.

89. Ehrlich, *Cinema of Paradox*, 7. Dalio, it will be recalled, played Rosenthal in Jean Renoir's *La Grande Illusion*. He had success finding work in wartime Hollywood, turning in a memorable performance as the croupier in Michael Curtiz's *Casablanca*. Nor was Dalio the only cast member from *La Grande Illusion* to follow the path of exile. Gabin also departed for the United States. He later joined Free French naval forces and went on to see service in North Africa. As noted, Renoir himself, unlike his brother Pierre, left France en route to the United States.

90. Ehrlich, *Cinema of Paradox*, 61. See also Richebé, *Au delà de l'Ecran*, 151–152, and Ehrlich, *Cinema of Paradox*, 68–69.

91. Léglise, *Histoire de la politique du cinéma*, II:61.

92. Morand would become Vichy's ambassador to Romania in the regime's final phase. This did not help his career at the Liberation, but he recovered in due course, ending his days as a member of the Académie française. Amaury, *Les Deux Premières Expériences*, 428; Jean-Pierre Jeancolas, *15 Ans d'années trente: Le cinéma des français, 1929–1944* (Paris, 1983), 303.

93. Laurent Mannoni, *Histoire de la Cinémathèque française* (Paris, 2006), 93, 102, 107; Patrick Olmeta, *La Cinémathèque française, de 1936 à nos jours* (Paris, 2002), 45ff., 56, 73–74.

94. L'Herbier, *La Tête qui tourne*, 288.

95. Mannoni, *Histoire de la Cinémathèque*, 108–111, 118; Olmeta, *La Cinémathèque*, 81.

96. Bertin-Maghit, *Le Cinéma français* (2002), 55.

97. Roger Régent, *Cinéma de France* (Paris, 1948), 237–238; Léglise, *Histoire de la politique du cinéma*, II:75.

98. Régent, *Cinéma*, 286, also 186–187; L'Herbier, *La Tête qui tourne*, 320–324.

99. Léglise, *Histoire de la politique du cinéma*, II: 72; Bertin-Maghit, *Le Cinéma français* (2002), 85–86.

100. Siclier, *La France de Pétain*, 32; Bertin-Maghit, *Le Cinéma français* (2002), 86.

101. Pierre Schaeffer, *Les Antennes de Jéricho* (Paris, 1978), 278; Leenhardt, *Les Yeux ouverts*, 134; Chabrol, "Jeune France—une expérience," 201, 254; Michael Kelly, "Catholic Cultural Policy from 1944 to 1950: '*Bande dessinée*' and Cinema," in Brian Rigby and Nicholas Hewitt, eds., *France and the Mass Media* (Basingstoke, 1991), 27.

102. Autant-Lara, cited in Bertin-Maghit, *Le Cinéma français* (1994), 10; Louis Daquin, *Le Cinéma, notre métier* (Paris, 1960), 115.

103. Siclier, *La France de Pétain*, 117.

104. Daquin, *Le Cinéma*, 117; Bertin-Maghit, *Le Cinéma français* (2002), 151–152.

105. Siclier, *La France de Pétain*, 185.

106. Régent, *Cinéma*, 241.

107. From the movie magazine *Vedettes*, as cited in Siclier, *La France de Pétain*, 97, 104–105.

108. Daquin cited in Ehrlich, *Cinema of Paradox*, 112. See also Siclier, *La France de Pétain*, 202n.

109. Régent, *Cinéma*, 238, 240–241; Ehrlich, *Cinema of Paradox*, 122–123.

110. Daquin, *Le Cinéma*, 117.

111. Ehrlich, *Cinema of Paradox*, 93ff.; Roy Armes, "Cinema of Paradox: French Film-Making during the Occupation," in Hirschfeld and Marsh, eds., *Collaboration in France*, 138.

112. Georges Sadoul has referred to the "anarchist skepticism" of the scene, and perhaps it is not unreasonable to characterize Clouzot, like Anouilh, as an anarchist of the Right. Sadoul, *Histoire générale*, VI:58.

113. See also Colin Crisp, *The Classic French Cinema, 1930–1960* (Bloomington, 1997), 44–63.

114. Hélène Eck, *La Guerre des ondes: Histoire des radios de langue française pendant la deuxième guerre mondiale* (Paris, 1985), 53; Jacques Chardonnier, "Radio-Paris, un foyer artistique très actif," *Cahiers d'histoire de la radiodiffusion*, no. 34 (September–November 1992): 58–73.

115. Christian Brochand, *Histoire générale de la radio et de la télévision en France* (Paris, 1994), I:594; Pascal Ory, *La Belle Illusion: Culture et politique sous le signe du Front populaire, 1935–1938* (Paris, 1994), 382; Eck, *La Guerre des ondes*, 56–57.

116. Aurélie Luneau, *Radio Londres, 1940–1944: Les voix de la liberté* (Paris, 2005), 46–50.

117. Luneau, *Radio Londres*, 63.

118. Dac was born André Isaac. See Luneau, *Radio Londres*, 219–220; and Eck, *La Guerre des ondes*, 61–62, 67–68.

119. Eck, *La Guerre des ondes*, 80.

120. Amaury, *Les Deux Premières Expériences*, 146–149.

121. Claude Autant-Lara, *Les Fourgons du malheur: Chronique cinématographique du XXe siècle* (Paris, 1987), 442. See also H. R. Kedward, "The Vichy of the Other Philippe," in Hirschfeld and Marsh, eds., *Collaboration in France*, 32–46.

122. Eck, *La Guerre des ondes*, 40–42.

123. On Trémoulet, see Ory, *La Belle Illusion*, 30, 591.

124. Brochand, *Histoire générale*, II:583–585; René Duval, *Histoire de la radio en France* (Paris, 1979), 349; Eck, *La Guerre des ondes*, 42.

125. Brochand, *Histoire générale*, II:585; Duval, *Histoire de la radio*, 351.

126. Jean-Noël Jeanneney, ed., *L'Echo du siècle: Dictionnaire radiophonique de la radio et de la télévision en France* (Paris, 2001), 116–117; Eck, *La Guerre des ondes*, 81; Ory, *La Belle Illusion*, 591.

127. Eck, *La Guerre des ondes*, 47–48, 99–100.

128. Brochand, *Histoire générale*, I:592–593; Eck, *La Guerre des ondes*, 99.

129. Hélène Eck, "Poète et directeur: Paul Gilson," *Cahiers d'histoire de la radiodiffusion*, no. 36 (March–May 1993): 62–63, 69–70; Jean Masson, "Les instants du Grand Paul," in Frédéric-Jacques Temple, ed., *Paul Gilson: Hommage et contribution bio-bibliographique* (Lausanne, 1983), 107. Gilson's personality is easier to pin down than his politics. He was the son of a general and nephew to Etienne Gilson, the neo-Thomist philosopher and historian. In the late twenties, Paul Gilson wrote film criticism for René Coty's right-wing newspaper *L'Ami du peuple*. And during the Ethiopian crisis of 1935, he backed then prime minister Laval's pro-Italian policies. Does all this make Gilson a man of the Right? Perhaps it is enough to say that he came from a conservative background. See Eck, "Poète et

directeur: Paul Gilson," 62; idem, "La Radiodiffusion française sous la IVe République: Monopole et service public (août 1944–décembre 1953)" (Thèse de doctorat, University of Paris–X, 1997), III:597 and 597n.

130. Claude Roy, *Moi, je: Essai d'autobiographie* (Paris, 1969), 391–392; Pierre Barbier, "Les nouvelles émissions littéraires de la radiodiffusion nationale," *Cahiers d'histoire de la radiodiffusion*, no. 34 (September–November 1992): 90–91; Leenhardt, *Les Yeux ouverts*, 134.

131. Chabrol, "Jeune France—une expérience," 16–17; CERPS, carton Libération, dossier Jeune France, sdr Association "Jeune France," Activités, letter of 1 December 1941 from Pierre Schaeffer and Paul Flamand to the Minster of the Interior, 4.

132. Pierre Barbier, "Radio-Jeunesse," *Cahiers d'histoire de la radiodiffusion*, no. 27 (December 1990): 65; Chabrol, "Jeune France—une expérience," 127; Francine Gaillard-Risler, *André Clavé: Théâtre et résistances, utopies et réalités* (Paris, 1998), 59.

133. Dallet, *Bibliographie commentée*, 34.

134. Schaeffer, *Antennes*, 283; Chabrol, "Jeune France—une expérience," 127; Eck, "La Radiodiffusion française," II:438.

135. Eck, *La Guerre des ondes*, 51.

136. Duval, *Histoire de la radio*, 332; Louis Merlin, *C'était formidable!* (Paris, 1966), 58–59.

137. Merlin, *C'était formidable!*, 61–65, 90–92.

138. Jeanneney, ed., *L'Echo du siècle*, 722; Eck, *La Guerre des ondes*, 83; and idem, "A la recherche d'un art radiophonique," in Rioux, ed., *La Vie culturelle*, 286–290.

139. Marc Pierret, *Entretiens avec Pierre Schaeffer* (Paris, 1969), 134–137; Brochand, *Histoire générale*, I:596–597; CERPS, carton Libération, dossier "Notes pour la commission d'épuration," 9 January 1945, "Note pour M. le Président de la Commission d'épuration de la radiodiffusion française," 2.

140. CERPS, carton Libération, dossier Programmes, "Activités de Pierre Schaeffer de 1940 à 1944," 3; Dallet, *Bibliographie commentée*, 36.

141. Dallet, *Bibliographie commentée*, 36.

142. CERPS, carton Libération, dossier Notes pour la Commission d'épuration, "Note pour M. Marc," 1 June 1944, 4.

143. Jeanneney, ed., *L'Echo du siècle*, 120.

144. Bergès, *Vichy contre Mounier*, 49.

CHAPTER 6. THE CULTURE STATE

1. Jean Vilar, *Le Théâtre, service public et autres textes* (Paris, 1986), 173.

2. Marion Denizot-Foulquier, *Jeanne Laurent, le théâtre et les arts* (Paris, 1997), 35–36, 40.

3. Raymond Josse, "La naissance de la résistance étudiante à Paris et la manifestation du 11 novembre 1940," *Revue d'histoire de la deuxième guerre mondiale*, no.

47 (July 1962): 1–31; Dudley Andrew, *André Bazin* (New York, 1978), 49ff.; Francine Gaillard-Risler, *André Clavé: Théâtre et résistances, utopies et réalités* (Paris, 1998), 106, 108; Pascale Goetschel, *Renouveau et décentralisation du théâtre (1945–1981)* (Paris, 2004), 76.

4. For the 1945 ordonnance, see Philippe Poirrier, ed., *Les Politiques culturelles en France* (Paris, 2002), 150; Serge Added, *Le Théâtre dans les années Vichy* (Paris, 1992), 87–88. For Laurent's views, see Goetschel, *Renouveau et décentralisation*, 65.

5. Goetschel, *Renouveau et décentralisation*, 54, 64–66, 76; Hubert Gignoux, *Histoire d'une famille théâtrale* (Lausanne, 1984), 316.

6. Goetschel, *Renouveau et décentralisation*, 49–52; Gaillard-Risler, *André Clavé*, 175–176.

7. Benigno Cacérès, *Histoire de l'éducation populaire* (Paris, 1964), 154; Gaillard-Risler, *André Clavé*, 157; Andrew, *André Bazin*, 85–86.

8. Cacérès, *Histoire*, 155; Goetschel, *Renouveau et décentralisation*, 76; Pascal Ory, *L'Aventure culturelle française, 1945–1989* (Paris, 1989), 55.

9. Pierre-Aimé Touchard, "Une chaîne sans fin," *Esprit* 113 (1 August 1945): 446–447.

10. John Hellman accents Uriage's Vichy connections, Bernard Comte its independent-mindedness. See Hellman, *The Knight-Monks of Vichy France: Uriage, 1940–1945* (Montreal, 1993); Comte, *Une Utopie combattante: L'Ecole des cadres d'Uriage, 1940–1942* (Paris, 1991).

11. Comte, *Utopie*, 526; Gilbert Gadoffre et al., *Vers le Style du XXe siècle* (Paris, 1945), avertissement.

12. Comte, *Utopie*, 531; Hellman, *Knight-Monks*, 222; Jean-Pierre Rioux, "Une nouvelle action culturelle? L'exemple de 'Peuple et Culture'," *Revue de l'économie sociale* (April–June 1985): 36–38.

13. Cacérès, *Histoire*, 140–141.

14. Gilbert Gadoffre, "Cristallisation des élites nouvelles," *Esprit* 107 (1 February 1945): 391–404; idem et al., *Vers le Style*, 171, 188, 252ff. See also Hubert Beuve-Méry's defense of Uriage in "Ecole de cadres," *Esprit* 115 (1 October 1945): 625. *Vers le Style* echoes with Vichy-era rhetoric in ways that are sometimes disturbing. The text describes the Ecole de Paris artists who gathered at Montparnasse in the thirties in these terms: "Escaped from the darkest quarters of Warsaw, of Bucharest, they arrive at the [Café de la] Rotonde in rags, in a chronic state of revolt." This in 1944, when it might have been thought such xenophobic expressions were a thing of the disreputable past. See *Vers le Style*, 195.

15. Brian Rigby, "The Reconstruction of Culture: Peuple et Culture and the Popular Education Movement," in Nicholas Hewitt, ed., *The Culture of Reconstruction: European Literature, Thought and Film, 1945–50* (London, 1989), 144.

16. Cited in Rioux, "Une nouvelle action culturelle?" 41. See also Evelyne Ritaine, *Les Stratégies de la culture* (Paris, 1983), 64–65; and Rigby, "Reconstruction of Culture," passim.

17. Jean Dasté, *Voyage d'un comédien* (Paris, 1977), 33 and 33n.

18. Dasté, *Voyage*, 34–35.

19. Cacérès, *Histoire*, 159.

20. See Jeanne Laurent's preface to Dasté, *Voyage*, 13–14, 17; and Goetschel, *Renouveau et décentralisation*, 52–54.

21. Goetschel, *Renouveau et décentralisation*, 54.

22. Goetschel, *Renouveau et décentralisation*, 55–56; Gignoux, *Histoire d'une famille théâtrale*, 316.

23. Gérard Lieber, "Gaston Baty et ses auteurs: le théâtre de l'évasion" (University of Paris–X, thèse d'Etat, 1987), I:131.

24. Jean Laurent, "Têtes de bois," *La Gerbe*, 10 February 1944; Gaston Baty, "Tremplin à rêves," *La Gerbe*, 4 May 1944.

25. Baty was also a southerner himself, having been born in Lyon.

26. Lieber, "Gaston Baty," I:147; Goetschel, *Renouveau et décentralisation*, 56–57.

27. Emmanuelle Loyer, *Le Théâtre citoyen de Jean Vilar: Une utopie d'après-guerre* (Paris, 1997), 17–18.

28. Loyer, *Le Théâtre citoyen*, 29; M. B. (Marc Beigbeder), "Un festival de théâtre à Avignon," *Esprit* 138 (October 1947): 581.

29. For the preceding, the essential reading is Loyer, *Le Théâtre citoyen*, 127ff.

30. Denizot-Foulquier, *Jeanne Laurent*, 70.

31. See the remarks by Clavé in Gaillard-Risler, *André Clavé*, 216.

32. See Schaeffer's epilogue, written in 1968, to Gaillard-Risler, *André Clavé*, 484.

33. Dasté, *Voyage*, 43–49, 115.

34. Dr. Butzbach, as cited in Gaillard-Risler, *André Clavé*, 182. See also Goetschel, *Renouveau et décentralisation*, 137, 142.

35. Dasté, *Voyage*, 120.

36. Goetschel, *Renouveau et décentralisation*, 142–143.

37. Dasté, *Voyage*, 116.

38. Gaillard-Risler, *André Clavé*, 215.

39. Denizot-Foulquier, *Jeanne Laurent*, 72.

40. Schaeffer epilogue, Gaillard-Risler, *André Clavé*, 484.

41. Goetschel, *Renouveau et décentralisation*, 104–105.

42. Roger Richebé, *Au delà de l'Ecran* (Monte Carlo, 1977), 174. See also Olivier Barrot, *L'Ecran français, 1943–1953: Histoire d'un journal et d'une époque* (Paris, 1979), 12; Georges Sadoul, *Histoire générale du cinéma, L'Epoque contemporaine: Le Cinéma pendant la guerre, 1939–1945* (Paris, 1954), VI:64–65.

43. See Daquin's article (June 1944) in *L'Ecran français*, cited by Barrot, *L'Ecran*, 34.

44. Jean-Pierre Bertin-Maghit, *Le Cinéma français sous l'Occupation: le monde du cinéma français de 1940 à 1946* (Paris, 2002), 242–246, 262–263; Barrot, *L'Ecran*, 35; Paul Léglise, *Histoire de la politique du cinéma français* (Paris, 1977), II:138.

45. Bertin-Maghit, *Le Cinéma français* (2002), 178–179, 254.

46. Philippe Mioche, *Le Plan Monnet: Genèse et élaboration, 1941–1947* (Paris, 1987), 218.

47. Léglise, *Histoire de la politique du cinéma*, II:132, 135.

48. Bertin-Maghit, "1945 l'épuration du cinéma français, mythe ou réalité,"

in Marc Ferro, ed., *Film et histoire* (Paris, 1984), 141–42; Léglise, *Histoire de la politique du cinéma*, II:148.

49. Bertin-Maghit, "1945 l'épuration du cinéma français," 141.

50. Cited in Jean-Pierre Jeancolas, "The Setting-up of a 'Method of Production' in the French Cinema, 1946–50," in Brian Rigby and Nicholas Hewitt, eds., *France and the Mass Media* (Paris, 1991), 61.

51. Bertin-Maghit, *Le Cinéma français* (2002), 246, 259–260; Barrot, *L'Ecran*, 53–54; Léglise, *Histoire de la politique du cinéma*, II:139–140.

52. Léglise, *Histoire de la politique du cinéma*, II:144–146.

53. Léglise, *Histoire de la politique du cinéma*, II:150–151.

54. Pierre Darmon, *Le Monde du cinéma sous l'Occupation* (Paris, 1997), 341; Colin Crisp, *The Classic French Cinema, 1930–1960* (Bloomington, 1997), 205; Pierre Billard, *Louis Malle, le rebelle solitaire* (Paris, 2003), 105; Léglise, *Histoire de la politique du cinéma*, II:178.

55. Claude Roy, *Moi, je: Essai d'autobiographie* (Paris, 1969), 193, 461–463.

56. Patricia Hubert-Lacroix, *Le Cinéma français dans la guerre froide: 1946–1956* (Paris, 1996), 25–42.

57. Jacques Portes, "Les origines de la légende noire des accords Blum-Byrnes sur le cinéma," *Revue d'histoire moderne et contemporaine* 33 (April–June 1986): 324–325.

58. Sadoul, *Histoire générale*, VI:157–160, 190–191; Louis Daquin, *Le Cinéma notre métier* (Paris, 1960), 70; Daquin cited in Bertin-Maghit, *Le Cinéma français* (2002), 275.

59. Gilson in the 12 June 1946 edition of *Le Monde*, as cited in Philippe Roger, *L'Ennemi américain, Généalogie de l'antiaméricanisme français* (Paris, 2002), 424; for Louis Jouvet's remark, see Jean-Noël Jeanneney, *Une Histoire des médias: des origines à nos jours* (Paris, 1996), 329.

60. Hubert-Lacombe, *Cinéma français dans la guerre froide*, 37–38.

61. Barrot, *L'Ecran*, 137.

62. Léglise, *Histoire de la politique du cinéma*, II:171–172; Portes, "Les origines de la légende noire," 326–327.

63. Alan Williams, *Republic of Images: A History of French Filmmaking* (Cambridge, MA, 1992), 278; Pierre Billard, *L'Age classique du cinéma français, du cinéma parlant à la Nouvelle Vague* (Paris, 1995), 505–507.

64. See Bresson's *Le Journal d'un curé de campagne* (1951) and *Un Condamné à mort s'est échappé* (1956), both quiet films with a minimum of dialogue. And see Becker's *Casque d'or* (1952) and *Ne touchez pas au grisbi* (1954), the former an evocation of the hard-luck lives of turn-of-the century Parisian Apaches, the latter an evocation (contemporary in setting) of the Parisian criminal milieu, featuring a star turn by Jean Gabin as a dapper, aging gangster out for one last score.

65. François Truffaut, "Une certaine tendance du cinéma français," *Cahiers du cinéma* 31 (January 1954): 15–28.

66. Crisp, *Classic French Cinema*, 114–115, 418.

67. Claude Autant-Lara, *Les Fourgons du malheur: Chronique cinématographique du XXe siècle* (Paris, 1987), 71.

68. Pierre Braunberger, *Cinémamémoire* (Paris, 1987), 129–130.

69. It is worth mentioning in this connection that Bost, like Autant-Lara himself, had a passing connection with 1930s nonconformism. Autant-Lara was linked to Philippe Lamour's *Plans*, Bost to Auguste Detoeuf's *Nouveaux Cahiers*. Bost has in fact been described as a "great friend" of Detoeuf's. See François Perthuis, *Auguste Detoeuf (1883–1947), l'ingénieur de l'impossible paix* (Paris, 1990), 51, 163.

70. Billard, *L'Age classique*, 537, 543–546.

71. Richard Kuisel, "The Fernandel Factor: The Rivalry between the French and American Cinema in the 1950s," *Yale French Studies* 98 (Fall 2000): 120–121, 128–129.

72. Bertin-Maghit, *Le Cinéma français* (2002), 288.

73. Crisp, *Classic French Cinema*, 75.

74. Marcel Dalio, *Mes Années folles* (Paris, 1976), 219. See also Williams, *Republic of Images*, 295.

75. Christian Brochand, *Histoire générale de la radio et de la télévision en France* (Paris, 1994), II:30–31; René Duval, *Histoire de la radio en France* (Paris, 1979), 358.

76. Hélène Eck, "La Radiodiffusion française sous la IVe République: Monopole et service public (août 1944–décembre 1953)" (Thèse de doctorat, University of Paris–X, 1997), I:53; idem, *La Guerre des ondes: Histoire des radios de langue française pendant la deuxième guerre mondiale* (Paris, 1985), 140–141; Pierre Schaeffer, *Les Antennes de Jéricho* (Paris, 1978), 255.

77. Schaeffer, *Antennes*, 269; Eck, "La Radiodiffusion française," I:53.

78. Schaeffer, *Antennes*, 270; Schaeffer in Marc Pierret, *Entretiens avec Pierre Schaeffer* (Paris, 1969), 132; CERPS, carton Libération, Radio, Paris 1944–45, dossier (untitled but green in color), "Note sur l'activité de Pierre Schaeffer à la Radio française," 2.

79. Sylvie Dallet, *Bibliographie commentée de l'oeuvre éditée de Pierre Schaeffer* (Paris, nd), 36; CERPS, carton Libération, Radio, Paris 1944–45, dossier (unnamed but salmon in color), exchange of correspondence: letter from Guignebert to Schaeffer, 4 October 1944; Schaeffer, "Note pour M. Jean Guignebert, 6 October 1944"; letter from Schaeffer to Guignebert, 6 October 1944.

80. Eck, "La Radiodiffusion française," I:40; Jean-Noël Jeanneney, ed., *L'Echo du siècle: Dictionnaire radiophonique de la radio et de la télévision en France* (Paris, 2001), 44.

81. Eck, "La Radiodiffusion française," I:90–91, 108; Roger Leenhardt, *Chroniques du cinéma* (Paris, 1986), 111.

82. Claude Bourdet, "Defferre m'a dit: 'Tu liquides tous ces Gaullistes et tous ces communistes,'" *Cahiers d'histoire de la radiodiffusion*, no. 50 (September–November 1996): 56; Bernard Lauzanne, "A la RDF, une équipe stable pour un régime instable," *Cahiers d'histoire de la radiodiffusion*, no. 50 (September–November 1996): 6; Eck, "La Radiodiffusion française," I:141.

83. Bourdet, "Defferre m'a dit," 56.

84. Lauzanne, "A la RDF," 7; Bourdet, "Defferre m'a dit," 59; Jeanneney, ed., *L'Echo du siècle*, 401–402.

85. Jacques Vasseur, "L'Information politique à la radio sous la IVe Répub-

lique: l'objectivité et ses limites," *Cahiers d'histoire de la radiodiffusion*, no. 36 (March–May 1993): 2–3; Brochand, *Histoire générale*, II:53–54.

86. Personal communication from Hélène Eck.

87. Wladimir Porché, "Fiat Lux, mémoires inédits, archives du Comité d'histoire de la télévision," *Bulletin du Comité d'histoire de la télévision*, no. 11 (December 1984–January 1985): 4–5; Cécile Méadel, *Histoire de la radio des années trente* (Paris, 1994), 61; Eck, "La Radiodiffusion française," I:172.

88. Vasseur, "L'Information politique," 3; Vital Gayman, "J'ai fabriqué une rédaction," *Cahiers d'histoire de la radiodiffusion*, no. 50 (September–November 1996): 106–109; Eck, "La Radiodiffusion française," II:318, 448.

89. Eck, "La Radiodiffusion française," III:598, 599n; idem, "Poète et directeur: Paul Gilson," *Cahiers d'histoire de la radiodiffusion*, no. 36 (March–May 1993): 61, 63–64.

90. Brochand, *Histoire générale*, II:567–568; Jeanneney, ed., *L'Echo du siècle*, 297.

91. Jeanneney, ed., *L'Echo du siècle*, 117.

92. Eck, "La Radiodiffusion française," I:84, 208–209, II:421; Brochand, *Histoire générale*, II:59–61.

93. Eck, "La Radiodiffusion française," I:214; II:396, 487, 489, 516; Jeanneney, ed., *L'Echo du siècle*, 287.

94. Henry Barraud, cited in Eck, "La Radiodiffusion française," III:603.

95. Eck, "La Radiodiffusion française," I:114–115.

96. Roger Pradalié, "Club d'essai, Centre d'Etudes, Modulation de fréquence: le triptyque radiophonique de Jean Tardieu," *Cahiers d'histoire de la radiodiffusion*, no. 48 (March–May 1996): 22, 23; Christian Brochand, "Du Studio d'essai au Club d'essai," *Cahiers d'histoire de la radiodiffusion*, no. 48 (March–May 1996): 31; André Francis, "De la poésie au jazz… et la suite," *Cahiers d'histoire de la radiodiffusion*, no. 48 (March–May 1996): 64–65.

97. Dallet, *Bibliographie commentée*, 44–45; Schaeffer interview with Tim Hodgkinson, http://silvertone.princeton.edu/paul/music242/shaefferinterview.html (accessed 9 March 2007).

98. Eck, "La Radiodiffusion française," I:113; II:479; III:573, 674, 677. See also Schaeffer, *Antennes*, 124; Brochand, *Histoire générale*, II:353–354.

99. Gaillard-Risler, *André Clavé*, 434; Eck, "La Radiodiffusion française," III: 631.

100. On these incidents, see Eck, "La Radiodiffusion française," II:479–483; Brochand, *Histoire générale*, II:346–347; Fernand Pouey, *Un Ingénu à la radio* (Paris, 1949), passim.

101. Jon Cowans, "Political Culture and Cultural Politics: The Reconstruction of French Radio after the Second World War," *Journal of Contemporary History* 31 (1996): 155. See also Cécile Méadel, "The Arrival of Opinion Polls in French Radio and Television 1945–60," in Rigby and Hewitt, eds., *France and the Mass Media*, 152.

102. Scize, as cited in Jean Thévenot, *L'Age de la télévision et l'avenir de la radio* (Paris, 1946), 79.

103. Robert Prot, "Avec Jean Tardieu et Paul Gilson," *Cahiers d'histoire de la radiodiffusion*, no. 36 (March–May 1993): 81.

104. Jeanneney, ed., *L'Echo du siècle*, 551; Eck, "La Radiodiffusion française," III:626.

105. Brochand, *Histoire générale*, II:342–343; Louis Merlin, *C'était formidable!* (Paris, 1962), 184–185.

106. Méadel, "Arrival of Opinion Polls," 150; Roger Veillé, *La Radio et les hommes* (Paris, 1952), 177, 182–183, 188.

107. Thévenot, *L'Âge de la télévision*, 130–131; Jeanneney, ed., *L'Echo du siècle*, 398.

108. Eck, "La Radiodiffusion française," II:438. For *Esprit*, see Persicaire, "Pourquoi la radio est si mauvaise," *Esprit* 109 (1 April 1945): 764–766; and Gabriel Venaissin (*Esprit*, September 1951), as cited in Eck, "La Radiodiffusion française," III:681.

109. Brochand, *Histoire générale*, II:345. See also Eck, "La Radiodiffusion française," I:3–4; Jeanneney, ed., *L'Echo du siècle*, 572–573.

110. Brochand, *Histoire générale*, II:346, 354–355.

111. Merlin, *C'était formidable!*, 115, 183, 237.

112. Merlin, *C'était formidable!*, 246. See more generally Brochand, *Histoire générale*, II:357–358. Radio Luxembourg did not rout the public airwaves on all fronts, however. Not on the musical front, for example, where its standard offerings—*la chanson française* with accordion accompaniment—were not so different from what might be heard on Paris-Inter. Here the challenge came not from Radio Luxembourg but from a newcomer, Europe no. 1. The station began broadcasting from the Saarland in 1955, and its impact was immediate for reasons of both style and content. Europe no. 1 announcers took a personal tone, low-key and insinuating, which contrasted not just with the declamatory mode of public radio but even with the hard-sell style of Radio Luxembourg. Yet it is for its musical programming that Europe no. 1 is best remembered, programming that targeted a baby-boom market just then coming into its own. And what kind of music appealed to the new youth market? Jazz in part, but above all and of course *le pop*, a rock 'n' roll sound in the making featured on a show that came to be the teenage favorite, Frank Ténot and Daniel Filipacchi's *Salut les copains*. It first aired in 1959, two years after its television equivalent in the United States, *American Bandstand*, went national on NBC. Brochand, *Histoire générale*, II:360; Merlin, *C'était formidable!*, 301, 319–320.

113. Méadel, "Arrival of Opinion Polls," 169–171.

114. Gilson, cited in Eck, "La Radiodiffusion française," III:640; Agathe Mella, "Témoignage," *Cahiers d'histoire de la radiodiffusion*, no. 36 (March–May 1993): 73.

115. Brochand, *Histoire générale*, II:49.

116. Eck, "La Radiodiffusion française," II:451.

117. Vasseur, "L'Information politique," 10. Vasseur was Gayman's lieutenant at RTF news.

118. Brochand, *Histoire générale*, II:341–342; Eck, "La Radiodiffusion française," II:434.

119. Vasseur, "L'Information politique," 11.

120. Eck, "La Radiodiffusion française," II:484–485; Veillé, *La Radio*, 195–196.

121. Eck, "La Radiodiffusion française," II:495–496, III:566–567, 570–571; Brochand, *Histoire générale*, II:64–65.

122. "Le 'Cahier noir' du journal parlé," *Cahiers d'histoire de la radiodiffusion*, no. 50 (September–November 1996): 123–124. Politics straitjacketed the public airwaves, and then came Europe no. 1, adding to the RTF's woes. Europe no. 1 did not fear spontaneity, quite the contrary. Its news announcers projected a relaxed demeanor; its journalists were sent out on assignment to report live from the news scene. For an on-the-spot account of the Hungarian uprising of 1956, it was to Europe no. 1 that listeners had to turn. The station's coverage of breaking news, moreover, included subjects, like the war in Algeria, that the RTF had a hard time dealing with. And the journalists Europe no. 1 recruited were an exceptional lot, not just skilled reporters but performers who understood the dramatic possibilities of news reporting, men like the onetime actor Pierre Sabbagh, who was en route to becoming a media personality in his own right. Merlin, *J'en ai vu des choses!* (Paris, 1962), 302; Brochand, *Histoire générale*, II:360, 362; Jeanneney, ed., *L'Echo du siècle*, 127–128, 417.

123. Philip Nord, "Catholic Culture in Interwar France," *French Politics, Culture & Society*, 21 (Fall 2003): 2–9.

124. For many French men and women, whether in the Resistance or not, the war did not bring an end to talk about a so-called Jewish question. On this point, see Renée Poznanski, *Propgandes et persécutions: La Résistance et le "problème juif"* (Paris, 2008).

CONCLUSION

1. *Journal de la France et des français, Chronologie politique, culturelle et religieuse de Clovis à 2000* (Paris, 2001), 2252.

2. Frison-Roche, *La Grande Crevasse* (Paris, 1948), 68.

3. Charles R. Morris, *American Catholic: The Saints and Sinners Who Built America's Most Powerful Church* (New York, 1997), 197.

4. Frison-Roche, *La Grande Crevasse*, 112.

5. Roger Frison-Roche, *Le Versant du soleil* (Paris, 1981), 194–197, 232, 418.

6. Stacy Schiff, *Saint-Exupéry: A Biography* (New York, 1994), 350–351; Antoine de Saint-Exupéry, *Ecrits de guerre, 1939–1944* (Paris, 1994), 120.

7. Antoine de Saint-Exupéry, *Le Petit Prince* (New York, 1943), 79.

8. For a fuller discussion, see Alan Perry, *The Don Camillo Stories of Giovannino Guareschi: A Humorist Portrays the Sacred* (Toronto, 2008).

9. Giovanni Guareschi, *Le Petit Monde de don Camillo* (Paris, 1951), 250. The 1950 English translation of the text ends on a less humorous, more irenic note: "But Peppone said nothing, and for a time the two men sat in the dim light looking at the little group of figures on the table and listening to the silence that had settled over the Little World of Don Camillo and which no longer seemed ominous but instead full of peace." *The Little World of Don Camillo*, tr. Una Vincenzo Troubridge (New York, 1950), 205.

10. Stanley Hoffmann, "The Paradoxes of the French Political Community," in Hoffmann et al., *In Search of France: The Economy, Society, and Political System in the Twentieth Century* (New York, 1965), 17.

11. Jean-Baptiste Duroselle, "Changes in French Foreign Policy Since 1945," in Hoffmann et al., *In Search of France*, 336.

12. Robert Paxton, *Vichy France: Old Guard and New Order, 1940–1944* (New York, 1972); see also Richard Kuisel, *Capitalism and the State in Modern France: Renovation and Economic Management in the Twentieth Century* (Cambridge, 1981).

13. Philip Nord, "Pierre Schaeffer and Jeune France: Cultural Politics in the Vichy Years," *French Historical Studies* 30 (Fall 2007): 685–709.

14. Olivier Dard, *Le Rendez-vous manqué des relèves des années trente* (Paris, 2002).

15. It is worth noting in this context that de La Rocque published a volume under the title *Service public* in 1934.

16. Martin Conway too is inclined to play down the exile experience in the shaping of postwar policy-making. See Conway, "Legacies of Exile: The Exile Governments in London during the Second World War and the Politics of Postwar Europe," in Conway and José Gotovitch, eds., *Europe in Exile: European Exile Communities in Britain, 1940–1945* (New York, 2001), 255–274.

17. For a good example of the ground-up perspective, see the work of Herrick Chapman, "The Liberation of France as a Moment in State-Making," in Kenneth Mouré and Martin S. Alexander, eds., *Crisis and Renewal in France, 1918–1962* (New York, 2002), 174–198.

18. Robert O. Paxton, *Parades and Politics at Vichy, The French Officer Corps under Marshal Pétain and Vichy* (Princeton, 1966), ch. 13; Claude d'Abzac-Epezy, "Epuration et rénovation de l'armée," in Marc Olivier Baruch, ed., *Une Poignée de misérables: L'Epuration de la société française après la Seconde Guerre mondiale* (Paris, 2003), 460–463.

19. Danièle Voldman, *La Reconstruction des villes françaises de 1940 à 1954* (Paris, 1997), 7, 48–50, 58, 125–126, 148–149, 395, 398, 427; see also Rosemary Wakeman, "Nostalgic Modernism and the Invention of Paris in the Twentieth Century," *French Historical Studies* 27 (Winter 2004): 131, 136–137.

20. Tantalizing on this subject are Götz Aly and Susanne Heim, *Architects of Annihilation: Auschwitz and the Logic of Destruction*, tr. A. G. Blunden (Princeton, 2002); and Mark Mazower, *Hitler's Empire: How the Nazis Ruled Europe* (New York, 2008). Both books cite examples of onetime Nazi experts who went on to successful postwar careers in economic policy-making and urban planning. For a study of writers and filmmakers who found ways to navigate the transition from fascism to postwar democracy in Italy, see Ruth Ben-Ghiat's excellent *Fascist Modernities: Italy, 1922–1945* (Berkeley and Los Angeles, 2001).

21. Philip H. Gordon and Sophie Meunier, *The French Challenge: Adapting to Globalization* (Washington, 2001), 13.

22. Claire Andrieu, *Pour l'Amour de la République: Le Club Jean Moulin, 1958–1970* (Paris, 2002).

Index

Compagnons de France, 112–13, 174, 278, 304–5

"concertedness," 154–55

Confédération française des travailleurs chrétiens (CFTC), 167, 171–72

Confédération générale de l'agriculture (CGA), 155–56, 168

Confédération générale de la production française (CGPF), 44–45

Confédération générale des cadres (CGC), 171–72

Confédération générale des petites et moyennes entreprises (CGPME), 155, 172

Confédération générale du patronat français (GGPF), 44–45

Confédération générale du travail (CGT): Blum Government and, 44, 46; communism and, 157, 160, 167–68, 172, 354; Daladier agenda and, 46–47, 62; FO as splinter group of, 168; HCCPF and, 175–76, 354; planning and, 28–29, 41, 155, 157; strike actions of, 46, 354

Conseil d'études économiques, 94

Conseil du Plan: membership and organizational culture of, 155–56

Conseil national de la Résistance (CNR), 4, 21, 101–2, 145, 207, 371

Conseil national économique (CNE), 28–29, 43–45, 239

Conseil supérieur de la Population, 116

Conseil supérieur de l'economie industrielle et commerciale, 93–94, 136

Conseil supérieur des émissions de la radiodiffusion, 248

consumerism, 7, 56, 382

Copeau, Jacques, 221–26, 229–31, 266, 273, 306–7, 323–24, 421n53

Copeau, Pascal, 105–6, 230

Corbeau, Le (film), 284, 293–95

Cornu, André, 324

corporatism, 20, 26, 35, 38–39; the Cartel and corporatism in film industry, 254, 257–59, 262; Laroque and framing of, 26, 29–31, 95, 146–47, 168–69, 172, 176, 186, 380; media reforms and, 228–29, 230, 311–12, 320, 358–59; Monnet and

corporatist influences on the Plan, 161, 166–67; néo-socialisme and, 29; opposition to left-based, 325, 330, 358–59; Perroux and, 39, 97–99; "technocorporatism," 10, 379 (*see also* Laroque and framing of *under this heading*); Vichy regime and, 95, 100–105, 142, 152, 168, 254, 256, 261–62, 277–79, 283, 296, 309–10, 320, 328, 330, 368; welfare policy and, 146–47, 168–69, 172, 186–88, 208, 371; X-Crise and, 39–41, 95

Cortot, Alfred, 266, 304

Cot, Pierre, 130–31, 191, 193

Courtin, René, 105, 106, 107

Cousteau, Jacques, 281

Coutrot, Jean, 40–41, 43, 49–50, 55–56, 60, 84

Couve de Murville, Maurice, 72, 89, 110, 370

Crémieux, Francis, 346, 354

Crochet radiophonique, Le (radio program), 245, 352

Croix de feu, 33, 43, 89, 105

cultural policy: Vichy-era (*See* cultural policy, Vichy-era). *See specific regimes; specific sectors, such as film, radio, television, theater*

cultural policy, Fourth Republic, 329–30, 331, 334, 345–46

cultural policy, Liberation and postwar, 311–12, 344, 356–59; anti-commercialism and, 344; as assertion of French identity, 315–16; Centres dramatiques nationaux and theater decentralization, 217, 316–24; christian democracy and, 145–46, 171, 356–57, 373, 376, 382; Comité de libération de la radio (CLR), 307; Comité de liberation du cinéma français (CLFC), 292, 311; Communist influence over cinema and, 325–26, 328; decentralization of theater, 313–24; democratization and, 268–69, 312; funding for the arts, 315; institution building and, 219–20, 356, 357; Lourmarin colloquium linked to, 268–69; proposed *statut de la radio,* 345; purge and renewal as objectives of, 311, 326; quality aes-